Ultimate Recipes

Low Fat

Ultimate Recipes

Low Fat

DP
DEMPSEY
PARR

This is a Dempsey Parr Book
This edition published in 2000

Dempsey Parr is an imprint of Parragon

Parragon
Queen Street House
4 Queen Street
Bath BA1 1HE, UK

ISBN 1-84084-970-3

Printed in Indonesia

Produced by Haldane Mason, London

Notes

Use all metric or all imperial quantities, as the two are not interchangeable.
Cup measurements in this book are for American cups. Tablespoons are assumed to be 15 ml.
Unless otherwise stated, milk is assumed to be full fat, eggs are medium and pepper is freshly
ground black pepper.

The nutritional information provided for each recipe is per serving or per portion.
Optional ingredients, variations or serving suggestions have not been included in the
calculations. The times given for each recipe are an approximate guide only as the
preparation times may differ as a result of the type of oven used.

Contents

Snacks & Light Meals

Meat & Game

Poultry

Poultry (continued)

Fish & Seafood

Vegetarian Dishes

Pasta, Grains, & Beans

Salads

Salads
(continued)

Side Dishes

Desserts

Introduction

Whether you are on a low fat diet or simply want to introduce healthier eating habits to your lifestyle, this is the book for you. Although the majority of recipes are low in fat, some have been included because they are highly nutritious and add an important variety of ingredients.

Nutritionists agree that typical modern diets usually contain too much fat and that this can be detrimental to health. Hardly a day passes without a television program or a magazine article giving advice on cutting down our intake of fat. In fact, so much attention is given to the subject that people could be forgiven for believing that all their health problems would be solved if they never ate another gram of fat in their lives. Nothing could be further from the truth. A moderate intake of fat is essential for good health. For example, the body requires fat-soluble vitamins. Fish oils are one of the richest sources of vitamins A and D, and vitamin E is found in vegetable oils. Fats are also a concentrated source of energy, providing over twice as much as carbohydrates or proteins. The aim should be to reduce fat in the diet, but not to cut it out altogether.

How much is too much?

The body's nutrient requirements, including how much fat is needed, vary with age, sex, general state of health, level of physical activity, and even genetic inheritance. However, the proportions in which the different nutrients are required are much the same from one person to another. The World Health Organization recommends that fats should not exceed 30 per cent of the daily intake of energy. (Energy is measured in calories, kilocalories, or kilojoules.)

Introduction

It has conducted studies in countries with an exceptionally high rate of heart disease and the research has revealed that this almost invariably coincides with a high-fat diet, where fats comprise as much as 40 per cent of the body's daily energy intake.

If 2,000 calories a day is taken as the average, then, for good health, only 600 of them should be supplied by fats. One gram of pure fat yields nine calories, whereas one gram of pure carbohydrate or pure protein yields only one calorie. Simple arithmetic, therefore, indicates that the maximum daily intake of fats should be 600 divided by nine, or 66.6 grams of fat.

Fats are broken down and digested in a different way from proteins and carbohydrates and the human body is designed to store them for times of need. In the Western world, food no longer becomes scarce every winter and we do not need to rely on stored fat to provide the energy for day-to-day life. So if a lot of fat is stored, the body becomes overweight, even obese. Worse still, a mechanism that is not yet properly understood can suddenly trigger fat deposits in the arteries, resulting in their becoming narrower and eventually leading to heart disease.

Anyone who is already overweight and keen to return to a healthier size can reduce their fat intake to well below the 30 per cent maximum. However, it is probably better and the long-term effects will be more permanent if the overall intake of calories is reduced, but the proportions of nutrients remains within the normal range. Everyone, overweight or not, should observe the no more than 30 per cent rule to ensure long-term health and vitality.

Types of Fat

When you are thinking about reducing your intake of fat, it is important to know that fats can broadly be divided into two categories: saturated and unsaturated fat. Although they are still fats, unsaturated fats are healthier than the saturated variety and it is important to consider this when buying food.

Fats are made up of a combination of fatty acids and glycerol. Fatty acids consist of a chain of carbon atoms linked to hydrogen atoms. The way these are linked determines the type of fat—saturated or unsaturated. The type of fat you eat is just as important as the amount.

Saturated fats

Saturated fatty acids contain as many hydrogen atoms as possible - there are no empty links on the chain. They are mainly found in animal products, such as meat and dairy foods, although some vegetable oils, including palm and coconut oil, also contain them. Foods labelled as containing hydrogenated vegetable oils, such as some types of margarine, also contain saturated fats as a by-product of their processing. They are easy to recognize as they are usually solid at room temperature.

These are the fats that the body has difficulty processing and which it tends to store. They also increase cholesterol levels in the bloodstream, which can increase the risk of heart disease. It is, therefore, sensible to reduce the level of saturated fats in the diet. They should comprise no more than 30 per cent of the total fat intake or no more than nine per cent of the total energy intake.

Unsaturated fats

These fatty acids have spare links in the carbon chain and some hydrogen atoms are missing. There are two types: monounsaturated fats which have one pair of hydrogen atoms missing and polyunsaturated fats which have more than one pair missing. They are normally liquid or soft at room temperature. They are both thought to reduce the level of cholesterol in the bloodstream.

Monounsaturated fats are mainly of vegetable origin, but are also found in oily fish, such as mackerel. Other rich sources include olive oil, many kinds of nuts, and avocados.

Types of Fat

There are two types of polyunsaturated fats: omega 3 is found in oily fish and omega 6 in seeds and seed oils, such as sunflower.

Cholesterol

The word cholesterol is almost certain to be heard in the course of virtually any discussion about diet and health, yet its role in the human body is far from being fully understood. Although increased levels of dietary and blood cholesterol have been linked with heart disease, this is not the full story.

Cholesterol is a sterol that is found in all animal fats and in some plants. It is also synthesized by the human liver from cholesterol-free substances, so it quite clearly serves some useful purpose. It seems to be important in the production of some of the body's natural steroids and a derivative is converted to vitamin D by the action of sunlight on the skin.

To complicate matters further, there are two types of proteins that carry cholesterol in the bloodstream: low-density and high-density lipoproteins. It seems that low-density lipoproteins promote atherosclerosis, the condition in which fats (lipids) are deposited on the inner walls of the arteries, narrowing them and constricting the flow of blood. This, in turn, increases the risk of heart attacks and heart disease. High-density lipoproteins, on the other hand, appear to retard atherosclerosis.

Research continues, but it is apparent that cholesterol is not always a villain. Its effects—good or bad—are controlled by other factors. It is probably more sensible, therefore, to think in terms of overall reduction of fat intake, especially saturated fats, than worry about the cholesterol content of individual foods.

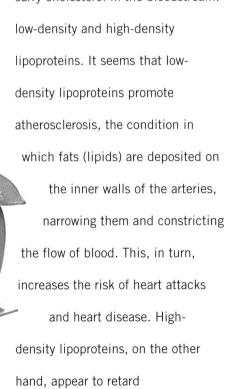

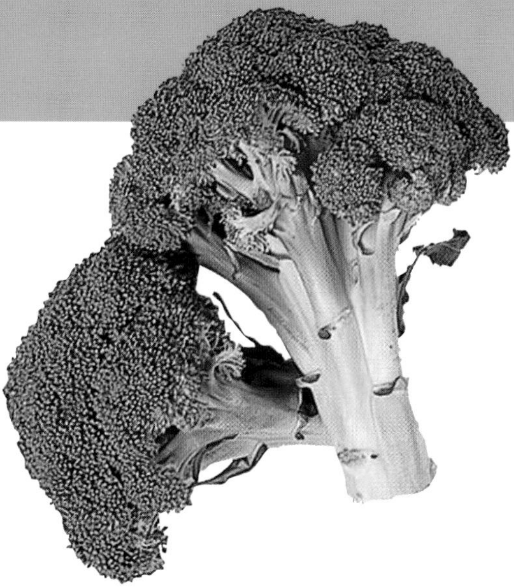

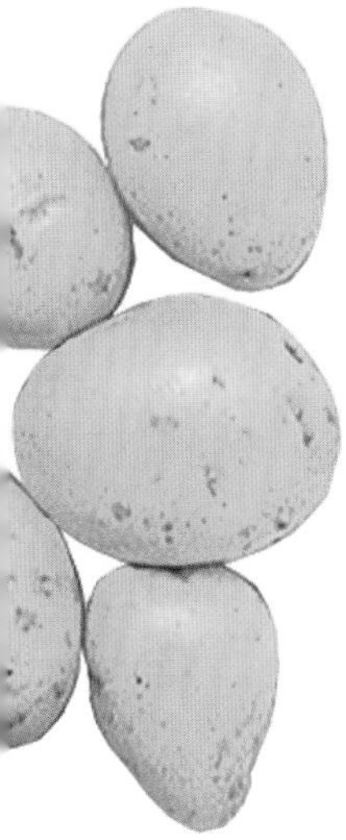

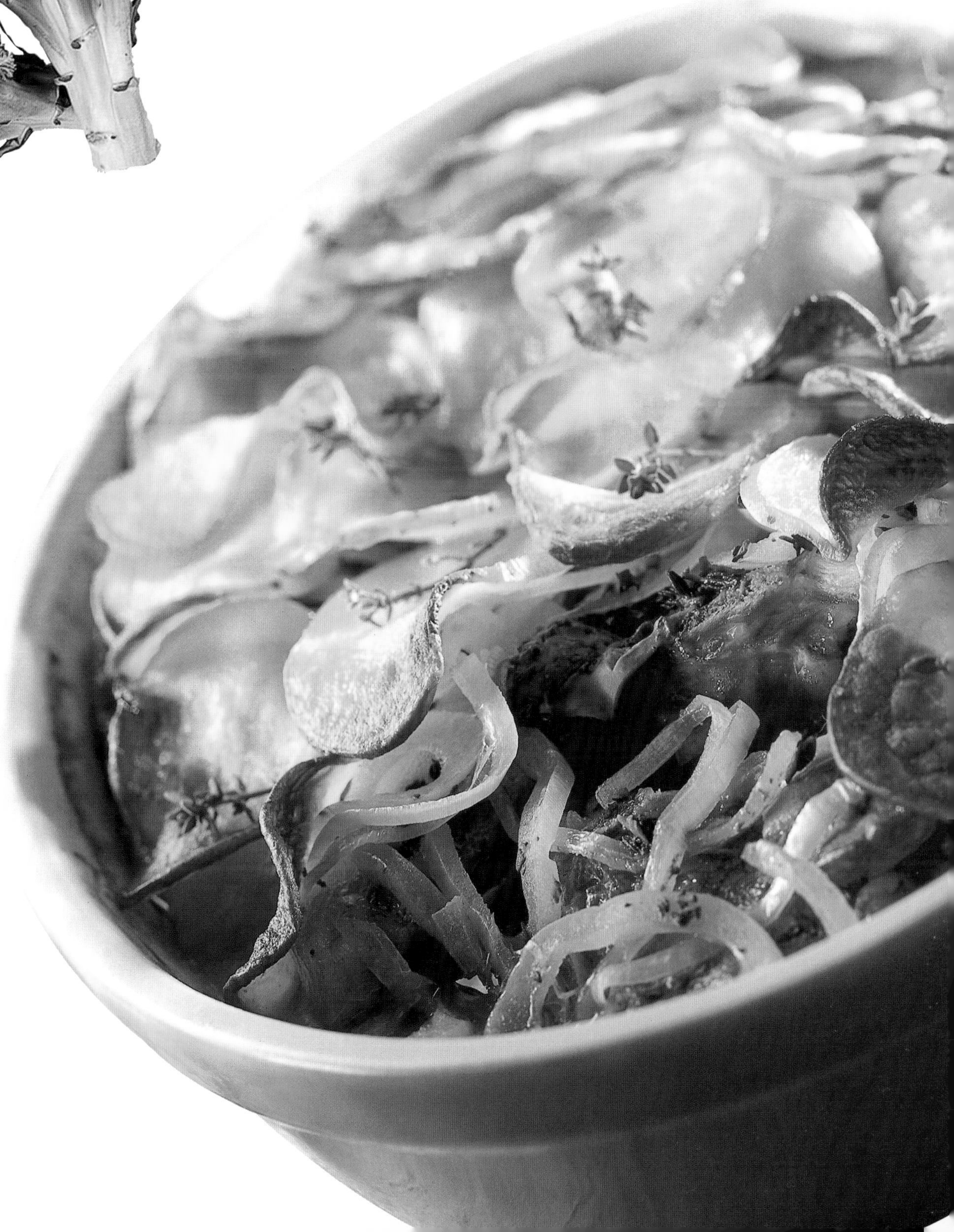

Cooking Techniques

One of the easiest and least disruptive ways to reduce your fat intake is to change the way you cook. Trying new recipes, even with familiar ingredients, is fun and will result in the pleasure of eating delicious meals that are also healthier.

Baking

Many baked dishes are virtually fat free. Foil-wrapped parcels of meat or fish are always delicious. Add a little fruit juice or wine, rather than oil or butter, for a moist texture and delicious flavor.

Braising and Stewing

Slow cooking techniques produce succulent dishes that are especially welcome in winter. Trim all visible fat from meat and always remove the skin from chicken. If red meat is to be browned first, consider dry-frying it in a heavy-based pan and drain off any fat before continuing with the recipe. Straining the cooking liquid, reducing it, and then skimming off the fat before serving is a classic way of preparing braised food and concentrates the flavor as well as reducing the fat content.

Broiling

This is a good alternative to frying, producing a similar crisp and golden coating while remaining moist and tender inside. Ingredients with a delicate texture and which can easily dry out, such as white fish or chicken breasts, will require brushing with oil, but more robust foods, such as red meat or oily fish, can usually be broiled without additional fat, if the temperature is not too high. Consider marinating meat and fish in wine, soy sauce, cider, sherry, beer, and herbs or spices. Not only will this tenderize meat and provide additional flavor, the marinade can be brushed on during broiling, so that additional fat will not be required. When broiling, always place the food on a rack, so that the fat drains away.

Frying

This is undoubtedly the technique that most dramatically raises the level of fats in the diet. You do not have to abandon fries or fried foods completely, but it is sensible to make sure that they are only occasional treats rather than the staple diet. Fried-food fans might find it helpful to know that ingredients absorb much more fat when pan-fried than they do during deep-frying, but even deep-frying should be used only occasionally. If you do enjoy a pan-fried dish once in a while, invest in a good quality, heavy-based, non-stick frying pan and you will then require much less oil. Use a vegetable oil, high in polyunsaturates, for frying rather than a solid fat and measure the quantity you add to the pan, rather than just pouring it in. A spray oil is a useful way of controlling how much you use. Try the Chinese cooking technique of stir-frying. The ingredients are cooked very rapidly over an extremely high heat, using a small amount of oil. Consequently, they absorb little fat and, as an additional advantage, largely retain their color, flavor, texture, and nutritional content.

Microwave

Food cooked in this way rarely requires additional fat.

Poaching

This is an ideal technique for ingredients with a delicate texture or subtle flavor, such as chicken and fish, and is fat-free. Poached food does not have to be bland and uninteresting. You can use all kinds of liquids, including stock, wine, and vinegar, flavored with fruit, vegetables and herbs. The cooking liquid can be used as the basis for a sauce to provide additional flavor, as well as preserving any dissolved nutrients.

Roasting

Fat is an integral part of this cooking technique. Without it, meat or fish would dry out and become too brown. If you are planning a roast dish, stand the meat on a rack over a tray or roasting pan so that the fat drains off. When making gravy, use stock or vegetable cooking water rather than the meat juices.

Steaming

Another fat-free technique, this is becoming an increasingly popular way of cooking meat, fish, chicken, and vegetables. Ingredients retain their color, flavor, and texture, fewer nutrients are dissolved, and it is very economical because steamers can be stacked on top of one another. The addition of herbs and other flavorings to the cooking liquid or the ingredients, results in a wonderfully aromatic dish. An additional advantage is that when meat is steamed, the fat melts and drips into the cooking liquid. In that case, do not use the cooking liquid for making gravy or sauces.

Ingredients

Many common foods are naturally low in fats: most vegetables and fruit, white fish, mushrooms, legumes, rice, and shellfish, for example. Some manufactured foods, such as pasta, noodles, dried fruit, and jam, also have a low fat content, whereas others, such as pâté, sausages, donuts, and crisps, have a very high fat content. Food manufacturers now produce a wide range of reduced fat, low fat, and fat free versions of otherwise high fat products, such as milk, cheese, and mayonnaise.

Food labeling

Laws concerning the nutritional information supplied on pre-packed food vary from country to country, but in these health-conscious days, the basic facts usually include the energy value and protein, carbohydrate, and fat content for a specific weight or quantity. This makes it easier to compare different products which may be packed in different size containers. The values of saturated and unsaturated fats are also often included. Always read the nutritional information, usually somewhere on the back of the packaging, rather than simply accepting claims about health-giving qualities plastered all over the front. This will also reveal whether a low fat product contains other ingredients that you may not want. Flavored yogurt, for example, may be low in fat but can also contain undesirably high quantities of sugar.

Bacon, ham, and preserved meats

These all have a high fat content, but some types are leaner than others. Extra lean bacon is available from most supermarkets. If you are going to include them in the diet occasionally, trim off the visible fat and use a low fat method of cooking rather than frying. Broil bacon, for example, and boil ham or gammon. Most preserved meats, such as pastrami, have a high fat content, but bresaola is usually lean. Buy extra thinly sliced bacon and preserved meats, so that your overall consumption is lower.

Cereals

An important source of complex carbohydrate, cereals also contain some fats, proteins, and vitamins. Some, such as bulghur wheat and rice, may be cooked as an accompaniment or as an integral part of the main dish, as in the case of risotto. Rice contains small amounts

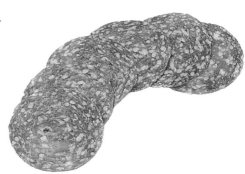

Ingredients

combined with meat or fish to "bulk up" a meal. Most dried peas and beans require soaking for several hours before cooking, sometimes for as long as eight hours. Lentils do not need to be soaked. After soaking, it is essential to boil dried red or black kidney beans for 15 minutes before simmering for the required time to cook until tender. This is because they contain a toxin which is destroyed by this treatment. Canned beans and peas are convenient and can simply be heated through, but they should be drained and rinsed first as they sometimes have salt or sugar added. The range of dried beans is extensive and they are excellent in soups, stews, casseroles, and curries. An easy way to reduce fat in your diet is to cook a vegetarian dish, based on beans, once every week or two.

Cereals

An important source of complex carbohydrate, cereals also contain some fats, proteins, and vitamins. Some, such as bulgur wheat and rice, may be cooked as an accompaniment or as an integral part of the main dish, as in the case of risotto. Rice contains only 0.6 grams of fat per 100 grams of food, so it is a useful staple in a low fat diet. Other cereals are usually ground to produce flour, which is then manufactured into other products, bread and pasta being two of the most important. Pasta contains less than one per cent fat and is rich in complex carbohydrates, B group vitamins, and some minerals. Besides being a healthy food, it is astonishingly versatile and goes well with just about everything.

Do not overlook the value of commercial breakfast cereals, which invariably have their nutritional content listed on the package and often include added vitamins and minerals. Corn flakes, for example, contain 0.8 grams of fat per 100 grams of food and of this 0.3 grams are saturated, 0.2 grams are monounsaturated and 0.3 grams are polyunsaturated. A single serving contains only traces of fat, although this depends on the kind of milk used.

Dairy products

Milk is a valuable source of protein, carbohydrates, vitamins, and minerals, especially calcium, but it has a very high fat content. It follows that most milk products, such as cream and cheese, have a similar nutritional make up. However, various reduced fat, low fat, and fat free products are widely available.

Semi-skimmed milk contains 1.5-1.8 per cent fat, while skimmed milk contains no more than 0.3 per cent fat, although typically it contains only 0.1 per cent. It is a matter of personal taste which you prefer in tea and coffee and both are equally suitable for cooking. The fat-soluble vitamins A and D are usually removed with the fat from skimmed milk, but some brands add them artificially afterwards. Skimmed milk is not suitable for babies and young children. Buttermilk is basically a skimmed milk produced as a result of the butter-making process. Condensed milk may be made from full-fat, semi-skimmed or skimmed milk. It is very sweet and highly concentrated and is often used for making fudge and other sweets. Evaporated milk, on the other hand, is concentrated full-fat milk. Soya milk, which has a very high nutritional value, may be used as a low fat substitute for milk in any circumstances, but it has quite a distinctive and different flavor.

The fat content of cream is always high, whether light, heavy, half, soured, or crème fraîche, as it is made from the liquid butterfat content of full-fat milk. Smetana, a soured cream made from skimmed milk, and low fat yogurt are both good substitutes. Silken tofu, a soya product, can also be successfully used in any recipes that require cream. Fromage frais and virtually fat free fromage frais are also useful substitutes.

Traditional cheeses vary considerably in their fat content, but many reduced fat and low fat versions are now available. Cottage cheese and skimmed milk cream cheese contain less than 1 gram of fat per 100 grams of food.

Eggs

The white of egg is protein, but the yolks contain some fat. Eggs also contain some useful vitamins and important minerals. A high consumption of eggs has been linked with increases in the cholesterol levels in the bloodstream, so they should be eaten in moderation. Because they are so nutritious, inexpensive, and easy to prepare, as well as being integral to many dishes, such as pancakes, soufflés, and sponge cakes, they are difficult to omit completely from the diet.

Ingredients

Fats

Hard fats, such as butter, margarine, lard, suet, drippings, ghee, and other cooking fats are high in saturated fats. Polyunsaturated vegetable oils are a wiser choice for cooking.

Soft margarine and low fat spreads, which contain polyunsaturates, may be used in place of butter on bread or crackers and some can be used for making pastry and cooking. However, very low fat spreads contain a high percentage of water and cannot be heated successfully. Hydrogenated fat is produced from inexpensive vegetable oils which are converted into a semi-solid fat, originally designed for deep-frying. In the process, polyunsaturated fats are converted into saturated fats. Vegetable ghee and hard margarine both contain hydrogenated fat.

Instead of using soft margarine and low fat spreads when making sandwiches or toast, try replacing them with low fat cream cheese, yeast extract, olive oil, fat free mayonnaise, or jellies and marmalades.

Packed with protein, B group vitamins, and minerals, such as calcium, fluorine, and iodine, fish is a highly nutritious food. Any fats present are unsaturated and white fish contains less than 1 gram of fat per 100 grams of food. Even oily fish, such as trout, contain less fat than meat or poultry. It is important to think carefully about cooking methods. It is no good choosing sole or cod because it is low in fat and then frying it in butter or smothering it in a cheese sauce. Poaching, steaming, and baking in foil are especially good methods, which allow plenty of scope for adding herbs and other flavorings and also preserve the delicate texture of the fish. Canned fish, such as tuna, is a useful household ingredient. If you choose it canned in water rather than oil, the fat content is still less than 1 gram per 100 grams of food.

Fruit

Rich in natural sugars, vitamins, minerals, and dietary fiber and low in fat or fat free, fruit is a useful ingredient. It is an ideal choice—raw or cooked—for desserts, but is also delicious in savory dishes, such as when combined with poultry and fish. Pork and apple, and lamb and red currants are classic combinations and mangoes feature in many Indian and West African curries. Dried fruit is a good source of dietary fiber and retains most of the nutrients present in fresh fruit, apart from vitamin C. The flavor is concentrated and it usually contains more calories than fresh fruit. When it is rehydrated, by soaking in water or some other liquid, the nutritional value is much the same. Dried fruit, especially prunes, apricots, and pears, goes well in savory, as well as sweet dishes. Lamb cooked with apricots is a traditional and flavorful North African dish, while pork and prunes is a regional speciality in the Loire valley in France. Fresh and dried fruits make excellent in-between-meal snacks.

The following common fruits contain less than 1 gram of fat per 100 grams of food: apples, bananas, dried mixed fruit, grapefruit, oranges, peaches, and pears.

Herbs

The nutritional value of herbs is negligible, although some do have medicinal properties. Their real value is in the way they add aroma and flavor to both salads and cooked dishes. They are particularly valuable in a low fat diet, which can become insipid and dull. Fresh herbs have a more delicious flavor and scent than dried but if they are unavailable, use half the quantity of dried herbs.

Meat

The nutritional content of meat varies depending on the cut and on the individual animal. It is a good source of nutrition, being packed with high-quality protein and providing many vitamins and minerals. It contains no carbohydrate. The fat content of lean meat can range from about 4.5 per cent in beef to 11.5 per cent in lamb. Fattier cuts have very much higher values and cuts, such as belly of pork, are best avoided. When preparing meat, whatever the method of cooking, always trim off any skin and visible fat. Place meat for roasting or broiling on a rack so that the fat drains off and make the most of marinades, rather than oil or fat, for basting. Before serving, always skim off any fat from the cooking liquid when braising or stewing. Drain off the oil used for browning meat or any fat that may have run before adding other ingredients when making dishes such as spaghetti bolognese. Some dishes—chili con carne and Irish stew being classic examples—improve if they are cooked the day before they are to be served. This also provides an

Ingredients

opportunity to remove some of the fat, as it solidifies on the top of the dish and can simply be lifted off. This technique is also useful when making stock. Try pot-roasting rather than oven-roasting for larger cuts. Braising, stewing, and broiling are other low fat techniques that suit most meats.

Mushrooms

Mushrooms contain protein, vitamins B1, B2, and niacin, and valuable minerals, such as potassium, but no fat, cholesterol, or carbohydrate. Their unique flavor makes them a valuable addition to many savory dishes.

Nuts

All nuts are high in fat, protein, and carbohydrate. Almonds, hazelnuts, walnuts, pine nuts, and coconut are widely used in sweet and savory dishes, but should not be combined

with other high fat ingredients.

Oils

These are necessary for many cooking techniques and provide fatty acids that are essential to the body. Choose an oil low in saturated fats and high in polyunsaturates for general cooking: safflower, grapeseed, soya, or corn, for example. Sunflower oil is ideal, as it is not only high in polyunsaturates, but contains 33 per cent monounsaturates. Do not assume that just because an oil is of vegetable origin, it necessarily falls into this category. Coconut oil and palm oil, both of which are solid at room temperature, are high in saturated fat. Oil simply described as "vegetable oil" often combines a wide range of constituents, which are not always listed on the label,

and these may include coconut or refined palm oil. Olive oil is a particularly valuable ingredient, not only because of its unique and delicious flavor, but also because it is high in monounsaturated fats, as well as vitamin A. The best quality is extra virgin, which is the cold-pressed oil obtained after the first pressing of the olives. This makes lovely salad dressings and is a good substitute for butter in mashed potato, on cooked vegetables, and for tossing pasta. Strong-tasting oils, such as sesame seed (high in polyunsaturates), are usually used sparingly for extra flavor rather than for cooking.

Poultry

An excellent source of high-quality protein and some important vitamins and minerals, poultry contains less

Ingredients

fat than red meat, especially if the skin is removed before cooking. It also contains less saturated fat than red meat and is often recommended for low cholesterol diets. Whole birds and portions lend themselves to most cooking techniques—poaching, steaming, broiling, and braising being especially suitable in the low fat diet. Goose and duck, which tend to be fattier, are best broiled or roasted and should be eaten only occasionally. Always place birds for roasting or broiling on a rack so the fat drains away.

Sausages and salami

Fat is an essential part of the ingredients, although low fat sausages are produced by some food manufacturers. Traditional sausages, especially European varieties, always have a high fat content. Indeed, there is no such thing as low fat salami.

Seafood

Shellfish, such as mussels and clams, crustaceans, such as shrimp and crab, and cephalopods, such as squid and octopus, are all low in fat. The classic cooking techniques for seafood —poaching, broiling, and stir-frying, for example—by happy coincidence are also low fat. There are, of course, exceptions. Many shrimp recipes call for butter and many lobster dishes involve rich, creamy sauces, but as these are unlikely to be typical family meals, avoiding them is not difficult.

Spices

Like herbs, spices are an excellent way of pepping up a low fat diet and preventing it from becoming bland and boring. Their culinary worth is immeasurable, but they have negligible nutritional value.

Sprouts

Mung bean sprouts are widely available from supermarkets, but many beans, peas and seeds can be easily sprouted. These include soya beans, aduki beans, alfalfa seeds, poppy seeds, sunflower seeds and chick-peas. They are rich in protein, complex carbohydrates, vitamins, minerals and fibre, but low in fat. As well as being healthy and nourishing, they add a nutty flavour and crunchy texture to salads and quick-cooked dishes.

Vegetables

High in beneficial complex carbohydrates but low in fat, vegetables form an important part of the low fat diet. They are rich in vitamins and minerals, including vitamins A, C, E and some of the B group, calcium, iron and phosphorus.

As they are also high in fibre, they satisfy the appetite. An easy way to cut down your fat intake is to cook at least one vegetarian dish, without dairy products, each week. Steaming, baking and braising are good techniques for cooking vegetables. When serving them as an accompaniment, sprinkle with chopped fresh herbs or ground spices, rather than adding a knob of butter. Serve baked potatoes with a spoonful of low fat cream cheese, cottage cheese or fromage frais, rather than butter or full fat cheese. Make your own salad dressings with low-fat yogurt or fromage frais rather than using full-fat mayonnaise. Raw vegetable sticks – celery, carrots or cucumber – make

excellent fat free nibbles, so substitute them for ready-made, high fat snacks, such as crisps and biscuits.

The major exception among vegetables is the avocado, although, strictly speaking, it is a fruit. It has a very high oil content, which can reach 30 per cent in some varieties. The good news is that this oil contains 75 per cent unsaturated fatty acids and no cholesterol. As avocados are so nourishing, containing between three and four per cent of the daily recommended protein requirement for adults, 14 minerals and 11 vitamins, the occasional treat may be allowed.

The following common vegetables contain less than 1 gram of fat per 100 grams of food: cabbage, carrots, cauliflower, celery, courgettes, cucumbers, onions, peas, potatoes and tomatoes.

Basic Recipes

Fresh Chicken Stock

MAKES: 7½ CUPS

2 lb 4 oz chicken, skinned

2 celery sticks

1 onion

2 carrots

1 garlic clove

few sprigs of fresh parsley

9 cups water

salt and pepper

1 Put all the ingredients into a large saucepan.

2 Bring to a boil. Skim away surface scum using a large flat spoon. Reduce the heat to a gentle simmer, partially cover, and cook for 2 hours. Allow to cool.

3 Line a strainer with clean cheesecloth and place over a large jug or bowl. Pour the stock through the strainer. The cooked chicken can be used in another recipe. Discard the other solids. Cover the stock and chill.

4 Skim away any fat that forms before using. Store in the refrigerator for 3–4 days, until required, or freeze in small batches.

Fresh Beef Stock

MAKES: 7½ CUPS

about 2 lb 4 oz bones from a cooked joint or raw chopped beef

2 onions, studded with 6 cloves, or sliced or chopped coarsely

2 carrots, sliced

1 leek, sliced

1–2 celery sticks, sliced

1 Bouquet Garni

about 2 quarts water

1 Use chopped marrow bones with a few strips of shin of beef if possible. Put in a roasting pan and cook in a preheated oven at 450°F for 30–50 minutes until browned.

2 Transfer to a large saucepan with the other ingredients. Bring to a boil and remove any scum from the surface with a perforated spoon.

3 Cover and simmer gently for 3–4 hours. Strain the stock and leave to cool. Remove any fat from the surface and chill. If stored for more than 24 hours the stock must be boiled every day, cooled quickly, and chilled again.

4 The stock may be frozen for up to 2 months; place in a large plastic bag and seal, leaving at least 1 inch of headspace to allow for expansion.

Fresh Fish Stock

MAKES: 7½ CUPS

2 lb 4 oz white fish bones, heads and scraps

1 large onion, chopped

2 carrots, chopped

2 celery sticks, chopped

½ tsp black peppercorns

½ tsp grated lemon rind

few sprigs of fresh parsley

9 cups water

salt and pepper

1 Rinse the fish trimmings well in cold water and place in a large saucepan with the other ingredients.

2 Bring to a boil and skim off any surface scum with a large flat spoon.

3 Reduce the heat to a gentle simmer and cook, partially covered, for 30 minutes. Allow to cool.

4 Line a strainer with clean cheesecloth and place over a large jug or bowl. Pour the stock through the strainer. Discard the solids. Cover the stock and store in the refrigerator for up to 3 days until required, or freeze in small batches.

Fresh Vegetable Stock

MAKES: 6¼ CUPS

1 large onion, sliced

1 large carrot, diced

1 stick celery, chopped

2 garlic cloves

1 dried bay leaf

few sprigs of fresh parsley

pinch of grated nutmeg

9 cups water

salt and pepper

1 Place all the ingredients in a large saucepan and bring to a boil.

2 Skim off surface scum using a flat spoon. Reduce the heat to a gentle simmer, partially cover, and cook for 45 minutes. Leave to cool.

3 Line a strainer with clean cheesecloth and place over a large jug or bowl. Pour the stock through the strainer. Discard the solids.

4 Cover the stock and store in the refrigerator for up to 3 days until required, or freeze in small batches.

Chinese Stock

MAKES: 10 CUPS

1 lb 10 oz chicken pieces

1 lb 10 oz pork spare ribs

15 cups cold water

3–4 pieces fresh ginger, crushed

3–4 green onions, each tied into knot

3–4 tbsp Chinese rice wine or dry sherry

1 Trim off any excess fat from the chicken and spare ribs; chop them into large pieces.

2 Place the chicken and pork in a large pan with water; add the ginger and green onion knots.

3 Bring to a boil and skim off the scum. Reduce the heat and simmer uncovered for at least 2–3 hours.

4 Strain the stock, discarding the chicken, pork, ginger, and green onions. Add the wine, return to a boil, and then simmer for 2–3 minutes.

5 Refrigerate the stock when cool, it will keep for up to 4–5 days. Alternatively, it can be frozen in small containers and be defrosted as required.

Cornstarch Paste

Mix 1 part cornstarch with about 1.5 parts of cold water. Stir until smooth. The paste is used to thicken sauces.

Fresh Bouquet Garni

1 fresh or dried bay leaf

few sprigs of fresh parsley

few sprigs of fresh thyme

Tie the herbs together with a length of string or cotton.

Dried Bouquet Garni

1 dried bay leaf

pinch of dried mixed herbs or any one herb

pinch of dried parsley

8–10 black peppercorns

2–4 cloves

1 garlic clove (optional)

Put all the ingredients in a small square of cheesecloth and secure with string or cotton, leaving a long tail so it can be tied to the handle of the pan for easy removal.

How to Use This Book

Each recipe contains a wealth of useful information, including a breakdown of nutritional quantities, preparation and cooking times, and level of difficulty. All of this information is explained in detail below.

The nutritional information provided for each recipe is per serving or per portion. Optional ingredients, variations, or serving suggestions have not been included in the calculations.

The number of chef's hats represents the difficulty of each recipe, ranging from easy (1 chef's hat) to difficult (5 chef's hats).

This amount of time represents the preparation of ingredients, including cooling, chilling, and soaking times.

This represents the cooking time.

The ingredients for each recipe are listed in the order that they are used.

74 Ultimate Low Fat Recipes

Tomato & (Bell) Pepper Soup
Sweet red (bell) peppers and tangy tomatoes are blended together in a smooth vegetable soup that makes a perfect starter or light lunch.

NUTRITIONAL INFORMATION

Calories ....52 Sugars 9g
Protein ....3g Fat 0.4g
Carbohydrate ...10g Saturates 0g

1¼ HOURS   35 MINS

SERVES 4

INGREDIENTS

2 large red (bell) peppers
1 large onion, chopped
2 sticks celery, trimmed and chopped
1 garlic clove, crushed
600 ml/1 pint/2½ cups Fresh Vegetable Stock (see page 29)
2 bay leaves
2 x 400 g/14 oz cans plum tomatoes
salt and pepper
2 spring onions (scallions), finely shredded, to garnish
crusty bread, to serve

1 Preheat the grill (broiler) to hot. Halve and deseed the (bell) peppers, arrange them on the grill (broiler) rack and cook, turning occasionally, for 8–10 minutes until softened and charred.

2 Leave to cool slightly, then carefully peel off the charred skin. Reserving a small piece for garnish, chop the (bell) pepper flesh and place in a large saucepan.

3 Mix in the onion, celery and garlic. Add the stock and the bay leaves. Bring to the boil, cover and simmer for 15 minutes. Remove from the heat.

4 Stir in the tomatoes and transfer to a blender. Process for a few seconds until smooth. Return to the saucepan.

5 Season to taste and heat for 3–4 minutes until piping hot. Ladle into warm bowls and garnish with the reserved (bell) pepper cut into strips and the spring onion (scallion). Serve with crusty bread.

COOK'S TIP

If you prefer a coarser, more robust soup, lightly mash the tomatoes with a wooden spoon and omit the blending process in step 4.

The method is clearly explained with step-by-step instructions that are easy to follow.

A full-color photograph of the finished dish.

The method is illustrated with step-by-step photographs, making the recipe easy to follow.

Cook's tips and variations provide useful information regarding ingredients or cooking techiques.

Soups

The traditional way to start a meal is with a soup, but they can also be a satisfying meal in themselves depending on their ingredients or if they are served with crusty bread. For best results use homemade stock—use the liquid left after cooking vegetables and the juices from fish and meat that have been used as the base of casseroles. Ready-made

stocks in the form of cubes or granules tend to contain large amounts of salt and flavorings which can overpower the soup. Although making fresh stock takes a little longer, it is well worth it for the superior taste. It is a good idea to make a large batch and freeze the remainder, in smaller quantities, for later use. Potato can be added to thicken soups rather than stirring in the traditional thickener of flour and water—or, worse, flour and fat.

Chicken & Asparagus Soup

This light, clear soup has a delicate flavor of asparagus and herbs. Use a good quality stock for best results.

NUTRITIONAL INFORMATION

Calories 224   Sugars 2g
Protein . . . . .27g   Fat 5g
Carbohydrate . . .12g   Saturates 1g

 2³/₄ HOURS   15 MINS

SERVES 4

INGREDIENTS

8 oz fresh asparagus

3¾ cups Fresh Chicken Stock (see page 30)

⅔ cup dry white wine

1 sprig each fresh parsley, dill, and
    tarragon

1 garlic clove

⅓ cup vermicelli rice noodles

12 oz lean cooked chicken, finely shredded

salt and white pepper

1 small leek

1 Wash the asparagus and trim away the woody ends. Cut each spear into pieces 1½ inches long.

2 Pour the stock and wine into a large saucepan and bring to a boil.

3 Wash the herbs and tie them with clean string. Peel the garlic clove and add, with the herbs, to the saucepan together with the asparagus and noodles. Cover and simmer for 5 minutes.

4 Stir in the chicken and plenty of seasoning. Simmer gently for a further 3-4 minutes until heated through.

5 Trim the leek, slice it down the center and wash under running water to remove any dirt. Shake dry and shred finely.

6 Remove the herbs and garlic from the pan and discard. Ladle the soup into warm bowls, sprinkle with shredded leek and serve at once.

VARIATION

You can use any of your favorite herbs in this recipe, but choose those with a subtle flavor so that they do not overpower the asparagus. Small, tender asparagus give the best results and flavor.

Tuscan Bean Soup

This thick, satisfying blend of beans and diced vegetables in a rich red wine and tomato stock makes an ideal simple supper dish.

NUTRITIONAL INFORMATION

Calories ....164 Sugars 10g
Protein ....9g Fat 1g
Carbohydrate ...26g Saturates 0g

1 HOUR   30 MINS

SERVES 4

I N G R E D I E N T S

1 medium onion, chopped

1 garlic clove, finely chopped

2 celery sticks, sliced

1 large carrot, diced

14 oz can chopped tomatoes

⅔ cup Italian dry red wine

5 cups Fresh Vegetable Stock
   (see page 31)

1 tsp dried oregano

15 oz can mixed beans

2 medium zucchini, diced

1 tbsp tomato paste

salt and pepper

TO SERVE

low-fat pesto sauce (see page 351)

crusty bread

1 Place the prepared onion, garlic, celery, and carrot in a large saucepan. Stir in the tomatoes, red wine, vegetable stock, and oregano.

2 Bring the vegetable mixture to a boil, cover, and simmer for 15 minutes.

3 Stir the mixed beans, and zucchini into the mixture in the saucepan, and continue to cook, uncovered, for 5 minutes.

4 Add the tomato paste to the mixture and season well with salt and pepper to taste. Heat through gently, stirring occasionally, for a further 2–3 minutes.

5 Ladle the soup into warm bowls and serve with a spoonful of low-fat pesto (see page 351) on each portion and accompanied with crusty bread. Serve immediately.

COOK'S TIP

For a more substantial soup, add 12 oz diced lean cooked chicken or turkey with the tomato paste in step 4.

Chicken & Leek Soup

This satisfying soup can be served as a main course. You can add rice and bell peppers to make it even more hearty, as well as colorful.

NUTRITIONAL INFORMATION

Calories 183	Sugar 4g	
Protein 21g	Fats 9g	
Carbohydrates 4g	Saturates 5g	

 5 MINS   1¹/₄ HOURS

SERVES 4–6

I N G R E D I E N T S

2 tbsp butter

12 oz boneless chicken

12 oz leeks, cut into 1-inch pieces

5 cups Fresh Chicken Stock
  (see page 30)

1 bouquet garni sachet

8 pitted prunes, halved

salt and white pepper

cooked rice and diced bell peppers
  (optional)

1 Melt the butter slowly in a large saucepan.

2 Add the chicken and leeks to the saucepan, and fry for 8 minutes.

3 Add the chicken stock and bouquet garni sachet to the chicken and stir well together.

4 Season well with salt and pepper to taste.

5 Bring the soup to a boil and simmer for 45 minutes.

6 Add the prunes to the saucepan with some cooked rice and diced bell peppers (if using) and simmer for about 20 minutes.

7 Remove the bouquet garni sachet from the soup and discard. Serve the chicken and leek soup immediately.

VARIATION

Instead of the bouquet garni sachet, you can use a bunch of fresh mixed herbs, tied together with string. Choose herbs such as parsley, thyme, and rosemary.

Shrimp Gumbo

This soup is thick with onions, red bell peppers, rice, shrimp, and okra, which both adds flavor and acts as a thickening agent.

NUTRITIONAL INFORMATION

Calories 177   Sugar 5g
Protein . . . . .12g   Fats 8g
Carbohydrates . . .15g   Saturates 1g

1 HOUR   45 MINS

SERVES 4–6

I N G R E D I E N T S

1 large onion, chopped finely

2 slices lean bacon, chopped finely (optional)

1–2 garlic cloves, crushed

2 tbsp olive oil

1 large or 2 small red bell peppers, chopped finely or minced coarsely

3½ cups Fish or Vegetable Stock (see pages 28–29)

1 fresh or dried bay leaf

1 blade mace

pinch of ground allspice

3 tbsp long-grain rice

1 tbsp white wine vinegar

4½–6 oz okra, trimmed and sliced very thinly

½–⅔ cup peeled shrimp

1 tbsp anchovy paste

2 tsp tomato paste

1–2 tbsp chopped fresh parsley

salt and pepper

T O   G A R N I S H

whole shrimp

sprigs of fresh parsley

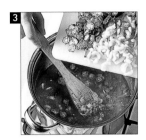

1 Gently fry the onion, bacon (if using), and garlic in the oil in a large saucepan for 4–5 minutes until soft. Add the bell peppers to the pan and continue to fry gently for a couple of minutes.

2 Add the stock, bay leaf, mace, allspice, rice, vinegar, and seasoning and bring to a boil. Cover and simmer gently for about 20 minutes, giving an occasional stir, until the rice is just tender.

3 Add the okra, shrimp, anchovy paste, and tomato paste, cover, and simmer gently for about 15 minutes until the okra is tender and the mixture slightly thickened.

4 Discard the bay leaf and mace from the soup and adjust the seasoning. Stir in the parsley and serve each portion garnished with a whole shrimp and fresh parsley sprigs.

Beef & Vegetable Soup

This comforting broth is perfect for a cold day and is just as delicious made with lean lamb or pork fillet.

NUTRITIONAL INFORMATION

Calories 138   Sugars 2g
Protein ....13g   Fat 3g
Carbohydrate ...15g   Saturates 1g

17¼ HOURS   40 MINS

SERVES 4

I N G R E D I E N T S

⅓ cup pearl barley, soaked overnight

5 cups Fresh Beef Stock (see page 30)

1 tsp dried mixed herbs

8 oz lean rump or sirloin beef

1 large carrot, diced

1 leek, shredded

1 medium onion, chopped

2 sticks celery, sliced

salt and pepper

2 tbsp fresh parsley, chopped, to garnish

crusty bread, to serve

1 Place the pearl barley in a large saucepan. Pour over the stock and add the mixed herbs. Bring to a boil, cover and simmer gently over a low heat for 10 minutes.

VARIATION

A vegetarian version can be made by omitting the beef and beef stock and using vegetable stock instead. Just before serving, stir in 6 oz fresh tofu, drained and diced.

2 Meanwhile, trim any fat from the beef and cut the meat into thin strips.

3 Skim away any scum that has risen to the top of the stock with a flat ladle.

4 Add the beef, carrot, leek, onion, and celery to the pan. Bring back to a boil, cover, and simmer for about 1 hour or until the barley, meat, and vegetables are just tender.

5 Skim away any remaining scum that has risen to the top of the soup with a flat ladle. Blot the surface with absorbent kitchen paper to remove any fat. Adjust the seasoning according to taste.

6 Ladle the soup into warm bowls and sprinkle with freshly chopped parsley. Serve piping hot, accompanied with fresh crusty bread.

Chicken & Corn Soup

A quick and satisfying soup, full of flavor and different textures. This will serve two people for one day or one person for two days.

NUTRITIONAL INFORMATION

Calories 200	Sugars 6g
Protein 10g	Fat 12g
Carbohydrate . . .13g	Saturates 5g

 10 MINS 40 MINS

SERVES 2

INGREDIENTS

2 tsp oil

¼ cup butter or margarine

1 small onion, chopped finely

1 chicken leg quarter or 2–3 drumsticks

1 tbsp all-purpose flour

2½ cups chicken stock

½ small red, yellow, or orange bell pepper, seeded and chopped finely

2 large tomatoes, peeled and chopped

2 tsp tomato paste

7 oz can corn kernels, drained

pinch of dried oregano

¼ tsp ground coriander

salt and pepper

chopped fresh parsley, to garnish

1 Heat the oil and butter or margarine in a saucepan and fry the onion until beginning to soften. Cut the chicken quarter (if using) into 2 pieces. Add the chicken and fry until golden brown.

2 Add the flour and cook for 1–2 minutes. Then add the stock, bring to a boil and simmer for 5 minutes.

3 Add the bell pepper, tomatoes, tomato paste, corn, oregano, coriander, and seasoning. Cover and simmer gently for about 20 minutes until the chicken is very tender.

4 Remove the chicken from the soup, strip off the flesh, and chop finely. Return the chopped meat to the soup.

5 Adjust the seasoning and simmer for a further 2–3 minutes before sprinkling with parsley and serving very hot with crusty bread.

COOK'S TIP

If preferred, the chicken may be removed from the soup when tender to serve separately.

Red Bell Pepper Soup

This soup has a real Mediterranean flavor, using sweet red bell peppers, tomato, chili, and basil. It is great served with warm olive bread.

NUTRITIONAL INFORMATION

Calories	55	Sugar	........10g
Protein	........2g	Fats	........0.5g
Carbohydrates	...11g	Saturates	.....0.1g

 5 MINS   🕐 25 MINS

SERVES 4

I N G R E D I E N T S

8 oz red bell peppers, seeded and sliced

1 onion, sliced

2 garlic cloves, crushed

1 green chili, chopped

1½ cups strained tomatoes

2½ cups vegetable stock

2 tbsp chopped basil

fresh basil sprigs, to garnish

1 Put the bell peppers in a large saucepan with the onion, garlic, and chili. Add the strained tomatoes and vegetable stock and bring to a boil, stirring well.

2 Reduce the heat to a simmer and cook for 20 minutes or until the bell peppers have softened. Drain, reserving the liquid and vegetables separately.

3 Strain the vegetables by pressing through a strainer with the back of a spoon. Alternatively, blend in a food processor until smooth.

4 Return the vegetable purée to a clean saucepan with the reserved cooking liquid. Add the basil and heat through until hot. Garnish the soup with fresh basil sprigs and serve.

VARIATION

This soup is also delicious served cold with 1¼ cup of plain yogurt swirled into it.

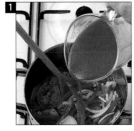

Potato & Mixed Fish Soup

Any mixture of fish is suitable for this recipe, from simple smoked and white fish to salmon or mussels, depending on the occasion.

NUTRITIONAL INFORMATION

Calories	458	Sugar	.........5g
Protein	........28g	Fats	..........25g
Carbohydrates	...22g	Saturates	.....12g

10 MINS   35 MINS

SERVES 4

INGREDIENTS

2 tbsp vegetable oil

1 lb small new potatoes, halved

1 bunch green onions, sliced

1 yellow bell pepper, sliced

2 garlic cloves, crushed

1 cup dry white wine

2½ cups fish stock

8 oz white fish fillet, skinned and cubed

8 oz smoked cod fillet, skinned and cubed

2 tomatoes, peeled, seeded, and chopped

3½ oz peeled cooked shrimp

⅔ cup heavy cream

2 tbsp shredded fresh basil

1 Heat the vegetable oil in a large saucepan and add the halved potatoes, sliced green onions, bell pepper, and the garlic. Sauté gently for 3 minutes, stirring constantly.

2 Add the white wine and fish stock to the saucepan and bring to a boil. Reduce the heat and simmer for 10-15 minutes.

3 Add the cubed fish fillets and the tomatoes to the soup and continue to cook for 10 minutes or until the fish is cooked through.

4 Stir in the shrimp, cream, and shredded basil and cook for 2-3 minutes. Pour the soup into warmed bowls and serve immediately.

COOK'S TIP

For a soup which is slightly less rich, omit the wine and stir plain yogurt into the soup instead of the heavy cream.

Garbanzo Bean & Tomato Soup

A thick vegetable soup which is a delicious meal in itself. Serve with Parmesan cheese and warm sun-dried tomato bread.

NUTRITIONAL INFORMATION

Calories 285	Sugar 11g
Protein 16g	Fats 12g
Carbohydrates ...29g	Saturates 3g

 5 MINS   15 MINS

SERVES 4

INGREDIENTS

2 tbsp olive oil

2 leeks, sliced

2 zucchini, diced

2 garlic cloves, crushed

2 x 14 oz cans chopped
   tomatoes

1 tbsp tomato paste

1 fresh bay leaf

3¾ cups chicken stock

14 oz can garbanzo beans, drained and
   rinsed

8 oz spinach

TO SERVE

Parmesan cheese, freshly-grated

sun-dried tomato bread

1 Heat the oil in a large saucepan, add the leeks and zucchini, and cook briskly for 5 minutes, stirring constantly.

2 Add the garlic, tomatoes, tomato paste, bay leaf, chicken stock, and garbanzo beans.

3 Bring to a boil and simmer for 5 minutes.

4 Shred the spinach finely, add to the soup and cook for 2 minutes. Season to taste.

5 Discard the bay leaf. Serve the soup immediately with freshly-grated Parmesan cheese and warm sun-dried tomato bread.

COOK'S TIP

Garbanzo beans are used extensively in North African cuisine and are also found in Spanish, Middle Eastern, and Indian cooking. They have a nutty flavor with a firm texture and are excellent canned.

Chicken & Coconut Soup

This fragrant, Thai-style soup combines citrus flavors with coconut and a hint of piquancy from chilies.

NUTRITIONAL INFORMATION

Calories	345	Sugar	.........2g
Protein	........28g	Fats	..........24g
Carbohydrates	....5g	Saturates	.....18g

2³/₄ HOURS   15 MINS

SERVES 4

I N G R E D I E N T S

1¾ cups cooked, skinned chicken breast

1⅓ cups unsweetened desiccated coconut

2 cups boiling water

2 cups Fresh Chicken Stock (see page 30)

4 green onions, white and green parts, sliced thinly

2 stalks lemon grass

1 lime

1 tsp grated ginger root

1 tbsp light soy sauce

2 tsp ground coriander

2 large fresh red chilies

1 tbsp chopped fresh cilantro

1 tbsp cornstarch mixed with 2 tbsp cold water

salt and white pepper

chopped red chili, to garnish

1 Slice the chicken into thin strips. Place the coconut in a heatproof bowl and pour the boiling water over.

2 Place a fine strainer over another bowl and pour in the coconut water. Work the coconut through the strainer.

3 Add the coconut water, the stock, and the green onions to a large saucepan. Slice the base of each lemon grass and discard damaged leaves. Bruise the stalks and add to the saucepan.

4 Peel the rind from the lime, keeping it in large strips. Slice the lime in half and extract the juice. Add the lime strips, juice, ginger, soy sauce, and ground coriander to the saucepan.

5 Bruise the chilies with a fork then add to the saucepan. Heat the pan to just below boiling point. Add the chicken and fresh cilantro to the saucepan, bring to a boil, then simmer for 10 minutes.

6 Discard the lemon grass, lime rind, and chilies. Pour the blended cornstarch mixture into the saucepan and stir until slightly thickened. Season, then garnish with the red chili.

Chilled Cucumber Soup

Serve this soup over ice on a warm summer day as a refreshing starter. It has the fresh tang of yogurt and a dash of spice from the Tabasco sauce.

NUTRITIONAL INFORMATION

Calories 83   Sugars 7g
Protein . . . . .12g   Fat 1g
Carbohydrate . . . .7g   Saturates 0.3g

 3¹/₂ HOURS   0 MINS

SERVES 4

I N G R E D I E N T S

1 cucumber, peeled and diced

1⅔ cups Fresh Fish Stock, chilled (see page 30)

⅔ cup tomato juice

⅔ cup low-fat plain yogurt

⅔ cup low-fat fromage frais (or double the quantity of plain yogurt)

4½ oz peeled shrimp, thawed if frozen, roughly chopped

few drops Tabasco sauce

1 tbsp fresh mint, chopped

salt and white pepper

ice cubes, to serve

T O   G A R N I S H

sprigs of mint

cucumber slices

whole peeled shrimp

1 Place the diced cucumber in a blender or food processor and work for a few seconds until smooth. Alternatively, chop the cucumber finely and push through a strainer.

2 Transfer the cucumber to a bowl. Stir in the stock, tomato juice, yogurt, fromage frais (if using), and shrimp, and mix well.

3 Add the Tabasco sauce and season to taste.

4 Stir in the chopped mint, cover, and chill for at least 2 hours.

5 Ladle the soup into glass bowls and add a few ice cubes. Serve garnished with mint, cucumber slices, and whole shrimp.

VARIATION

Instead of shrimp, add white crab meat or minced chicken. For a vegetarian version of this soup, omit the shrimp and add an extra 4½ oz finely diced cucumber. Use fresh vegetable stock instead of fish stock.

Beet root & Potato Soup

A deep red soup makes a stunning first course. Adding a swirl of sour cream and a few sprigs of dill gives a very pretty effect.

NUTRITIONAL INFORMATION

Calories	120	Sugars	........11g
Protein	.........4g	Fat	...........2g
Carbohydrate	...22g	Saturates	......1g

 20 MINS   30 MINS

SERVES 6

INGREDIENTS

1 onion, chopped

12 oz potatoes, diced

1 small cooking apple, peeled, cored, and grated

3 tbsp water

1 tsp cumin seeds

1 lb 2 oz cooked beet root, peeled and diced

1 dried bay leaf

pinch of dried thyme

1 tsp lemon juice

2½ cups hot vegetable stock

4 tbsp sour cream

salt and pepper

few sprigs of fresh dill, to garnish

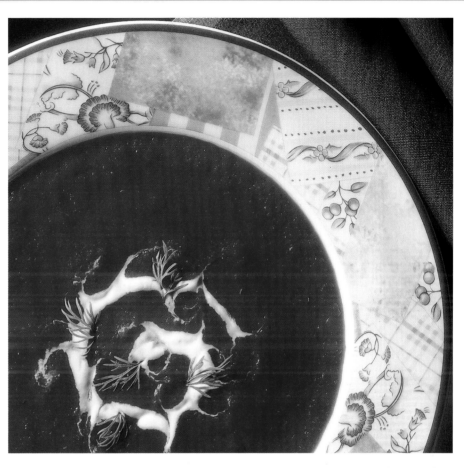

1 Place the onion, potatoes, apple, and water in a large bowl. Cover and cook on HIGH power for 10 minutes.

2 Stir in the cumin seeds and cook on HIGH power for 1 minute.

3 Stir in the beet root, bay leaf, thyme, lemon juice, and stock. Cover and cook on HIGH power for 12 minutes, stirring halfway through. Leave to stand, uncovered, for 5 minutes.

4 Remove and discard the bay leaf. Strain the vegetables and reserve the liquid in a jug.

5 Purée the vegetables with a little of the reserved liquid in a food processor or blender, until they are smooth and creamy. Alternatively, either mash the soup or press it through a strainer.

6 Pour the vegetable purée into a clean bowl with the reserved liquid and mix well. Season to taste. Cover and cook on HIGH power for 4–5 minutes or until piping hot.

7 Serve the soup in warmed bowls. Swirl 1 tablespoon of sour cream into each serving and garnish with a few sprigs of fresh dill.

Spiced Fruit Soup

This delicately flavored apple and apricot soup is gently spiced with ginger and allspice, and finished with a swirl of sour cream.

NUTRITIONAL INFORMATION

Calories 147	Sugar 28g	
Protein 3g	Fats 0.4g	
Carbohydrates ...29g	Saturates 0g	

7³/₄ HOURS   25 MINS

SERVES 4–6

INGREDIENTS

⅔ cup dried apricots, soaked overnight or no-need-to-soak dried apricots

1 lb 2 oz dessert apples, peeled, cored, and chopped

1 small onion, chopped

1 tbsp lemon or lime juice

3 cups Fresh Chicken Stock (see page 30)

⅔ cup dry white wine

¼ tsp ground ginger

pinch of ground allspice

salt and pepper

TO GARNISH

4–6 tbsp sour cream or natural fromage frais

little ground ginger or ground allspice

1 Drain the apricot, if necessary, and then chop.

2 Put in a saucepan and add the apples, onion, lemon or lime juice, and stock. Bring to a boil, cover, and simmer gently for about 20 minutes.

3 Leave the soup to cool a little, then press through a strainer or blend in a food processor or blender until very smooth. Pour the fruit soup into a clean saucepan.

4 Add the wine and spices and season to taste. Bring back to a boil, then leave to cool. If too thick, add a little more stock or water and then chill thoroughly.

5 Put a spoonful of sour cream or fromage frais on top of each portion and lightly dust with ginger or allspice.

VARIATION

Other fruits can be combined with apples to make fruit soups—try raspberries, blackberries, blackcurrants, or cherries. If the fruits have a lot of seeds or pits, the soup should be strained after puréeing.

Beef Soup with Rice

Strips of tender lean beef are combined with crisp water chestnuts and cooked rice in a tasty beef broth with a tang of orange.

NUTRITIONAL INFORMATION

Calories 210	Sugar 4g
Protein 20g	Fats 5g
Carbohydrates . . .21g	Saturates 2g

  25 MINS   25 MINS

SERVES 4

INGREDIENTS

12 oz lean beef (such as rump or sirloin)

1 quart beef stock

1 cinnamon stick, broken

2 star anise

2 tbsp dark soy sauce

2 tbsp dry sherry

3 tbsp tomato paste

4 oz can water chestnuts, drained and sliced

3 cups cooked white rice

1 tsp zested orange rind

6 tbsp orange juice

salt and pepper

TO GARNISH

strips of orange rind

2 tbsp chives, snipped

1 Carefully trim away any fat from the beef. Cut the beef into thin strips and then place into a large saucepan.

2 Pour over the stock and add the cinnamon, star anise, soy sauce, sherry, tomato paste, and water chestnuts. Bring to a boil, skimming away any surface scum with a flat ladle. Cover the pan and simmer gently for about 20 minutes.

3 Skim the soup with a flat ladle to remove any more scum. Remove and discard the cinnamon and star anise and blot the surface with absorbent kitchen paper to remove any fat.

4 Stir in the rice, orange rind, and juice. Check the seasoning. Heat through for 2–3 minutes before ladling into warm bowls. Serve garnished with strips of orange rind and snipped chives.

COOK'S TIP

Omit the rice for a lighter soup that is an ideal starter for an Oriental meal of many courses. For a more substantial soup that would be a meal in itself, add vegetables such as carrot, bell pepper, corn kernels, or zucchini.

Mixed Bean Soup

This is a really hearty soup, filled with color, flavor, and goodness, which may be adapted to any vegetables that you have available.

NUTRITIONAL INFORMATION

Calories	190	Sugars	.........9g
Protein	........10g	Fat	...........4g
Carbohydrate	...30g	Saturates	.....0.5g

5 MINS | 40 MINS

SERVES 4

I N G R E D I E N T S

1 tbsp vegetable oil

1 red onion, halved and sliced

⅔ cup potato, diced

1 carrot, diced

1 leek, sliced

1 green chili, sliced

3 garlic cloves, crushed

1 tsp ground coriander

1 tsp chili powder

4 cups vegetable stock

1 lb mixed canned beans, such as red kidney, borlotti, black eye, or flageolet, drained

salt and pepper

2 tbsp chopped cilantro, to garnish

1 Heat the vegetable oil in a large saucepan and add the prepared onion, potato, carrot, and leek. Sauté for about 2 minutes, stirring, until the vegetables are slightly softened.

2 Add the sliced chili and crushed garlic and cook for 1 minute.

3 Stir in the ground coriander, chili powder, and the vegetable stock.

4 Bring the soup to a boil, reduce the heat, and cook for 20 minutes or until the vegetables are tender.

5 Stir in the beans, season well with salt and pepper, and cook for a further 10 minutes, stirring occasionally.

6 Transfer the soup to a warm tureen or individual bowls, garnish with chopped cilantro, and serve.

COOK'S TIP

Serve this soup with slices of warm corn bread or a cheese loaf.

Yogurt & Spinach Soup

Whole young spinach leaves add vibrant color to this unusual soup.
Serve with hot, crusty bread for a nutritious, light meal.

NUTRITIONAL INFORMATION

Calories 227   Sugars 13g
Protein . . . . .14g   Fat 7g
Carbohydrate . . .29g   Saturates 2g

 15 MINS    30 MINS

SERVES 4

INGREDIENTS

2½ cups chicken stock

4 tbsp long-grain rice, rinsed and drained

4 tbsp water

1 tbsp cornstarch

2½ cups low-fat plain yogurt

juice of 1 lemon

3 egg yolks, lightly beaten

12 oz young spinach leaves, washed and
    drained

salt and pepper

1 Pour the stock into a large pan, season and bring to a boil. Add the rice and simmer for 10 minutes, until barely cooked. Remove from the heat.

2 Combine the water and cornstarch to make a smooth paste.

3 Pour the yogurt into a second pan and stir in the cornstarch mixture. Set the pan over a low heat and bring the yogurt slowly to a boil, stirring with a wooden spoon in one direction only. This will stabilize the yogurt and prevent it from separating or curdling on contact with the hot stock. When the yogurt has reached boiling point, stand the pan on a heat diffuser, and leave to simmer slowly for 10 minutes. Remove the pan from the heat and allow the mixture to cool slightly before stirring in the beaten egg yolks.

4 Pour the yogurt mixture into the stock, stir in the lemon juice, and stir to blend thoroughly. Keep the soup warm, but do not allow it to boil.

5 Blanch the washed and drained spinach leaves in a large pan of boiling, salted water for 2–3 minutes until they begin to soften but have not collapsed. Pour the spinach into a colander, drain well, and stir it into the soup. Let the spinach warm through. Taste the soup and adjust the seasoning if necessary. Serve in wide shallow soup plates, with hot, crusty bread.

Mediterranean Fish Soup

Juicy chunks of fish and sumptuous shellfish are cooked in a flavorful stock. Serve with toasted bread rubbed with garlic.

NUTRITIONAL INFORMATION

Calories	316	Sugar	.........4g
Protein	........53g	Fats	...........7g
Carbohydrates	....5g	Saturates	......1g

 1 HOUR   15 MINS

SERVES 4

INGREDIENTS

1 tbsp olive oil

1 large onion, chopped

2 garlic cloves, finely chopped

1¾ cups Fresh Fish Stock (see page 30)

⅔ cup dry white wine

1 bay leaf

1 sprig each fresh thyme, rosemary and
oregano

1 lb firm white fish fillets (such as cod,
swordfish, or halibut), skinned and cut
into 1 inch cubes

1 lb fresh mussels, prepared

14 oz can chopped tomatoes

8 oz peeled shrimp, thawed if frozen

salt and pepper

sprigs of thyme, to garnish

TO SERVE

lemon wedges

4 slices toasted French bread, rubbed with
cut garlic clove

1 Heat the olive oil in a large saucepan and gently fry the onion and garlic for 2–3 minutes or until just softened.

2 Pour in the stock and wine and bring to a boil.

3 Tie the bay leaf and herbs together with clean string and add to the saucepan together with the fish and mussels. Stir well, cover, and simmer for 5 minutes.

4 Stir in the tomatoes and shrimp and continue to cook for a further 3–4 minutes until piping hot and the fish is cooked through.

5 Discard the herbs and any mussels that have not opened. Season to taste, then ladle into warm bowls.

6 Garnish with sprigs of fresh thyme and serve with lemon wedges and toasted bread.

Chicken & Pasta Broth

This satisfying soup makes a good lunch or supper dish and you can use any vegetables that you have available.

NUTRITIONAL INFORMATION

Calories 295	Sugar 8g	
Protein 25g	Fats 10g	
Carbohydrates . . .29g	Saturates 2g	

5 MINS   20 MINS

SERVES 4

I N G R E D I E N T S

12 oz boneless chicken breasts

2 tbsp sunflower oil

1 medium onion, diced

1½ cups carrots, diced

8 oz cauliflower florets

3¾ cups chicken stock

2 tsp dried mixed herbs

4½ oz small pasta shapes

salt and pepper

Parmesan cheese (optional) and crusty
   bread, to serve

1 Finely dice the chicken, discarding any skin.

2 Heat the oil and quickly sauté the chicken and vegetables until they are lightly colored.

3 Stir in the stock and herbs. Bring to a boil and add the pasta. Return to a boil, cover, and simmer for 10 minutes.

4 Season to taste and sprinkle with Parmesan cheese (if using). Serve with crusty bread.

Cucumber & Tomato Soup

Although this chilled soup is not an authentic Indian dish, it is wonderful served as a "cooler" between hot, spicy courses.

NUTRITIONAL INFORMATION

Calories 73   Sugar 16g
Protein ....2g   Fats 1g
Carbohydrates ...16g   Saturates 0.2g

 12 HOURS   0 MINS

SERVES 6

I N G R E D I E N T S

4 tomatoes, peeled and deseeded

3 lb 5 oz watermelon, seedless if available

4 inch piece cucumber, peeled and deseeded

2 green onions, green part only, chopped

1 tbsp chopped fresh mint

salt and pepper

fresh mint sprigs, to garnish

1 Using a sharp knife, cut 1 tomato into ½ inch dice.

2 Remove the rind from the melon, and remove the seeds if it is not seedless.

3 Put the 3 remaining tomatoes into a blender or food processor and, with the motor running, add the deseeded cucumber, chopped green onions, and watermelon. Blend until smooth.

4 If not using a food processor, push the deseeded watermelon through a strainer. Stir the diced tomatoes and mint into the melon mixture. Adjust the seasoning to taste. Chop the cucumber, green onions, and the 3 remaining tomatoes finely and add to the melon.

5 Chill the cucumber and tomato soup overnight in the refrigerator. Check the seasoning and transfer to a serving dish. Garnish with mint sprigs.

COOK'S TIP

Although this soup does improve if chilled overnight, it is also delicious as a quick appetizer if whipped up just before a meal, and served immediately.

Coconut & Crab Soup

Thai red curry paste is quite fiery, but adds a superb flavor to this dish. It is available in jars or packets from supermarkets.

NUTRITIONAL INFORMATION

Calories 122   Sugar 9g
Protein ....11g   Fats 4g
Carbohydrates ...11g   Saturates 1g

5 MINS   10 MINS

SERVES 4

INGREDIENTS

1 tbsp peanut oil

2 tbsp Thai red curry paste

1 red bell pepper, deseeded and sliced

2½ cups coconut milk

2½ cups fish stock

2 tbsp fish sauce

8 oz canned or fresh white crab meat

8 oz fresh or frozen crab claws

2 tbsp chopped fresh cilantro

3 green onions, trimmed and sliced

1 Heat the oil in a large preheated wok.

2 Add the red curry paste and red bell pepper to the wok and stir-fry for 1 minute.

3 Add the coconut milk, fish stock, and fish sauce and bring to a boil.

4 Add the crab meat, crab claws, cilantro, and green onions to the wok.

5 Stir the mixture well and heat thoroughly for 2–3 minutes or until everything is warmed through.

6 Transfer the soup to warm bowls and serve hot.

COOK'S TIP

Clean the wok after use by washing it with water, using a mild detergent if necessary, and a soft cloth or brush. Do not scrub or use any abrasive cleaner as this will scratch the surface. Dry thoroughly then wipe the surface all over with a little oil to protect the surface.

Dickensian Chicken Broth

This soup is made with traditional Scottish ingredients. It should be left for at least two days before being re-heated.

NUTRITIONAL INFORMATION

Calories	357	Sugars	.........5g
Protein	........53g	Fat	...........8g
Carbohydrate	...19g	Saturates	......2g

48¼ HOURS   2¾ HOURS

SERVES 4

INGREDIENTS

⅓ cup pre-soaked dried peas

2 lb diced lean chicken, fat removed

5 cups chicken stock

2½ cups water

¼ cup barley

1 large carrot, peeled and diced

1 small turnip, peeled and diced

1 large leek, thinly sliced

1 red onion, chopped finely

salt and white pepper

oatmeal cakes or bread to serve

COOK'S TIP

Use either whole grain barley or pearl barley. Only the outer husk is removed from whole grain barley and when cooked, it has a nutty flavor and a chewy texture.

1 Put the pre-soaked peas and diced chicken into a pan, then add the stock and water, and bring slowly to a boil.

2 Skim the stock as it boils.

3 Wash the barley thoroughly and put to one side.

4 When all the scum is removed, add the washed barley and salt, and simmer for 35 minutes.

5 Add the rest of the ingredients, simmer for 2 hours, and skim again.

6 Let the broth stand for at least 48 hours. Reheat, adjust the seasoning and serve with oatmeal cakes or bread.

Red Lentil Soup with Yogurt

Tasty red lentil soup flavored with chopped cilantro. The yogurt adds a light piquancy to the soup.

NUTRITIONAL INFORMATION

Calories	280	Sugars	.........6g
Protein	........17g	Fat	...........7g
Carbohydrate	...40g	Saturates	......4g

 5 MINS   30 MINS

SERVES 4

I N G R E D I E N T S

2 tbsp butter

1 onion, chopped finely

1 celery stick, chopped finely

1 large carrot, grated

1 dried bay leaf

1 cup red lentils

5 cups hot vegetable or chicken stock

2 tbsp chopped fresh cilantro

4 tbsp low-fat plain yogurt

salt and pepper

fresh cilantro sprigs, to garnish

1 Place the butter, onion, and celery in a large bowl. Cover and cook on HIGH power for 3 minutes.

2 Add the carrot, bay leaf, and lentils. Pour over the stock. Cover and cook on HIGH power for 15 minutes, stirring halfway through.

3 Remove from the microwave oven and stand, covered, for 5 minutes.

4 Remove the bay leaf, then blend in batches in a food processor, until smooth. Alternatively, press the soup through a strainer.

5 Pour into a clean bowl. Season with salt and pepper to taste and stir in the cilantro. Cover and cook on HIGH power for 4–5 minutes until piping hot.

6 Serve in warmed bowls. Stir 1 tablespoon of yogurt into each serving and garnish with sprigs of fresh cilantro.

COOK'S TIP

For an extra creamy soup, try adding low-fat crème fraîche or sour cream instead of yogurt.

Cock-a-Leekie Soup

A traditional Scottish soup in which a whole chicken is cooked with the vegetables to add extra flavor to the stock.

NUTRITIONAL INFORMATION

Calories 45   Sugars 4g
Protein . . . . .5g   Fat 1g
Carbohydrate . . . .5g   Saturates 0.2g

2½ HOURS   2 HOURS

SERVES 4–6

I N G R E D I E N T S

2 lb 4 oz–3 lb 5 oz oven-ready chicken plus giblets, if available

8–9 cups Chicken Stock (see page 30)

1 onion, sliced

4 leeks, sliced thinly

pinch of ground allspice or ground coriander

1 Bouquet Garni (see page 31)

12 no-need-to-soak prunes, halved and pitted

salt and pepper

warm crusty bread to serve

1 Put the chicken, giblets (if using) stock, and onion in a large saucepan.

2 Bring to a boil and remove any scum from the surface.

3 Add the leeks, seasoning, allspice or coriander, and bouquet garni to the pan, cover, and simmer gently for about 1½ hours until the chicken is falling off the bones.

4 Remove the chicken and bouquet garni from the pan and skim any fat from the surface of the soup.

5 Chop some of the chicken flesh and return to the pan.

6 Add the prunes, bring back to a boil, and simmer, uncovered, for about 20 minutes.

7 Adjust the seasoning and serve with warm, crusty bread.

VARIATION

You can replace the chicken stock with 3 chicken stock cubes dissolved in the same amount of water, if you prefer.

Spicy Lentil Soup

For a warming, satisfying meal on a cold day, this lentil dish is packed full of taste and goodness.

NUTRITIONAL INFORMATION

Calories 155   Sugars 4g
Protein ....11g   Fat 3g
Carbohydrate ...22g   Saturates 0.4g

1 HOUR   1¼ HOURS

SERVES 4

INGREDIENTS

½ cup red lentils

2 tsp vegetable oil

1 large onion, chopped finely

2 garlic cloves, crushed

1 tsp ground cumin

1 tsp ground coriander

1 tsp garam masala

2 tbsp tomato paste

4½ cups Fresh Vegetable Stock (see page 31)

12 oz can corn kernels, drained

salt and pepper

TO SERVE

low-fat plain yogurt

chopped fresh parsley

warmed pita bread

  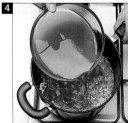

1 Rinse the red lentils in cold water. Drain the lentils well and put to one side.

2 Heat the oil in a large non-stick saucepan and fry the onion and garlic gently until softened, but not browned.

3 Stir in the cumin, coriander, garam masala, tomato paste, and 4 tablespoons of the stock. Mix well and simmer gently for 2 minutes.

4 Add the lentils and pour in the remaining stock. Bring to a boil, reduce the heat, and simmer, covered, for 1 hour until the lentils are tender and the soup thickened. Stir in the corn and heat through for 5 minutes. Season well.

5 Ladle into warmed soup bowls and top each with a spoonful of yogurt and a sprinkling of parsley. Serve with warmed pita bread.

COOK'S TIP

Many of the ready-prepared ethnic breads available today either contain fat or are brushed with oil before baking. Always check the ingredients list for fat content.

Partan Bree

This traditional Scottish soup is thickened with a purée of rice and crab meat cooked in milk. Add sour cream, if liked, at the end of cooking.

NUTRITIONAL INFORMATION

Calories 112	Sugars 5g
Protein 7g	Fat 2g
Carbohydrate ...18g	Saturates 0.3g

🍲 1 HOUR 🕐 35 MINS

SERVES 6

INGREDIENTS

1 medium-sized boiled crab

½ cup long-grain rice

2½ cups skim milk

2½ cups Fish Stock
(see page 30)

1 tbsp anchovy paste

2 tsp lime or lemon juice

1 tbsp chopped fresh parsley or I tsp
chopped fresh thyme

3–4 tbsp sour cream optional

salt and pepper

snipped chives, to garnish

1 Remove and reserve all the brown and white meat from the crab, then crack the claws, and remove and chop that meat; reserve the claw meat.

COOK'S TIP

If you are unable to buy a whole crab, use about 6 oz frozen crab meat and thaw thoroughly before use; or a 6 oz can of crab meat which just needs thorough draining.

2 Put the rice and milk into a saucepan and bring slowly to a boil. Cover and simmer gently for about 20 minutes.

3 Add the reserved white and brown crab meat and seasoning and simmer for a further 5 minutes.

4 Cool a little, then press through a strainer, or work in a food processor or blender until smooth.

5 Pour the soup into a clean saucepan and add the fish stock and the reserved claw meat. Bring slowly to a boil, then add the anchovy paste and lime or lemon juice, and adjust the seasoning.

6 Simmer for a further 2–3 minutes. Stir in the parsley or thyme and then swirl sour cream (if using) through each serving. Garnish with snipped chives.

Split Pea & Ham Soup

You can use either yellow or green split peas in this recipe but both types must be well washed and soaked overnight before use.

NUTRITIONAL INFORMATION

Calories	323	Sugars 9g
Protein	........17g	Fat 9g
Carbohydrate	...45g	Saturates 4g

12¼ HOURS   2¾ HOURS

SERVES 6

INGREDIENTS

1¼ cups dried yellow split peas

7½ cups water

2 onions, chopped finely

1 small turnip, chopped finely

2 carrots, chopped finely

2–4 celery sticks, chopped finely

1 lean ham bone

1 Bouquet Garni (see page 31)

½ tsp dried thyme

½ tsp ground ginger

1 tbsp white wine vinegar

salt and pepper

1 Wash the dried peas thoroughly, then place in a bowl with half the water, and leave to soak overnight.

2 Put the soaked peas and their liquid, the remaining water, the onions, turnip, carrots, and celery into a large saucepan, then add the ham bone, bouquet garni, dried thyme, and ginger. Bring slowly to a boil.

3 Remove any scum from the surface of the soup, cover the pan, and simmer gently for 2–2½ hours until the peas are very tender.

4 Remove the ham bone and bouquet garni. Strip about ³/₄–1 cup meat from the bone and chop it finely.

5 Add the chopped ham and vinegar to the soup and season to taste.

6 Bring back to a boil and simmer for 3–4 minutes. Serve.

VARIATION

If preferred, this soup can be strained or blended in a food processor or blender until smooth. You can vary the vegetables, depending on what is available. Leeks, celery root, or chopped or canned tomatoes are particularly good.

Veg & Garbanzo Bean Soup

A tasty soup, full of vegetables, chicken, and garbanzo beans, with just a hint of spiciness, to serve on any occasion.

NUTRITIONAL INFORMATION

Calories 271   Sugar 6g
Protein . . . . .17g   Fats 13g
Carbohydrates . . .24g   Saturates 2g

 10 MINS   55 MINS

SERVES 4–6

I N G R E D I E N T S

3 tbsp olive oil

1 large onion, chopped finely

2–3 garlic cloves, crushed

½–1 red chili, deseeded and chopped very finely

1 skinless, boneless chicken breast, about 5½ oz, sliced thickly

2 celery stalks, chopped finely

6 oz carrots, grated coarsely

2¼ pints chicken stock

2 bay leaves

½ tsp dried oregano

¼ tsp ground cinnamon

14 oz can garbanzo beans, drained

2 medium tomatoes, peeled, deseeded, and chopped

1 tbsp tomato paste

salt and pepper

chopped fresh cilantro or parsley, to garnish

corn or wheat tortillas, to serve

1 Heat the oil in a large saucepan and fry the onion, garlic, and chili very gently until they are softened but not colored.

2 Add the chicken to the saucepan and continue to cook until well sealed and lightly browned.

3 Add the celery, carrots, stock, bay leaves, oregano, cinnamon, and salt and pepper. Bring to a boil, then cover, and simmer gently for about 20 minutes, or until the chicken is tender and cooked through.

4 Remove the chicken from the soup and chop it finely, or cut it into narrow strips.

5 Return the chicken to the pan with the garbanzo beans, tomatoes, and tomato paste. Simmer, covered, for a further 15–20 minutes. Discard the bay leaves, then adjust the seasoning.

6 Serve very hot sprinkled with cilantro or parsley and accompanied by warmed tortillas.

Hot & Sour Soup

This is the favorite soup in Chinese restaurants throughout the world. Strain the soaking liquid and use in other soups, sauces, and casseroles.

NUTRITIONAL INFORMATION

Calories 118   Sugar 0.3g
Protein . . . . .14g   Fats 4g
Carbohydrates . . . .7g   Saturates 1g

4¹/₄ HOURS   10 MINS

SERVES 4

I N G R E D I E N T S

4-6 dried Chinese mushrooms (Shiitake), soaked

4½ oz cooked lean pork or chicken

1 cake tofu (bean curd)

2 oz canned sliced bamboo shoots, drained

2½ cups Chinese Stock (see page 30) or water

1 tbsp Chinese rice wine or dry sherry

1 tbsp light soy sauce

2 tbsp rice vinegar

1 tbsp cornstarch paste (see page 31)

salt, to taste

½ tsp ground white pepper

2-3 green onions, thinly sliced, to serve

1 Drain the mushrooms, squeeze dry, and discard the hard stalks. Thinly slice the mushrooms. Slice the meat, tofu, and bamboo shoots into narrow shreds.

2 Bring the stock or water to a rolling boil in a wok or large pan and add all the ingredients. Bring back to a boil, then simmer for about 1 minute.

3 Add the wine, soy sauce, and vinegar to the wok or pan.

4 Bring back to a boil once more, and add the cornstarch paste to thicken the soup. Gently stir the soup while it is thickening. Serve the soup hot, sprinkled with the sliced green onions.

COOK'S TIP

There are many varieties of dried mushrooms, which add a particular flavor to Chinese cooking. Shiitake mushrooms are one of the best kinds. Soak in hot water for 25-30 minutes before use and cut off the hard stems.

Lentil & Ham Soup

This is a good hearty soup, based on a stock made from a ham bone, with plenty of vegetables and red lentils to thicken it and add flavor.

NUTRITIONAL INFORMATION

Calories	.219	Sugars	.4g
Protein	.17g	Fat	.3g
Carbohydrate	.33g	Saturates	.1g

 2¼ HOURS   1¾ HOURS

SERVES 4–6

INGREDIENTS

1 cup red lentils

6¼ cups stock or water

2 onions, chopped

1 garlic clove, crushed

2 large carrots, chopped

1 lean ham bone or 6 oz lean bacon, chopped

4 large tomatoes, skinned and chopped

2 fresh or dried bay leaves

9 oz potatoes, chopped

1 tbsp white wine vinegar

¼ tsp ground allspice

salt and pepper

chopped green onions or chopped fresh parsley, to garnish

1 Put the lentils and stock or water in a saucepan and leave to soak for 1–2 hours.

2 Add the onions, garlic, carrots, ham bone or bacon, tomatoes, bay leaves, and seasoning.

3 Bring the mixture in the saucepan to a boil, cover, and simmer for about 1 hour until the lentils are tender, stirring

occasionally to prevent the lentils from sticking to the bottom of the pan.

4 Add the potatoes and continue to simmer for about 20 minutes until the potatoes and ham are tender.

5 Discard the bay leaves. Remove the ham bone and chop ¾ cup of the meat and reserve. If liked, press half of the soup through a strainer or blend in a food processor or blender until smooth. Return to the pan with the rest of the soup.

6 Adjust the seasoning, add the vinegar, allspice, and the reserved chopped ham. Simmer gently for a further 5–10 minutes. Serve sprinkled liberally with green onions or chopped parsley.

Minted Pea & Yogurt Soup

A deliciously refreshing soup that is full of goodness. It is also extremely tasty served chilled.

NUTRITIONAL INFORMATION

Calories 208   Sugars 9g
Protein ....10g   Fat 7g
Carbohydrate ...26g   Saturates 2g

10 MINS   25 MINS

SERVES 4

INGREDIENTS

2 tbsp vegetable ghee or oil

2 onions, peeled and coarsely chopped

8 oz potato, peeled and coarsely chopped

2 garlic cloves, peeled

1 inch fresh ginger, peeled and chopped

1 tsp ground coriander

1 tsp ground cumin

1 tbsp plain flour

3½ cups vegetable stock

1 lb 2 oz frozen peas

2-3 tbsp chopped fresh mint, to taste

salt and freshly ground black pepper

⅔ cup low-fat plain yogurt

½ tsp cornstarch

¼ cup skim milk

a little extra yogurt, for serving (optional)

mint sprigs, to garnish

1 Heat the ghee or oil in a saucepan, add the onions and potato, and cook gently for 3 minutes. Stir in the garlic, ginger, coriander, cumin, and flour and cook for 1 minute, stirring. Add the stock, peas, and half the mint and bring to a boil, stirring. Reduce the heat, cover, and simmer gently for 15 minutes.

2 Purée the soup in a blender or food processor. Return the mixture to the pan and season with salt and pepper to taste. Blend the yogurt with the cornstarch and stir into the soup.

3 Add the milk and bring almost to a boil, stirring all the time. Cook very gently for 2 minutes. Serve hot, sprinkled with the remaining mint and a swirl of extra yogurt, if wished.

COOK'S TIP

The yogurt is mixed with a little cornstarch before being added to the hot soup—this helps to stabilize the yogurt and prevents it separating when heated.

Sweet Potato & Onion Soup

This simple recipe uses the sweet potato with its distinctive flavor and color, combined with a hint of orange and cilantro.

NUTRITIONAL INFORMATION

Calories ....320 Sugars 26g
Protein ....7g Fat 7g
Carbohydrate ...62g Saturates 1g

15 MINS   30 MINS

SERVES 4

INGREDIENTS

2 tbsp vegetable oil

2 lb sweet potatoes, diced

1 carrot, diced

2 onions, sliced

2 garlic cloves, crushed

2½ cups vegetable stock

1¼ cups unsweetened orange juice

1 cup low-fat plain yogurt

2 tbsp chopped fresh cilantro

salt and pepper

TO GARNISH

cilantro sprigs

orange rind

1 Heat the vegetable oil in a large saucepan and add the diced sweet potatoes and carrot, sliced onions, and garlic. Sauté the vegetables gently for 5 minutes, stirring constantly.

2 Pour in the vegetable stock and orange juice and bring them to a boil.

3 Reduce the heat to a simmer, cover the saucepan, and cook the vegetables for 20 minutes or until the sweet potato and carrot cubes are tender.

4 Transfer the mixture to a food processor or blender in batches and process for 1 minute until puréed. Return the purée to the rinsed-out saucepan.

5 Stir in the plain yogurt and chopped cilantro and season to taste.

6 Serve the soup in warm bowls and garnish with cilantro sprigs and orange rind.

VARIATION

This soup can be chilled before serving, if preferred. If chilling it, stir the yogurt into the dish just before serving. Serve in chilled bowls.

Consommé

A traditional clear soup made from beef bones and lean ground beef. Thin strips of vegetables provide a colorful garnish.

 6¼ HOURS   1¼ HOURS

SERVES 4–6

I N G R E D I E N T S

5 cups strong Beef Stock (see page 30)

1 cup extra lean ground beef

2 tomatoes, skinned, seeded, and chopped

2 large carrots, chopped

1 large onion, chopped

2 celery sticks, chopped

1 turnip, chopped (optional)

1 Bouquet Garni (see page 31)

2–3 egg whites

shells of 2–4 eggs, crushed

1–2 tbsp sherry (optional)

salt and pepper

Melba toast, to serve

TO GARNISH

julienne strips of raw carrot, turnip, celery, or celery root or a one-egg omelet, cut into julienne strips

1 Put the stock and ground beef in a saucepan. Leave for 1 hour. Add the tomatoes, carrots, onion, celery, turnip (if using), bouquet garni, 2 of the egg whites, the crushed shells of 2 of the eggs, and plenty of seasoning. Bring to almost boiling point, whisking hard all the time with a flat whisk.

2 Cover and simmer for 1 hour, taking care not to allow the layer of froth on top of the soup to break.

3 Pour the soup through a jelly bag or scalded fine cloth, keeping the froth back until the last, then pour the ingredients through the cloth again into a clean pan. The resulting liquid should be clear.

4 If the soup is not quite clear, return it to the pan with another egg white and the crushed shells of 2 more eggs. Repeat the whisking process as before and then boil for 10 minutes; strain again.

5 Add the sherry (if using) to the soup and reheat gently. Place the garnish in the warmed soup bowls and carefully pour in the soup. Serve with Melba toast.

Corn & Lentil Soup

This pale-colored soup is made with corn and green lentils, and is similar in style to the traditional Chinese crab and corn soup.

NUTRITIONAL INFORMATION

Calories	.171	Sugars	.9g
Protein	.5g	Fat	.2g
Carbohydrate	.30g	Saturates	.0.3g

5 MINS   30 MINS

SERVES 4

INGREDIENTS

2 tbsp green lentil, washed

4 cups vegetable stock

½ inch piece fresh ginger, chopped finely

2 tsp soy sauce

1 tsp sugar

1 tbsp cornstarch

3 tbsp dry sherry

11½ oz can corn kernels

1 egg white

1 tsp sesame oil

salt and pepper

TO GARNISH

strips green onion

strips red chili

1 Place the lentils in a saucepan with the stock, ginger root, soy sauce, and sugar. Boil rapidly, uncovered, for 10 minutes. Skim the liquid. Reduce the heat, cover, and simmer for 15 minutes.

2 Mix the cornstarch with the sherry in a small bowl and add to the saucepan. Add the corn and its liquid. Simmer for 2 minutes.

3 Whisk the egg white lightly with the sesame oil. Pour the egg mixture into the soup in a thin stream, remove from the heat, and stir. The egg white will form white strands.

4 Season to taste. Pour into 4 warmed soup bowls and garnish with strips of green onion and chili before serving.

COOK'S TIP

Ginger should be smooth and fresh looking. Keep unused ginger in a plastic bag and store in the refrigerator.

Chunky Potato & Beef Soup

This is a real winter warmer—pieces of tender beef and chunky, mixed vegetables are cooked in a broth flavored with sherry.

NUTRITIONAL INFORMATION

Calories . . . . . . .187 Sugars 3g
Protein . . . . .14g Fat 9g
Carbohydrate . . .12g Saturates 2g

   5 MINS   35 MINS

SERVES 4

I N G R E D I E N T S

2 tbsp vegetable oil

8 oz lean braising or frying steak, cut into strips

8 oz new potatoes, halved

1 carrot, diced

2 celery sticks, sliced

2 leeks, sliced

3¾ cups beef stock

8 baby corn-on-the-cobs, sliced

1 bouquet garni

2 tbsp dry sherry

salt and pepper

chopped fresh parsley, to garnish

1 Heat the vegetable oil in a large saucepan.

2 Add the strips of meat to the saucepan and cook for 3 minutes, turning constantly.

3 Add the halved potatoes, diced carrot, and sliced celery and leeks. Cook for a further 5 minutes, stirring.

4 Pour the beef stock into the saucepan and bring to a boil. Reduce the heat until the liquid is simmering, then add the sliced baby corn-on-the-cobs and the bouquet garni.

5 Cook the soup for a further 20 minutes or until cooked through.

6 Remove the bouquet garni from the saucepan and discard. Stir the dry sherry into the soup and then season to taste with salt and pepper.

7 Pour the soup into warmed bowls and garnish with the chopped fresh parsley. Serve at once with crusty bread.

COOK'S TIP

Make double the quantity of soup and freeze the remainder in a rigid container for later use. When ready to use, leave in the refrigerator to defrost thoroughly, then heat until piping hot.

Fish & Crab Chowder

Packed full of flavor, this delicious fish dish is a meal in itself, but it is ideal accompanied with a crisp side salad.

NUTRITIONAL INFORMATION

Calories 440   Sugars 10g
Protein ....49g   Fat 7g
Carbohydrate ...43g   Saturates 1g

 1¼ HOURS   25 MINS

SERVES 4

INGREDIENTS

1 large onion, chopped finely

2 celery sticks, chopped finely

⅔ cup dry white wine

2½ cups Fresh Fish Stock (see page 30)

2½ cups skim milk

1 dried bay leaf

1½ cups smoked cod fillets, skinned and cut into 1 inch cubes

8 oz undyed smoked haddock fillets, skinned and cut into 1 inch cubes

6 oz can crab meat, drained

8 oz blanched green beans, sliced into 1 inch pieces

1½ cups cooked brown rice

4 tsp cornstarch mixed with 4 tablespoons cold water

salt and pepper

chopped fresh parsley, to garnish

mixed green salad, to serve

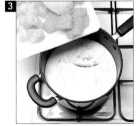

1 Place the onion, celery, and wine in a large non-stick saucepan. Bring to a boil, cover, and cook for 5 minutes.

2 Uncover and cook for 5 minutes until the liquid has evaporated.

3 Pour in the stock and milk and add the bay leaf. Bring to a simmer and stir in the cod and haddock. Simmer gently, uncovered, for 5 minutes.

4 Add the crab meat, green beans, and rice and cook gently for 2–3 minutes until heated through. Remove the bay leaf with a perforated spoon.

5 Stir in the cornstarch mixture until thickened slightly. Season to taste and ladle into 4 warmed soup bowls. Garnish with chopped parsley and serve with a mixed salad.

Lentil & Parsnip Soup

Smooth and thick, this soup has the most glorious golden color and a fabulous flavor.

NUTRITIONAL INFORMATION

Calories 82   Sugars 4g
Protein . . . . .6g   Fat 1g
Carbohydrate . . .13g   Saturates 0.3g

 5 MINS   55 MINS

SERVES 4

INGREDIENTS

3 slices lean streaky bacon, chopped

1 onion, chopped

2 carrots, chopped

2 parsnips, chopped

⅓ cup red lentils

4 cups vegetable stock or water

salt and pepper

chopped fresh chives to garnish

1 Heat a large saucepan, add the bacon, and dry-fry for 5 minutes until crisp and golden.

2 Add the onion, carrots, and parsnips and cook for about 5 minutes without browning.

3 Add the lentils to the saucepan and stir to mix with the vegetables.

4 Add the stock or water to the pan and bring to a boil. Cover and simmer for 30–40 minutes until tender.

5 Transfer the soup to a blender or food processor and blend for about 15 seconds until smooth. Alternatively, press the soup through a strainer.

6 Return to the saucepan and reheat gently until almost boiling.

7 Season the soup with salt and pepper to taste.

8 Garnish the lentil and parsnip soup with chopped fresh chives and serve at once.

COOK'S TIP

For a meatier soup, use a ham bone in place of the streaky bacon. Cook it for 1¹/₂–2 hours before adding the vegetables and lentils and use the ham's cooking liquid as the stock.

Mushroom & Ginger Soup

Thai soups are very quickly and easily put together, and are cooked so that each ingredient can still be tasted in the finished dish.

NUTRITIONAL INFORMATION

Calories	74	Sugars	.........1g
Protein	.........3g	Fat	...........3g
Carbohydrate	....9g	Saturates	.....0.4g

1½ HOURS   15 MINS

SERVES 4

INGREDIENTS

¼ cup dried Chinese mushrooms or
　1⅓ cups field mushrooms

4 cups hot Fresh Vegetable Stock (see page
　31)

4½ oz thread egg noodles

2 tsp sunflower oil

3 garlic cloves, crushed

1 inch piece fresh ginger,
　shredded finely

½ tsp mushroom ketchup

1 tsp light soy sauce

2 cups bean sprouts

cilantro leaves, to garnish

1　Soak the dried Chinese mushrooms (if using) for at least 30 minutes in 1¼ cups of the hot vegetable stock. Remove the stalks and discard, then slice the mushrooms. Reserve the stock.

2　Cook the noodles for 2–3 minutes in boiling water. Drain and rinse. Set them aside.

3　Heat the oil over a high heat in a wok or large, heavy skillet. Add the garlic and ginger, stir, and add the mushrooms. Stir over a high heat for 2 minutes.

4　Add the remaining vegetable stock with the reserved stock and bring to a boil. Add the mushroom ketchup and soy sauce.

5　Stir in the bean sprouts and cook until tender. Put some noodles in each bowl and ladle the soup on top. Garnish with cilantro leaves and serve immediately.

COOK'S TIP

Rice noodles contain no fat and are ideal for anyone on a low-fat diet.

Smoked Haddock Soup

Smoked haddock gives this soup a wonderfully rich flavor, while the mashed potatoes and cream thicken and enrich the stock.

NUTRITIONAL INFORMATION

Calories 169   Sugars 8g
Protein . . . . .16g   Fat 5g
Carbohydrate . . .16g   Saturates 3g

25 MINS   40 MINS

SERVES 4–6

INGREDIENTS

8 oz smoked haddock fillet

1 onion, chopped finely

1 garlic clove, crushed

2½ cups water

2½ cups skim milk

1–1½ cups hot mashed potatoes

2 tbsp butter

1 tbsp lemon juice

6 tbsp low-fat natural fromage frais

4 tbsp fresh parsley, chopped

salt and pepper

1 Put the fish, onion, garlic and water into a saucepan. Bring to a boil, cover, and simmer for 15–20 minutes.

2 Remove the fish from the pan, strip off the skin, and remove all the bones. Flake the flesh finely.

3 Return the skin and bones to the cooking liquid and simmer for 10 minutes. Strain, discarding the skin and bone. Pour the liquid into a clean pan.

4 Add the milk, flaked fish, and seasoning to the pan, bring to a boil and simmer for about 3 minutes.

5 Gradually whisk in sufficient mashed potato to form a fairly thick soup, then stir in the butter, and adjust the taste with lemon juice.

6 Add the fromage frais and 3 tablespoons of the chopped parsley. Reheat gently and adjust the seasoning. Sprinkle with the remaining parsley and serve immediately.

COOK'S TIP

Undyed smoked haddock may be used in place of the bright yellow fish; it will give a paler color but just as much flavor. Alternatively, use smoked cod or smoked white fish.

Tomato & Bell Pepper Soup

Sweet red bell peppers and tangy tomatoes are blended together in a smooth vegetable soup that makes a perfect starter or light lunch.

NUTRITIONAL INFORMATION

Calories 52	Sugars 9g
Protein 3g	Fat 0.4g
Carbohydrate . . .10g	Saturates 0g

1¼ HOURS   35 MINS

SERVES 4

I N G R E D I E N T S

2 large red bell peppers

1 large onion, chopped

2 sticks celery, trimmed and chopped

1 garlic clove, crushed

2½ cups Fresh Vegetable Stock (see page 31)

2 bay leaves

2 x 14 oz cans plum tomatoes

salt and pepper

2 green onions, finely shredded, to garnish

crusty bread, to serve

1 Preheat the broiler to hot. Halve and deseed the bell peppers, arrange them on the broiler rack, and cook, turning occasionally, for 8–10 minutes until softened and charred.

2 Leave to cool slightly, then carefully peel off the charred skin. Reserving a small piece for garnish, chop the bell pepper flesh, and place in a large saucepan.

3 Mix in the onion, celery, and garlic. Add the stock and the bay leaves. Bring to a boil, cover, and simmer for 15 minutes. Remove from the heat.

4 Stir in the tomatoes and transfer to a blender. Process for a few seconds until smooth. Return to the saucepan.

5 Season to taste and heat for 3–4 minutes until piping hot. Ladle into warm bowls and garnish with the reserved bell pepper cut into strips and the green onion. Serve with crusty bread.

COOK'S TIP

If you prefer a coarser, more robust soup, lightly mash the tomatoes with a wooden spoon and omit the blending process in step 4.

Salmon Bisque

A filling soup which is ideal for all types of occasions, from an elegant dinner to a picnic. For a touch of luxury, garnish with smoked salmon.

NUTRITIONAL INFORMATION

Calories 272   Sugars 1g
Protein ....17g   Fat 19g
Carbohydrate ....5g   Saturates 8g

 5 MINS   40 MINS

SERVES 4–6

INGREDIENTS

1–2 salmon heads (depending on size) or a tail piece of salmon weighing about 1 lb 2 oz

3½ cups water

1 fresh or dried bay leaf

1 lemon, sliced

a few black peppercorns

2 tbsp butter or margarine

2 tbsp finely chopped onion or green onions

¼ cup all-purpose flour

⅔ cup dry white wine or Fish Stock (see page 30)

⅔ cup light cream

1 tbsp chopped fresh fennel or dill

2–3 tsp lemon or lime juice

salt and pepper

TO GARNISH

1–1½ oz smoked salmon pieces, chopped (optional)

sprigs of fresh fennel or dill

1 Put the salmon, water, bay leaf, lemon, and peppercorns into a saucepan. Bring to a boil, remove any scum from the surface, then cover the pan and simmer gently for 20 minutes until the fish is cooked through.

2 Remove from the heat, strain the stock and reserve 2¹/₂ cups. Remove and discard all the skin and bones from the salmon and flake the flesh, removing all the pieces from the head, if using.

3 Melt the butter or margarine in a saucepan and fry the onion or green onions gently for about 5 minutes until soft. Stir in the flour and cook for 1 minute then stir in the reserved stock and wine or fish stock. Bring to a boil, stirring. Add the salmon, season well, then simmer gently for about 5 minutes.

4 Add the cream and the chopped fennel or dill and reheat gently, but do not boil. Adjust the taste with lemon or lime juice and season again. Serve hot or chilled, garnished with smoked salmon (if using) and sprigs of fennel or dill.

Carrot & Cumin Soup

Carrot soups are very popular and here cumin, tomato, potato, and celery give the soup both richness and depth.

NUTRITIONAL INFORMATION

Calories	114	Sugars	. . . . .8g
Protein	. . . . .3g	Fat	. . . . .6g
Carbohydrate	. . .12g	Saturates	. . . . . .4g

2¹/₂ HOURS   45 MINS

SERVES 4–6

INGREDIENTS

3 tbsp butter or margarine

1 large onion, chopped

1–2 garlic cloves, crushed

12 oz carrots, sliced

3½ cups Chicken or Vegetable Stock (see pages 28–29)

¾ tsp ground cumin

2 celery sticks, sliced thinly

4½ oz potato, diced

2 tsp tomato paste

2 tsp lemon juice

2 fresh or dried bay leaves

1¼ cups skim milk

salt and pepper

celery leaves, to garnish

1 Melt the butter or margarine in a large saucepan. Add the onion and garlic and fry very gently until the onion begins to soften.

2 Add the carrots and continue to fry gently for a further 5 minutes, stirring frequently and taking care they do not brown.

3 Add the stock, cumin, seasoning, celery, potato, tomato paste, lemon juice, and bay leaves and bring to a boil. Cover and simmer gently for about 30 minutes until all the vegetables are very tender.

4 Discard the bay leaves, cool the soup a little, and then press it through a strainer or blend in a food processor or blender until smooth.

5 Pour the soup into a clean pan, add the milk, and bring slowly to a boil. Taste and adjust the seasoning.

6 Garnish each serving with a small celery leaf and serve.

COOK'S TIP

This soup can be frozen for up to 3 months. Add the milk when reheating.

Mulligatawny Soup

This soup, based on Madras curry, became popular with army officers in India at the beginning of the century.

NUTRITIONAL INFORMATION

Calories ....154 Sugars 6g
Protein ....6g Fat 7g
Carbohydrate ...17g Saturates 4g

5½ HOURS   1 HOUR

SERVES 4-6

INGREDIENTS

3 tbsp butter or margarine

1 large onion, chopped

2 carrots, chopped

2–3 celery sticks, chopped

1 dessert apple, peeled, cored, and chopped

1 tbsp all-purpose flour

1–2 tsp Madras curry powder

1–2 tsp curry paste

½ tsp ground coriander

5 cups Beef, Chicken, or Vegetable Stock (see pages 28–29)

8 oz can chopped tomatoes

½ cup cooked long grain rice (optional)

⅓–½ cup cooked chicken, beef, or lamb, chopped very finely

salt and pepper

poppadoms, to serve (optional)

1 Melt the butter or margarine in a large saucepan and fry the onion, carrots, celery, and apple, stirring occasionally, until just soft and lightly browned.

2 Stir in the flour, curry powder, curry paste, and coriander and cook for 1 minute or so, stirring all the time.

3 Gradually add the stock and bring to a boil, stirring constantly.

4 Add the tomatoes and plenty of seasoning, cover the pan, and simmer for about 45 minutes until the vegetables and apple are tender.

5 Cool the soup a little, then press through a strainer or blend in a food processor or blender until smooth. Pour the soup into a clean pan.

6 Add the rice (if using) and the chicken or meat, adjust the seasoning, and bring to a boil. Simmer gently for 5 minutes.

7 Serve the soup in warmed bowls, with poppadoms (if using).

Carrot, Apple, & Celery Soup

For this fresh-tasting soup, use your favorite dessert apple rather than a cooking variety, which will give too tart a flavor.

NUTRITIONAL INFORMATION

Calories . . . . . . .153g   Sugars 34g
Protein . . . . .2g   Fat 1g
Carbohydrate . . .36g   Saturates 0.2g

1¼ HOURS   40 MINS

SERVES 4

INGREDIENTS

2 lb carrots, finely diced

1 medium onion, chopped

3 sticks celery, trimmed and diced

1 quart Fresh Vegetable Stock (see page 31)

3 medium-sized dessert apples

2 tbsp tomato paste

1 bay leaf

2 tsp sugar

¼ large lemon

salt and pepper

celery leaves, washed and shredded, to garnish

1 Place the prepared carrots, onion, and celery in a large saucepan and add the stock. Bring to a boil, cover, and simmer for 10 minutes.

2 Meanwhile, peel, core, and dice 2 of the apples. Add the pieces of apple, tomato paste, bay leaf, and sugar to the saucepan and bring to a boil. Reduce the heat, half cover, and allow to simmer for 20 minutes. Remove and discard the bay leaf.

3 Meanwhile, wash, core, and cut the remaining apple into thin slices, leaving on the skin.

4 Place the apple slices in a small saucepan and squeeze over the lemon juice. Heat the apple slices gently and simmer for 1–2 minutes until tender.

5 Drain the apple slices and set aside until required.

6 Place the carrot and apple mixture in a blender or food processor and blend until smooth. Alternatively, press the mixture through a strainer with the back of a wooden spoon.

7 Gently re-heat the soup if necessary and season with salt and pepper to taste. Serve the soup topped with the reserved apple slices and shredded celery leaves.

Indian Potato & Pea Soup

A slightly hot and spicy Indian flavor is given to this soup with the use of garam masala, chili, cumin, and coriander.

NUTRITIONAL INFORMATION

Calories	153	Sugars	.........6g
Protein	.........6g	Fat	...........6g
Carbohydrate	...18g	Saturates	......1g

5 MINS   35 MINS

SERVES 4

INGREDIENTS

2 tbsp vegetable oil

8 oz russet or Idaho potatoes, diced

1 large onion, chopped

2 garlic cloves, crushed

1 tsp garam masala

1 tsp ground coriander

1 tsp ground cumin

3¾ cups vegetable stock

1 red chili, chopped

3½ oz frozen peas

4 tbsp low-fat plain yogurt

salt and pepper

chopped fresh cilantro, to garnish

1 Heat the vegetable oil in a large saucepan and add the diced potatoes, onion, and garlic. Sauté gently for about 5 minutes, stirring constantly. Add the ground spices and cook for 1 minute, stirring all the time.

2 Stir in the vegetable stock and chopped red chili and bring the mixture to a boil. Reduce the heat, cover the pan, and simmer for 20 minutes.

3 Add the peas and cook for a further 5 minutes. Stir in the yogurt and season to taste.

4 Pour the soup into warmed bowls, garnish with the chopped fresh cilantro, and serve hot with warm bread.

COOK'S TIP

For slightly less heat, deseed the chili before adding it to the soup. Always wash your hands after handling chilies as they contain volatile oils that can irritate the skin and make your eyes burn if you touch your face.

Bacon, Bean, & Garlic Soup

A mouthwateringly healthy vegetable, bean, and bacon soup with a garlic flavor. Serve with multigrain or whole wheat bread.

NUTRITIONAL INFORMATION

Calories . . . . .261 Sugars 5g
Protein . . . . .23g Fat 8g
Carbohydrate . . .25g Saturates 2g

5 MINS   20 MINS

SERVES 4

INGREDIENTS

8 oz smoked back lean
   bacon slices

1 carrot, sliced thinly

1 celery stick, sliced thinly

1 onion, chopped

1 tbsp oil

3 garlic cloves, sliced

3 cups hot vegetable stock

7 oz can chopped tomatoes

1 tbsp chopped fresh thyme

14 oz can cannellini beans, drained

1 tbsp tomato paste

salt and pepper

grated Cheddar cheese, to garnish

COOK'S TIP

For a more substantial soup add 2 oz small pasta shapes or short lengths of spaghetti when you add the stock and tomatoes. You will also need to add an extra cup of vegetable stock.

1 Chop 2 slices of the bacon and place in a bowl. Cook on HIGH power for 3–4 minutes until the fat runs and the bacon is well cooked. Stir the bacon halfway through cooking to separate the pieces. Transfer to a plate lined with kitchen towels and leave to cool. When cool, the bacon pieces should be crisp and dry. Place the carrot, celery, onion, and oil in a large bowl. Cover and cook on HIGH power for 4 minutes.

2 Chop the remaining bacon and add to the bowl with the garlic. Cover and cook on HIGH power for 2 minutes.

3 Add the stock, the tomatoes, the thyme, beans, and tomato paste. Cover and cook on HIGH power for 8 minutes, stirring halfway through. Season to taste. Ladle the soup into warmed bowls and sprinkle with the crisp bacon and grated cheese.

Chicken Consommé

This is a very flavorful soup, especially if you make it from real chicken stock. Egg shells are used to give a crystal clear appearance.

NUTRITIONAL INFORMATION

Calories 96	Sugars 1g
Protein 11g	Fat 1g
Carbohydrate 1g	Saturates 0.4g

1¼ HOURS   15 MINS

SERVES 4

INGREDIENTS

8 cups chicken stock

⅔ cup medium sherry

4 egg whites, plus egg shells

4½ oz cooked lean chicken, sliced thinly

salt and pepper

1 Place the chicken stock and sherry in a large saucepan and heat gently for 5 minutes.

2 Add the egg whites and the egg shells to the chicken stock and whisk until the mixture begins to boil.

3 When the mixture boils, remove the pan from the heat and allow the mixture to subside for 10 minutes. Repeat this process three times.

4 This allows the egg white to trap the sediments in the chicken stock to clarify the soup.

5 Let the chicken consommé cool for 5 minutes.

6 Carefully place a piece of fine cheesecloth over a clean saucepan.

Ladle the soup over the cheesecloth and strain into the saucepan.

7 Repeat this process twice, then gently re-heat the consommé. Season with salt and pepper to taste, add the chicken slices to the consommé, and serve immediately.

COOK'S TIP

For extra color, add a garnish to the soup. Use a tablespoon each of finely diced carrot, celery, and turnip or some finely chopped herbs, such as parsley or tarragon.

Lentil & Pasta Soup

Packed with the flavor of garlic, this soup is a filling supper dish when it is served with crusty bread and a crisp salad.

NUTRITIONAL INFORMATION

Calories 390	Sugars 12g	
Protein 20g	Fat 5g	
Carbohydrate 71g	Saturates 1g	

1¼ HOURS   55 MINS

SERVES 4

INGREDIENTS

1 tbsp olive oil

1 medium onion, chopped

4 garlic cloves, finely chopped

12 oz carrot, sliced

1 stick celery, sliced

1¼ cups red lentils

2½ cups Fresh Vegetable Stock (see page 31)

3 cups boiling water

1 cup pasta

⅔ cup low-fat plain yogurt, plus extra to serve

salt and pepper

2 tbsp fresh parsley, chopped, to garnish

1 Heat the oil in a large saucepan and gently fry the prepared onion, garlic, carrot, and celery, stirring gently, for 5 minutes or until the vegetables begin to soften.

2 Add the lentils, stock, and boiling water. Season well, stir, and bring back to a boil. Simmer, uncovered, for 15 minutes until the lentils are completely tender. Allow to cool for 10 minutes.

3 Meanwhile, bring another saucepan of water to a boil and cook the pasta according to the instructions on the packet. Drain well and set aside.

4 Place the soup in a blender and process until smooth. Return to a saucepan and add the pasta. Bring back to a simmer and heat for 2–3 minutes until piping hot. Remove from the heat and stir in the yogurt. Adjust the seasoning if necessary.

5 Serve sprinkled with freshly ground black pepper and chopped parsley and with extra yogurt if wished.

COOK'S TIP

Avoid boiling the soup once the yogurt has been added. Otherwise it will separate and become watery, spoiling the appearance of the soup.

Spicy Dal & Carrot Soup

This delicious, warming, and nutritious soup includes a selec_ spices to give it a "kick." It is simple to make and extremely goo_

NUTRITIONAL INFORMATION

Calories 173	Sugars 11g
Protein 9g	Fat 5g
Carbohydrate ...24g	Saturates 1g

10 MINS   50 MINS

SERVES 6

INGREDIENTS

4½ oz split red lentils

5 cups vegetable stock

12 oz carrots, peeled and sliced

2 onions, peeled and chopped

9 oz can chopped tomatoes

2 garlic cloves, peeled and chopped

2 tbsp vegetable ghee or oil

1 tsp ground cumin

1 tsp ground coriander

1 fresh green chili, seeded and chopped,
   or use 1 tsp minced chili (from a jar)

½ tsp ground turmeric

1 tbsp lemon juice

salt

1¼ cups skim milk

2 tbsp chopped fresh cilantro

yogurt, to serve

1 Place the lentils in a sieve and wash well under cold running water. Drain and place in a large saucepan with 3½ cups of the vegetable stock, the carrots, onions, tomatoes, and garlic. Bring the mixture to a boil, reduce the heat, cover, and simmer for 30 minutes.

2 Meanwhile, heat the ghee or oil in a small pan, add the cumin, coriander, chili, and turmeric and fry gently for 1 minute.

3 Remove from the heat and stir in the lemon juice and salt to taste.

4 Purée the soup in batches in a blender or food processor. Return the soup to the saucepan, add the spice mixture and the remaining 1¼ cups stock or water, and simmer for 10 minutes.

5 Add the milk to the soup and adjust the seasoning according to taste.

6 Stir in the chopped cilantro and reheat gently. Serve hot, with a swirl of yogurt.

ouisiana Seafood Gumbo

Gumbo is a hearty, thick soup, almost a stew. This New Orleans classic must be served with a scoop of hot, fluffy, cooked rice.

NUTRITIONAL INFORMATION

Calories	267	Sugars	.........6g
Protein	........27g	Fat	...........8g
Carbohydrate	...24g	Saturates	......1g

5 MINS   35 MINS

SERVES 4

INGREDIENTS

1 tbsp flour

1 tsp paprika

12 oz swordfish fillets, cut into chunks

2 tbsp olive oil

1 onion, chopped

1 green bell pepper, cored, seeded, and chopped

3 celery sticks, finely chopped

2 garlic cloves, crushed

6 oz okra, sliced

2½ cups vegetable stock

15 oz can chopped tomatoes

1 bouquet garni

4½ oz peeled shrimp

juice of 1 lemon

dash of Tabasco

2 tsp Worcestershire sauce

1 cup cooked long-grain rice

1 Mix the flour with the paprika. Add the swordfish chunks and toss to coat well.

2 Heat the olive oil in a large, heavy-based pan. Add the swordfish pieces and fry until browned on all sides. Remove from the pan with a slotted spoon and set aside.

3 Add the onion, green bell pepper, celery, garlic, and okra and fry gently for 5 minutes until softened.

4 Add the stock, tomatoes, and bouquet garni. Bring to a boil, reduce the heat, and simmer for 15 minutes.

5 Return the swordfish to the pan with the shrimp, lemon juice, Tabasco, and Worcestershire sauces. Simmer for a further 5 minutes.

6 To serve, place a mound of cooked rice in each warmed, serving bowl, then ladle over the seafood gumbo.

Creamy Corn Soup

This filling combination of tender corn kernels and a creamy stock is extra delicious with lean diced ham sprinkled on top.

NUTRITIONAL INFORMATION

Calories 307   Sugars 15g
Protein . . . . .19g   Fat 14g
Carbohydrate . . .28g   Saturates 5g

15 MINS   25 MINS

SERVES 4

INGREDIENTS

1 large onion, chopped

1 large potato, peeled and diced

1 quart skim milk

1 bay leaf

½ tsp ground nutmeg

1 lb corn kernels, canned or frozen, drained or thawed

1 tbsp cornstarch

3 tbsp cold water

4 tbsp low-fat plain yogurt

salt and pepper

TO GARNISH

3½ oz lean ham, diced

2 tbsp fresh chives, snipped

1 Place the onion and potato in a large saucepan and pour over the milk.

2 Add the bay leaf, nutmeg, and half of the corn to the saucepan. Bring to a boil, cover, and simmer gently for 15 minutes until the potato is softened. Stir the soup occasionally and keep the heat low so that the milk does not burn on the bottom of the pan.

3 Discard the bay leaf and leave the liquid to cool for 10 minutes. Transfer to a blender and process for a few seconds. Alternatively, rub through a sieve.

4 Pour the smooth liquid into a saucepan. Blend the cornstarch with the cold water to make a paste and stir it into the soup.

5 Bring the soup back to a boil, stirring until it thickens, and add the remaining corn kernels. Heat through for 2–3 minutes until piping hot.

6 Remove the soup from the heat and season well with salt and pepper to taste. Stir in the yogurt until well blended.

7 Ladle the creamy corn soup into warm bowls and serve sprinkled with the diced ham and snipped chives.

Lamb & Barley Broth

Warming and nutritious, this broth is perfect for a cold winter's day. The slow cooking allows you to use one of the cheaper cuts of meat.

NUTRITIONAL INFORMATION

Calories	304	Sugars	.........4g
Protein	........29g	Fat	..........14g
Carbohydrate	...16g	Saturates	......6g

 15 MINS   2¼ HOURS

SERVES 4

INGREDIENTS

1 tbsp vegetable oil

1 lb 2 oz lean neck of lamb

1 large onion, sliced

2 carrots, sliced

2 leeks, sliced

4 cups vegetable stock

1 bay leaf

few sprigs of fresh parsley

⅓ cup pearl barley

1 Heat the vegetable oil in a large, heavy-based saucepan and add the pieces of lamb, turning them to seal and brown on both sides.

2 Lift the lamb out of the pan and set aside until required.

3 Add the onion, carrots, and leeks to the saucepan and cook gently for about 3 minutes.

4 Return the lamb to the saucepan and add the vegetable stock, bay leaf, parsley, and pearl barley to the saucepan.

5 Bring the mixture in the pan to a boil, then reduce the heat. Cover and simmer for 1½–2 hours.

6 Discard the parsley sprigs. Lift the pieces of lamb from the broth and allow them to cool slightly.

7 Remove the bones and any fat and chop the meat. Return the lamb to the broth and reheat gently.

8 Ladle the lamb and parsley broth into warmed bowls and serve immediately.

COOK'S TIP

This broth will taste even better if made the day before, as this allows the flavors to fully develop. It also means that any fat will solidify on the surface so you can then lift it off. Keep the broth in the refrigerator until required.

Spiced Cauliflower Soup

A thick puréed soup flavored with Indian spices and yogurt. Serve with hot naan bread.

NUTRITIONAL INFORMATION

Calories 123   Sugars 13g
Protein ....8g   Fat 4g
Carbohydrate ...14g   Saturates 1g

 10 MINS   25 MINS

SERVES 4

INGREDIENTS

12 oz cauliflower, divided into small florets

12 oz rutabaga, diced

1 onion, chopped

1 tbsp oil

3 tbsp water

1 garlic clove, crushed

2 tsp grated ginger root

1 tsp cumin seeds

1 tsp black mustard seeds

2 tsp ground coriander

2 tsp ground turmeric

3½ cups hot vegetable stock

1¼ cups low-fat plain yogurt

salt and pepper

chopped fresh cilantro, to garnish

1 Place the cauliflower, rutabaga, onion, oil, and water in a large bowl. Cover and cook on HIGH power for 10 minutes, stirring halfway through.

2 Add the garlic, ginger, and spices. Stir well, cover, and cook on HIGH power for 2 minutes.

3 Pour in the stock, cover, and cook on HIGH power for 10 minutes. Leave to stand, covered, for 5 minutes.

4 Strain the vegetables and reserve the liquid. Purée the vegetables with a little of the reserved liquid in a food processor or blender, until smooth and creamy. Alternatively, either mash the soup or press it through a strainer.

5 Pour the vegetable purée and remaining reserved liquid into a clean bowl and mix well. Season to taste.

6 Stir in the yogurt and cook on HIGH power for 3–4 minutes until hot but not boiling, otherwise the yogurt will curdle. Ladle into warmed bowls and serve garnished with chopped fresh cilantro.

Starters & Appetizers

If you prefer not to start your meal with soup, then this chapter contains a range of starters to whet the appetite. There are low-fat starters from around the world such as

Italian Platter, a mouthwatering assortment of figs, mango, artichokes, and Parma ham-wrapped Mozzarella sticks, or Gazpacho Water Ice, a starter of puréed, frozen tomatoes, ideal for a hot summer's day with virtually no fat! There are also attractive starters to impress your guests at a dinner party for example Rosy Melon & Strawberries and Spinach Cheese Molds. There is a selection of pâtés including Tuna & Anchovy, Lentil, and Smoked Fish & Potato.

Rosy Melon & Strawberries

The combination of sweet melon and strawberries macerated in rosé wine and a hint of rose water is a delightful start to a special meal.

NUTRITIONAL INFORMATION

Calories 59	Sugars 8g	
Protein 1g	Fat 0.1g	
Carbohydrate 8g	Saturates 0g	

 2¹/₂ HOURS   0 MINS

SERVES 4

INGREDIENTS

¼ honeydew melon

½ cantaloupe melon

⅔ cup rosé wine

2–3 tsp rose water

6 oz small strawberries, washed and hulled

rose petals, to garnish

1 Scoop out the seeds from both melons with a spoon. Then carefully remove the skin, taking care not to remove too much flesh.

2 Cut the melon flesh into thin strips and place in a bowl. Pour over the wine and sufficient rose water to taste. Mix together gently, cover, and leave to chill in the refrigerator for at least 2 hours.

3 Halve the strawberries and carefully mix into the melon.

4 Allow the melon and strawberries to stand at room temperature for about 15 minutes for the flavors to develop—if the melon is too cold, there will be little flavor.

5 Arrange on individual serving plates and serve sprinkled with a few rose petals, if wished.

COOK'S TIP

Rose water is generally available from large pharmacies and leading supermarkets as well as from speciality food suppliers.

Turkey & Vegetable Loaf

This impressive-looking turkey loaf is flavored with herbs and a layer of juicy tomatoes, and covered with zucchini ribbons.

NUTRITIONAL INFORMATION

Calories 165   Sugars 1g
Protein . . . . .36g   Fat 2g
Carbohydrate . . . .1g   Saturates 0.5g

10 MINS   1¼ HOURS

SERVES 6

I N G R E D I E N T S

1 medium onion, finely chopped

1 garlic clove, crushed

2 lb lean turkey, minced (ground)

1 tbsp fresh parsley, chopped

1 tbsp fresh chives, chopped

1 tbsp fresh tarragon, chopped

1 medium egg white, lightly beaten

2 zucchini, 1 medium, 1 large

2 medium tomatoes

salt and pepper

tomato and herb sauce, to serve

1 Preheat the oven to 375°F and line a non-stick loaf pan with baking parchment. Place the onion, garlic, and turkey in a bowl, add the herbs, and season well. Mix together with your hands, then add the egg white to bind.

2 Press half of the turkey mixture into the base of the pan. Thinly slice the medium zucchini and the tomatoes and arrange the slices over the meat. Top with the rest of the turkey and press down firmly.

3 Cover with a layer of kitchen foil and place in a roasting pan. Pour in enough boiling water to come half-way up the sides of the pan. Bake in the oven for

1–1¼ hours, removing the foil for the last 20 minutes of cooking. Test the loaf is cooked by inserting a skewer into the centre—the juices should run clear. The loaf will also shrink away from the sides of the pan.

4 Meanwhile, trim the large zucchini. Using a vegetable peeler or hand-held metal cheese slicer, cut the zucchini into thin slices. Bring a saucepan of water to a boil and blanch the zucchini ribbons for 1–2 minutes until just tender. Drain and keep warm.

5 Remove the turkey loaf from the pan and transfer to a warm platter. Drape the zucchini ribbons over the turkey loaf and serve with a tomato and herb sauce.

Tuna & Anchovy Pâté

An excellent tangy combination which can be used for a sandwich filling or as a dip. The pâté will keep well in the refrigerator for up to one week.

NUTRITIONAL INFORMATION

Calories ....183 Sugars 3g
Protein ....25g Fat 6g
Carbohydrate ....9g Saturates 2g

 1¼ HOURS   25 MINS

SERVES 6

INGREDIENTS

PATE

1¾ oz can anchovy fillets, drained

14 oz can tuna fish in water, drained

¾ cup low-fat cottage cheese

½ cup low-fat cream cheese

1 tbsp horseradish relish

½ tsp grated orange rind

white pepper

MELBA CROUTONS

4 slices, thick sliced wholewheat bread

TO GARNISH

orange slices

fresh dill sprigs

1 To make the pâté, separate the anchovy fillets and pat well with paper towels to remove all traces of oil.

2 Place the anchovy fillets and remaining pâté ingredients into a blender or food processor. Blend for a few seconds until smooth. Alternatively, finely chop the anchovy fillets and flake the tuna, then beat together with the remaining ingredients; this will make a more textured pâté.

3 Transfer to a mixing bowl, cover, and chill for 1 hour.

4 To make the melba croutons, place the bread slices under a preheated medium broiler for 2–3 minutes on each side until lightly browned.

5 Using a serrated knife, slice off the crusts and slide the knife between the toasted edges of the bread.

6 Stamp out circles using a 2 inch round cutter and place on a cookie sheet. Alternatively, cut each piece of toast in half diagonally. Bake in a preheated oven at 300°F for 15–20 minutes until curled and dry.

7 Spoon the pâté on to serving plates and garnish with orange slices and fresh dill sprigs. Serve with the freshly baked melba croutons.

Minted Onion Bhajis

Gram flour (also known as besan flour) is a fine yellow flour made from garbanzo beans and is available from supermarkets and Asian food shops.

NUTRITIONAL INFORMATION

Calories 251   Sugars 7g
Protein . . . . .7g   Fat 8g
Carbohydrate . . .39g   Saturates 1g

 5 MINS   15 MINS

MAKES 12

I N G R E D I E N T S

1 cup gram flour

¼ tsp cayenne pepper

¼–½ tsp ground coriander

¼–½ tsp ground cumin

1 tbsp chopped fresh mint

4 tbsp strained thick low-fat plain yogurt

¼ cup cold water

1 large onion, quartered and thinly sliced

vegetable oil, for frying

salt and pepper

sprigs of mint, to garnish

1   Put the gram flour into a bowl, add the cayenne pepper, coriander, cumin, and mint and season with salt and pepper to taste. Stir in the yogurt, water, and sliced onion and mix well together.

2   One-third fill a large, deep frying pan with oil and heat until very hot. Drop heaped spoonfuls of the mixture, a few at a time, into the hot oil and use two forks to neaten the mixture into rough ball-shapes.

3   Fry the bhajis until golden brown and cooked through, turning frequently.

4   Drain the bhajis on absorbent paper towels and keep warm while cooking the remainder in the same way.

5   Arrange the bhajis on a platter and garnish with sprigs of fresh mint. Serve hot or warm.

COOK'S TIP

Gram flour is excellent for making batter and is used in India in place of flour. It can be made from ground split peas as well as garbanzo beans.

Italian Platter

This popular hors d'oeuvre usually consists of vegetables soaked in olive oil and rich, creamy cheeses. Try this great low-fat version.

NUTRITIONAL INFORMATION

Calories 198   Sugars 12g
Protein ....12g   Fat 6g
Carbohydrate ...25g   Saturates 3g

 10 MINS   🕐 0 MINS

SERVES 4

INGREDIENTS

4½ oz reduced-fat Mozzarella cheese, drained

2 oz lean Parma ham (prosciutto)

14 oz can artichoke hearts, drained

4 ripe figs

1 small mango

few plain bread sticks, to serve

DRESSING

1 small orange

1 tbsp strained tomatoes

1 tsp wholegrain mustard

4 tbsp low-fat plain yogurt

fresh basil leaves

salt and pepper

1 Cut the cheese into 12 sticks, 2½ inches long. Remove the fat from the ham and slice the meat into 12 strips. Carefully wrap a strip of ham around each stick of cheese and arrange neatly on a serving platter.

2 Halve the artichoke hearts and cut the figs into quarters. Arrange them on the serving platter in groups.

3 Peel the mango, then slice it down each side of the large, flat central stone. Slice the flesh into strips and arrange them so that they form a fan shape on the serving platter.

4 To make the dressing, pare the rind from half the orange using a vegetable peeler. Cut the rind into small strips and place them in a bowl. Extract the juice from the orange and add it to the bowl containing the rind.

5 Add the strained tomatoes, mustard, yogurt, and seasoning to the bowl and mix together. Shred the basil leaves and mix them into the dressing.

6 Spoon the dressing into a small dish and serve with the Italian Platter, accompanied with bread sticks.

VARIATION

For a change serve with a French stick or an Italian bread, widely available from supermarkets, and use to mop up the delicious dressing.

Potato & Bean Pâté

This pâté is easy to prepare and may be stored in the refrigerator for up to two days. Serve with small toasts, Melba toast, or crudités.

NUTRITIONAL INFORMATION

Calories ....94 Sugars 5g
Protein ....6g Fat 1g
Carbohydrate ...17g Saturates 0.2g

🥔 5 MINS   🕙 10 MINS

SERVES 4

INGREDIENTS

3½ oz russet or Idaho potatoes, diced

8 oz mixed canned beans, such as borlotti, flageolet, and kidney beans, drained

1 garlic clove, crushed

2 tsp lime juice

1 tbsp chopped fresh cilantro

2 tbsp low-fat plain yogurt

salt and pepper

chopped fresh cilantro, to garnish

1 Cook the potatoes in a saucepan of boiling water for 10 minutes until tender. Drain well and mash.

2 Transfer the potato to a food processor or blender and add the beans, garlic, lime juice, and the fresh cilantro.

3 Season the mixture with salt and pepper and process for 1 minute to make a smooth purée. Alternatively, mix the beans with the potato, garlic, lime juice, and cilantro and mash.

4 Turn the purée into a bowl and add the yogurt. Mix well and season with salt and pepper to taste.

5 Spoon the pâté into a serving dish and garnish with the chopped cilantro. Serve at once or leave to chill.

COOK'S TIP

If you do not have a food processor or you would prefer to make a chunkier pâté, simply mash the ingredients with a fork.

Potato Skins with Guacamole

Although avocados do contain fat, if they are used in small quantities you can still enjoy their creamy texture.

NUTRITIONAL INFORMATION

Calories 399	Sugars 4g
Protein 10g	Fat 15g
Carbohydrate ...59g	Saturates 4g

45 MINS   1³/₄ HOURS

SERVES 4

I N G R E D I E N T S

4 x 8 oz baking potatoes

2 tsp olive oil

coarse sea salt and pepper

chopped fresh chives, to garnish

G U A C A M O L E   D I P

6 oz ripe avocado

1 tbsp lemon juice

2 ripe, firm tomatoes, chopped finely

1 tsp grated lemon rind

½ cup low-fat cream cheese
  with herbs and garlic

4 green onions, chopped
  finely

a few drops of Tabasco sauce

salt and pepper

COOK'S TIP

Mash the leftover potato flesh with plain yogurt and seasoning, and serve as an accompaniment to meat, fish, and vegetarian dishes.

1 Bake the potatoes in a preheated oven at 400°F for 1¼ hours. Remove from the oven and allow to cool for 30 minutes. Reset the oven to 425°F.

2 Halve the potatoes lengthwise and scoop out 2 tablespoons of the flesh. Slice in half again. Place on a cookie sheet and brush the flesh side lightly with oil. Sprinkle with salt and pepper. Bake for a further 25 minutes until golden and crisp.

3 To make the guacamole dip, mash the avocado with the lemon juice. Add the remaining ingredients and mix.

4 Drain the potato skins on paper towels and transfer to a warmed serving platter. Garnish with chives. Pile the avocado mixture into a serving bowl.

Gazpacho Water Ice

Try serving this refreshing appetizer at a dinner party—it's certain to impress and contains virtually no fat.

NUTRITIONAL INFORMATION

Calories . . . . .33 Sugars 6g
Protein . . . . .1g Fat 1g
Carbohydrate . . . .6g Saturates 0.2g

5½ HOURS   0 MINS

SERVES 4

I N G R E D I E N T S

1 lb 2 oz tomatoes
2½ cups boiling water
4 green onions, chopped
2 celery sticks, chopped
1 small red bell pepper, chopped
1 garlic clove, crushed
1 tbsp tomato paste
1 tbsp chopped fresh parsley
salt and pepper
fresh parsley sprigs, to garnish

TO SERVE

shredded iceberg lettuce
bread sticks

1 Prick the skin of the tomatoes with a fork at the stalk end and place in a large heatproof bowl. Pour over enough boiling water to cover them. Leave for 5–10 minutes. After this time, the skin should start peeling away from the flesh.

2 Skewer the tomatoes with a fork and peel away the skin. Slice the tomatoes in half, scoop out the seeds, and discard. Chop the flesh.

3 Place the chopped tomatoes, green onions, celery, bell pepper, garlic, and tomato paste in a food processor or blender. Blend for a few seconds until smooth. Alternatively, finely chop or mince the vegetables then mix with the tomato paste. Pour into a freezerproof container and freeze.

4 Remove from the freezer and leave at room temperature for 30 minutes. Break up with a fork and place in a blender or food processor. Blend for a few seconds to break up the ice crystals and form a smooth mixture. Alternatively, beat with a wooden spoon until smooth.

5 Transfer to a mixing bowl and stir in the parsley and seasoning. Return to the freezer container and freeze for a further 30 minutes. Fork through the water ice again and serve with shredded iceberg lettuce and bread sticks, and garnish with parsley.

Lentil Pâté

Red lentils are used in this spicy recipe for speed as they do not require pre-soaking. If you use other lentils, soak and pre-cook them first.

NUTRITIONAL INFORMATION

Calories ....267 Sugars 12g
Protein ....14g Fat 8g
Carbohydrate ...37g Saturates 1g

25 MINS   1¼ HOURS

SERVES 4

INGREDIENTS

1 tbsp vegetable oil, plus extra for greasing

1 onion, chopped

2 garlic cloves, crushed

1 tsp garam masala

½ tsp ground coriander

1¼ cups vegetable stock

¾ cup red lentils

1 small egg

2 tbsp milk

2 tbsp mango chutney

2 tbsp chopped parsley

chopped parsley, to garnish

salad leaves and warm toast, to serve

1 Heat the vegetable oil in a large saucepan and sauté the onion and garlic for 2–3 minutes, stirring gently.

Add the spices and cook for a further 30 seconds. Stir in the stock and lentils and bring the mixture to a boil. Reduce the heat and simmer for 20 minutes until the lentils are cooked and softened. Remove the pan from the heat and drain off any excess moisture.

2 Put the mixture in a food processor and add the egg, milk, mango chutney, and parsley. Blend until smooth.

3 Grease and line the base of a 1lb loaf pan and spoon the mixture into the pan. Cover and cook in a preheated oven at 400°F for 40–45 minutes or until firm.

4 Allow the pâté to cool in the pan for 20 minutes, then transfer to the refrigerator to cool completely. Slice the pâté and garnish with chopped parsley. Serve with salad leaves and warm toast.

VARIATION

Use other spices, such as chili powder or Chinese five-spice powder, to flavor the pâté and add tomato relish or chili relish instead of the mango chutney, if you prefer.

Vegetables with Tahini Dip

This tasty dip is great for livening-up simply cooked vegetables.
You can vary the vegetables according to the season.

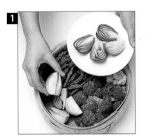

NUTRITIONAL INFORMATION

Calories 126   Sugars 7g
Protein . . . . .11g   Fat 6g
Carbohydrate . . . .8g   Saturates 1g

 5 MINS   20 MINS

SERVES 4

I N G R E D I E N T S

8 oz small broccoli florets

8 oz small cauliflower florets

8 oz asparagus, sliced into 2 inch lengths

2 small red onions, quartered

1 tbsp lime juice

2 tsp toasted sesame seeds

1 tbsp chopped fresh chives, to garnish

HOT TAHINI & GARLIC DIP

1 tsp sunflower oil

2 garlic cloves, crushed

½–1 tsp chili powder

2 tsp tahini (sesame seed paste)

⅔ cup low-fat plain yogurt

2 tbsp chopped fresh chives

salt and pepper

1 Line the base of a steamer with baking parchment and arrange the vegetables on top.

2 Bring a wok or large saucepan of water to a boil, and place the steamer on top. Sprinkle with lime juice and steam for 10 minutes.

3 To make the hot tahini (sesame seed paste) & garlic dip, heat the sunflower oil in a small non-stick saucepan, add the garlic, chili powder, and seasoning to taste and fry gently for 2–3 minutes until the garlic is softened.

4 Remove the saucepan from the heat and stir in the tahini (sesame seed paste) and yogurt. Return to the heat and cook gently for 1–2 minutes without boiling. Stir in the chives.

5 Remove the vegetables from the steamer and place on a warmed serving platter. Sprinkle with the sesame seeds and garnish with chopped chives. Serve with the hot dip.

Parsley, Chicken, & Ham Pâté

Pâté is easy to make at home, and this combination of lean chicken and ham mixed with herbs is especially straightforward.

NUTRITIONAL INFORMATION

Calories	119	Sugars	........2g
Protein	........20g	Fat	..........3g
Carbohydrate	....2g	Saturates	......1g

55 MINS   0 MINS

SERVES 4

INGREDIENTS

8 oz lean, skinless chicken, cooked

3½ oz lean ham, trimmed

small bunch fresh parsley

1 tsp lime rind, grated

2 tbsp lime juice

1 garlic clove, peeled

½ cup low-fat plain yogurt

salt and pepper

1 tsp lime zest, to garnish

TO SERVE

wedges of lime

crisp bread

green salad

VARIATION

This pâté can be made successfully with other kinds of minced, lean, cooked meat such as turkey, beef, and pork. Alternatively, replace the meat with peeled shrimp and/or white crab meat, or with canned tuna in water, drained.

1 Dice the chicken and ham and place in a blender or food processor.

2 Add the parsley, lime rind and juice, and garlic to the chicken and ham, and process well until finely minced. Alternatively, finely chop the chicken, ham, parsley, and garlic and place in a bowl. Mix gently with the lime rind and juice.

3 Transfer the mixture to a bowl and mix in the yogurt. Season with salt and pepper to taste, cover, and leave to chill in the refrigerator for about 30 minutes.

4 Pile the pâté into individual serving dishes and garnish with lime zest. Serve the pâtés with lime wedges, crisp bread, and a fresh green salad.

Spinach Cheese Molds

These flavor-packed little molds are a perfect starter or a tasty light lunch. Serve them with warm pita bread.

NUTRITIONAL INFORMATION

Calories 119   Sugars 2g
Protein . . . . .6g   Fat 9g
Carbohydrate . . . .2g   Saturates 6g

 1¼ HOURS   50 MINS

SERVES 4

INGREDIENTS

3½ oz fresh spinach leaves

10½ oz low-fat cream cheese

2 garlic cloves, crushed

sprigs of fresh parsley, tarragon, and chives, finely chopped

salt and pepper

TO SERVE

salad leaves and fresh herbs

pita bread

1 Trim the stalks from the spinach leaves and rinse the leaves under running water. Pack the leaves into a saucepan while still wet, cover, and cook for 3–4 minutes until wilted—they will cook in the steam from the wet leaves (do not overcook). Drain well and pat dry with absorbent paper towels.

2 Base-line 4 small pudding dishes or individual ramekin dishes with baking parchment. Line the dishes or ramekins with spinach leaves so that the leaves overhang the edges if they are large enough to do so.

3 Place the cheese in a bowl and add the garlic and herbs. Mix together thoroughly and season to taste.

4 Spoon the cheese and herb mixture into the dishes or ramekins and pull over the overlapping spinach to cover the cheese, or lay extra leaves to cover the top. Place a waxed paper circle on top of each dish and weigh down with a 3½ oz weight. Leave to chill in the refrigerator for 1 hour.

5 Remove the weights and peel off the paper. Loosen the molds gently by running a small spatula around the edges of each dish and turn them out on to individual serving plates. Serve the molds with a mixture of salad leaves and fresh herbs, and warm pita bread.

Bruschetta

Traditionally, this Italian savoury is enriched with olive oil. Here, sun-dried tomatoes are a good substitute and only a little oil is used.

NUTRITIONAL INFORMATION

Calories 178	Sugars 2g
Protein 8g	Fat 6g
Carbohydrate ...24g	Saturates 2g

45 MINS   5 MINS

SERVES 4

INGREDIENTS

¼ cup dry-pack sun-dried tomatoes

1¼ cups boiling water

14 inch long multigrain or whole wheat stick of French bread

1 large garlic clove, halved

¼ cup pitted black olives in brine, drained and quartered

2 tsp olive oil

2 tbsp chopped fresh basil

⅓ cup grated low-fat Italian Mozzarella cheese

salt and pepper

fresh basil leaves, to garnish

1 Place the sun-dried tomatoes in a heatproof bowl and pour over the boiling water.

2 Set aside for 30 minutes to soften. Drain well and pat dry with paper towels. Slice into thin strips and set aside.

3 Trim and discard the ends from the bread and cut into 12 slices. Arrange on a broiler rack and place under a preheated hot broiler and cook for 1–2 minutes on each side until lightly golden.

4 Rub both sides of each piece of bread with the cut sides of the garlic. Top with strips of sun-dried tomato and olives.

5 Brush lightly with olive oil and season well. Sprinkle with the basil and Mozzarella cheese and return to the broiler for 1–2 minutes until the cheese is melted and bubbling.

6 Transfer to a warmed serving platter and garnish with fresh basil leaves.

COOK'S TIP

If you use sun-dried tomatoes packed in oil, drain them, rinse well in warm water and drain again on paper towels to remove as much oil as possible. Sun-dried tomatoes give a rich, full flavor to this dish, but thinly-sliced fresh tomatoes can be used instead.

Smoked Fish & Potato Pâté

This smoked fish pâté is given a tart fruity flavor by the gooseberries, which complement the fish perfectly.

NUTRITIONAL INFORMATION

Calories 418	Sugars 4g
Protein 18g	Fat 25g
Carbohydrate ...32g	Saturates 6g

20 MINS   10 MINS

SERVES 4

INGREDIENTS

1 lb 7 oz russet or Idaho potatoes, diced

10½ oz smoked mackerel, skinned and flaked

2¾ oz cooked gooseberries

2 tsp lemon juice

2 tbsp low-fat crème fraîche

1 tbsp capers

1 gherkin, chopped

1 tbsp chopped dill pickle

1 tbsp chopped fresh dill

salt and pepper

lemon wedges, to garnish

toast or warm crusty bread, to serve

1 Cook the diced potatoes in a saucepan of boiling water for 10 minutes until tender, then drain well.

2 Place the cooked potatoes in a food processor or blender.

3 Add the skinned and flaked smoked mackerel and process for 30 seconds until fairly smooth. Alternatively, place the ingredients in a bowl and mash with a fork.

4 Add the cooked gooseberries, lemon juice, and crème fraîche to the fish and potato mixture. Blend for a further 10 seconds or mash well.

5 Stir in the capers, chopped gherkin, dill pickle, and chopped fresh dill. Season well with salt and pepper.

6 Turn the fish pâté into a serving dish, garnish with lemon wedges, and serve with slices of toast or warm crusty bread cut into chunks or slices.

COOK'S TIP

Use stewed, canned or bottled cooked gooseberries for convenience and to save time, or when fresh gooseberries are out of season.

Snacks & Light Meals

Instead of reaching for a bag of chips or a bar of chocolate when you are feeling hungry, why not opt for one of the delicious low fat snacks in this chapter, for example

Breakfast Muffins which are quick and easy to prepare, or Cheese & Chive Scones which take longer but can be made in large quantities and stored in the freezer until ready to eat. This chapter also contains a selection of light meals for when you are not feeling enormously hungry—Soufflé Omelet, as its name suggests, is a light fluffy omelet filled with a mouthwatering combination of sweet cherry tomatoes, mushrooms, and peppery arugula leaves.

Breakfast Muffins

Try this filling breakfast or brunch—a toasted muffin, topped with lean bacon, broiled tomato, mushrooms, and a poached egg.

NUTRITIONAL INFORMATION

Calories 159	Sugars 1g
Protein 12g	Fat 7g
Carbohydrate ...12g	Saturates 2g

  1 HOUR   25 MINS

SERVES 4

I N G R E D I E N T S

2 Whole Wheat muffins

8 slices lean back bacon, rinds removed

4 medium eggs

2 large tomatoes

2 large flat mushrooms

4 tbsp Fresh Vegetable Stock (see page 31)

salt and pepper

1 small bunch fresh chives, snipped, to garnish

1 Preheat the broiler to medium. Cut the muffins in half and lightly toast them for 1–2 minutes on the open side. Set aside and keep warm.

2 Trim off all visible fat from the bacon and broil for 2–3 minutes on each side until cooked through. Drain on absorbent paper towels and keep warm.

3 Place 4 egg-poaching rings in a skillet and pour in enough water to cover the base of the pan. Bring to a boil and reduce the heat to a simmer. Break one egg into each ring and poach gently for 5–6 minutes until set.

4 Cut the tomatoes into 8 thick slices and arrange on a piece of kitchen foil on the broiler rack. Broil for 2–3 minutes until just cooked. Season to taste. Peel and thickly slice the mushrooms. Place in a saucepan with the stock, bring to a boil, cover, and simmer for 4–5 minutes. Drain and keep warm.

5 Arrange the tomato and mushroom slices on the toasted muffins and top each with 2 slices of bacon. Carefully place an egg on top of each and sprinkle with a little pepper. Garnish with snipped fresh chives and serve at once.

VARIATION

Omit the bacon for a vegetarian version and use more tomatoes and mushrooms instead. Alternatively, include a broiled low-fat tofu burger.

Crêpes with Curried Crab

Home-made crêpes are delicious—here, white crab meat is lightly flavored with curry spices and tossed in a low-fat dressing.

NUTRITIONAL INFORMATION

Calories 279   Sugars 9g
Protein ....25g   Fat 7g
Carbohydrate ...31g   Saturates 1g

40 MINS   25 MINS

SERVES 4

INGREDIENTS

4 oz Whole Wheat flour

1 large egg, beaten

1¼ cups skim milk

4½ oz frozen spinach, thawed, well-drained, and chopped

2 tsp vegetable oil

FILLING

12 oz white crab meat

1 tsp mild curry powder

1 tbsp mango chutney

1 tbsp reduced-calorie mayonnaise

2 tbsp low-fat plain yogurt

2 tbsp fresh cilantro, chopped

TO SERVE

green salad

lemon wedges

1 Sift the flour into a bowl. Make a well in the center of the flour and add the egg. Whisk in the milk, then blend in the spinach. Transfer to a jug and leave for 30 minutes.

2 To make the filling, mix together all the ingredients, except the cilantro, in a bowl, cover, and chill until required. Whisk the batter. Brush a small crêpe pan with a little oil, heat until hot, and pour in enough batter to cover the base thinly.

Cook for 1–2 minutes, turn over, and cook for 1 minute until golden. Repeat to make 8 pancakes, layering them on a plate with baking parchment.

3 Stir the cilantro into the crab mixture. Fold each pancake into quarters. Open one fold and fill with the crab mixture. Serve warm, with a green salad and lemon wedges.

VARIATION

Try lean diced chicken in a light white sauce or peeled shrimp instead of the crab.

Spicy Garbanzo Bean Snack

You can use fresh garbanzo beans, soaked overnight, for this popular Indian snack, but the canned variety is just as flavorful.

NUTRITIONAL INFORMATION

Calories 190   Sugars 4g
Protein ....9g   Fat 3g
Carbohydrate ...34g   Saturates 0.3g

5 MINS   10 MINS

SERVES 4

INGREDIENTS

14 oz can garbanzo beans, drained

2 medium potatoes

1 medium onion

2 tbsp tamarind paste

6 tbsp water

1 tsp chili powder

2 tsp sugar

1 tsp salt

TO GARNISH

1 tomato, sliced

2 fresh green chilies, chopped

fresh cilantro leaves

1 Place the garbanzo beans in a bowl.

  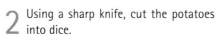 

2 Using a sharp knife, cut the potatoes into dice.

3 Place the potatoes in a saucepan of water and boil until cooked through. Test by inserting the tip of a knife into the potatoes—they should feel soft and tender. Set the potatoes aside.

4 Using a sharp knife, finely chop the onion. Set aside until required.

5 Mix together the tamarind paste and water. Add the chili powder, sugar, and salt and mix again. Pour the mixture over the garbanzo beans.

6 Add the onion and the diced potatoes, and stir to mix. Season to taste.

7 Transfer to a serving bowl and garnish with tomatoes, chilies, and fresh cilantro leaves.

COOK'S TIP

Garbanzo beans have a nutty flavor and slightly crunchy texture. Indian cooks also grind these to make a flour called gram or besan, which is used to make breads, thicken sauces, and to make batters for deep-fried dishes.

Baked Stuffed Onions

Spanish onions are ideal for this recipe, as they have a milder, sweeter flavor that is not too overpowering.

NUTRITIONAL INFORMATION

Calories 182   Sugars 6g
Protein ....10g   Fat 9g
Carbohydrate ...18g   Saturates 5g

  15 MINS   2¼ HOURS

SERVES 4

I N G R E D I E N T S

4 large Spanish onions

2 slices streaky bacon, diced

½ red bell pepper, deseeded and diced

4½ oz lean ground beef

1 tbsp chopped mixed fresh herbs
    such as parsley, thyme, and rosemary
    or 1 tsp dried mixed herbs

½ cup fresh white breadcrumbs

1¼ cups beef stock

salt and pepper

chopped fresh parsley, to garnish

long grain rice, to serve

G R A V Y

2 tbsp butter

4½ oz mushrooms, chopped finely

1¼ cups beef stock

2 tbsp cornstarch

2 tbsp water

1 Put the onions in a saucepan of lightly salted water. Bring to a boil, then simmer for 15 minutes until tender.

2 Remove the onions from the pan, drain and cool slightly, then hollow out the centers and finely chop.

3 Heat a skillet and cook the bacon until the fat runs. Add the chopped onion and bell pepper and cook for 5–7 minutes, stirring frequently.

4 Add the beef to the skillet and cook, stirring, for 3 minutes, until browned. Remove from the heat and stir in the herbs, breadcrumbs, and seasoning.

5 Grease an ovenproof dish and stand the whole onions in it. Pack the beef mixture into the centers and pour the stock around them.

6 Bake the stuffed onions in a preheated oven at 350°F for 1–1½ hours or until tender.

7 To make the gravy, heat the butter in a small saucepan and fry the mushrooms for 3–4 minutes. Strain the liquid from the onions and add to the pan with the stock. Cook for 2–3 minutes.

8 Mix the cornstarch with the water then stir into the gravy and heat, stirring, until thickened and smooth. Season with salt and pepper to taste. Serve the onions with the gravy and rice, garnished with chopped fresh parsley.

Cheese & Chive Scones

These tea-time classics have been given a healthy twist by the use of low-fat cream cheese and reduced-fat Cheddar cheese.

NUTRITIONAL INFORMATION

Calories	...297	Sugars	...3g
Protein	...13g	Fat	...7g
Carbohydrate	...49g	Saturates	...4g

 10 MINS   20 MINS

MAKES 10

INGREDIENTS

8 oz self-raising flour

1 tsp powdered mustard

½ tsp cayenne pepper

½ tsp salt

3½ oz low-fat cream cheese with added herbs

2 tbsp fresh snipped chives, plus extra to garnish

3½ fl oz and 2 tbsp skim milk

2 oz reduced-fat sharp Cheddar cheese, grated

low-fat cream cheese, to serve

1 Preheat the oven to 400°F. Sift the flour, mustard, cayenne, and salt into a mixing bowl.

2 Add the cream cheese to the mixture and mix together until well incorporated. Stir in the snipped chives.

3 Make a well in the center of the ingredients and gradually pour in 3½ fl oz milk, stirring as you pour, until the mixture forms a soft dough.

4 Turn the dough on to a floured surface and knead lightly. Roll out until ¾ inch thick and use a 2 inch plain pastry cutter to stamp out as many rounds as you can. Transfer the rounds to a cookie sheet.

5 Re-knead the dough trimmings together and roll out again. Stamp out more rounds—you should be able to make 10 scones in total.

6 Brush the scones with the remaining milk and sprinkle with the grated cheese. Bake in the oven for 15–20 minutes until risen and golden. Transfer to a wire rack to cool. Serve warm with low-fat cream cheese, garnished with chives.

VARIATION

For sweet scones, omit the mustard, cayenne pepper, chives, and grated cheese. Replace the flavored cream cheese with plain low-fat cream cheese. Add 2¾ oz currants and 1 oz sugar. Serve with low-fat cream cheese and fruit spread.

Potato & Mushroom Hash

This is a quick one-pan dish which is ideal for a quick snack. Packed with color and flavor, you can add any other vegetable you have available.

NUTRITIONAL INFORMATION

Calories ....378 Sugars 14g
Protein ....18g Fat 26g
Carbohydrate ...20g Saturates 7g

10 MINS   35 MINS

SERVES 4

INGREDIENTS

1½ lb potatoes, cubed

1 tbsp olive oil

2 garlic cloves, crushed

1 green bell pepper, cubed

1 yellow bell pepper, cubed

3 tomatoes, diced

1 cup small white mushrooms, halved

1 tbsp Worcestershire sauce

2 tbsp chopped basil

salt and pepper

fresh basil sprigs, to garnish

warm, crusty bread, to serve

1 Cook the potatoes in a saucepan of boiling salted water for 7–8 minutes. Drain well and reserve.

2 Heat the oil in a large, heavy-based skillet and cook the potatoes for 8–10 minutes, stirring until browned.

3 Add the garlic and bell peppers to the skillet and cook for 2–3 minutes.

4 Stir in the tomatoes and mushrooms and cook, stirring, for 5–6 minutes.

5 Stir in the Worcestershire sauce and basil and season well. Garnish with the fresh basil and serve with crusty bread.

COOK'S TIP

Most brands of Worcestershire sauce contain anchovies. If cooking for vegetarians, make sure you choose a vegetarian variety.

Sweet & Sour Drumsticks

Chicken drumsticks are marinated to impart a tangy, sweet, and sour flavor and a shiny glaze before being cooked on a barbecue.

NUTRITIONAL INFORMATION

Calories 171   Sugars 9g
Protein . . . . .23g   Fat 5g
Carbohydrate . . .10g   Saturates 1g

 1¼ HOURS   20 MINS

SERVES 4

INGREDIENTS

8 chicken drumsticks

4 tbsp red wine vinegar

2 tbsp tomato paste

2 tbsp soy sauce

2 tbsp clear honey

1 tbsp Worcestershire sauce

1 garlic clove

pinch of cayenne

salt and pepper

crisp salad leaves, to serve

1 Skin the chicken if desired and slash 2–3 times with a sharp knife.

2 Put the chicken drumsticks into a non-metallic container.

  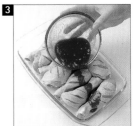

3 Mix all the remaining ingredients and pour over the chicken.

4 Leave to marinate in the refrigerator for 1 hour. Cook the drumsticks on a preheated barbecue for about 20 minutes, brushing with the glaze several times during cooking until the chicken is well browned and the juices run clear when pierced with a skewer. Serve with crisp salad leaves.

COOK'S TIP

For a tangy flavor, add the juice of 1 lime to the marinade. While the drumsticks are grilling, check regularly to ensure that they are not burning.

Oat-Crusted Chicken Pieces

A very low-fat chicken recipe with a refreshingly light, mustard-spiced sauce, which is ideal for a healthy lunchbox or a light meal with salad.

NUTRITIONAL INFORMATION

Calories	120	Sugars	.........3g
Protein	........15g	Fat	...........3g
Carbohydrate	....8g	Saturates	......1g

 5 MINS   40 MINS

SERVES 4

I N G R E D I E N T S

⅓ cup rolled oats

1 tbsp chopped fresh rosemary

4 skinless chicken quarters

1 egg white

½ cup plain low-fat yogurt

2 tsp wholegrain mustard

salt and pepper

grated carrot salad, to serve

1 Mix together the rolled oats, chopped fresh rosemary, and salt and pepper to taste in a bowl.

2 Brush each piece of chicken evenly with egg white, then coat in the oat mixture.

3 Place the chicken pieces on a cookie sheet and bake in a preheated oven, 400°F, for about 40 minutes. Test to see if the chicken is cooked by inserting a skewer into the thickest part of the chicken—the juices should run clear without a trace of pink.

4 Mix together the yogurt and mustard, and season with salt and pepper to taste.

5 Serve the chicken, hot or cold, with the sauce and a grated carrot salad.

Cranberry Turkey Burgers

This recipe is bound to be popular with children and is easy to prepare for their supper.

NUTRITIONAL INFORMATION

Calories 209	Sugars 15g
Protein 22g	Fat 5g
Carbohydrate ...21g	Saturates 1g

 45 MINS   25 MINS

SERVES 4

INGREDIENTS

1½ cups lean ground turkey

1 onion, chopped finely

1 tbsp chopped fresh sage

6 tbsp dry white breadcrumbs

4 tbsp cranberry sauce

1 medium egg white, lightly beaten

2 tsp sunflower oil

salt and pepper

TO SERVE

4 toasted multigrain or whole wheat burger buns

½ lettuce, shredded

4 tomatoes, sliced

4 tsp cranberry sauce

1 Mix together the turkey, onion, sage, seasoning, breadcrumbs, and cranberry sauce, then bind with egg white.

2 Press into 4 x 4 inch rounds, about ¾ inch thick. Chill the burgers for 30 minutes.

3 Line a broiler rack with baking parchment, making sure the ends are secured underneath the rack to ensure they don't catch fire. Place the burgers on top and brush lightly with oil. Put under a preheated moderate broiler and cook for 10 minutes. Turn the burgers over, brush again with oil. Cook for a further 12–15 minutes until cooked through.

4 Fill the burger rolls with lettuce, tomato, and a burger, and top with cranberry sauce.

COOK'S TIP

Look out for a variety of ready ground meats at your butcher shop or supermarket. If unavailable, you can grind your own by choosing lean cuts and processing them in a blender or food processor.

Stuffed Mushrooms

Large mushrooms have more flavor than the smaller button mushrooms. Serve these mushrooms as a side vegetable or appetizer.

NUTRITIONAL INFORMATION

Calories 148   Sugars 1g
Protein . . . . .11g   Fat 7g
Carbohydrate . . . .11g   Saturates 3g

10 MINS   15 MINS

SERVES 4

INGREDIENTS

12 open-cap mushrooms

4 green onions, chopped

4 tsp olive oil

3½ oz fresh brown breadcrumbs

1 tsp fresh oregano, chopped

3½ oz low-fat sharp
 Cheddar cheese

1 Wash the mushrooms and pat dry with paper towels. Remove the stalks and chop the stalks finely.

2 Sauté the mushroom stalks and green onions in half of the oil.

3 In a large bowl, mix together the mushroom stalks and green onions.

4 Add the breadcrumbs and oregano to the mushrooms and green onions, mix, and set aside.

5 Crumble the cheese into small pieces in a small bowl. Add the cheese to the breadcrumb mixture and mix well. Spoon the stuffing mixture into the mushroom caps.

6 Drizzle the remaining oil over the mushrooms. Barbecue on an oiled rack over medium hot coals for 10 minutes or until cooked through.

7 Transfer the mushrooms to serving plates and serve hot.

VARIATION

For a change replace the cheese with finely-chopped chorizo sausage (remove the skin first), chopped hard-boiled eggs, chopped olives, or chopped anchovy fillets. Mop up the juices with some crusty bread.

Savory Bell Pepper Bread

This flavorsome bread contains only the minimum amount of fat.
Serve with a bowl of hot soup for a filling and nutritious light meal.

NUTRITIONAL INFORMATION

Calories 468	Sugars 11g	
Protein 16g	Fat 5g	
Carbohydrate . . .97g	Saturates 1g	

 2 HOURS   50 MINS

SERVES 4

INGREDIENTS

1 small red bell pepper

1 small green bell pepper

1 small yellow bell pepper

2 oz dry-pack sun-dried tomatoes

¼ cup boiling water

2 tsp dried yeast

1 tsp superfine sugar

⅔ cup tepid water

4 cups strong white bread flour

2 tsp dried rosemary

2 tbsp tomato paste

⅔ cup low-fat natural unsweetened yogurt

1 tbsp coarse salt

1 tbsp olive oil

COOK'S TIP

For a quick, filling snack serve the
bread with a bowl of hot soup in
winter, or a crisp leaf salad
in summer.

1 Preheat the oven to 425°F and the broiler to hot. Halve and seed the bell peppers, arrange on the broiler rack, and cook until the skin is charred. Leave to cool for 10 minutes, peel off the skin, and chop the flesh. Slice the tomatoes into strips, place in a bowl, and pour over the boiling water. Leave to soak.

2 Place the yeast and sugar in a small jug, pour over the tepid water, and leave for 10–15 minutes until frothy. Sift the flour into a bowl and add 1 tsp dried rosemary. Make a well in the center and pour in the yeast mixture.

3 Add the tomato paste, tomatoes, and soaking liquid, bell peppers, yogurt, and half the salt. Mix to form a soft dough. Turn out on to a lightly floured surface and knead for 3–4 minutes until smooth and elastic. Place in a lightly floured bowl, cover, and leave in a warm room for 40 minutes until doubled in size.

4 Knead the dough again and place in a lightly greased 9 inch round spring-clip pan. Using a wooden spoon, form "dimples" in the surface. Cover and leave for 30 minutes. Brush with oil and sprinkle with rosemary and salt. Bake for 35–40 minutes, cool for 10 minutes and release from the pan. Leave to cool on a rack and serve.

Sticky Chicken Drummers

The mango salsa contrasts well with the spicy chicken. Pack leftover chicken in lunchboxes for a tasty alternative to sandwiches.

NUTRITIONAL INFORMATION

Calories	159	Sugars	........3g
Protein	........22g	Fat	..........6g
Carbohydrate	....4g	Saturates	......2g

10 MINS   40 MINS

SERVES 4

INGREDIENTS

8 skinless chicken drumsticks

3 tbsp mango chutney

2 tsp Dijon mustard

2 tsp oil

1 tsp paprika

1 tsp black mustard seeds, roughly crushed

½ tsp turmeric

2 garlic cloves, chopped

salt and pepper

SALSA

1 mango, diced

1 tomato, chopped finely

½ red onion, sliced thinly

2 tbsp chopped fresh cilantro

1 Using a small, sharp knife, slash each drumstick three or four times then place in a roasting pan.

2 Mix together the mango chutney, mustard, oil, spices, garlic, and salt and pepper and spoon over the chicken drumsticks, turning until they are coated all over with the glaze.

3 Cook in a preheated oven, 400°F, for 40 minutes, brushing with the glaze several times during cooking until the chicken is well browned and the juices run clear when pierced with a skewer.

4 Meanwhile, mix together the mango, tomato, onion, and cilantro for the mango salsa. Season to taste and chill until needed.

5 Arrange the chicken drumsticks on a serving plate and serve hot or cold with the mango salsa.

VARIATION

Use mild curry powder instead of the turmeric for a stronger flavor.

Thai Potato Crab Cakes

These small crab cakes are based on a traditional Thai recipe. They make a delicious snack when served with this sweet and sour cucumber sauce.

NUTRITIONAL INFORMATION

Calories . . . . . . .254 Sugars 9g
Protein . . . . .12g Fat 6g
Carbohydrate . . .40g Saturates 1g

10 MINS   30 MINS

SERVES 4

I N G R E D I E N T S

1 lb russet or Idaho potatoes, diced

6 oz white crab meat, drained if canned

4 green onions, chopped

1 tsp light soy sauce

½ tsp sesame oil

1 tsp chopped lemon grass

1 tsp lime juice

3 tbsp all-purpose flour

2 tbsp vegetable oil

salt and pepper

S A U C E

4 tbsp finely chopped cucumber

2 tbsp clear honey

1 tbsp garlic wine vinegar

½ tsp light soy sauce

1 chopped red chili

T O   G A R N I S H

1 red chili, sliced

cucumber slices

1 Cook the diced potatoes in a saucepan of boiling water for 10 minutes until cooked through. Drain well and mash.

2 Mix the crab meat into the potato with the green onions, soy sauce, sesame oil, lemon grass, lime juice, and flour. Season with salt and pepper.

3 Divide the potato mixture into 8 portions of equal size and shape them into small rounds, using floured hands.

4 Heat the oil in a wok or skillet and cook the cakes, 4 at a time, for 5-7 minutes, turning once. Keep warm and repeat with the remaining crab cakes.

5 Meanwhile, make the sauce. In a small serving bowl, mix the cucumber, honey, vinegar, soy sauce, and chopped red chili.

6 Garnish the cakes with the sliced red chili and cucumber slices and serve with the sauce.

Rice & Tuna Bell Peppers

Broiled mixed sweet bell peppers are filled with tender tuna, corn, nutty brown and wild rice, and grated, reduced-fat cheese.

NUTRITIONAL INFORMATION

Calories	332	Sugars	.......13g
Protein	........27g	Fat	...........8g
Carbohydrate	...42g	Saturates	......4g

 10 MINS 🕐 35 MINS

SERVES 4

INGREDIENTS

⅓ cup wild rice

⅓ cup brown rice

4 assorted medium bell peppers

7 oz can tuna fish in water,
   drained and flaked

11½ oz can corn kernels (with no added
   sugar or salt), drained

3½ oz reduced-fat sharp Cheddar cheese,
   grated

1 bunch fresh basil leaves, shredded

2 tbsp dry white breadcrumbs

1 tbsp Parmesan cheese, freshly
   grated

salt and pepper

fresh basil leaves, to garnish

crisp salad leaves, to serve

1 Place the wild rice and brown rice in different saucepans, cover with water, and cook for about 15 minutes or according to the instructions on the package. Drain the rice well.

2 Meanwhile, preheat the broiler to medium. Halve the bell peppers, remove the seeds and stalks, and arrange the bell peppers on the broiler rack, cut side down. Cook for 5 minutes, turn over, and cook for a further 4–5 minutes.

3 Transfer the cooked rice to a mixing bowl and add the flaked tuna and drained corn. Gently fold in the grated cheese. Stir the basil leaves into the rice mixture and season with salt and pepper to taste.

4 Divide the tuna and rice mixture into 8 equal portions. Pile each portion into each cooked bell pepper half. Mix together the breadcrumbs and Parmesan cheese and sprinkle over each bell pepper.

5 Return the bell peppers to the broiler for 4–5 minutes until hot and golden-brown.

6 Serve the bell peppers immediately, garnished with basil, and accompanied with fresh, crisp salad leaves.

Potato-Filled Naan Breads

This is a filling Indian sandwich. Spicy potatoes fill the naan breads, which are served with a cool cucumber raita and lime pickle.

NUTRITIONAL INFORMATION

Calories 244	Sugars 7g
Protein 8g	Fat 8g
Carbohydrate ...37g	Saturates 1g

 10 MINS   25 MINS

SERVES 4

INGREDIENTS

8 oz new potatoes, scrubbed and diced

1 tbsp vegetable oil

1 onion, chopped

2 garlic cloves, crushed

1 tsp ground cumin

1 tsp ground coriander

½ tsp chili powder

1 tbsp tomato paste

3 tbsp vegetable stock

2¾ oz baby spinach, shredded

4 small or 2 large naan breads

lime pickle, to serve

RAITA

⅔ cup low-fat plain yogurt

4 tbsp diced cucumber

1 tbsp chopped mint

1 Cook the diced potatoes in a saucepan of boiling water for 10 minutes. Drain thoroughly.

2 Heat the vegetable oil in a separate saucepan and cook the onion and garlic for 3 minutes, stirring. Add the spices and cook for a further 2 minutes.

3 Stir in the potatoes, tomato paste, vegetable stock, and spinach. Cook for 5 minutes until the potatoes are tender.

4 Warm the naan breads in a preheated oven, 300°F, for about 2 minutes.

5 To make the raita, mix the yogurt, cucumber, and mint together in a small bowl.

6 Remove the naan breads from the oven. Using a sharp knife, cut a pocket in the side of each naan bread. Spoon the spicy potato mixture into each pocket.

7 Serve the filled naan breads at once, accompanied by the raita and lime pickle.

COOK'S TIP

To give the raita a much stronger flavor, make it in advance and leave to chill in the refrigerator until ready to serve.

Cheesy Ham Savory

Lean ham wrapped around crisp celery, topped with a light crust of cheese and green onions, makes a delicious light lunch.

NUTRITIONAL INFORMATION

Calories 188   Sugars 5g
Protein ....15g   Fat 12g
Carbohydrate ....5g   Saturates 7g

🥔 10 MINS   🕐 10 MINS

SERVES 4

I N G R E D I E N T S

4 stalks celery, with leaves

12 thin slices of lean ham

1 bunch green onions

6 oz low-fat cream cheese with garlic and herbs

6 tbsp low-fat unsweetened yogurt

4 tbsp Parmesan cheese, freshly grated

celery salt and pepper

T O   S E R V E

tomato salad

crusty bread

1 Wash the celery, remove the leaves and reserve (if wished). Slice each celery stalk into 3 equal portions.

2 Cut any visible fat off the ham and lay the slices on a chopping board. Place a piece of celery on each piece of ham and roll up. Place 3 ham and celery rolls in each of 4 small, heatproof dishes.

3 Trim the green onions, then finely shred both the white and green parts. Sprinkle the green onions over the ham and celery rolls and season with celery salt and pepper.

4 Mix the cream cheese and yogurt and spoon over the ham and celery rolls.

5 Preheat the broiler to medium. Sprinkle each portion with 1 tbsp grated Parmesan cheese and broil for 6–7 minutes until hot and the cheese has formed a crust. If the cheese starts to brown too quickly, lower the broiler setting slightly.

6 Garnish with celery leaves (if using) and serve with a tomato salad and crusty bread.

COOK'S TIP

Parmesan is useful in low-fat recipes because its intense flavor means you need to use only a small amount.

Snapper & Coconut Loaf

This fish and coconut loaf is ideal to take along on picnics, as it can be served cold as well as hot.

NUTRITIONAL INFORMATION

Calories 138	Sugars 12g	
Protein 11g	Fat 1g	
Carbohydrate ...23g	Saturates 0g	

 15 MINS   1¼ HOURS

SERVES 4–6

INGREDIENTS

8 oz Snapper fillets, skinned

2 small tomatoes, deseeded and chopped finely

2 green bell peppers, chopped finely

1 onion, chopped finely

1 fresh red chili, chopped finely

2½ cups breadcrumbs

2½ cups coconut liquid

salt and pepper

HOT PEPPER SAUCE

½ cup tomato ketchup

1 tsp West Indian hot pepper sauce

¼ tsp hot mustard

TO GARNISH

lemon twists

sprigs of fresh chervil

1 Finely chop the fish and mix with the tomatoes, bell peppers, onion, and chili.

2 Stir in the breadcrumbs, coconut liquid, and seasoning. If using fresh coconut, use a hammer and screwdriver or the tip of a sturdy knife to poke out the three eyes in the top of the coconut and pour out the liquid.

3 Grease and base-line a 1 lb 2 oz loaf tin and add the fish.

4 Bake in a preheated oven at 400°F for 1–1¼ hours or until set.

5 To make the hot pepper sauce, mix together the tomato ketchup, hot pepper sauce, and mustard until smooth and creamy.

6 To serve, cut the loaf into slices, garnish with lemon twists and chervil, and serve hot or cold with the hot pepper sauce.

COOK'S TIP

Be careful when preparing chilies because the juices can irritate the skin, especially the face. Wash your hands after handling them or wear clean rubber gloves to prepare them if preferred.

Soufflé Omelet

The sweet cherry tomatoes, mushrooms, and peppery arugula leaves make a mouthwatering filling for these light, fluffy omelets.

NUTRITIONAL INFORMATION

Calories ....146 Sugars 2g
Protein ....10g Fat 11g
Carbohydrate ....2g Saturates 2g

 1¼ HOURS   45 MINS

SERVES 4

I N G R E D I E N T S

6 oz cherry tomatoes

8 oz mixed mushrooms (such as white, shiitake, oyster, and field mushrooms)

4 tbsp Fresh Vegetable Stock (see page 31)

small bunch fresh thyme

4 medium eggs, separated

4 medium egg whites

4 tsp olive oil

1 oz arugula leaves

salt and pepper

fresh thyme sprigs, to garnish

1 Halve the tomatoes and place them in a saucepan. Wipe the mushrooms with kitchen paper, trim if necessary, and slice if large. Place the tomatoes and mushrooms in the saucepan.

2 Add the stock and thyme to the pan. Bring to a boil, cover, and simmer for 5–6 minutes until tender. Drain, remove the thyme and discard, and keep the mixture warm.

3 Meanwhile, separate the eggs and whisk the egg yolks with 8 tbsp water until frothy. In a clean, grease-free bowl, mix the 8 egg whites until stiff and dry.

4 Spoon the egg yolk mixture into the egg whites and, using a metal spoon, fold together until well mixed. Take care not to release too much of the air.

5 For each omelet, brush a small omelet pan with 1 tsp oil and heat until hot. Pour in a quarter of the egg mixture and cook for 4–5 minutes until the mixture has set.

6 Preheat the broiler to medium and finish cooking the omelet for 2–3 minutes.

7 Transfer the omelet to a warm serving plate. Fill the omelet with a few arugula leaves, and a quarter of the mushroom and tomato mixture. Flip over the top of the omelet, garnish with sprigs of thyme, and serve.

Paprika Chips

These wafer-thin potato chips are great cooked over a grill and served with spicy chicken or pork. They also work well broiled.

NUTRITIONAL INFORMATION

Calories 149	Sugars 0.6g
Protein 2g	Fat 8g
Carbohydrate . . .17g	Saturates 1g

 5 MINS   7 MINS

SERVES 4

I N G R E D I E N T S

2 large potatoes

3 tbsp olive oil

½ tsp paprika

salt

1 Using a sharp knife, slice the potatoes very thinly so that they are almost transparent. Drain the potato slices thoroughly and pat dry with paper towels.

2 Heat the oil in a large skillet and add the paprika, stirring constantly to ensure that the paprika doesn't catch and burn.

3 Add the potato slices to the skillet and cook them in a single layer for about 5 minutes or until the potato slices just begin to curl slightly at the edges.

VARIATION

You could use curry powder or any other spice to flavor the chips instead of the paprika, if you prefer.

4 Remove the potato slices from the pan using a slotted spoon and transfer them to paper towels to drain thoroughly.

5 Thread the potato slices on to several wooden kabob skewers.

6 Sprinkle the potato slices with a little salt and cook over a medium hot grill or under a medium broiler, turning frequently, for 10 minutes, until the potato slices begin to crispen. Sprinkle with a little more salt, if preferred, and serve immediately.

Spicy Chicken Tortillas

The chicken filling for these easy-to-prepare tortillas has a mild, mellow spicy heat and a fresh salad makes a perfect accompaniment.

NUTRITIONAL INFORMATION

Calories 650   Sugars 15g
Protein . . . . .48g   Fat 31g
Carbohydrate . . .47g   Saturates 10g

10 MINS   35 MINS

SERVES 4

I N G R E D I E N T S

2 tbsp oil

8 skinless, boneless chicken thighs, sliced

1 onion, chopped

2 garlic cloves, chopped

1 tsp cumin seeds, roughly crushed

2 large dried chilies, sliced

14 oz can tomatoes

14 oz can red kidney beans, drained

⅔ cup chicken stock

2 tsp sugar

salt and pepper

lime wedges, to garnish

TO SERVE

1 large ripe avocado

1 lime

8 soft tortillas

1 cup low-fat plain yogurt

1 Heat the oil in a large skillet or wok, add the chicken and fry for 3 minutes.

2 Add the chopped onion and fry for 5 minutes, stirring until browned.

3 Add the chopped garlic, cumin, and chilies, with their seeds, and cook for about 1 minute.

4 Add the tomatoes, kidney beans, stock, sugar, and salt and pepper. Bring to a boil, breaking up the tomatoes. Cover and simmer for 15 minutes. Remove the lid and cook for 5 minutes, stirring occasionally until the sauce has thickened.

5 Halve the avocado, discard the stone, and scoop out the flesh onto a plate. Mash the avocado with a fork.

6 Cut half of the lime into 8 thin wedges. Now squeeze the juice from the remaining lime over the mashed avocado.

7 Warm the tortillas according to the directions on the package. Put two tortillas on each serving plate, fill with the chicken mixture, and top with spoonfuls of avocado and yogurt. Garnish the tortillas with lime wedges.

Chicken & Almond Rissoles

Cooked potatoes and cooked chicken are combined to make tasty rissoles rolled in chopped almonds then served with stir-fried vegetables.

NUTRITIONAL INFORMATION

Calories 161	Sugars 3g
Protein 12g	Fat 9g
Carbohydrate 8g	Saturates 1g

35 MINS   20 MINS

SERVES 4

INGREDIENTS

4½ oz par-boiled potatoes

½ cup carrots

1 cup cooked chicken meat

1 garlic clove, crushed

½ tsp dried tarragon or thyme

pinch of ground allspice or ground coriander seeds

1 egg yolk, or ½ egg, beaten

¼ cup slivered almonds

salt and pepper

STIR-FRIED VEGETABLES

1 celery stalk

2 green onions, trimmed

1 tbsp oil

8 baby corn-on-the-cobs

10–12 snow peas or sugar snap peas, trimmed

2 tsp balsamic vinegar

salt and pepper

1 Grate the boiled potatoes and raw carrots coarsely into a bowl. Chop finely or grind the chicken. Add to the vegetables with the garlic, herbs, spices, and plenty of salt and pepper.

2 Add the egg and bind the ingredients together. Divide in half and shape into sausages. Chop the almonds and then evenly-coat each rissole in the nuts. Place the rissoles in a greased ovenproof dish and cook in a preheated oven, 400°F, for about 20 minutes until browned.

3 To prepare the stir-fried vegetables, cut the celery and green onions on the diagonal into narrow slices. Heat the oil in a skillet and toss in the vegetables. Cook over a high heat for 1–2 minutes, then add the corn-on-the-cobs and peas, and cook for 2–3 minutes. Finally, add the balsamic vinegar and season well with salt and pepper .

4 Place the rissoles on to a platter and add the stir-fried vegetables.

Minty Lamb Burgers

A tasty alternative to traditional hamburgers, these lamb burgers are flavored with mint and are accompanied with a smooth minty dressing.

NUTRITIONAL INFORMATION

Calories	320	Sugars	........11g
Protein	........28g	Fat	..........10g
Carbohydrate	...33g	Saturates	......4g

40 MINS   20 MINS

SERVES 4

INGREDIENTS

12 oz lean lamb, ground

1 medium onion, finely chopped

4 tbsp dry whole wheat breadcrumbs

2 tbsp mint jelly

salt and pepper

TO SERVE

4 whole wheat buns, split

2 large tomatoes, sliced

small piece of cucumber, sliced

lettuce leaves

RELISH

4 tbsp low-fat plain yogurt

1 tbsp mint jelly, softened

2 inch piece cucumber, finely diced

1 tbsp chopped fresh mint

1 Place the lamb in a large bowl and mix in the onion, breadcrumbs, and mint jelly. Season well, then mold the ingredients together with your hands to form a firm mixture.

2 Divide the mixture into 4 and shape each portion into a round measuring 4 inches across. Place the rounds on a plate lined with baking parchment and leave to chill for 30 minutes.

3 Preheat the broiler to medium. Line a broiler rack with baking parchment, securing the ends under the rack, and place the burgers on top. Cook for 8 minutes, then turn over the burgers, and cook for a further 7 minutes or until cooked through.

4 Meanwhile, make the relish. In a small bowl, mix together the plain yogurt, mint jelly, cucumber, and freshly chopped mint. Cover the relish with plastic wrap and leave to chill in the refrigerator for 1 hour or until required.

5 Drain the burgers on absorbent paper towels. Serve the burgers inside the buns with sliced tomatoes, cucumber, lettuce, and relish.

Potato & Tuna Quiche

The base for this quiche is made from mashed potato instead of pastry, giving a softer textured shell for the tasty tuna filling.

NUTRITIONAL INFORMATION

Calories 383   Sugars 5g
Protein ....25g   Fat 15g
Carbohydrate ...40g   Saturates 6g

 20 MINS   1 HOUR

SERVES 4

INGREDIENTS

1 lb russet or Idaho potatoes, diced

2 tbsp butter

6 tbsp all-purpose flour

FILLING

1 tbsp vegetable oil

1 shallot, chopped

1 garlic clove, crushed

1 red bell pepper, diced

6 oz can tuna in water, drained

1¾ oz canned corn kernels, drained

⅔ cup skim milk

3 eggs, beaten

1 tbsp chopped fresh dill

1¾ oz sharp low-fat cheese, grated

salt and pepper

TO GARNISH

fresh dill sprigs

lemon wedges

1 Cook the potatoes in a pan of boiling water for 10 minutes or until tender. Drain and mash the potatoes. Add the butter and flour and mix to form a dough.

2 Knead the potato dough on a floured surface and press the mixture into a 8 inch flan tin. Prick the base with a fork.

Line with baking parchment and baking beans and bake in a preheated oven, 400°F, for 20 minutes.

3 Heat the oil in a skillet, add the shallot, garlic, and bell pepper, and fry gently for 5 minutes. Drain well and spoon the mixture into the flan shell. Flake the tuna and arrange it over the top with the corn.

4 In a bowl, mix the milk, eggs, and chopped dill and season.

5 Pour the egg and dill mixture into the flan shell and sprinkle the grated cheese on top.

6 Bake in the oven for 20 minutes or until the filling has set. Garnish the quiche with fresh dill and lemon wedges. Serve with mixed vegetables or salad.

Spicy Jacket Potatoes

These crisp, twice-baked potatoes have an unusual filling of the Middle Eastern flavors of garbanzo beans, cumin, and coriander.

NUTRITIONAL INFORMATION

Calories 451	Sugars 6g	
Protein 18g	Fat 4g	
Carbohydrate . . .91g	Saturates 0.5g	

 20 MINS   1½ HOURS

SERVES 4

I N G R E D I E N T S

4 baking potatoes, each about 10½ oz

1 tbsp vegetable oil (optional)

15½ oz can garbanzo beans, drained

1 tsp ground coriander

1 tsp ground cumin

4 tbsp fresh cilantro, chopped

⅔ cup low-fat plain yogurt

salt and pepper

S A L A D

2 tomatoes

4 tbsp fresh cilantro

½ cucumber

½ red onion

4 Meanwhile, place the garbanzo beans in a large mixing bowl and mash with a fork or potato masher.

5 Stir in the ground coriander, cumin, and half the chopped fresh cilantro. Cover the bowl with plastic wrap and set aside.

6 Halve the cooked potatoes and scoop the flesh into a bowl, keeping the shells intact. Mash the flesh until smooth and gently mix into the garbanzo bean mixture with the plain yogurt. Season well with salt and pepper to taste.

7 Place the potato shells on a cookie sheet and fill with the potato and garbanzo bean mixture. Return the potatoes to the oven and bake for 10–15 minutes until heated through.

8 Meanwhile, make the salad. Using a sharp knife, chop the tomatoes and fresh cilantro. Slice the cucumber and cut the red onion into thin slices. Toss all the ingredients together in a serving dish.

9 Serve the potatoes sprinkled with the remaining chopped cilantro and the prepared salad.

1 Preheat the oven to 400°F.

2 Scrub the potatoes and pat them dry with absorbent paper towels. Prick the potatoes all over with a fork, brush with oil (if using), and season with salt and pepper.

3 Place the potatoes on a cookie sheet and bake for 1–1¼ hours or until cooked through. Cool for 10 minutes.

Chicken & Cheese Jackets

Use the breasts from a roasted chicken to make these delicious potatoes and serve as a light lunch or supper dish.

NUTRITIONAL INFORMATION

Calories 417	Sugars 4g
Protein 28g	Fat 10g
Carbohydrate . . .57g	Saturates 5g

 10 MINS   50 MINS

SERVES 4

I N G R E D I E N T S

4 large baking potatoes

8 oz cooked, boneless chicken breasts

4 green onions

1 cup low-fat cream cheese
   or Quark

pepper

1 Scrub the potatoes and pat dry with absorbent paper towels.

2 Prick the potatoes all over with a fork. Bake in a preheated oven, 400°F, for about 50 minutes until tender, or cook in a microwave on HIGH/100% power for 12–15 minutes.

3 Using a sharp knife, dice the chicken and trim and thickly slice the green onions. Place the chicken and green onions in a bowl.

4 Add the low-fat cream cheese or Quark to the chicken and green onions and stir well to combine.

5 Cut a cross through the top of each potato and pull slightly apart. Spoon the chicken filling into the potatoes and sprinkle with pepper.

6 Serve the chicken and cheese jackets immediately with coleslaw, green salad, or a mixed salad.

COOK'S TIP

Look for Quark in the chilled section. It is a low-fat, white, fresh curd cheese made from cow's milk with a delicate, slightly sour flavor.

Cheese, Herb, & Onion Rolls

A great texture and flavor are achieved by mixing white and granary flours together with minced onion, grated cheese, and fresh herbs.

NUTRITIONAL INFORMATION

Calories	529	Sugars 2g
Protein	........24g	Fat 7g
Carbohydrate	...98g	Saturates 4g

  2 HOURS 15 MINS

SERVES 4

I N G R E D I E N T S

2 cups all-purpose flour

1½ tsp salt

1 tsp dried mustard powder

pinch of pepper

2 cups multigrain or malted
   wheat flour

2 tbsp chopped fresh mixed herbs

2 tbsp finely chopped green onions

1–1½ cups sharp low-fat Cheddar cheese,
   grated

½ cake compressed yeast; or 1½ tsp dried
   yeast plus 1 tsp sugar; or 1 sachet easy-
   blend yeast plus 1 tbsp oil

1¼ cups warm water

 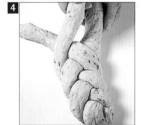 

1 Sift the flour with the salt, mustard, and pepper into a bowl. Mix in the multigrain flour, herbs, green onions, and most of the cheese.

2 Blend the fresh yeast with the warm water or, if using dried yeast, dissolve the sugar in the water, sprinkle the yeast on top and leave in a warm place for about 10 minutes until frothy. Add the yeast mixture of your choice to the dry ingredients and mix to form a firm dough, adding more flour if necessary.

3 Knead until smooth and elastic. Cover with an oiled polythene bag and leave in a warm place to rise for 1 hour or until doubled in size. Punch down and knead the dough until smooth. Divide into 10–12 pieces and shape into round or long rolls, coils, or knots.

4 Alternatively, make one large plaited loaf. Divide the dough into 3 even pieces and roll each into a long thin sausage and join at one end. Beginning at the joined end, plait to the end and secure. Place on greased cookie sheets, cover with an oiled sheet of polythene, and leave to rise until doubled in size. Remove the polythene.

5 Sprinkle with the rest of the cheese. Bake in a preheated oven at 400°F for 15–20 minutes for the rolls, or 30–40 minutes for the loaf.

Pasta Provençale

A combination of Italian vegetables tossed in a tomato dressing, served on a bed of assorted salad leaves, makes an appetizing meal.

NUTRITIONAL INFORMATION

Calories	197	Sugars	.........5g
Protein	........10g	Fat	..........5g
Carbohydrate	...30g	Saturates	......1g

10 MINS   15 MINS

SERVES 4

INGREDIENTS

8 oz penne (pasta quills)

1 tbsp olive oil

1 oz pitted black olives, drained and chopped

1 oz dry-pack sun-dried tomatoes, soaked, drained, and chopped

14 oz can artichoke hearts, drained and halved

4 oz baby zucchini, trimmed and sliced

4 oz baby plum tomatoes, halved

3½ oz assorted baby salad leaves

salt and pepper

shredded basil leaves, to garnish

DRESSING

4 tbsp strained tomatoes

2 tbsp low-fat plain yogurt

1 tbsp unsweetened orange juice

1 small bunch fresh basil, shredded

1 Cook the penne (pasta quills) according to the instructions on the package. Do not overcook the pasta—it should still have "bite". Drain well and return to the pan.

2 Stir in the olive oil, salt and pepper, olives, and sun-dried tomatoes. Leave to cool.

3 Gently mix the artichokes, zucchini, and plum tomatoes into the cooked pasta. Arrange the salad leaves in a serving bowl.

4 To make the dressing, mix all the ingredients together and toss into the vegetables and pasta.

5 Spoon the mixture on top of the salad leaves and garnish with shredded basil leaves.

Lamb & Tomato Koftas

These little meatballs, served with a minty yogurt dressing, can be prepared well in advance, ready to cook when required.

NUTRITIONAL INFORMATION

Calories	183	Sugars	........5g
Protein	........15g	Fat	...........11g
Carbohydrate	....5g	Saturates	......4g

15 MINS   10 MINS

SERVES 4

INGREDIENTS

8 oz finely minced lean lamb

1½ onions, peeled

1-2 garlic cloves, peeled and crushed

1 dried red chili, finely chopped (optional)

2-3 tsp garam masala

2 tbsp chopped fresh mint

2 tsp lemon juice

salt

2 tbsp vegetable oil

4 small tomatoes, quartered

mint sprigs, to garnish

YOGURT DRESSING

⅔ cup low-fat plain yogurt

2 inch piece cucumber, grated

2 tbsp chopped fresh mint

½ tsp toasted cumin seeds (optional)

1 Place the minced lamb in a bowl. Finely chop 1 onion and add to the bowl with the garlic and chili (if using). Stir in the garam masala, mint, and lemon juice and season well with salt. Mix well.

2 Divide the mixture in half, then divide each half into 10 equal portions, and form each into a small ball. Roll balls in the oil to coat. Quarter the remaining onion half and separate into layers.

3 Thread 5 of the spicy meatballs, 4 tomato quarters, and some of the onion layers on to each of 4 pre-soaked bamboo or metal skewers.

4 Brush the vegetables with the remaining oil and cook the koftas under a hot broiler for about 10 minutes, turning frequently until they are browned all over and cooked through.

5 Meanwhile, prepare the yogurt dressing for the koftas. In a small bowl mix together the yogurt, grated cucumber, mint, and toasted cumin seeds (if using).

6 Garnish the lamb and tomato koftas with mint sprigs and place on a large serving platter. Serve the koftas hot with the yogurt dressing.

Meat & Game

The growing awareness of the importance of healthy eating means that supermarkets and butchers now offer leaner, lower-fat cuts of meat. Although these are slightly

more expensive than standard cuts, you do not need to buy as much if you combine them with lots of tasty vegetables and low-fat sauces. It is also worth spending a little extra time cooking the meat carefully to enhance its flavor. Always remember to cut any visible fat from beef and pork before you cook it. Liver, kidney, and venison are relatively low in fat. Look out for extra lean ground meats which can be dry-fried without the addition of oil or fat.

Pork with Fennel & Aniseed

Lean pork chops, stuffed with an aniseed and orange filling, are pan-cooked with fennel in an aniseed-flavored sweet sauce.

NUTRITIONAL INFORMATION

Calories	298	Sugars	........10g
Protein	........30g	Fat	..........10g
Carbohydrate	...18g	Saturates	......3g

20 MINS   35 MINS

SERVES 4

I N G R E D I E N T S

4 lean pork chops, 4½ oz each

⅓ cup brown rice, cooked

1 tsp orange rind, grated

4 green onions, trimmed and finely chopped

½ tsp aniseed

1 tbsp olive oil

1 fennel bulb, trimmed and thinly sliced

2 cups unsweetened orange juice

1 tbsp cornstarch

2 tbsp Pernod

salt and pepper

fennel fronds, to garnish

cooked vegetables, to serve

1 Trim away any excess fat from the pork chops. Using a small, sharp knife, make a slit in the center of each chop to create a pocket.

2 Mix the rice, orange rind, green onions, seasoning, and aniseed together in a bowl.

3 Push the rice mixture into the pocket of each chop, then press gently to seal.

4 Heat the oil in a skillet and fry the pork chops on each side for 2–3 minutes until lightly browned.

5 Add the sliced fennel and orange juice to the pan, bring to a boil, and simmer for 15–20 minutes until the meat is tender and cooked through. Remove the pork and fennel with a slotted spoon and transfer to a serving plate.

6 Blend the cornstarch and Pernod together in a small bowl. Add the cornstarch mixture to the pan and stir into the pan juices. Cook for 2–3 minutes, stirring, until the sauce thickens.

7 Pour the Pernod sauce over the pork chops, garnish with fennel fronds, and serve with some cooked vegetables.

Lamb with Rosemary

This is a pretty dish of pink tender lamb tenderloin served on a light green bed of mashed leeks and potatoes.

NUTRITIONAL INFORMATION

Calories	388	Sugars	........11g
Protein	........35g	Fat	..........12g
Carbohydrate	...38g	Saturates	......5g

  1¼ HOURS   55 MINS

SERVES 4

I N G R E D I E N T S

1 lb 2 oz lean lamb tenderloin

4 tbsp red currant jelly

1 tbsp chopped fresh rosemary

1 garlic clove, crushed

1 lb potatoes, diced

1 lb leeks, sliced

⅔ cup Fresh Vegetable Stock, (see page 31)

4 tsp low-fat natural fromage frais

salt and pepper

freshly steamed vegetables, to serve

TO GARNISH

chopped fresh rosemary

red currants

1 Put the lamb in a shallow baking pan. Blend 2 tablespoons of the red currant jelly with the rosemary, garlic, and seasoning. Brush over the lamb and cook in a preheated oven at 450°F, brushing occasionally with any cooking juices, for 30 minutes.

2 Meanwhile, place the potatoes in a saucepan and cover with water. Bring to a boil and cook for 8 minutes until softened. Drain well.

3 Put the leeks in a saucepan with the stock. Cover and simmer for 7–8 minutes or until soft. Drain, reserving the cooking liquid.

4 Place the potato and leeks in a bowl and mash with a potato masher. Season to taste and stir in the fromage frais. Pile on to a warmed platter and keep warm.

5 In a saucepan, melt the remaining red currant jelly and stir in the leek cooking liquid. Bring to a boil for 5 minutes.

6 Slice the lamb and arrange over the mashed mixture. Spoon the sauce over the top. Garnish the lamb with rosemary and red currants and serve with freshly steamed vegetables.

Fish-flavored Pork

"Fish-flavored" is a Szechuan cooking term meaning that the dish is prepared with seasonings normally used in fish dishes.

NUTRITIONAL INFORMATION

Calories	183	Sugars	.......0.2g
Protein	........14g	Fat	..........13g
Carbohydrate	....3g	Saturates	.......3g

25 MINS   10 MINS

SERVES 4

INGREDIENTS

about 2 tbsp dried wood ears

9-10½ oz pork tenderloin

1 tsp salt

2 tsp cornstarch paste
(see page 31)

3 tbsp vegetable oil

1 garlic clove, finely chopped

½ tsp finely chopped gingerroot

2 scallions, finely chopped, with the white
and green parts separated

2 celery stalks, thinly sliced

½ tsp sugar

1 tbsp light soy sauce

1 tbsp chili bean sauce

2 tsp rice vinegar

1 tsp rice wine or dry sherry

a few drops of sesame oil

1 Soak the wood ears in warm water for about 20 minutes, then rinse in cold water until the water is clear. Drain well, then cut into thin shreds.

2 Cut the pork into thin shreds, then mix in a bowl with a pinch of salt and about half of the cornstarch paste until well coated.

3 Heat 1 tablespoon of vegetable oil in a preheated wok. Add the pork strips and stir-fry for about 1 minute, or until the color changes, then remove with a draining spoon and set aside until required.

4 Heat the remaining oil in the wok. Add the garlic, ginger, the white parts of the scallions, the wood ears, and celery and stir-fry for about 1 minute.

5 Return the pork strips together with the salt, sugar, soy sauce, chili bean sauce, vinegar, and wine or sherry. Blend well and continue stirring for 1 minute.

6 Finally, add the green parts of the scallions and blend in the remaining cornstarch paste and sesame oil. Stir until the sauce has thickened. Transfer the fish-flavored pork to a warm serving dish and serve immediately.

COOK'S TIP

Also known as cloud ears, wood ears are a dried gray-black fungus widely used in Szechuan cooking. They are always soaked in warm water before using. Wood ears have a crunchy texture and a mild flavor.

Chili con Carne

Probably the best-known Mexican dish and one that is a great favorite with all. The chili content can be increased to suit your taste.

NUTRITIONAL INFORMATION

Calories	443	Sugars	........11g
Protein	........48g	Fat	..........15g
Carbohydrate	...30g	Saturates	......4g

5 MINS   2¹/₂ HOURS

SERVES 4

INGREDIENTS

1 lb 10 oz lean braising or stewing steak

2 tbsp oil

1 large onion, sliced

2–4 garlic cloves, crushed

1 tbsp all-purpose flour

¾ pint tomato juice

14 oz can tomatoes

1–2 tbsp sweet chili sauce

1 tsp ground cumin

salt and pepper

15 oz can red kidney beans, drained

½ teaspoon dried oregano

1–2 tbsp chopped fresh parsley

chopped fresh herbs, to garnish

boiled rice and tortillas, to serve

1 Cut the beef into cubes of about ¾ inch. Heat the oil in a flameproof casserole and fry the beef until well sealed. Remove from the casserole.

2 Add the onion and garlic to the casserole and fry until lightly browned; then stir in the flour and cook for 1–2 minutes.

3 Stir in the tomato juice and tomatoes and bring to a boil. Replace the beef and add the chili sauce, cumin, and seasoning. Cover and place in a preheated oven at 325°F for 1¹/₂ hours, or until almost tender.

4 Stir in the kidney beans, oregano, and parsley, and adjust the seasoning to taste. Cover the casserole and return to the oven for 45 minutes. Serve sprinkled with chopped fresh herbs and with boiled rice and tortillas.

COOK'S TIP

Because chili con carne requires quite a lengthy cooking time, it saves time and fuel to prepare double the quantity you need and freeze half of it to serve on another occasion. Defrost and use within 3–4 weeks.

Turkish Lamb Stew

A delicious blend of flavors with lamb, onions, and tomatoes, complete with potatoes to make the perfect one-pot dish for two.

NUTRITIONAL INFORMATION

Calories 442	Sugars 5g
Protein 41g	Fat 17g
Carbohydrate . . .35g	Saturates 7g

 10 MINS   1¼ HOURS

SERVES 2

I N G R E D I E N T S

12 oz lean boneless lamb

1 large or 2 small onions

1 garlic clove, crushed

½ red, yellow or green bell pepper, diced roughly

1¼ cups stock

1 tbsp balsamic vinegar

2 tomatoes, peeled and chopped roughly

1½ tsp tomato paste

1 bay leaf

½ tsp dried sage

½ tsp dried dillweed

12 oz potatoes

6–8 black olives, halved and pitted

salt and pepper

1 Cut the piece of lamb into cubes of about ³/₄ inch, discarding any excess fat or gristle.

2 Place in a non-stick saucepan with no extra fat and heat gently until the fat runs and the meat begins to seal.

3 Cut the onion into 8 wedges. Add to the lamb with the garlic and fry for a further 3–4 minutes.

4 Add the bell pepper, stock, vinegar, tomatoes, tomato paste, bay leaf, sage, dillweed, and seasoning. Cover and simmer gently for 30 minutes.

5 Peel the potatoes and cut into ³/₄ inch cubes. Add to the stew and stir well. If necessary, add a little more boiling stock or water if it seems a little dry. Cover the pan again and simmer for a further 25–30 minutes, or until tender.

6 Add the olives and adjust the seasoning. Simmer for a further 5 minutes and serve with vegetables or a salad and crusty bread.

COOK'S TIP

A good accompaniment would be a salad made of shredded white cabbage, lettuce, coarsely grated carrot, diced avocado or cucumber, and green onions.

Beef & Orange Curry

A citrusy, spicy blend of tender chunks of beef with the tang of orange and the warmth of Indian spices.

NUTRITIONAL INFORMATION

Calories	345	Sugars 24g
Protein	........28g	Fat 13g
Carbohydrate	...31g	Saturates 3g

5¹/₄ HOURS   1¹/₄ HOURS

SERVES 4

I N G R E D I E N T S

1 tbsp vegetable oil

8 oz shallots, halved

2 garlic cloves, crushed

1 lb lean rump or sirloin beef, trimmed and cut into ¾ inch cubes

3 tbsp curry paste

2 cups Fresh Beef Stock (see page 30)

4 medium oranges

2 tsp cornstarch

salt and pepper

2 tbsp fresh cilantro, chopped, to garnish

basmati rice, freshly boiled, to serve

R A I T A

½ cucumber, finely diced

3 tbsp chopped fresh mint

⅔ cup low-fat plain yogurt

1 Heat the oil in a large saucepan. Gently fry the shallots, garlic, and the cubes of beef for 5 minutes, stirring occasionally, until the beef is evenly browned all over.

2 Blend together the curry paste and stock. Add the mixture to the beef and stir to mix thoroughly. Bring to a boil, cover, and simmer for about 1 hour.

3 Grate the rind of one orange. Extract the juice from the orange and from one other. Peel the other two oranges, removing the pith. Slice between each segment and remove the flesh.

4 Blend the cornstarch with the orange juice. At the end of the cooking time, stir the orange rind into the beef along with the orange and cornstarch mixture. Bring to a boil and simmer, stirring, for

3–4 minutes until the sauce thickens. Season to taste and stir in the orange segments.

5 To make the raita, mix the cucumber with the mint and stir in the yogurt. Season with salt and pepper to taste.

6 Serve the curry with rice and the cucumber raita, garnished with the chopped cilantro.

Lamb Hotpot

This classic recipe using lamb cutlets layered between sliced potatoes, kidneys, onions, and herbs makes a perfect meal on a cold winter's day.

NUTRITIONAL INFORMATION

Calories ....420 Sugars 2g
Protein ....41g Fat 15g
Carbohydrate ...31g Saturates 8g

15 MINS   2 HOURS

SERVES 4

INGREDIENTS

1½ lb lean lamb neck cutlets

2 lamb's kidneys

1½ lb new potatoes, scrubbed and sliced thinly

1 large onion, sliced thinly

2 tbsp chopped fresh thyme

⅔ cup lamb stock

2 tbsp butter, melted

salt and pepper

fresh thyme sprigs, to garnish

1 Remove any excess fat from the lamb. Skin and core the kidneys and cut them into slices.

2 Arrange a layer of potatoes in the base of a 3½ cup ovenproof dish.

3 Arrange the lamb neck cutlets on top of the potatoes and cover with the sliced kidneys, onion, and chopped thyme.

4 Pour the lamb stock over the meat and season to taste with salt and pepper.

5 Layer the remaining potato slices on top, overlapping to completely cover the meat and sliced onion.

6 Brush the potato slices with the butter, cover the dish, and cook in a preheated oven, 350°F, for 1½ hours.

7 Remove the lid and cook for a further 30 minutes until golden brown on top.

8 Garnish with fresh thyme sprigs and serve hot.

VARIATION

Traditionally, oysters are also included in this tasty hotpot. Add them to the layers along with the kidneys, if wished.

Baked Ham with Sauce

Ham is first par-boiled then baked with a mustard topping. Serve hot or cold with this tangy Cumberland sauce.

NUTRITIONAL INFORMATION

Calories 414	Sugars 4g	
Protein 70g	Fat 13g	
Carbohydrate 4g	Saturates 5g	

10 MINS   5³/4 HOURS

SERVES 4–6

INGREDIENTS

4–6 lb lean ham

2 bay leaves

1–2 onions, quartered

2 carrots, sliced thickly

6 cloves

GLAZE

1 tbsp red currant jelly

1 tbsp wholegrain mustard

CUMBERLAND SAUCE

1 orange

3 tbsp red currant jelly

2 tbsp lemon or lime juice

2 tbsp orange juice

2–4 tbsp port

1 tbsp wholegrain mustard

TO GARNISH

salad leaves

orange slices

1 Put the meat in a large saucepan. Add the bay leaves, onion, carrots, and cloves and cover with cold water. Bring slowly to a boil, cover, and simmer for half the cooking time, allowing 30 minutes per 1 lb 2 oz plus 30 minutes.

2 Drain the meat and remove the skin. Put the meat in a roasting pan or dish and score the fat.

3 To make the glaze, combine the ingredients and spread over the fat. Cook in a preheated oven at 350°F for the remainder of the cooking time. Baste at least once.

4 To make the sauce, thinly pare the rind from half the orange and cut into narrow strips. Cook in boiling water for 3 minutes, then drain.

5 Place all the remaining sauce ingredients in a small saucepan and heat gently until the red currant jelly dissolves. Add the orange rind and simmer gently for 3–4 minutes.

6 Slice the ham and serve with the Cumberland sauce, garnished with salad leaves and orange slices.

Carrot-Topped Beef Pie

This is a variation of an old favorite, where a creamy mashed potato and carrot topping is piled thickly onto a delicious beef pie filling.

NUTRITIONAL INFORMATION

Calories 352	Sugars 6g	
Protein 28g	Fat 11g	
Carbohydrate . . .38g	Saturates 6g	

 10 MINS   1¼ HOURS

SERVES 4

INGREDIENTS

1 lb lean ground beef

1 onion, chopped

1 garlic clove, crushed

1 tbsp all-purpose flour

1¼ cups beef stock

2 tbsp tomato paste

1 celery stalk, chopped

3 tbsp chopped fresh parsley

1 tbsp Worcestershire sauce

1½ lb russet or Idaho potatoes, diced

2 large carrots, diced

2 tbsp butter

3 tbsp skim milk

salt and pepper

1 Dry fry the beef in a large pan set over a high heat for 3-4 minutes or until sealed. Add the onion and garlic and cook for a further 5 minutes, stirring.

2 Add the flour and cook for 1 minute. Gradually blend in the beef stock and tomato paste. Stir in the celery, 1 tbsp of the parsley, and the Worcestershire sauce. Season to taste.

3 Bring the mixture to a boil, then reduce the heat and simmer for 20-25 minutes. Spoon the beef mixture into a 2 pint pie dish.

4 Meanwhile, cook the potatoes and carrots in a saucepan of boiling water for 10 minutes. Drain and mash them together.

5 Stir the butter, milk, and the remaining parsley into the potato and carrot mixture and season with salt and pepper to taste. Spoon the potato on top of the beef mixture to cover it completely; alternatively, pipe the potato with a pastry bag.

6 Cook the carrot-topped beef pie in a preheated oven, 375°F, for 45 minutes or until cooked through. Serve piping hot.

Rogan Josh

This is one of the best-known curries. Rogan Josh means "red curry", and is so-called because of the red chilies in the recipe.

NUTRITIONAL INFORMATION

Calories	248	Sugar	........2g
Protein	35	Fats	..........11g
Carbohydrate	....2g	Saturates	......5g

10 MINS 1³/₄ HOURS

SERVES 6

INGREDIENTS

2 tbsp ghee

2 lb 4 oz lean braising steak, cut into 1 inch cubes

1 onion, chopped finely

3 garlic cloves

1 inch piece gingerroot, grated

4 fresh red chilies, chopped

4 green cardamom pods

4 cloves

2 tsp coriander seeds

2 tsp cumin seeds

1 tsp paprika

1 tsp salt

1 bay leaf

¼ cup low-fat yogurt

1 inch piece cinnamon stick

⅔ cup hot water

¼ tsp garam masala

pepper

1 Heat the ghee in a large flameproof casserole and brown the meat in batches. Remove the meat from the casserole and set aside in a bowl.

2 Add the chopped onion to the ghee and stir over a high heat for 3–4 minutes.

3 Grind together the garlic, ginger, chilies, cardamom, cloves, coriander, cumin, paprika, and salt. Add the spice paste and bay leaf to the casserole and stir until fragrant.

4 Return the meat and any juices in the bowl to the casserole and simmer for 2–3 minutes. Gradually stir the yogurt into the casserole keeping the sauce simmering.

5 Stir in the cinnamon stick and hot water, and pepper to taste.

6 Cover the casserole and cook in a preheated oven, 350°F, for 1¼ hours until the meat is very tender and the sauce is slightly reduced. Discard the cinnamon stick and stir in the garam masala. Remove surplus oil from the surface of the casserole before serving.

Mexican Beef

Strips of beef cooked with bell peppers, onion, and carrot in a tomato and chili sauce are prepared quickly in the microwave.

NUTRITIONAL INFORMATION

Calories	...513	Sugars	...7g
Protein	...33g	Fat	...23g
Carbohydrate	...46g	Saturates	...8g

 30 MINS   35 MINS

SERVES 4

INGREDIENTS

1 cup brown rice

3 cups boiling water

½ tsp salt

2 tbsp oil

1 onion, sliced into rings

1 carrot, cut into thin matchsticks

½ each red, green and yellow bell peppers

½–1 fresh green chili, deseeded and chopped

1 garlic clove, crushed

1 lb 2 oz rump steak, cut into strips

1 cup canned tomatoes

1 tbsp tomato paste

2 tsp cornstarch

sprigs of fresh cilantro, to garnish

salt and pepper

SALSA

tomatoes, skinned and chopped

2 green onions, chopped

1 small fresh green chili, deseeded and chopped

2 tbsp lime juice

1 tbsp chopped fresh cilantro

8 flour tortillas

1 Place the rice in a large bowl. Add the boiling water and salt. Cover and cook on HIGH power for 15 minutes. Leave to stand, covered, for 5 minutes before draining.

2 Place the oil, onion, and carrot in a large bowl. Cover and cook on HIGH power for 2 minutes. Slice the bell peppers and add with the chili, garlic, and steak to the bowl. Cover and cook on HIGH power for 4 minutes, stirring once.

3 Add the canned tomatoes, tomato paste, and seasoning. Mix the cornstarch with a little water, then stir into the bowl. Cover and cook on MEDIUM power for 10 minutes.

4 To make the salsa, mix together the tomatoes, green onions, chili, lime juice, and cilantro. Season and leave to stand for 10 minutes.

5 Heat the tortillas on HIGH power for 40 seconds, covered, or according to the package instructions.

6 Garnish the beef with fresh cilantro sprigs and serve with the tortillas, rice, and salsa.

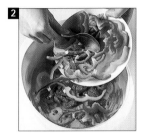

Stir-Fried Lamb with Orange

Oranges and lamb are a great combination because the citrus flavor offsets the fattier, fuller flavor of the lamb.

NUTRITIONAL INFORMATION

Calories 209	Sugars 4g	
Protein 25g	Fat 10g	
Carbohydrate 5g	Saturates 5g	

5 MINS   30 MINS

SERVES 4

INGREDIENTS

1 lb ground lamb

2 cloves garlic, crushed

1 tsp cumin seeds

1 tsp ground coriander

1 red onion, sliced

finely grated zest and juice of
    1 orange

2 tbsp soy sauce

1 orange, peeled and segmented

salt and pepper

snipped fresh chives, to garnish

1 Heat a wok or large, heavy-bottomed skillet, without adding any oil.

2 Add the ground lamb to the wok. Dry fry the ground lamb for 5 minutes, or until the lamb is evenly browned. Drain away any excess fat from the wok.

3 Add the garlic, cumin seeds, coriander, and red onion to the wok and stir-fry for another 5 minutes.

4 Stir in the finely grated orange zest and juice and the soy sauce, mixing until thoroughly combined. Cover, reduce the heat, and leave to simmer, stirring occasionally, for 15 minutes.

5 Remove the lid, increase the heat, and add the oranges. Stir to mix.

6 Season with salt and pepper to taste and heat through for another 2–3 minutes.

7 Transfer the stir-fry to warm serving plates and garnish with snipped fresh chives. Serve immediately.

COOK'S TIP

If you wish to serve wine with your meal, try light, dry white wines and lighter Burgundy-style red wines as they blend well with Oriental food.

Red Roast Pork in Soy Sauce

In this traditional Chinese dish the pork turns "red" during cooking because it is basted in dark soy sauce.

NUTRITIONAL INFORMATION

Calories 268   Sugars 20g
Protein ....26g   Fat 8g
Carbohydrate ...22g   Saturates 3g

 1¼ HOURS   1¼ HOURS

SERVES 4

INGREDIENTS

1 lb lean pork tenderloin

6 tbsp dark soy sauce

2 tbsp dry sherry

1 tsp five-spice powder

2 garlic cloves, minced

1 inch piece gingerroot, finely chopped

1 large red bell pepper

1 large yellow bell pepper

1 large orange bell pepper

4 tbsp superfine sugar

2 tbsp red wine vinegar

TO GARNISH

scallions, shredded

fresh chives, snipped

1 Trim away excess fat and silver skin from the pork and place in a shallow dish.

2 Mix together the soy sauce, sherry, five-spice powder, garlic, and ginger. Spoon over the pork, cover, and marinate in the refrigerator for at least 1 hour or until required.

3 Preheat the oven to 375°F. Drain the pork, reserving the marinade.

4 Place the pork on a roasting rack over a roasting pan. Cook in the oven, occasionally basting with the marinade, for 1 hour or until cooked through.

5 Meanwhile, halve and seed the bell peppers. Cut each bell pepper half into 3 equal portions. Arrange them on a baking sheet and bake alongside the pork for the last 30 minutes of cooking time.

6 Place the superfine sugar and vinegar in a saucepan and heat gently until the sugar dissolves. Bring to a boil and simmer for 3–4 minutes, until syrupy.

7 When the pork is cooked, remove it from the oven and brush with the sugar syrup. Leave for about 5 minutes, then slice and arrange on a serving platter with the bell peppers, garnished with the scallions and chives.

Kibbeh

This Lebanese barbeque dish is similar to the Turkish kofte and the Indian kofta, but the spices used to flavor the meat are quite different.

NUTRITIONAL INFORMATION

Calories 232	Sugars 3g
Protein 19g	Fat 13g
Carbohydrate 9g	Saturates 4g

  1 HOUR ⏱ 15 MINS

SERVES 4

I N G R E D I E N T S

2¾ oz couscous

1 small onion

12 oz lean minced lamb

½ tsp ground cinnamon

¼ tsp cayenne

4 tsp ground allspice

green salad and onion rings, to serve

B A S T E

2 tbsp tomato ketchup

2 tbsp sunflower oil

1 Place the couscous in a large bowl, cover with cold water, and leave to stand for 30 minutes or until the couscous has swelled and softened. Alternatively, soak the couscous according to the instructions on the package.

2 Drain the couscous through a sieve and squeeze out as much moisture as you can.

3 If you have a food processor, add the onion and chop finely. Add the lamb and process briefly to chop the mince further. If you do not have a processor, grate the onion, then add to the lamb.

4 Combine the couscous, lamb, and spices and mix well together. Divide the mixture into 8 equal sized portions. Press and shape the mixture around 8 skewers, pressing the mixture together firmly so that it holds it shape. Leave to chill for at least 30 minutes or until required.

5 To make the baste, combine the oil and ketchup.

6 Barbecue the kibbeh over hot coals for 10–15 minutes, turning and basting frequently. Serve with barbecued onion rings and green salad leaves.

Pork Stroganoff

Tender, lean pork, cooked in a tasty, rich tomato sauce, is flavored with the extra tang of unsweetened yogurt.

NUTRITIONAL INFORMATION

Calories ....223 Sugars 7g
Protein ....22g Fat 10g
Carbohydrate ...12g Saturates 3g

2¼ HOURS   30 MINS

SERVES 4

INGREDIENTS

12 oz lean pork fillet

1 tbsp vegetable oil

1 medium onion, chopped

2 garlic cloves, crushed

1 oz all-purpose flour

2 tbsp tomato paste

1¾ cups Fresh Chicken or Vegetable stock
   (see page 30-31)

4½ oz small white mushrooms, sliced

1 large green bell pepper, deseeded and
   diced

½ tsp ground nutmeg

4 tbsp low-fat plain yogurt, plus extra to
   serve

salt and pepper

white rice, freshly boiled, to serve

ground nutmeg, to garnish

1 Trim away any excess fat and silver skin from the pork, then cut the meat into slices ½ inch thick.

2 Heat the oil in a large saucepan and gently fry the pork, onion, and garlic for 4–5 minutes until lightly browned.

3 Stir in the flour and tomato paste, pour in the stock and stir to mix thoroughly.

4 Add the mushrooms, bell pepper, seasoning, and nutmeg. Bring to a boil, cover, and simmer for 20 minutes until the pork is tender and cooked through.

5 Remove the saucepan from the heat and stir in the yogurt.

6 Serve the pork and sauce on a bed of rice with an extra spoonful of yogurt, and garnish with a dusting of ground nutmeg.

COOK'S TIP

You can buy ready-made stock from leading supermarkets. Although more expensive, they are more nutritious than stock cubes, which are high in salt and artificial flavorings.

Boiled Beef & Carrots

Serve this old favorite with vegetables and herb dumplings for a substantial one-pot meal.

NUTRITIONAL INFORMATION

Calories 459	Sugars 2g	
Protein 31g	Fat 22g	
Carbohydrate . . .35g	Saturates 10g	

15 MINS   2³/₄ HOURS

SERVES 6

INGREDIENTS

about 3½ lb joint of salted silverside or topside

2 onions, quartered, or 5–8 small onions

8–10 cloves

2 bay leaves

1 cinnamon stick

2 tbsp brown sugar

4 large carrots, sliced thickly

1 turnip, quartered

½ rutabaga sliced thickly

1 large leek, sliced thickly

2 tbsp butter or margarine

4 tbsp all-purpose flour

½ tsp dried mustard powder

salt and pepper

DUMPLINGS

2 cups self-raising flour

½ tsp dried sage

½ cup shredded vegetable suet

about ⅔ cup water

1 Put the beef in a large saucepan, add the onions, cloves, bay leaves, cinnamon, and sugar and sufficient water to cover the meat. Bring slowly to a boil, remove any scum from the surface, cover, and simmer gently for 1 hour.

2 Add the carrots, turnip, rutabaga, and leeks, cover, and simmer for a further 1¼ hours until the beef is tender.

3 Meanwhile, make the dumplings. Sift the flour into a bowl, season well, and mix in the herbs and suet. Add sufficient water to mix to a softish dough.

4 Divide the dough into 8 pieces, roughly shape into balls, and place on top of the beef and vegetables. Replace the lid and simmer for 15–20 minutes.

5 Place the beef, vegetables and dumplings in a serving dish. Measure 1¼ cups of the cooking liquid into a pan. Blend the margarine with the flour then gradually whisk into the pan. Bring to a boil and simmer until thickened. Stir in the mustard, adjust the seasoning, and serve with the beef.

Shepherd's Pie

Ground lamb or beef cooked with onions, carrots, herbs, and tomatoes and with a topping of piped creamed potatoes.

NUTRITIONAL INFORMATION

Calories	378	Sugars	.........8g
Protein	........33g	Fat	..........12g
Carbohydrate	...37g	Saturates	......4g

 10 MINS   🕐 1¹/₂ HOURS

SERVES 4–5

I N G R E D I E N T S

1 lb 9 oz lean ground lamb or beef

2 onions, chopped

8 oz carrots, diced

1–2 garlic cloves, crushed

1 tbsp all-purpose flour

1 cup beef stock

7 oz can chopped tomatoes

1 tsp Worcestershire sauce

1 tsp chopped fresh sage or oregano or
  ½ tsp dried sage or oregano

1½–2 lb potatoes

2 tbsp margarine

3–4 tbsp skim milk

4½ oz small white mushrooms, sliced
  (optional)

salt and pepper

1 Place the meat in a heavy-based saucepan with no extra fat and cook gently, stirring frequently, until the meat begins to brown.

2 Add the onions, carrots, and garlic and continue to cook gently for about 10 minutes. Stir in the flour and cook for 1 minute or so, then gradually stir in the stock and tomatoes, and bring to a boil.

3 Add the Worcestershire sauce, seasoning, and herbs, cover the pan, and simmer gently for about 25 minutes, giving an occasional stir.

4 Cook the potatoes in boiling salted water until tender, then drain thoroughly and mash, beating in the margarine, seasoning, and sufficient milk to give a piping consistency. Place in a piping bag fitted with a large star tip.

5 Stir the mushrooms (if using) into the meat and adjust the seasoning. Turn into a shallow ovenproof dish.

6 Pipe the potatoes evenly over the meat. Cook in a preheated oven at 400°F for about 30 minutes until piping hot and the potatoes are golden brown.

VARIATION

If liked, a mixture of boiled potatoes and parsnips or rutabaga may be used for the topping.

Minty Lamb Kabobs

These spicy lamb kabobs go well with the cool cucumber and yogurt dip.
In the summer you can barbecue the kabobs outside.

NUTRITIONAL INFORMATION

Calories	295	Sugars	........4g
Protein	........29g	Fat	..........18g
Carbohydrate	....4g	Saturates	......9g

5 MINS | 20 MINS

SERVES 4

INGREDIENTS

2 tsp coriander seeds

2 tsp cumin seeds

3 cloves

3 green cardamom pods

6 black peppercorns

½ inch piece ginger root

2 garlic cloves

2 tbsp chopped fresh mint

1 small onion, chopped

1¾ cups ground lamb

½ tsp salt

lime slices to serve

DIP

⅔ cup low-fat plain yogurt

2 tbsp chopped fresh mint

3 inch piece of cucumber, grated

1 tsp mango chutney

1 Heat a skillet and dry-fry the coriander, cumin, cloves, cardamom pods, and peppercorns until they turn a shade darker and release a roasted aroma.

2 Grind the spices in a coffee grinder, spice mill, or a pestle and mortar.

3 Put the ginger and garlic into a food processor or blender and process to a purée. Add the ground spices, mint, onion, lamb, and salt and process until chopped finely. Alternatively, finely chop the garlic and ginger and mix with the ground spices and remaining kabob ingredients.

4 Mold the kabob mixture into small sausage shapes on 4 kabob skewers.

Cook under a preheated hot broiler for 10–15 minutes, turning the skewers occasionally.

5 To make the dip, mix together the yogurt, mint, cucumber and mango chutney.

6 Serve the kabobs with lime slices and the dip.

Fruity Lamb Casserole

The sweet spicy blend of cinnamon, coriander, and cumin is the perfect foil for the tender lamb and apricots in this warming casserole.

NUTRITIONAL INFORMATION

Calories	384	Sugars	........16g
Protein	........32g	Fat	..........22g
Carbohydrate	...17g	Saturates	......9g

5 MINS   1¼ HOURS

SERVES 4

INGREDIENTS

1 lb lean lamb, trimmed and cut into 1 inch cubes

1 tsp ground cinnamon

1 tsp ground coriander

1 tsp ground cumin

2 tsp olive oil

1 medium red onion, finely chopped

1 garlic clove, crushed

14 oz can chopped tomatoes

2 tbsp tomato paste

4½ oz no-soak dried apricots

1 tsp sugar

1¼ cups vegetable stock

salt and pepper

1 small bunch fresh cilantro, to garnish

brown rice, steamed couscous or bulgar wheat, to serve

1 Preheat the oven to 350°F. Place the meat in a mixing bowl and add the spices and oil. Mix thoroughly so that the lamb is well coated in the spices.

2 Heat a non-stick skillet for a few seconds until it is hot, then add the spiced lamb. Reduce the heat and cook for 4–5 minutes, stirring, until browned all over. Using a slotted spoon, remove the lamb and transfer to a large ovenproof casserole.

3 In the same skillet, cook the onion, garlic, tomatoes and tomato paste for 5 minutes. Season to taste. Stir in the apricots and sugar, add the stock, and bring to a boil.

4 Spoon the sauce over the lamb and mix well. Cover and cook in the oven for 1 hour, removing the lid for the last 10 minutes.

5 Roughly chop the cilantro and sprinkle over the casserole to garnish. Serve with brown rice, steamed couscous, or bulgar wheat.

Beef Teriyaki

This Japanese-style teriyaki sauce complements barbecued beef, but it can also be used to accompany chicken or salmon.

NUTRITIONAL INFORMATION

Calories 184   Sugars 6g
Protein . . . . .24g   Fat 5g
Carbohydrate . . . .8g   Saturates 2g

2¼ HOURS   15 MINS

SERVES 4

INGREDIENTS

1 lb extra thin lean beef steaks

8 green onions, trimmed and cut into short lengths

1 yellow bell pepper, deseeded and cut into chunks

green salad, to serve

SAUCE

1 tsp cornstarch

2 tbsp dry sherry

2 tbsp white wine vinegar

3 tbsp soy sauce

1 tbsp brown sugar

1 clove garlic, crushed

½ tsp ground cinnamon

½ tsp ground ginger

1 Place the meat in a shallow, non-metallic dish.

2 To make the sauce, combine the cornstarch with the sherry, then stir in the remaining sauce ingredients. Pour the sauce over the meat and leave to marinate for at least 2 hours.

3 Remove the meat from the sauce. Pour the sauce into a small saucepan.

4 Cut the meat into thin strips and thread these, concertina-style, onto pre-soaked wooden skewers, alternating each strip of meat with the prepared pieces of green onion and bell pepper.

5 Gently heat the sauce until it is just simmering, stirring occasionally.

6 Barbecue the kabobs over hot coals for 5–8 minutes, turning and basting the beef and vegetables occasionally with the reserved teriyaki sauce.

7 Arrange the skewers on serving plates and pour the remaining sauce over the kabobs. Serve with a green salad.

Pork with Ratatouille Sauce

Serve this delicious combination of meat and vegetables with baked potatoes for an appetizing supper dish.

NUTRITIONAL INFORMATION

Calories 230	Sugars 8g
Protein 29g	Fat 9g
Carbohydrate 8g	Saturates 3g

10 MINS   35 MINS

SERVES 4

INGREDIENTS

4 lean, boneless pork chops, about
   4½ oz each

1 tsp dried mixed herbs

salt and pepper

baked potatoes, to serve

SAUCE

1 medium onion

1 garlic clove

1 small green bell pepper, deseeded

1 small yellow bell pepper, deseeded

1 medium zucchini, trimmed

3½ oz small white mushrooms

14 oz can chopped tomatoes

2 tbsp tomato paste

1 tsp dried mixed herbs

1 tsp sugar

COOK'S TIP

This vegetable sauce could
be served with any other broiled or
baked meat or fish. It would also
make an excellent alternative filling
for savoury crêpes.

1 To make the sauce, peel and chop the onion and garlic. Dice the bell peppers. Dice the zucchini. Wipe and halve the mushrooms.

2 Place all of the vegetables in a saucepan and stir in the chopped tomatoes and tomato paste. Add the dried herbs, sugar, and plenty of seasoning. Bring to a boil, cover, and simmer for 20 minutes.

3 Meanwhile, preheat the broiler to medium. Trim away any excess fat from the chops, then season on both sides, and rub in the dried mixed herbs. Cook the chops for 5 minutes, then turn over, and cook for a further 6–7 minutes or until cooked through.

4 Drain the chops on absorbent kitchen paper and serve accompanied with the sauce and baked potatoes.

Pathan Beef Stir-Fry

Although the meat can be left in the marinade overnight, this is a quick and tasty dish to make.

2¹/₄ HOURS   15 MINS

SERVES 4

INGREDIENTS

1 lb 10 oz fillet of lean beef, cut into 1 inch strips

2 tbsp vegetable oil

1 onion

1 inch piece ginger root, cut into strips

1 fresh red chili, deseeded and sliced

2 carrots, cut into strips

1 green bell pepper, cut into strips

1 tsp garam masala

1 tbsp toasted sesame seeds

MARINADE

1 tsp dried fenugreek

1 tsp brown mustard seeds, ground

1 tsp ground cinnamon

1 tsp ground cumin

1 garlic clove, crushed

⅔ cup low-fat yogurt

1 To make the marinade, mix the ingredients together in a bowl.

2 Mix the beef with the marinade, then cover, and leave to marinate for 1–2 hours, or overnight in the refrigerator.

3 Heat the oil in a wok, add the onion, and stir-fry until softened.

4 Stir in the ginger, chili, carrots, and green bell pepper and stir-fry for 1 minute.

5 Add the garam masala and beef with its marinade to the vegetables, and stir-fry for 8–10 minutes until the beef is tender; it is best if it is still pinkish inside.

6 Stir in the toasted sesame seeds and serve the stir-fry immediately.

VARIATION

Any selection of vegetables can be added to the stir-fry, which is a good way to use up any vegetables left over in the refrigerator, but add them to the beef for just long enough to heat through.

Moroccan Lamb Kabobs

Marinated in Moroccan spices, these barbecued kabobs have a mild, spicy flavor. Add the chili if you like a bit of heat to your meat.

NUTRITIONAL INFORMATION

Calories	348	Sugars 2g
Protein	........30g	Fat 24g
Carbohydrate	....2g	Saturates 10g

2¼ HOURS   10 MINS

SERVES 4

I N G R E D I E N T S

1 lb lean lamb

1 lemon

1 red onion

4 small zucchini

couscous, to serve (see Cook's Tip)

M A R I N A D E

grated rind and juice of 1 lemon

2 tbsp olive oil

1 clove garlic, crushed

1 red chili, sliced (optional)

1 tsp ground cinnamon

1 tsp ground ginger

½ tsp ground cumin

½ tsp ground coriander

1 Cut the lamb into large, evenly sized chunks.

2 To make the marinade, combine the lemon rind and juice, oil, garlic, chili (if using), ground cinnamon, ginger, cumin, and coriander in a large non-metallic dish.

3 Add the meat to the marinade, tossing to coat the meat completely. Cover and leave to marinate in the refrigerator for at least 2 hours or preferably overnight.

4 Cut the lemon into 8 pieces. Cut the onion into wedges, then separate each wedge into 2 pieces.

5 Using a canelle knife (or potato peeler), cut thin strips of peel from the zucchini, then cut the zucchini into chunks.

6 Remove the meat from the marinade, reserving the liquid for basting. Thread the meat on to skewers alternating with the onion, lemon, and zucchini.

7 Barbecue over hot coals for 8–10 minutes, turning, and basting with the reserved marinade. Serve on a bed of couscous (see Cook's Tip).

COOK'S TIP

Serve these kabobs with couscous. Allowing 2 oz couscous per person, soak the couscous in cold water for about 20 minutes until softened. Drain and steam for 10 minutes or until piping hot.

Fruity Stuffed Bacon Chops

This combination of green lentils, celery, and apricots stuffed into bacon chops, served with a sweet sauce is a speedy dish for the microwave.

NUTRITIONAL INFORMATION

Calories	148	Sugars	.........5g
Protein	........15g	Fat	..........6g
Carbohydrate	....9g	Saturates	......3g

  20 MINS   30 MINS

SERVES 4

INGREDIENTS

¼ cup green lentils, washed

1 celery stalk, sliced

2 green onions, chopped

4 thick cut tendersweet lean bacon chops

1 tbsp chopped fresh sage

4 apricot halves canned in natural juice, drained and chopped

1 tsp cornstarch

4 tbsp natural juice from can of apricots

2 tbsp fresh orange juice

1 tsp grated orange rind

1 tbsp low-fat crème fraîche

salt and pepper

TO GARNISH

orange slices

sprigs of fresh sage

1 Place the lentils and celery in a bowl. Pour on boiling water to cover them. Cover and cook on HIGH power for 18–20 minutes until tender, adding extra water if necessary. Add the green onions for the last minute of cooking. Leave to stand, covered, for 10 minutes.

2 Using a sharp knife, slit the meaty end of each chop nearly through to the fat side, to form a pocket.

3 Drain the lentils and mix with half of the sage and the apricots. Season to taste.

4 Spoon the lentil stuffing into the pockets in the bacon chops. Arrange 2 on a plate. Cover with a paper towel. Cook on HIGH power for 4 minutes until cooked through. Transfer to warmed plates, cover, and keep warm while cooking the remaining stuffed chops.

5 Mix the cornstarch with a little water in a bowl, then stir in the juice from the apricots, and the orange juice and rind. Cover and cook on HIGH power for 2 minutes, stirring every 30 seconds. Stir in the crème fraîche and remaining sage. Season and reheat on HIGH power for 30 seconds.

6 Serve the chops with the sauce. Garnish with orange slices and sage.

Beef Goulash

Slow, gentle cooking is the secret to this superb goulash—it really brings out the flavor of the ingredients.

NUTRITIONAL INFORMATION

Calories 386	Sugars 10g
Protein 44g	Fat 16g
Carbohydrate ...17g	Saturates 5g

10 MINS   2¼ HOURS

SERVES 4

INGREDIENTS

2 tbsp vegetable oil

1 large onion, chopped

1 garlic clove, crushed

1 lb 10 oz lean stewing steak

2 tbsp paprika

15 oz can chopped tomatoes

2 tbsp tomato paste

1 large red bell pepper, deseeded and chopped

6 oz mushrooms, sliced

2½ cups beef stock

1 tbsp cornstarch

1 tbsp water

4 tbsp low-fat plain yogurt

salt and pepper

paprika for sprinkling

chopped fresh parsley, to garnish

long grain rice and wild rice, to serve

1 Heat the vegetable oil in a large skillet and cook the onion and garlic for 3–4 minutes.

2 Cut the stewing steak into chunks and cook over a high heat for 3 minutes until browned all over. Add the paprika and stir well, then add the chopped tomatoes, tomato paste, bell pepper, and mushrooms. Cook for 2 minutes, stirring frequently.

3 Pour in the beef stock. Bring to a boil, then reduce the heat. Cover and simmer for 1½–2 hours or until the meat is tender.

4 Blend the cornstarch with the water, then add to the saucepan, stirring until thickened and smooth. Cook for 1 minute, then season with salt and pepper to taste.

5 Put the plain yogurt in a serving bowl and sprinkle with a little paprika.

6 Transfer the beef goulash to a warm serving dish, garnish with chopped fresh parsley, and serve with rice and yogurt.

Venison & Garlic Mash

Rich game is best served with a sweet fruit sauce. Here the venison steaks are cooked with sweet, juicy prunes and red currant jelly.

NUTRITIONAL INFORMATION

Calories	602	Sugars	........18g
Protein	........51g	Fat	..........14g
Carbohydrate	...62g	Saturates	......1g

  10 MINS   35 MINS

SERVES 4

I N G R E D I E N T S

8 medallions of venison, 2¾ oz each

1 tbsp vegetable oil

1 red onion, chopped

⅔ cup Fresh Beef Stock (see page 30)

⅔ cup red wine

3 tbsp red currant jelly

3½ oz no-need-to-soak dried, pitted prunes

2 tsp cornstarch

2 tbsp brandy

salt and pepper

G A R L I C   M A S H

2 lb potatoes, peeled and diced

½ tsp garlic paste

2 tbsp low-fat plain yogurt

4 tbsp fresh parsley, chopped

1 Trim off any excess fat from the meat and season with salt and pepper on both sides. Heat the oil in a skillet and fry the venison with the onions for 2 minutes on each side until brown.

2 Lower the heat and pour in the stock and wine. Add the red currant jelly and prunes and stir until the jelly melts. Cover and simmer for 10 minutes.

3 Meanwhile, make the garlic mash. Place the potatoes in a saucepan and cover with water. Bring to a boil and cook for 8–10 minutes. Drain well and mash until smooth. Add the garlic paste, yogurt, and parsley and blend thoroughly. Season, set aside, and keep warm.

4 Remove the medallions from the skillet with a slotted spoon and keep warm.

5 Blend the cornstarch with the brandy in a small bowl and add to the pan juices. Heat, stirring, until thickened. Season with salt and pepper to taste. Serve the venison with the red currant and prune sauce and the garlic mash.

Pan-Fried Liver with Thyme

This elegant dish is very simple to make. You can use either calf's or lamb's liver for the main ingredient.

NUTRITIONAL INFORMATION

Calories 462	Sugars 1g
Protein 27g	Fat 31g
Carbohydrate ...14g	Saturates 6g

5 MINS   10 MINS

SERVES 1

INGREDIENTS

1 slice calf's liver, about 4½ oz, or
    2 smaller slices, or 2 slices lamb's liver

1 tbsp seasoned flour

2 tsp oil

1 tbsp butter or margarine

2 tbsp white wine

½ tsp chopped fresh thyme or a large pinch
    of dried thyme

pinch of finely grated lime or lemon rind

2 tsp lemon juice

1 tsp capers

1–2 tbsp heavy cream (optional)

salt and pepper

TO GARNISH

lemon or lime slices

fresh thyme or parsley

COOK'S TIP

Liver is traditionally served with bacon and onions. Broiled bacon and crisply fried onions can be used as an extra garnish, if desired.

1 Trim the liver if necessary and toss in the seasoned flour until evenly coated.

2 Heat the oil and margarine in a frying pan. When foaming, add the liver and fry for 2–3 minutes on each side until well sealed and just cooked through. Take care not to overcook or the liver will become tough and hard. Transfer to a plate and keep warm.

3 Add the wine, 1 tablespoon of water, the thyme, citrus rind, lemon juice, capers, and seasoning to the pan juices, and heat through gently until bubbling and syrupy. Add the cream (if using) to the sauce and reheat gently. Adjust the seasoning and spoon over the liver.

5 Serve the liver, garnished with lemon or lime slices and thyme or parsley, with new potatoes and a salad.

Fruity Pork Skewers

Prunes and apricots bring color and flavor to these tasty pork kabobs.
They are delicious eaten straight off the barbecue.

1¹/₄ HOURS   15 MINS

MAKES 4

I N G R E D I E N T S

4 boneless lean pork loin steaks

8 ready-to-eat prunes

8 ready-to-eat dried apricots

4 bay leaves

slices of orange and lemon, to garnish

M A R I N A D E

4 tbsp orange juice

2 tbsp olive oil

1 tsp ground bay leaves

salt and pepper

1 Trim the visible fat from the pork and cut the meat into evenly-sized chunks.

2 Place the pork in a shallow, non-metallic dish and add the prunes and apricots.

3 To make the marinade, mix together the orange juice, oil, and bay leaves in a bowl. Season with salt and pepper to taste.

4 Pour the marinade over the pork and fruit and toss until well coated. Leave to marinate in the refrigerator for at least 1 hour or preferably overnight.

5 Soak 4 wooden skewers in cold water to prevent them from catching alight on the barbecue.

6 Remove the pork and fruit from the marinade, using a perforated spoon, reserving the marinade for basting. Thread the pork and fruit on to the skewers, alternating with the bay leaves.

7 Barbecue the skewers on an oiled rack over medium hot coals for 10–15 minutes, turning and frequently basting with the reserved marinade, or until the pork is cooked through.

8 Transfer the pork and fruit skewers to warm serving plates. Garnish with slices of orange and lemon and serve hot.

Lamb & Potato Moussaka

Ground lamb makes a very tasty and authentic moussaka. For a change, use ground beef.

NUTRITIONAL INFORMATION

Calories 422	Sugars 8g
Protein 32g	Fat 18g
Carbohydrate ...35g	Saturates 8g

45 MINS   1¼ HOURS

SERVES 4

INGREDIENTS

1 large eggplant, sliced

1 tbsp olive or vegetable oil

1 onion, chopped finely

1 garlic clove, crushed

12 oz lean ground lamb

9 oz mushrooms, sliced

15 oz can chopped tomatoes with herbs

⅔ cup lamb or vegetable stock

2 tbsp cornstarch

2 tbsp water

1 lb 2 oz potatoes, parboiled for
   10 minutes and sliced

2 eggs

½ cup low-fat cream cheese

⅔ cup low-fat plain yogurt

½ cup grated low-fat sharp Cheddar cheese

salt and pepper

fresh flat-leaf parsley, to garnish

green salad, to serve

1 Lay the eggplant slices on a clean surface and sprinkle liberally with salt, to extract the bitter juices. Leave for 10 minutes, then turn the slices over and repeat. Put in a colander, rinse, and drain well.

2 Meanwhile, heat the oil in a saucepan and fry the onion and garlic for 3–4 minutes. Add the lamb and mushrooms and cook for 5 minutes, until browned. Stir in the tomatoes and stock, bring to a boil, and simmer for 10 minutes. Mix the cornstarch with the water and stir into the pan. Cook, stirring, until thickened.

3 Spoon half of the mixture into an ovenproof dish. Cover with the eggplant slices, then the remaining lamb mixture. Arrange the sliced potatoes on top.

4 Beat together the eggs, cream cheese, yogurt, and seasoning. Pour over the potatoes to cover them completely. Sprinkle with the grated cheese.

5 Bake in a preheated oven at 375°F for 45 minutes until the topping is set and golden brown. Garnish with flat-leaf parsley and serve with a green salad.

Pan-Cooked Pork Medallions

In this dish these lean and tender cuts of meat are perfectly complemented by the dessert apples and apple cider.

NUTRITIONAL INFORMATION

Calories	256	Sugars	........12g
Protein	........21g	Fat	..........13g
Carbohydrate	...12g	Saturates	......3g

 2¹/₂ HOURS   40 MINS

SERVES 4

I N G R E D I E N T S

8 lean pork medallions, about 1¾ oz each

2 tsp vegetable oil

1 medium onion, finely sliced

1 tsp sugar

1 tsp dried sage

⅔ cup apple cider

⅔ cup Fresh Chicken or Vegetable Stock (see page 30–31)

1 green-skinned apple

1 red-skinned apple

1 tbsp lemon juice

salt and pepper

fresh sage leaves, to garnish

freshly cooked vegetables, to serve

1 Discard the string from the pork and trim away any excess fat. Re-tie with clean string and set aside until required.

2 Heat the oil in a frying pan and gently fry the onion for 5 minutes until softened. Add the sugar and cook for 3–4 minutes until golden. Add the pork to the pan and cook for 2 minutes on each side until browned.

3 Add the sage, cider, and stock. Bring to a boil and then simmer for 20 minutes.

4 Meanwhile, core and cut each apple into 8 wedges. Toss the apple wedges in lemon juice so that they do not turn brown.

5 Add the apples to the pork and mix gently. Season and cook for a further 3–4 minutes until tender.

6 Remove the string from the pork and serve immediately, garnished with fresh sage, and accompanied with freshly cooked vegetables.

Tamarind Beef Balti

Tamarind has been used in Asian cooking for centuries and gives a sour, fruity flavor to the sauce.

NUTRITIONAL INFORMATION

Calories	280	Sugars	........7g
Protein	........35g	Fat	..........12g
Carbohydrate	....7g	Saturates	......4g

12 HOURS   35 MINS

SERVES 4

INGREDIENTS

4½ oz tamarind block, broken into pieces

⅔ cup water

2 tbsp tomato paste

1 tbsp sugar

1 inch piece fresh ginger, chopped

1 garlic clove, chopped

½ tsp salt

1 onion, chopped

2 tbsp oil

1 tsp cumin seeds

1 tsp coriander seeds

1 tsp brown mustard seeds

4 curry leaves

1 lb 10 oz lean braising steak, cut into
  1 inch cubes and par-cooked

1 red bell pepper, cut in half, sliced

2 fresh green chilies, deseeded and sliced

1 tsp garam masala

1 tbsp chopped fresh cilantro,
  to garnish

1 Soak the tamarind overnight in the water. Strain the soaked tamarind, keeping the liquid.

2 Put the tamarind, tomato paste, sugar, ginger, garlic, salt, and onion into a food processor or blender and mix to a smooth purée. Alternatively, mash the ingredients together in a bowl.

3 Heat the oil in a wok, add the cumin, coriander seeds, mustard seeds, and curry leaves, and cook until the spices start popping.

4 Stir the beef into the spices and stir-fry for 2–4 minutes until the meat is browned.

5 Add the red bell pepper, chilies, garam masala, tamarind mixture, and reserved tamarind liquid and cook for 20–25 minutes.

6 Serve the beef balti garnished with fresh cilantro.

Lamb Couscous

Couscous is a dish that originated among the Berbers of North Africa. When steamed, it is a plump grain, ideal for serving with stews.

NUTRITIONAL INFORMATION

Calories	537	Sugars	........11g
Protein	........32g	Fat	..........14g
Carbohydrate	...73g	Saturates	......4g

15 MINS   35 MINS

SERVES 4

INGREDIENTS

2 medium red onions, sliced

juice of 1 lemon

1 large red bell pepper, deseeded and thickly sliced

1 large green bell pepper, deseeded and thickly sliced

1 large orange bell pepper, deseeded and thickly sliced

pinch of saffron strands

cinnamon stick, broken

1 tbsp clear honey

1¼ cups vegetable stock

2 tsp olive oil

12 oz lean lamb fillet, trimmed and sliced

1 tsp Harissa paste

7 oz can chopped tomatoes

15 oz can garbanzo beans, drained

12 oz precooked couscous

2 tsp ground cinnamon

salt and pepper

1 Toss the onions in the lemon juice and transfer to a saucepan. Mix in the bell peppers, saffron, cinnamon stick, and honey. Pour in the stock, bring to a boil, cover, and simmer for 5 minutes.

2 Meanwhile, heat the oil in a frying pan and gently fry the lamb for 3–4 minutes until browned all over.

3 Using a slotted spoon, drain the lamb and transfer it to the pan with the onions and bell peppers. Season and stir in the Harissa paste, tomatoes, and garbanzo beans. Mix well, bring back to a boil, and simmer, uncovered, for 20 minutes.

4 Soak the couscous, following the package instructions. Bring a saucepan of water to a boil. Put the couscous in a steamer or strainer lined with cheesecloth over the pan of boiling water. Cover and steam.

5 Transfer the couscous to a serving platter and dust with ground cinnamon. Discard the cinnamon stick and spoon the stew over the couscous.

Masala Kabobs

Indian kabob dishes are not necessarily cooked on a skewer; they can also be served in a dish and are always dry dishes with no sauce.

NUTRITIONAL INFORMATION

Calories	294	Sugars	.........0g
Protein	........35g	Fat	..........17g
Carbohydrate	....0g	Saturates	......7g

 1¼ HOURS 20 MINS

SERVES 4

I N G R E D I E N T S

1 dried bay leaf

1 inch piece fresh ginger, chopped

1 inch cinnamon stick

1 tsp coriander seeds

½ tsp salt

1 tsp fennel seeds

1 tsp chili powder

1 tsp garam masala

1 tsp lemon juice

1 tsp ground turmeric

1 tbsp oil

1 lb 10 oz lamb neck fillet

TO GARNISH

sprigs of fresh cilantro

lemon wedges

TO SERVE

bread

chutney

1 Use a food processor, blender or pestle and mortar to grind together the bay leaf, ginger, cinnamon, coriander seeds, salt, fennel seeds, and chili powder.

2 Combine this spice mix with the garam masala, lemon juice, turmeric, and oil in a large bowl.

3 Cut the lamb into ¼ inch slices. Add to the spice mix and leave to marinate at room temperature for 1 hour, or in the refrigerator for 3 hours or overnight.

4 Spread out the pieces of lamb on a cookie sheet and cook in a preheated oven, 400°F, for 20 minutes until well done. Transfer the pieces of lamb to paper towels to drain any excess fat.

5 Thread 3 or 4 pieces of meat on to each skewer and garnish with sprigs of fresh cilantro and lemon wedges.

6 Serve the masala kabobs hot with bread and chutney.

Tangy Pork Fillet

Barbecued in a parcel of kitchen foil, these tasty pork fillets are served with a tangy orange sauce.

NUTRITIONAL INFORMATION

Calories	230	Sugars	........16g
Protein	........19g	Fat	...........9g
Carbohydrate	...20g	Saturates	......3g

 10 MINS   55 MINS

SERVES 4

I N G R E D I E N T S

14 oz lean pork fillet

3 tbsp orange marmalade

grated rind and juice of 1 orange

1 tbsp white wine vinegar

dash of Tabasco sauce

salt and pepper

S A U C E

1 tbsp olive oil

1 small onion, chopped

1 small green bell pepper, deseeded and thinly sliced

1 tbsp cornstarch

⅔ cup orange juice

TO SERVE

cooked rice

tossed salad leaves

1 Place a large piece of double thickness foil in a shallow dish. Put the pork fillet in the center of the foil and season.

2 Heat the marmalade, orange rind and juice, vinegar, and Tabasco sauce in a small pan, stirring until the marmalade melts and the ingredients combine. Pour the mixture over the pork and wrap the meat in foil, making sure that the parcel is well sealed so that the juices cannot run

out. Place over hot coals and barbecue for about 25 minutes, turning the parcel occasionally.

3 For the sauce, heat the oil and cook the onion for 2–3 minutes. Add the bell pepper and cook for 3–4 minutes.

4 Remove the pork from the kitchen foil and place on to the rack. Pour the juices into the pan with the sauce.

5 Barbecue the pork for a further 10–20 minutes, turning, until cooked through and golden on the outside.

6 In a small bowl, mix the cornstarch with a little orange juice to form a paste. Add to the sauce with the remaining cooking juices. Cook, stirring, until the sauce thickens. Slice the pork, spoon over the sauce, and serve with rice and tossed salad leaves.

Pork Chops & Spicy Beans

A tasty and substantial dish, and the spicy bean mixture, served on its own, also makes a good accompaniment to other meat or chicken dishes.

NUTRITIONAL INFORMATION

Calories ......388 Sugars 5g
Protein ....20g Fat 27g
Carbohydrate ...17g Saturates 8g

 5 MINS   50 MINS

SERVES 4

INGREDIENTS

3 tbsp vegetable oil

4 lean pork chops, rind removed

2 onions, peeled and thinly sliced

2 garlic cloves, peeled and crushed

2 fresh green chilies, seeded and chopped or use 1-2 tsp minced chili (from a jar)

1 inch piece fresh ginger, peeled and chopped

1½ tsp cumin seeds

1½ tsp ground coriander

2½ cups stock or water

2 tbsp tomato paste

½ eggplant, trimmed and cut into ½ inch dice

salt

1 x 14 oz can red kidney beans, drained

4 tbsp heavy cream

sprigs of cilantro, to garnish

2 Add the sliced onions, garlic, chilies, ginger, and spices and fry gently for 2 minutes. Stir in the stock or water, tomato paste, diced eggplant, and season with salt and pepper.

3 Bring the mixture to a boil, place the pork chops on top, then cover, and simmer gently over medium heat for 30 minutes.

4 Remove the chops for a moment and stir the red kidney beans and heavy cream into the mixture. Return the chops to the pan, cover, and heat through gently for 5 minutes.

5 Taste and adjust the seasoning, if necessary. Serve hot, garnished with cilantro sprigs.

1 Heat the vegetable oil in a large frying pan, add the pork chops, and fry until sealed and browned on both sides. Remove from the pan and set aside until required.

Pork Fry with Vegetables

This is a very simple dish which lends itself to almost any combination of vegetables that you have available.

5 MINS   15 MINS

SERVES 4

I N G R E D I E N T S

12 oz pork tenderloin

2 tbsp vegetable oil

2 garlic cloves, crushed

½ inch piece fresh ginger, cut into slivers

1 carrot, cut into thin strips

1 red bell pepper, seeded and diced

1 fennel bulb, sliced

1 oz water chestnuts, halved

2 ¾ oz bean sprouts

2 tbsp Chinese rice wine

1¼ cups pork or chicken stock

pinch of dark brown sugar

1 tsp cornstarch

2 tsp water

1 Cut the pork into thin slices. Heat the oil in a preheated wok. Add the garlic, ginger, and pork and stir-fry for 1–2 minutes, until the meat is sealed.

2 Add the carrot, bell pepper, fennel, and water chestnuts to the wok and stir-fry for about 2-3 minutes.

3 Add the bean sprouts and stir-fry for 1 minute. Remove the pork and vegetables from the wok and keep warm.

4 Add the Chinese rice wine, pork or chicken stock, and sugar to the wok. Blend the cornstarch to a smooth paste with the water and stir it into the sauce. Bring to a boil, stirring constantly until thickened and clear.

5 Return the meat and vegetables to the wok and cook for 1–2 minutes, until heated through and coated with the sauce. Serve immediately.

VARIATION

Use dry sherry instead of the Chinese rice wine if you have difficulty obtaining it.

Lamb & Potato Masala

To create delicious Indian dishes at home—simply open a can of curry sauce, add a few interesting ingredients and you have a splendid meal.

NUTRITIONAL INFORMATION

Calories	.513	Sugars	.6g
Protein	.40g	Fat	.27g
Carbohydrate	.30g	Saturates	.8g

 15 MINS   🕐 1½ HOURS

SERVES 4

I N G R E D I E N T S

1 lb 10 oz lean lamb (from the leg)

3 tbsp ghee or vegetable oil

1 lb 2 oz potatoes, peeled and cut into large 1 inch pieces

1 large onion, peeled, quartered, and sliced

2 garlic cloves, peeled and crushed

6 oz mushrooms, thickly sliced

1 x 10 oz can Tikka Masala Curry Sauce

1¼ cups water

salt

3 tomatoes, halved and cut into thin slices

4½ oz spinach, washed and stalks trimmed

sprigs of mint, to garnish

1 Cut the lamb into 1 inch cubes. Heat the ghee or oil in a large pan, add the lamb, and fry over moderate heat for 3 minutes or until sealed all over. Remove the lamb from the pan.

2 Add the potatoes, onion, garlic, and mushrooms and fry for 3-4 minutes, stirring frequently.

3 Stir the curry sauce and water into the pan, add the lamb, mix well, and season with salt to taste. Cover and cook very gently for 1 hour or until the lamb is tender and cooked through, stirring occasionally.

4 Add the sliced tomatoes and the spinach to the pan, pushing the leaves well down into the mixture, then cover, and cook for a further 10 minutes until the spinach is cooked and tender.

5 Garnish with mint sprigs and serve hot.

COOK'S TIP

Spinach leaves wilt quickly during cooking, so if the leaves are young and tender add them whole to the mixture; larger leaves may be coarsely shredded, if wished, before adding to the pan.

Pork & Apple Skewers

Flavored with mustard and served with a mustard sauce, these kabobs make an ideal lunch.

NUTRITIONAL INFORMATION

Calories	290	Sugars	........11g
Protein	........24g	Fat	..........17g
Carbohydrate	....11g	Saturates	......5g

10 MINS   15 MINS

SERVES 4

INGREDIENTS

1 lb pork fillet

2 dessert apples

a little lemon juice

1 lemon

2 tsp wholegrain mustard

2 tsp Dijon mustard

2 tbsp apple or orange juice

2 tbsp sunflower oil

crusty brown bread, to serve

MUSTARD SAUCE

1 tbsp wholegrain mustard

1 tsp Dijon mustard

6 tbsp light cream

1 To make the mustard sauce, combine the wholegrain and Dijon mustards in a small bowl and slowly blend in the cream. Leave to stand until required.

2 Cut the pork fillet into bite-size pieces and set aside until required.

3 Core the apples, then cut them into thick wedges. Toss the apple wedges in a little lemon juice—this will prevent any discoloration. Slice the lemon.

4 Thread the pork, apple, and lemon slices alternately on to 4 metal or pre-soaked wooden skewers.

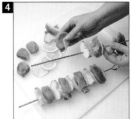

5 Mix together the mustards, apple or orange juice, and sunflower oil. Brush the mixture over the kabobs and barbecue over hot coals for 10–15 minutes, until cooked through, frequently turning and basting the kabobs with the mustard marinade.

6 Transfer the kabobs to warm serving plates and spoon over a little of the mustard sauce. Serve the kabobs with fresh, crusty brown bread.

Meatball Brochettes

Children will love these tasty meatballs on a skewer, which are economical and easy to make on the barbecue.

NUTRITIONAL INFORMATION

Calories 120	Sugars 2g	
Protein 17g	Fat 5g	
Carbohydrate 2g	Saturates 2g	

1 HOUR   10 MINS

SERVES 4

I N G R E D I E N T S

1 oz cracked wheat

12 oz lean minced beef

1 onion, chopped very finely (optional)

1 tbsp tomato ketchup

1 tbsp brown fruity sauce

1 tbsp chopped, fresh parsley

beaten egg, to bind

8 cherry tomatoes

8 small white mushrooms

oil, to baste

8 bread finger rolls, to serve

1 Place the cracked wheat in a bowl and cover with boiling water. Leave to soak for 20 minutes or until softened. Drain thoroughly and leave to cool.

2 Place the soaked wheat, minced beef, onion (if using), ketchup, brown fruity sauce, and chopped fresh parsley together in a mixing bowl and mix well until all the ingredients are well combined. Add a little beaten egg if necessary to bind the mixture together.

3 Using your hands, shape the meat mixture into 18 even-sized balls. Leave to chill in the refrigerator for 30 minutes.

4 Thread the meatballs on to 8 pre-soaked wooden skewers, alternating them with the cherry tomatoes and mushrooms.

5 Brush the brochettes with a little oil and barbecue over hot coals for about 10 minutes, until cooked through, turning occasionally and brushing with a little more oil if the meat starts to dry out.

6 Transfer the meatball brochettes to warm serving plates. Cut open the bread finger rolls and push the meat and vegetables off the skewer into the open rolls, using a fork. Serve immediately.

Savory Hotpot

This hearty lamb stew is full of vegetables and herbs, and is topped with a layer of crisp, golden potato slices.

NUTRITIONAL INFORMATION

Calories 365	Sugars 5g
Protein 23g	Fat 11g
Carbohydrate . . .48g	Saturates 4g

 15 MINS   2 HOURS

SERVES 4

I N G R E D I E N T S

8 middle neck lean lamb chops, neck of lamb or any lean stewing lamb on the bone

1–2 garlic cloves, crushed

2 lamb's kidneys (optional)

1 large onion, sliced thinly

1 leek, sliced

2–3 carrots, sliced

1 tsp chopped fresh tarragon or sage, or ½ tsp dried tarragon or sage

2 lb 4 oz potatoes, sliced thinly

1¼ cups stock

2 tbsp margarine, melted, or 1 tbsp vegetable oil

salt and pepper

chopped fresh parsley, to garnish

1 Trim any excess fat from the lamb, season well with salt and pepper, and arrange in a large ovenproof casserole. Sprinkle with the garlic.

2 If using kidneys, remove the skin, halve, and cut out the cores. Chop into small pieces and sprinkle over the lamb.

3 Place the vegetables over the lamb, allowing the pieces to slip in between the meat, then sprinkle with the herbs.

4 Arrange the potato slices over the meat and vegetables, in an overlapping pattern.

5 Bring the stock to a boil, season to taste, then pour over the casserole.

6 Brush the potatoes with the melted margarine or vegetable oil, cover with greased foil or a lid, and cook in a preheated oven at 350°F for 1½ hours.

7 Remove the foil or lid from the potatoes, increase the temperature to 425°F, and return the casserole to the oven for about 30 minutes until the potatoes are browned.

8 Garnish the hotpot with the chopped fresh parsley and serve immediately.

Pork with Plums

Plum sauce is often used in Chinese cooking with duck or rich, fattier meat to counteract the flavor.

NUTRITIONAL INFORMATION

Calories 281   Sugars 6g
Protein . . . . .25g   Fat 14g
Carbohydrate . . .10g   Saturates 4g

35 MINS   25 MINS

SERVES 4

I N G R E D I E N T S

1 lb pork tenderloin

1 tbsp cornstarch

2 tbsp light soy sauce

2 tbsp Chinese rice wine

4 tsp light brown sugar

pinch of ground cinnamon

5 tsp vegetable oil

2 garlic cloves, crushed

2 green onions, chopped

4 tbsp plum sauce

1 tbsp hoisin sauce

⅔ cup water

dash of chili sauce

fried plum quarters and green onions, to garnish

1 Cut the pork tenderloin into thin slices.

2 Combine the cornstarch, soy sauce, rice wine, sugar, and cinnamon in a small bowl.

3 Place the pork in a shallow dish and pour the cornstarch mixture over it. Toss the meat in the marinade until it is completely coated. Cover and leave to marinate for at least 30 minutes.

4 Remove the pork from the dish, reserving the marinade.

5 Heat the oil in a preheated wok or large skillet. Add the pork and stir-fry for 3–4 minutes, until a light golden color.

6 Stir in the garlic, green onions, plum sauce, hoisin sauce, water, and chili sauce. Bring the sauce to a boil. Reduce the heat, cover, and leave to simmer for

8–10 minutes, or until the pork is cooked through and tender.

7 Stir in the reserved marinade and cook, stirring, for about 5 minutes.

8 Transfer the pork stir-fry to a warm serving dish and garnish with fried plum quarters and green onions. Serve immediately.

Lamb Kabobs with Herbs

Serve the kabobs sizzling hot, and the cucumber and yogurt sauce as cool as can be—it is a delicious partnership.

NUTRITIONAL INFORMATION

Calories	238	Sugars	.........7g
Protein	........21g	Fat	..........14g
Carbohydrate	....7g	Saturates	......5g

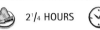

🍖 2¼ HOURS   🕐 15 MINS

SERVES 4

I N G R E D I E N T S

2 lb 4 oz lean leg of lamb, trimmed of fat

3 tbsp olive oil

1 tbsp red wine vinegar

juice of ½ lemon

3 tbsp low-fat plain yogurt

1 tbsp dried oregano

2 large garlic cloves, crushed

2 dried bay leaves, crumbled

4 fresh bay leaves

2 tbsp chopped parsley

salt and pepper

S A U C E

1¼ cups low-fat plain yogurt

1 garlic clove, crushed

¼ tsp salt

½ small cucumber, peeled and finely chopped

3 tbsp finely chopped mint

pinch of paprika

1 Cut the lamb into cubes about 1½–2 inches square. Pat dry with paper towels to ensure that the meat stays crisp and firm on the outside when broiled.

2 Whisk together the olive oil, wine vinegar, lemon juice, and yogurt. Stir in the oregano, garlic, and crumbled bay leaves and season with salt and pepper. Place the meat cubes in the marinade and stir until well coated in the mixture. Cover and place in the refrigerator for at least 2 hours.

3 Meanwhile, make the sauce. Place the plain yogurt in a large bowl. Stir in the garlic, salt, cucumber, and mint. Cover with plastic wrap and set aside in the refrigerator until required.

4 Heat the broiler to high. With a slotted spoon, lift the meat from the marinade and shake off any excess liquid. Divide the meat into 4 equal portions. Thread the meat and the fresh bay leaves on to 4 skewers.

5 Broil the kabobs for about 4 minutes on each side, basting frequently with the marinade. At this stage the meat should be crisp on the outside and slightly pink on the inside. If you prefer lamb well done, cook the kabobs for a little longer.

6 Sprinkle the kabobs with parsley and serve at once. Sprinkle the paprika over the sauce and serve chilled.

Beef & Tomato Gratin

A satisfying bake of lean ground beef, zucchini, and tomatoes cooked in a low-fat "custard" with a cheesy crust.

NUTRITIONAL INFORMATION

Calories	278	Sugars	........10g
Protein	........29g	Fat	..........10g
Carbohydrate	...20g	Saturates	......5g

10 MINS   1¼ HOURS

SERVES 4

I N G R E D I E N T S

12 oz lean beef, ground

1 large onion, finely chopped

1 tsp dried mixed herbs

1 tbsp all-purpose flour

1¼ cups beef stock

1 tbsp tomato paste

2 large tomatoes, thinly sliced

4 medium zucchini, thinly sliced

2 tbsp cornstarch

1¼ cups skim milk

⅔ cup low-fat plain yogurt

1 medium egg yolk

4 tbsp Parmesan cheese, freshly grated

salt and pepper

TO SERVE

crusty bread

steamed vegetables

2 Stir in the dried mixed herbs, flour, beef stock, and tomato paste, and season. Bring to a boil and simmer for 30 minutes until the mixture has thickened.

3 Transfer the beef mixture to an ovenproof gratin dish. Cover with a layer of the sliced tomatoes and then add a layer of sliced zucchini. Blend the cornstarch with a little milk. Pour the remaining milk into a saucepan and bring to a boil. Add the cornstarch mixture and cook, stirring, for 1–2 minutes until

thickened. Remove from the heat and beat in the yogurt and egg yolk. Season well.

4 Spread the white sauce over the layer of zucchini. Place the dish on to a cookie sheet and sprinkle with grated Parmesan. Bake in the oven for 25–30 minutes until golden-brown. Serve with crusty bread and vegetables.

1 Preheat the oven to 375°F. In a large frying pan, dry-fry the beef and onion for 4–5 minutes until browned.

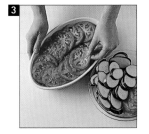

Sweet Lamb Fillet

Lamb fillet, enhanced by a sweet and spicy glaze, is cooked on the barbecue in a kitchen foil parcel for deliciously moist results.

NUTRITIONAL INFORMATION

Calories ....258 Sugars 13g
Protein ....24g Fat 13g
Carbohydrate ...13g Saturates 5g

 5 MINS   1 HOUR

SERVES 4

INGREDIENTS

2 fillets of neck of lean lamb, each 8 oz

1 tbsp olive oil

½ onion, chopped finely

1 clove garlic, crushed

1 inch piece fresh ginger, grated

5 tbsp apple juice

3 tbsp smooth apple sauce

1 tbsp brown sugar

1 tbsp tomato ketchup

½ tsp mild mustard

salt and pepper

green salad leaves, croutons, and fresh
crusty bread, to serve

1 Place the lamb fillet on a large piece of double thickness kitchen foil. Season with salt and pepper to taste.

2 Heat the oil in a small pan and fry the onion and garlic for 2–3 minutes until softened, but not browned. Stir in the grated ginger and cook for 1 minute, stirring occasionally.

3 Stir in the apple juice, apple sauce, sugar, ketchup, and mustard and bring to a boil. Boil rapidly for about 10 minutes until reduced by half. Stir the mixture occasionally so that it does not burn and stick to the base of the pan.

4 Brush half of the sauce over the lamb, then wrap up the lamb in the kitchen foil to completely enclose it. Barbecue the lamb parcels over hot coals for about 25 minutes, turning the parcel occasionally.

5 Open up the kitchen foil and brush the lamb with some of the sauce. Continue to barbecue for a further 15–20 minutes or until cooked through.

6 Place the lamb on a chopping board, remove the foil, and cut into thick slices. Transfer to serving plates and spoon over the remaining sauce. Serve with green salad leaves, croutons, and fresh crusty bread.

Ginger Beef with Chili

Serve these fruity, hot, and spicy steaks with noodles. Use a non-stick ridged frying pan to cook with a minimum of fat.

NUTRITIONAL INFORMATION

Calories 179   Sugars 8g
Protein ....21g   Fat 6g
Carbohydrate ....8g   Saturates 2g

40 MINS   10 MINS

SERVES 4

INGREDIENTS

4 lean beef steaks (such as rump, sirloin, or fillet), 3½ oz each

2 tbsp ginger wine

1 inch piece fresh ginger, finely chopped

1 garlic clove, crushed

1 tsp ground chili

1 tsp vegetable oil

salt and pepper

red chili strips, to garnish

TO SERVE

freshly cooked noodles

2 green onions, shredded

RELISH

8 oz fresh pineapple

1 small red bell pepper

1 red chili

2 tbsp light soy sauce

1 piece stem ginger in syrup, drained and chopped

1 Trim any excess fat from the beef, if necessary. Using a meat mallet or covered rolling pin, pound the steaks until ½ inch thick. Season on both sides and place in a shallow dish.

2 Mix the ginger wine, fresh ginger, garlic, and chili and pour over the meat. Cover and chill for 30 minutes.

3 Meanwhile, make the relish. Peel and finely chop the pineapple and place it in a bowl. Halve, deseed, and finely chop the bell pepper and chili. Stir into the pineapple together with the soy sauce and stem ginger. Cover and chill until required.

4 Brush a broiler pan with the oil and heat until very hot. Drain the beef and add to the pan, pressing down to seal. Lower the heat and cook for 5 minutes. Turn the steaks over and cook for a further 5 minutes.

5 Drain the steaks on kitchen paper and transfer to serving plates. Garnish with chili strips, and serve with noodles, green onions, and the relish.

Irish Stew with Dumplings

This traditional recipe makes a hearty stew with fluffy parsley dumplings. Cubes of lean lamb shoulder could be used in place of the cutlets.

NUTRITIONAL INFORMATION

Calories 576   Sugars 4g
Protein ....27g   Fat 28g
Carbohydrate ...55g   Saturates 12g

10 MINS   1¼ HOURS

SERVES 4

INGREDIENTS

2 tbsp vegetable oil

2 large onions, sliced

1 leek, sliced

1 large carrot, sliced

2 celery sticks, sliced

3¾ cups lamb stock

1 lb 10 oz lean lamb cutlets, trimmed

⅓ cup pearl barley

2 large potatoes, peeled and cut into large chunks

salt and pepper

chopped fresh parsley, to garnish

DUMPLINGS

3 oz self-raising flour

¼ cup porridge oats

2 tbsp chopped fresh parsley

pinch of salt

2 oz vegetable suet

chilled water, to mix

1 First make the dumplings. Put the flour, oats, parsley, and salt into a large mixing bowl. Stir in the suet. Add sufficient chilled water to make a soft, but not sticky, dough. Shape into 8 dumplings, cover with a tea towel and set aside.

2 Heat the vegetable oil in a large saucepan and gently fry the onions, leek, carrot, and celery for 5 minutes, without browning.

3 Add the stock, lamb, and pearl barley to the saucepan. Bring to a boil and then reduce the heat. Cover and simmer for 20 minutes.

4 Add the potatoes and cook for a further 20 minutes. Add the dumplings to the saucepan. Cover and simmer for 15–20 minutes until the dumplings are light and fluffy.

5 Season the stew with salt and pepper, garnish with parsley, and serve immediately while still hot.

Lamb with a Spice Crust

Lamb neck fillet is a tender cut that is not too thick and is, therefore, ideal for cooking on the barbecue.

NUTRITIONAL INFORMATION

Calories 203	Sugars 9g
Protein 16g	Fat 10g
Carbohydrate ...12g	Saturates 4g

 5 MINS   45 MINS

SERVES 4

I N G R E D I E N T S

1 tbsp olive oil

2 tbsp brown sugar

2 tbsp wholegrain mustard

1 tbsp horseradish sauce

1 tbsp all-purpose flour

12 oz neck fillet of lamb

salt and pepper

T O   S E R V E

coleslaw

slices of tomato

1 Combine the oil, sugar, mustard, horseradish sauce, flour, and salt and pepper to taste in a shallow, non-metallic dish until they are well mixed.

2 Roll the lamb in the spice mixture until well coated.

COOK'S TIP

If preferred, the lamb can be completely removed from the kitchen foil for the second part of the cooking. Barbecue the lamb directly over the coals for a smokier barbecue flavor, basting with extra oil if necessary.

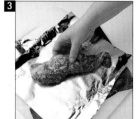

3 Lightly oil one or two pieces of foil or a large, double thickness of foil. Place the lamb on the foil and wrap it up so that the meat is completely enclosed.

4 Place the foil parcel over hot coals for 30 minutes, turning the parcel over occasionally.

5 Open the kitchen foil, spoon the cooking juices over the lamb, and continue to barbecue for a further 10-15 minutes or until cooked through.

6 Place the lamb on a platter and remove the foil. Cut into thick slices and serve with coleslaw and tomato slices.

Steak in a Wine Marinade

Fillet, sirloin, rump, and entrecôte are all suitable cuts for this dish, although rump retains the most flavor.

NUTRITIONAL INFORMATION

Calories 356	Sugars 2g	
Protein 41g	Fat 9g	
Carbohydrate 2g	Saturates 4g	

 3 HOURS   15 MINS

SERVES 4

INGREDIENTS

4 rump steaks, about 9 oz each

2½ cups red wine

1 onion, quartered

2 tbsp Dijon mustard

2 garlic cloves, crushed

salt and pepper

4 large field mushrooms

olive oil for brushing

branch of fresh rosemary (optional)

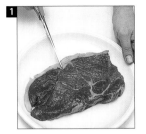

1 Snip through the fat strip on the steaks in 3 places, so that the steak retains its shape when barbecued.

2 Combine the red wine, onion, mustard, garlic, salt and pepper. Lay the steaks in a shallow non-porous dish and pour over the marinade. Cover and chill for 2–3 hours.

3 Remove the steaks from the refrigerator 30 minutes before you intend to cook them to let them come to room temperature. This is especially important if the steak is thick, so that it cooks more evenly and is not well done on the outside and raw in the middle.

4 Sear both sides of the steak—about 1 minute on each side—over a hot barbecue. If it is about 1 inch thick, keep it over a hot barbecue, and cook for about 4 minutes on each side. This will give a medium-rare steak—cook it more or less, to suit your taste. If the steak is a thicker cut, move it to a less hot part of the barbecue or further away from the coals. To test the readiness of the meat while cooking, simply press it with your finger—the more the meat yields, the less it is cooked.

5 Brush the mushrooms with the olive oil and cook them alongside the steak, for 5 minutes, turning once. When you put the mushrooms on the barbecue, put the rosemary branch (if using) in the fire to flavor the meat slightly.

6 Remove the steak and leave to rest for a minute or two before serving. Slice the mushrooms and serve alongside the meat.

Pork with Apple & Berries

We are accustomed to certain meat/fruit combinations, but this one really is a delicious dish of tender cooked meat with luscious juicy fruits.

NUTRITIONAL INFORMATION

Calories	298	Sugars	. . . . .16g
Protein	. . . . .27g	Fat	. . . . .11g
Carbohydrate	. . .18g	Saturates	. . . . . .3g

🍲 1 HOUR ⏱ 20 MINS

SERVES 4

I N G R E D I E N T S

1 lb 2 oz piece lean pork tenderloin

2 tsp sunflower oil

⅔ cup Fresh Vegetable Stock (see page 31)

⅔ cup dry rosé wine

1 tbsp chopped fresh thyme

1 tbsp clear honey

2 green-skinned dessert apples,
    cored and sliced, and tossed in
    1 tbsp lemon juice

1¼ cups prepared fresh or frozen
    blackberries, or 7½ oz can blackberries in
    natural juice, drained

2 tsp cornstarch mixed with
    4 tsp cold water

salt and pepper

freshly cooked vegetables, to serve

1 Trim away any fat and silvery skin from the pork fillet and cut into ½ inch thick slices, taking care to keep the slices a good shape.

2 Heat the oil in a non-stick frying pan, add the pork slices, and fry for 4–5 minutes until browned all over. Using a perforated spoon, transfer the pork to paper towels. Reserve the pan juices.

3 Pour the stock and wine into the pan with the juices and add the thyme and honey. Mix well, bring to a simmer, and add the pork and apples. Continue to simmer, uncovered, for 5 minutes.

4 Add the blackberries, season to taste, and simmer for a further 5 minutes.

5 Stir in the cornstarch mixture until thickened. Serve with freshly cooked vegetables.

VARIATION

This dish works very well with fresh raspberries or even blueberries, but frozen or canned berries in natural juice make a suitable substitute.

Beef & Potato Goulash

In this recipe, the potatoes are actually cooked in the goulash. For a change, you may prefer to substitute small, scrubbed new potatoes.

NUTRITIONAL INFORMATION

Calories	477	Sugars	........11g
Protein	........47g	Fat	..........16g
Carbohydrate	...39g	Saturates	......5g

15 MINS   2¼ HOURS

SERVES 4

INGREDIENTS

2 tablespoons vegetable oil

1 large onion, sliced

2 garlic cloves, crushed

1 lb 10 oz lean stewing steak

2 tbsp paprika

14 oz can chopped tomatoes

2 tbsp tomato paste

1 large red bell pepper, cored, deseeded, and chopped

6 oz mushrooms, wiped and sliced

2½ cups beef stock

1 lb 2 oz potatoes, peeled and cut into large chunks

1 tbsp cornstarch

salt and pepper

TO GARNISH

4 tbsp low-fat plain yogurt

paprika

chopped fresh parsley

1 Heat the oil in a large saucepan and fry the onion and garlic for 3–4 minutes until softened.

2 Cut the steak into chunks and cook over a high heat for about 3 minutes until browned all over.

3 Add the paprika and stir well. Add the tomatoes, tomato paste, red bell pepper, and mushrooms. Cook the vegetables for 2 minutes, stirring constantly.

4 Pour in the stock. Bring to a boil, then reduce the heat. Cover and simmer for about 1½ hours until the meat is tender.

5 Add the potatoes and cook, covered, for 20–30 minutes until tender.

6 Blend the cornstarch with a little water and add to the saucepan, stirring until thickened and blended. Cook for 1 minute then season with salt and pepper. Top with the yogurt, sprinkle over the paprika, garnish with chopped fresh parsley, and serve.

Persian Lamb

Chargrilling and lamb seem to be made for each other, and all over the Middle East both lamb and mutton are enjoyed in this way.

NUTRITIONAL INFORMATION

Calories ....235 Sugars 4g
Protein ....15g Fat 9g
Carbohydrate ...25g Saturates 3g

 3¹/₄ HOURS   25 MINS

SERVES 4–6

INGREDIENTS

2 tbsp chopped fresh mint

1 cup low-fat plain yogurt

4 garlic cloves, crushed

¼ tsp pepper

6 lean lamb chops

2 tbsp lemon juice

TABBOULEH

2 cups couscous

2 cups boiling water

2 tbsp olive oil

2 tbsp lemon juice

½ onion, chopped finely

4 tomatoes, chopped

½ cup fresh cilantro, chopped

2 tbsp chopped fresh mint

salt and pepper

1 For the marinade, combine the mint, yogurt, garlic, and pepper.

2 Put the chops into a non-porous dish and rub all over with the lemon juice. Pour the marinade over the chops. Cover and marinate for 2–3 hours.

3 To make the tabbouleh, put the couscous into a heatproof bowl and pour over the boiling water. Leave for 5 minutes. Drain and put into a strainer. Steam over a pan of barely simmering water for 8 minutes. Toss in the oil and lemon juice. Add the onion, tomato, and herbs. Season and set aside.

4 Cook the lamb over a medium barbecue for 15 minutes, turning once. Serve with the tabbouleh.

COOK'S TIP

Yogurt is a useful ingredient as a base for a marinade. The bland taste is a good medium for many flavors such as herbs, citrus fruit, spices, and oils.

Beef Daube

This dish is very French but also very, very New Orleans, especially when the beef is perked up with Tabasco and Cajun spices.

NUTRITIONAL INFORMATION

Calories 251	Sugars 2g
Protein 31g	Fat 10g
Carbohydrate 8g	Saturates 3g

 10 MINS   🕐 3¹/₄ HOURS

SERVES 6–8

I N G R E D I E N T S

2 tbsp olive oil

1 large onion, cut into wedges

2 celery sticks, chopped

1 green bell pepper, cored, seeded, and chopped

2¼ lb lean braising steak, cubed

½ cup all-purpose flour, seasoned with salt and pepper

2½ cups beef stock

2 garlic cloves, crushed

⅔ cup red wine

2 tbsp red wine vinegar

2 tbsp tomato paste

½ tsp Tabasco

1 tsp chopped fresh thyme

2 bay leaves

½ tsp Cajun Spice Mixture

French bread, to serve

1 Heat the oil in a large, heavy-based, flameproof casserole. Add the onion wedges and cook until browned on all sides. Remove with a slotted spoon and set aside.

2 Add the celery and bell pepper to the pan and cook until softened. Remove the vegetables with a slotted spoon and set aside.

3 Coat the meat in the seasoned flour, add to the pan, and sauté until browned on all sides.

4 Add the stock, garlic, wine, vinegar, tomato paste, Tabasco, and thyme and heat gently.

5 Return the onions, celery, and bell peppers to the pan. Tuck in the bay leaves and sprinkle with the Cajun seasoning.

6 Bring to a boil, transfer to the oven, and cook for 2½–3 hours, or until the meat and vegetables are tender.

7 Serve the beef daube with fresh French bread.

Hot Pot Chops

A Hot Pot is a lamb casserole, made with carrots and onions and with a potato topping. The chops used here are an interesting alternative.

NUTRITIONAL INFORMATION

Calories	250	Sugars	.........2g
Protein	........27g	Fat	..........12g
Carbohydrate	....8g	Saturates	......5g

10 MINS   30 MINS

SERVES 4

I N G R E D I E N T S

4 lean, boneless lamb leg steaks, about 4½ oz each

1 small onion, thinly sliced

1 medium carrot, thinly sliced

1 medium potato, thinly sliced

1 tsp olive oil

1 tsp dried rosemary

salt and pepper

fresh rosemary, to garnish

freshly steamed green vegetables, to serve

1 Preheat the oven to 350°F. Using a sharp knife, trim any excess fat from the lamb steaks.

2 Season both sides of the steaks with salt and pepper and arrange them on a cookie sheet.

3 Alternate layers of sliced onion, carrot, and potato on top of each lamb steak.

4 Brush the tops of the potato lightly with oil, season well with salt and pepper to taste, and then sprinkle with a little dried rosemary.

5 Bake the hot pot chops in the oven for 25–30 minutes until the lamb is tender and cooked through.

6 Drain the lamb on absorbent paper towels and transfer to a warmed serving plate.

7 Garnish with fresh rosemary and serve accompanied with a selection of green vegetables.

VARIATION

This recipe would work equally well with boneless chicken breasts. Pound the chicken slightly with a meat mallet or covered rolling pin so that the pieces are the same thickness throughout.

Lamb Do Pyaza

Do Pyaza usually indicates a dish of meat cooked with plenty of onions, and in this recipe the onions are cooked in two different ways.

NUTRITIONAL INFORMATION

Calories ....433 Sugars 6g
Protein ....42g Fat 27g
Carbohydrate ....7g Saturates 8g

10 MINS   1¾ HOURS

SERVES 4

INGREDIENTS

2 tbsp ghee or vegetable oil

2 large onions, sliced finely

4 garlic cloves, 2 of them crushed

1 lb 10 oz lean boneless lamb, cut into
   1 inch cubes

1 tsp chili powder

1 inch piece fresh ginger, grated

2 fresh green chilies, chopped

½ tsp ground turmeric

½ cup low-fat plain yogurt

2 cloves

1 inch piece cinnamon stick

1¼ cups water

2 tbsp chopped fresh cilantro

3 tbsp lemon juice

salt and pepper

naan bread, to serve

1 Heat the ghee or oil in a large saucepan and add 1 of the onions and all of the garlic. Cook for 2–3 minutes, stirring constantly.

2 Add the lamb and brown all over. Remove and set aside. Add the chili powder, ginger, chilies, and turmeric and stir for a further 30 seconds.

3 Add plenty of salt and pepper, the yogurt, cloves, cinnamon, and water.

4 Return the lamb to the pan. Bring to a boil, then simmer for 10 minutes.

5 Transfer the mixture to an ovenproof dish and cook, uncovered, in a preheated oven, 350°F, for 40 minutes.

6 Adjust the seasoning, if necessary, stir in the remaining onion, and cook, uncovered, for a further 40 minutes.

7 Add the fresh cilantro and lemon juice.

8 Transfer the lamb do pyaza to a warm serving dish and serve with naan bread.

Poultry

Chicken and turkey contain less fat than red meats, and even less if you remove the skin first. Duck is a rich meat with a distinctive flavor, and you only need a small amount to create flavorsome dishes which are healthy too. Because chicken itself does not have a very strong flavor, it marries well with other ingredients and the recipes in this

chapter exploit that quality. Fruit features heavily in low fat diets and it works particularly well with chicken. In this chapter there are several examples: Spiced Apricot Chicken, Chicken & Plum Casserole, and Lime Fricassée of Chicken. Broiling or barbecuing are very healthy ways of cooking as they require little or no fat, and they produce deliciously succulent meat with a crispy coating, for example Tasmanian Duck.

Chicken with a Yogurt Crust

A spicy, Indian-style coating is baked around lean chicken to give a full flavor. Serve with a tomato, cucumber, and cilantro relish.

NUTRITIONAL INFORMATION

Calories ....176 Sugars 5g
Protein ....30g Fat 4g
Carbohydrate ....5g Saturates 1g

10 MINS   35 MINS

SERVES 4

I N G R E D I E N T S

1 garlic clove, crushed

1 inch piece fresh ginger, finely chopped

1 fresh green chili, deseeded and finely chopped

6 tbsp low-fat plain yogurt

1 tbsp tomato paste

1 tsp ground turmeric

1 tsp garam masala

1 tbsp lime juice

4 boneless, skinless chicken breasts, each 4½ oz

salt and pepper

wedges of lime or lemon, to serve

R E L I S H

4 medium tomatoes

¼ cucumber

1 small red onion

2 tbsp fresh cilantro, chopped

1 Preheat the oven to 375°F.

2 Place the garlic, ginger, chili, yogurt, tomato paste, spices, lime juice, and seasoning in a bowl and mix to combine all the ingredients.

3 Wash and pat dry the chicken breasts with absorbent paper towels and place them on a cookie sheet.

4 Brush or spread the spicy yogurt mix over the chicken and bake in the oven for 30–35 minutes until the meat is tender and cooked through.

5 Meanwhile, make the relish. Finely chop the tomatoes, cucumber, and onion and mix together with the cilantro. Season with salt and pepper to taste, cover, and chill in the refrigerator until required.

6 Drain the cooked chicken on absorbent paper towels and serve hot with the relish and lemon or lime wedges. Alternatively, allow to cool, chill for at least 1 hour, and serve sliced as part of a salad.

Thai Red Chicken

This is a really colorful dish, the red of the tomatoes perfectly complementing the orange of the sweet potato.

NUTRITIONAL INFORMATION

Calories	249	Sugars	14g
Protein	26g	Fat	7g
Carbohydrate	22g	Saturates	2g

10 MINS 35 MINS

SERVES 4

INGREDIENTS

- 1 tbsp sunflower oil
- 1 lb lean boneless, skinless chicken
- 2 cloves garlic, crushed
- 2 tbsp Thai red curry paste
- 2 tbsp fresh grated galangal or fresh ginger
- 1 tbsp tamarind paste
- 4 lime leaves
- 8 oz sweet potato
- 2½ cups coconut milk
- 8 oz cherry tomatoes, halved
- 3 tbsp chopped fresh cilantro
- cooked jasmine or Thai fragrant rice, to serve

1 Heat the sunflower oil in a large preheated wok.

2 Thinly slice the chicken. Add the chicken to the wok and stir-fry for 5 minutes.

3 Add the garlic, curry paste, galangal or fresh ginger, tamarind, and lime leaves to the wok and stir-fry for about 1 minute.

4 Using a sharp knife, peel and dice the sweet potato. Add the coconut milk and sweet potato to the mixture in the wok and bring to a boil. Allow to bubble over a medium heat for 20 minutes, or until the juices start to thicken and reduce.

5 Add the cherry tomatoes and cilantro to the curry and cook for a further 5 minutes, stirring occasionally. Transfer to serving plates and serve hot with cooked jasmine or Thai fragrant rice.

COOK'S TIP

Galangal is a spice very similar to ginger and is used to replace the latter in Thai cuisine. It can be bought fresh from Oriental food stores but is also available dried and as a powder. The fresh root, which is not as pungent as ginger, needs to be peeled before slicing to use.

Sticky Chicken Wings

These need to be eaten with your fingers so serve them at an informal supper.

NUTRITIONAL INFORMATION

Calories 165	Sugars 12g
Protein 14g	Fat 7g
Carbohydrate ...12g	Saturates 1g

3¼ HOURS   1 HOUR

SERVES 4–6

I N G R E D I E N T S

2 tbsp olive oil

1 small onion, finely chopped

2 garlic cloves, crushed

¾ pint strained tomatoes

2 tsp dried thyme

1 tsp dried oregano

pinch fennel seeds

3 tbsp red wine vinegar

2 tbsp Dijon mustard

pinch ground cinnamon

2 tbsp brown sugar

1 tsp chili flakes

2 tbsp molasses

16 chicken wings

salt and pepper

TO GARNISH

celery stalks

cherry tomatoes

1 Heat the olive oil in a large frying pan and fry the onion and garlic for about 10 minutes.

2 Add the strained tomatoes, dried herbs, fennel, red wine vinegar, mustard, and cinnamon to the frying pan along with the sugar, chili flakes, molasses, and salt and pepper. Bring to a boil, then reduce the heat, and simmer gently for about 15 minutes, or until the sauce is slightly reduced.

3 Put the chicken wings in a large dish, and coat liberally with the sauce. Leave to marinate for 3 hours or as long as possible, turning the wings over often in the marinade.

4 Transfer the wings to a clean cookie sheet, and roast in a preheated oven, 425°F, for 10 minutes. Reduce the heat to 375°F and cook for 20 minutes, basting often.

5 Serve the wings piping hot, garnished with celery stalks and cherry tomatoes.

Steamed Chicken Parcels

A healthy recipe with a delicate oriental flavor. Use large spinach leaves to wrap around the chicken, but make sure they are young leaves.

NUTRITIONAL INFORMATION

Calories . . . . .216 Sugars 7g
Protein . . . . .31g Fat 7g
Carbohydrate . . . .7g Saturates 2g

20 MINS   30 MINS

SERVES 4

INGREDIENTS

4 lean boneless, skinless chicken
 breasts

1 tsp ground lemon grass

2 green onions, chopped finely

1 cup young carrots

1¾ cups young zucchini

2 stalks celery

1 tsp light soy sauce

¾ cup spinach leaves

2 tsp sesame oil

salt and pepper

1 With a sharp knife, make a slit through one side of each chicken breast, to open out a large pocket.

2 Sprinkle the inside of the pocket with lemon grass, salt and pepper. Tuck the green onions into the chicken pockets.

3 Trim the carrots, zucchini, and celery then cut into small matchsticks. Plunge them into a pan of boiling water for 1 minute, then drain, and toss in the soy sauce.

4 Pack into the pockets in each chicken breast and fold over firmly to enclose. Reserve the remaining vegetables. Wash and dry the spinach leaves then wrap the chicken breasts firmly in the leaves to enclose completely. If the leaves are too firm, steam them for a few seconds until they are softened and flexible.

5 Place the wrapped chicken in a steamer and steam over rapidly boiling water for 20–25 minutes, depending on size.

6 Stir-fry any leftover vegetable sticks and spinach for 1–2 minutes in the sesame oil and serve with the chicken.

Teppanyaki

This simple, Japanese style of cooking is ideal for thinly-sliced breast of chicken. You can use thin turkey escalopes, if you prefer.

NUTRITIONAL INFORMATION

Calories	206	Sugars	.........4g
Protein	........30g	Fat	...........7g
Carbohydrate	....6g	Saturates	......2g

🍲 5 MINS   🕐 10 MINS

SERVES 4

I N G R E D I E N T S

4 boneless chicken breasts

1 red bell pepper

1 green bell pepper

4 green onions

8 baby corn-on-the-cobs

½ cup bean sprouts

1 tbsp sesame or sunflower oil

4 tbsp soy sauce

4 tbsp mirin

1 tbsp grated fresh ginger

1 Remove the skin from the chicken and slice at a slight angle, to a thickness of about ¼ inch.

2 Deseed and thinly slice the bell peppers and trim and slice the green onions and baby corn-on-the-cobs.

3 Arrange the bell peppers, green onions, corn, and bean sprouts on a plate with the sliced chicken.

4 Heat a large griddle or heavy frying pan then lightly brush with oil. Add the vegetables and chicken slices in small batches, allowing space between them so that they cook thoroughly.

5 Combine the soy sauce, mirin, and ginger and serve as a dip with the chicken and vegetables.

COOK'S TIP

Mirin is a rich, sweet rice wine which you can buy in oriental shops, but if it is not available add 1 tablespoon of soft light brown sugar to the sauce instead.

Spiced Apricot Chicken

Spiced chicken legs are partially boned and packed with dried apricot.
A golden, spiced, low-fat yogurt coating keeps the chicken moist.

NUTRITIONAL INFORMATION

Calories	305	Sugars	........21g
Protein	........15g	Fat	..........8g
Carbohydrate	...45g	Saturates	......1g

10 MINS 　　40 MINS

SERVES 4

INGREDIENTS

4 large, lean skinless chicken leg quarters

finely grated rind of 1 lemon

1 cup ready-to-eat dried apricots

1 tbsp ground cumin

1 tsp ground turmeric

½ cup low-fat plain yogurt

salt and pepper

TO SERVE

1½ cups brown rice

2 tbsp flaked hazelnuts, toasted

2 tbsp sunflower seeds, toasted

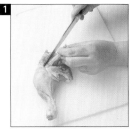

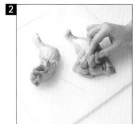

1 Remove any excess fat from the chicken legs. Use a small, sharp knife to carefully cut the flesh away from the thigh bone. Scrape the meat away down as far as the knuckle. Grasp the thigh bone firmly and twist it to break it away from the drumstick.

2 Open out the boned part of the chicken and sprinkle with lemon rind and pepper. Pack the dried apricots into each piece of chicken.

3 Fold over to enclose, and secure with cocktail sticks. Mix together the cumin, turmeric, yogurt, and salt and pepper, then brush this mixture over the chicken to coat evenly. Place the chicken in an ovenproof dish and bake in a preheated oven, 375°F, for 35–40 minutes, or until the chicken juices run clear, not pink, when pierced through the thickest part with a skewer.

4 Meanwhile, cook the rice in boiling, lightly salted water until just tender, then drain well. Stir the hazelnuts and sunflower seeds into the rice and serve.

VARIATION

For a change use dried herbs instead of spices to flavor the coating. Use dried oregano, tarragon, or rosemary—but remember dried herbs are more powerful than fresh, so you will only need a little.

Sweet-Sour Chicken

This sweet-citrusy chicken is delicious hot or cold. Sesame-flavored noodles are the ideal accompaniment for the hot version.

NUTRITIONAL INFORMATION

Calories	.... .248	Sugars	.... .8g
Protein	.... .30g	Fat	.... .8g
Carbohydrate	...16g	Saturates	...... .2g

5 MINS   25 MINS

SERVES 4

INGREDIENTS

4 boneless chicken breasts, about 4½ oz each

2 tbsp clear honey

1 tbsp dark soy sauce

1 tsp lemon rind, finely grated

1 tbsp lemon juice

salt and pepper

TO GARNISH

1 tbsp fresh chives, chopped

lemon rind, grated

NOODLES

8 oz rice noodles

2 tsp sesame oil

1 tbsp sesame seeds

1 tsp lemon rind, finely grated

1 Preheat the broiler to medium. Skin and trim the chicken breasts to remove any excess fat, then wash, and pat them dry with absorbent paper towels. Using a sharp knife, score the chicken breasts with a criss-cross pattern on both sides (making sure that you do not cut all the way through the meat).

2 Mix together the honey, soy sauce, lemon rind, and juice in a small bowl, and then season well with black pepper.

3 Arrange the chicken breasts on the broiler rack and brush with half of the honey mixture. Cook for 10 minutes, turn over, and brush with the remaining mixture. Cook for a further 8–10 minutes or until cooked through.

4 Meanwhile, prepare the noodles according to the instructions on the package. Drain well and transfer to a warm serving bowl. Mix the noodles with the sesame oil, sesame seeds, and the lemon rind. Season and keep warm.

5 Drain the chicken and serve with a small mound of noodles, garnished with chopped chives and grated lemon rind.

VARIATION

For a different flavor, replace the lemon with orange or lime. If you prefer, serve the chicken with boiled rice or pasta, which you can flavor with sesame seeds and citrus rind in the same way.

Ginger Chicken & Corn

Chicken wings and corn in a sticky ginger marinade are designed to be eaten with the fingers—there's no other way!

NUTRITIONAL INFORMATION

Calories	123	Sugars	.........3g
Protein	........14g	Fat	..........6g
Carbohydrate	....3g	Saturates	......1g

🍳 10 MINS   🕐 20 MINS

SERVES 6

INGREDIENTS

3 fresh corn cobs

12 chicken wings

1 inch piece fresh ginger

6 tbsp lemon juice

4 tsp sunflower oil

1 tbsp light brown sugar

baked potatoes or salad, to serve

1 Remove the husks and silks from the corn. Using a sharp knife, cut each cob into 6 slices.

2 Place the corn in a large bowl with the chicken wings.

3 Peel and grate the fresh ginger or chop finely. Place in a bowl and add the lemon juice, sunflower oil, and light brown sugar. Mix together until well combined.

4 Toss the corn and chicken in the ginger mixture to coat evenly.

5 Thread the corn and chicken wings alternately on to metal or pre-soaked wooden skewers, to make turning easier.

6 Cook under a preheated moderately hot broiler or barbecue for 15–20 minutes, basting with the gingery glaze, and turning frequently until the corn is golden brown and tender and the chicken is cooked. Serve with baked potatoes or salad.

COOK'S TIP

Cut off the wing tips before broiling as they burn very easily. Or you can cover them with small pieces of foil.

Poussin with Dried Fruits

Game hens are ideal for a one or two portion meal, and cook very easily and quickly for a special dinner—either in the oven or microwave.

NUTRITIONAL INFORMATION

Calories 316   Sugars 23g

Protein . . . . .23g   Fat 15g

Carbohydrate . . .23g   Saturates 2g

35 MINS   30 MINS

SERVES 2

I N G R E D I E N T S

¾ cup dried apples, peaches, and prunes

½ cup boiling water

2 game hens

⅓ cup walnut halves

1 tbsp honey

1 tsp ground allspice

1 tbsp walnut oil

salt and pepper

vegetables and new potatoes, to serve

1 Place the fruits in a bowl, cover with the water, and leave to stand for about 30 minutes.

2 Cut the game hens in half down the breastbone using a sharp knife, or leave whole.

3 Mix the fruit and any juices with the walnuts, honey, and allspice and divide between two small roasting bags or squares of foil.

4 Brush the game hens with walnut oil, sprinkle with salt and pepper, and then place on top of the fruits.

5 Close the roasting bags or fold the foil over to enclose the game hens and bake on a cookie sheet in a preheated oven, 375°F, for 25–30 minutes or until the juices run clear. To cook in a microwave, use microwave roasting bags and cook on HIGH/100% power for 6–7 minutes each, depending on size.

6 Transfer the poussin to a warm plate and serve hot with fresh vegetables and new potatoes.

VARIATION

Alternative dried fruits that can be used in this recipe are cherries, mangoes, or papayas.

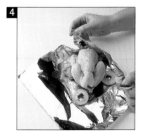

Harlequin Chicken

This colorful dish will tempt the appetites of all the family—it is ideal for toddlers, who enjoy the fun shapes of the multi-colored bell peppers.

NUTRITIONAL INFORMATION

Calories 183	Sugar 8g	
Protein 24g	Fats 6g	
Carbohydrates 8g	Saturates 1g	

 5 MINS   25 MINS

SERVES 4

INGREDIENTS

10 skinless, boneless chicken thighs

1 medium onion

1 each medium red, green, and yellow bell peppers

1 tbsp sunflower oil

14 oz can chopped tomatoes

2 tbsp chopped fresh parsley

pepper

whole wheat bread and salad, to serve

1 Using a sharp knife, cut the chicken thighs into bite-sized pieces.

2 Peel and thinly slice the onion. Halve and deseed the bell peppers and cut into small diamond shapes.

3 Heat the sunflower oil in a shallow pan, then quickly fry the chicken and onion until golden.

4 Add the bell peppers, cook for 2–3 minutes, then stir in the tomatoes and chopped fresh parsley, and season with pepper.

5 Cover tightly and simmer for about 15 minutes, until the chicken and vegetables are tender. Serve hot with whole wheat bread and a green salad.

COOK'S TIP
If you are making this dish for small children, the chicken can be finely chopped or ground first.

Chicken Tikka Kabobs

Chicken tikka is a low-fat Indian dish. Recipes vary but you can try your own combination of spices to suit your personal taste.

NUTRITIONAL INFORMATION

Calories 191   Sugars 8g
Protein . . . . .30g   Fat 4g
Carbohydrate . . . .8g   Saturates 2g

2¼ HOURS   15 MINS

SERVES 4

INGREDIENTS

4 × 4½ oz boneless, skinless
  chicken breasts,

1 garlic clove, crushed

1 tsp grated fresh ginger

1 fresh green chili, seeded and chopped
  finely

6 tbsp low-fat plain yogurt

1 tbsp tomato paste

1 tsp ground cumin

1 tsp ground coriander

1 tsp ground turmeric

1 large ripe mango

1 tbsp lime juice

salt and pepper

fresh cilantro leaves, to garnish

TO SERVE

boiled white rice

lime wedges

tossed salad

warmed naan bread

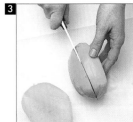

1 Cut the chicken into 1 inch cubes and place in a shallow dish.

2 Mix together the garlic, ginger, chili, yogurt, tomato paste, spices, and seasoning. Spoon over the chicken, cover, and chill for 2 hours.

3 Using a vegetable peeler, peel the skin from the mango. Slice down either side of the pit and cut the mango flesh into cubes. Toss in lime juice, cover, and chill until required.

4 Thread the chicken and mango pieces alternately on to 8 skewers. Place the skewers on a broiler rack and brush the chicken with the yogurt marinade and the lime juice left from the mango.

5 Place under a preheated moderate broiler for 6–7 minutes. Turn over, brush again with the marinade and lime juice, and cook for a further 6–7 minutes or until the chicken juices run clear when pierced with a sharp knife.

6 Serve on a bed of rice on a warmed platter, garnished with fresh cilantro leaves, and accompanied by lime wedges, salad, and naan bread.

Chicken in Spicy Yogurt

Make sure the barbecue is really hot before you start cooking. The coals should be white and glow red when fanned.

NUTRITIONAL INFORMATION

Calories ....74 Sugars 2g
Protein ....9g Fat 4g
Carbohydrate ....2g Saturates 1g

4³/₄ HOURS   25 MINS

SERVES 6

I N G R E D I E N T S

3 dried red chilies

2 tbsp coriander seeds

2 tsp turmeric

2 tsp garam masala

4 garlic cloves, crushed

½ onion, chopped

1 inch piece fresh ginger, grated

2 tbsp lime juice

1 tsp salt

½ cup low-fat plain yogurt

1 tbsp oil

4 lb 8 oz lean chicken, cut into
    6 pieces, or 6 chicken portions

T O   S E R V E

chopped tomatoes

diced cucumber

sliced red onion

cucumber and yogurt

1 Grind together the chilies, coriander seed, turmeric, garam masala, garlic, onion, ginger, lime juice, and salt with a pestle and mortar or grinder.

2 Gently heat a frying pan and add the spice mixture. Stir until fragrant, about 2 minutes, and turn into a shallow non-porous dish.

3 Add the plain yogurt and the oil to the spice paste and mix well to combine.

4 Remove the skin from the chicken portions and make three slashes in the flesh of each piece. Add the chicken to the dish containing the yogurt and spice mixture and coat the pieces completely in the marinade. Cover with plastic wrap and chill for at least 4 hours. Remove the dish from the refrigerator and leave covered at room temperature for 30 minutes before cooking.

5 Wrap the chicken pieces in foil, sealing well so the juices cannot escape.

6 Cook the chicken pieces over a very hot barbecue for about 15 minutes, turning once.

7 Remove the foil, with tongs and brown the chicken on the barbecue for 5 minutes.

8 Serve the chicken with the chopped tomatoes, diced cucumber, sliced red onion, and the yogurt and cucumber mixture.

Thai-style Chicken Skewers

The chicken is marinated in an aromatic sauce before being cooked on the barbecue. Use bay leaves if kaffir lime leaves are unavailable.

NUTRITIONAL INFORMATION

Calories 218   Sugars 4g
Protein . . . . .28g   Fat 10g
Carbohydrate . . . .5g   Saturates 2g

 2¼ HOURS   20 MINS

SERVES 4

I N G R E D I E N T S

lean chicken breasts, skinned and
  boned

1 onion, peeled and cut into wedges

1 large red bell pepper, deseeded

1 large yellow bell pepper deseeded

12 kaffir lime leaves

2 tbsp sunflower oil

2 tbsp lime juice

tomato halves, to serve

M A R I N A D E

1 tbsp Thai red curry paste

⅔ cup canned coconut milk

1 To make the marinade, place the red curry paste in a small pan over medium heat and cook for 1 minute. Add half of the coconut milk to the pan and bring the mixture to a boil. Boil for 2–3 minutes until the liquid has reduced by about two-thirds.

2 Remove the pan from the heat and stir in the remaining coconut milk. Set aside to cool.

3 Cut the chicken into 1 inch pieces. Stir the chicken into the cold marinade, cover, and leave to chill for at least 2 hours.

4 Cut the onion into wedges and the bell peppers into 1 inch pieces.

5 Remove the chicken pieces from the marinade and thread them on to skewers, alternating the chicken with the vegetables and lime leaves.

6 Combine the oil and lime juice in a small bowl and brush the mixture over the kabobs. Barbecue the skewers over hot coals, turning and basting frequently for 10–15 minutes until the chicken is cooked through. Barbecue the tomato halves and serve with the chicken skewers.

COOK'S TIP

Cooking the marinade first intensifies the flavor. It is important to allow the marinade to cool before adding the chicken, or bacteria may breed in the warm temperature.

Chicken & Ginger Stir-fry

The pomegranate seeds add a sharp Chinese flavor to this Indian stir-fry. Serve in the summer with a spicy rice salad or a tossed green salad.

NUTRITIONAL INFORMATION

Calories 291	Sugars 0g	
Protein 41g	Fat 14g	
Carbohydrate 0g	Saturates 3g	

10 MINS   25 MINS

SERVES 4

INGREDIENTS

3 tbsp oil

1 lb 9 oz lean skinless, boneless chicken breasts, cut into 2 inch strips

3 garlic cloves, crushed

1½ inch piece fresh ginger, cut into strips

1 tsp pomegranate seeds, crushed

½ tsp ground turmeric

1 tsp garam masala

2 fresh green chilies, sliced

½ tsp salt

4 tbsp lemon juice

grated rind of 1 lemon

6 tbsp chopped fresh cilantro

½ cup chicken stock

naan bread, to serve

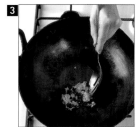
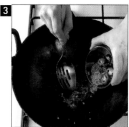

1 Heat the oil in a wok or large frying pan and stir-fry the chicken until golden brown all over. Remove from the pan and set aside.

2 Add the garlic, ginger strips, and pomegranate seeds to the pan and fry in the oil for 1 minute taking care not to let the garlic burn.

3 Stir in the turmeric, garam masala, and chilies and fry for 30 seconds.

4 Return the chicken to the pan and add the salt, lemon juice, lemon rind, cilantro, and stock. Stir the chicken well to make sure it is coated in the sauce.

5 Bring the mixture to a boil, then lower the heat, and simmer for 10–15 minutes until the chicken is thoroughly cooked. Serve with naan bread.

COOK'S TIP

Stir-frying is perfect for low-fat diets as only a little oil is needed. Cooking the food over a high temperature ensures that food is sealed and cooked quickly to hold in the flavor.

Chicken with Two Sauces

With its red and yellow bell pepper sauces, this quick and simple dish is colorful and healthy, and perfect for an impromptu lunch or supper.

NUTRITIONAL INFORMATION

Calories ....257 Sugars 7g

Protein ....29g Fat 10g

Carbohydrate ....8g Saturates 2g

🧊 10 MINS   🕐 1¹/₂ HOURS

SERVES 4

I N G R E D I E N T S

2 tbsp olive oil

2 medium onions, chopped finely

2 garlic cloves, crushed

2 red bell peppers, chopped

pinch cayenne pepper

2 tsp tomato paste

2 yellow bell peppers, chopped

pinch of dried basil

4 lean skinless, boneless chicken breasts

⅔ cup dry white wine

⅔ cup chicken stock

bouquet garni

salt and pepper

fresh herbs, to garnish

1 Heat 1 tablespoon of olive oil in each of two medium saucepans. Place half the chopped onions, 1 of the garlic cloves, the red bell peppers, the cayenne pepper, and the tomato paste in one of the saucepans. Place the remaining onion, garlic, yellow bell peppers, and basil in the other pan.

2 Cover each pan and cook over a very low heat for 1 hour until the bell peppers are very soft. If either mixture becomes dry, add a little water. Process then strain the contents of each pan separately.

3 Return to the pans and season with salt and pepper. Gently reheat the two sauces while the chicken is cooking.

4 Put the chicken breasts into a frying pan and add the wine and stock. Add the bouquet garni and bring the liquid to a simmer. Cook the chicken for about 20 minutes until tender.

5 To serve, put a pool of each sauce on to four serving plates, slice the chicken breasts, and arrange on the plates. Garnish with fresh herbs.

Pot-Roast Orange Chicken

This colorful, nutritious pot-roast could be served for a family meal or for a special dinner. Add more vegetables if you're feeding a crowd.

NUTRITIONAL INFORMATION

Calories 302   Sugar 17g
Protein . . . . .29g   Fats 11g
Carbohydrates . . .22g   Saturates 2g

 10 MINS   2 HOURS

SERVES 4

I N G R E D I E N T S

2 tbsp sunflower oil

1 chicken, weighing about 3 lb 5 oz

2 large oranges

2 small onions, quartered

2 cups small whole carrots or thin carrots, cut into 2 inch lengths

⅔ cup orange juice

2 tbsp brandy

2 tbsp sesame seeds

1 tbsp cornstarch

salt and pepper

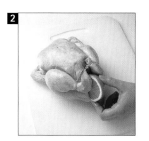

1 Heat the oil in a large flameproof casserole and fry the chicken, turning occasionally until evenly browned.

2 Cut one orange in half and place half inside the cavity of the chicken. Place the chicken in a large, deep casserole. Arrange the onions and carrots around the chicken. Season with salt and pepper and pour over the orange juice.

3 Cut the remaining oranges into thin wedges and tuck around the chicken, among the vegetables.

4 Cover and cook in a preheated oven, 350°F, for about 1½ hours, or until the chicken juices run clear when pierced, and the vegetables are tender. Remove the lid and sprinkle with the brandy and sesame seeds. Return to the oven for 10 minutes.

5 To serve, lift the chicken on to a large platter and add the vegetables. Skim any excess fat from the juices. Blend the cornstarch with 1 tablespoon cold water, then stir into the juices, and bring to a boil, stirring all the time. Adjust to taste, then serve the sauce with the chicken.

Two-in-One Chicken

Cook four chicken pieces and serve two hot, topped with a crunchy herb mixture. Serve the remainder as a salad in a delicious curry sauce.

NUTRITIONAL INFORMATION

Calories 421	Sugars 20g
Protein 31g	Fat 18g
Carbohydrate . . .34g	Saturates 4g

2¹/₂ HOURS   45 MINS

SERVES 2

INGREDIENTS

4 lean chicken thighs

oil for brushing

garlic powder

½ eating apple, grated coarsely

1½ tbsp dry parsley and thyme stuffing mix

salt and pepper

pasta shapes, to serve

SAUCE

1 tbsp butter or margarine

2 tsp all-purpose flour

5 tbsp skim milk

2 tbsp dry white wine or stock

½ tsp dried mustard powder

1 tsp capers or chopped gherkins

SPICED CHICKEN SALAD

½ small onion, chopped finely

1 tbsp oil

1 tsp tomato paste

½ tsp curry powder

1 tsp apricot jelly

1 tsp lemon juice

2 tbsp low-fat mayonnaise

1 tbsp low-fat plain yogurt

¾ cup seedless grapes, halved

¼ cup white long-grain rice, cooked, to serve

1 Place the chicken in a shallow ovenproof dish. Brush with oil, sprinkle with garlic powder, and season with salt and pepper. Place in a preheated oven, 400°F, for 25 minutes, or until almost cooked through. Combine the apple with the stuffing mix. Baste the chicken, then spoon the mixture over two of the pieces. Return all the chicken pieces to the oven for about 10 minutes until the chicken is cooked.

2 To make the sauce, melt the magarine in a pan, stir in the flour, and cook for 1–2 minutes. Add the milk gradually, then the wine or stock, and bring to a boil. Stir in the mustard, capers or gherkins, and seasoning. Simmer for 1 minute. Serve the two crunchy-topped pieces of chicken with the sauce and pasta shapes.

3 For the salad, fry the onion gently in the oil until barely colored. Add the tomato paste, curry powder, and jelly and cook for 1 minute. Leave the mixture to cool. Blend the mixture in a food processor, or press through a strainer. Beat in the lemon juice, mayonnaise, and yogurt. Season to taste with salt and pepper.

4 Cut the chicken into strips and add to the sauce with the grapes. Mix well and chill. Serve with the rice.

Karahi Chicken

A karahi is an extremely versatile two-handled metal pan, similar to a wok. Food is always cooked over a high heat in a karahi.

NUTRITIONAL INFORMATION

Calories 270   Sugars 1g
Protein . . . . .41g   Fat 11g
Carbohydrate . . . .1g   Saturates 2g

 5 MINS   20 MINS

SERVES 4

INGREDIENTS

2 tbsp ghee or vegetable oil

3 garlic cloves, crushed

1 onion, chopped finely

2 tbsp garam masala

1 tsp coriander seeds, ground

½ tsp dried mint

1 bay leaf

1 lb 10 oz lean boneless chicken meat, diced

1 cup chicken stock

1 tbsp fresh cilantro, chopped

salt

warm naan bread or chapatis, to serve

1 Heat the ghee or oil in a karahi, wok, or a large, heavy frying pan. Add the garlic and onion. Stir-fry for about 4 minutes until the onion is golden.

2 Stir in the garam masala, ground coriander, mint, and bay leaf.

3 Add the chicken and cook over a high heat, stirring occasionally, for about 5 minutes. Add the stock and simmer for 10 minutes, until the sauce has thickened

and the chicken juices run clear when the meat is tested with a sharp knife.

4 Stir in the fresh cilantro and salt to taste and mix well. Serve immediately with warm naan bread or chapatis.

COOK'S TIP

Always heat a karahi or wok before you add the oil to help maintain the high temperature.

Lime Chicken Kabobs

These succulent chicken kabobs are coated in a sweet lime dressing and are served with a lime and mango relish. They make an ideal light meal.

NUTRITIONAL INFORMATION

Calories	199	Sugars	........14g
Protein	........28g	Fat	...........4g
Carbohydrate	...14g	Saturates	......1g

15 MINS   10 MINS

SERVES 4

I N G R E D I E N T S

4 lean boneless chicken breasts, skinned, about 4½ oz each

3 tbsp lime marmalade

1 tsp white wine vinegar

½ tsp lime rind, finely grated

1 tbsp lime juice

salt and pepper

T O   S E R V E

lime wedges

boiled white rice, sprinkled with chili powder

S A L S A

1 small mango

1 small red onion

1 tbsp lime juice

1 tbsp fresh cilantro, chopped

1 Slice the chicken breasts into thin pieces and thread onto 8 skewers so that the meat forms an S-shape down each skewer.

2 Preheat the broiler to medium. Arrange the chicken kabobs on the broiler rack. Mix together the lime marmalade, vinegar, lime rind, and juice. Season with salt and pepper to taste. Brush the dressing generously over the chicken and broil for 5 minutes. Turn the chicken over, brush with the dressing again, and broil for a further 4-5 minutes until the chicken is cooked through.

3 Meanwhile, prepare the salsa. Peel the mango and slice the flesh off the smooth, central pit. Dice the flesh into small pieces and place in a small bowl.

4 Peel and finely chop the onion and mix into the mango, together with the lime juice and chopped cilantro. Season, cover, and chill until required.

5 Serve the chicken kabobs with the salsa, accompanied with wedges of lime and boiled rice sprinkled with chili powder.

COOK'S TIP

To prevent sticking, lightly oil metal skewers or dip bamboo skewers in water before threading the chicken on to them.

Filipino Chicken

Tomato ketchup is a very popular ingredient in Asian dishes, as it imparts a zingy sweet-sour flavor.

NUTRITIONAL INFORMATION

Calories 197   Sugars 7g
Protein ....28g   Fat 4g
Carbohydrate ....8g   Saturates 1g

2³/₄ HOURS   20 MINS

SERVES 4

INGREDIENTS

1 can lemonade or lime-and-lemonade

2 tbsp gin

4 tbsp tomato ketchup

2 tsp garlic salt

2 tsp Worcestershire sauce

4 lean chicken breast fillets

salt and pepper

TO SERVE

thread egg noodles

1 green chili, chopped finely

2 green onions, sliced

1 Combine the lemonade or lime-and-lemonade, gin, tomato ketchup, garlic salt, Worcestershire sauce, and seasoning in a large non-porous dish.

2 Put the chicken into the dish and make sure that the marinade covers them completely.

3 Leave to marinate in the refrigerator for 2 hours. Remove and leave covered at room temperature for 30 minutes.

4 Place the chicken over a medium barbecue and cook for 20 minutes.

5 Turn the chicken once, halfway through the cooking time.

6 Remove from the barbecue and leave to rest for 3–4 minutes before serving.

7 Serve with egg noodles, tossed with a little green chili and green onions.

COOK'S TIP

Cooking the meat on the bone after it has reached room temperature means that it cooks in a shorter time, which ensures that the meat remains moist right through to the bone.

Jerk Chicken

This is perhaps one of the best known Caribbean dishes. The jerk in the name refers to the hot, spicy coating.

NUTRITIONAL INFORMATION

Calories 158	Sugars 0.4g
Protein 29g	Fat 4g
Carbohydrate 2g	Saturates 1g

24 HOURS   30 MINS

SERVES 4

INGREDIENTS

4 lean chicken portions

1 bunch green onions, trimmed

1–2 chilies, deseeded

1 garlic clove

2 inch piece fresh ginger, peeled and
    roughly chopped

½ tsp dried thyme

½ tsp paprika

¼ tsp ground allspice

pinch ground cinnamon

pinch ground cloves

4 tbsp white wine vinegar

3 tbsp light soy sauce

pepper

1 Rinse the chicken portions and pat them dry on absorbent paper towels. Place them in a shallow dish.

2 Place the green onions, chilies, garlic, ginger, thyme, paprika, allspice, cinnamon, cloves, wine vinegar, soy sauce, and pepper to taste in a food processor and process until smooth.

3 Pour the spicy mixture over the chicken. Turn the chicken portions

over so that they are well coated in the marinade.

4 Transfer the chicken portions to the refrigerator and leave to marinate for up to 24 hours.

5 Remove the chicken from the marinade and barbecue over medium

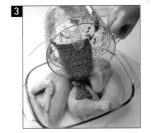

hot coals for about 30 minutes, turning the chicken over and basting occasionally with any remaining marinade, until the chicken is browned and cooked through.

6 Transfer the chicken portions to individual serving plates and serve at once.

Chicken & Potato Bake

Make this recipe when new potatoes are in season. A medium onion or a few shallots can be substituted for the green onions.

NUTRITIONAL INFORMATION

Calories 323	Sugars 9g
Protein 30g	Fat 10g
Carbohydrate ...29g	Saturates 2g

🥔 10 MINS 🕐 1¼ HOURS

SERVES 4

INGREDIENTS

2 tbsp olive oil

4 lean chicken breasts

1 bunch green onions, trimmed and chopped

12 oz young spring carrots, scrubbed and sliced

4½ oz dwarf green beans, trimmed and sliced

2½ cups chicken stock

12 oz small new potatoes, scrubbed

1 small bunch mixed fresh herbs, such as thyme, rosemary, bay, and parsley

salt and pepper

2 tbsp cornstarch

2–3 tbsp cold water

sprigs of fresh mixed herbs, to garnish

1 Heat the oil in a large flameproof casserole and add the chicken breasts. Gently fry for 5-8 minutes until browned on both sides. Lift from the casserole with a perforated spoon and set aside.

2 Add the green onions, carrots, and green beans and gently fry for 3–4 minutes.

3 Return the chicken to the casserole and pour in the stock. Add the potatoes and herbs. Season, bring to a boil, then cover the casserole, and transfer to the oven. Bake in a preheated oven at 375°F for 40-50 minutes until the potatoes are tender.

4 Blend the cornstarch with the cold water. Add to the casserole, stirring until blended and thickened. Cover and cook for a further 5 minutes. Garnish with fresh herbs and serve.

COOK'S TIP

Use your favorite combination of herbs for this dish. If fresh herbs are unavailable, use half the quantity of dried mixed herbs. Alternatively, use a bouquet garni sachet which is usually a combination of bay, thyme, and parsley.

Roast Duck with Apple

The richness of the duck meat contrasts well with the apricot sauce. If duckling portions are unavailable, use a whole bird cut into joints.

NUTRITIONAL INFORMATION

Calories 316	Sugars 38g
Protein 25g	Fat 6g
Carbohydrate . . .40g	Saturates 1g

 10 MINS   1¹/₂ HOURS

SERVES 4

I N G R E D I E N T S

4 duckling portions, 12 oz each

4 tbsp dark soy sauce

2 tbsp brown sugar

2 red-skinned apples

2 green-skinned apples

juice of 1 lemon

2 tbsp clear honey

few bay leaves

salt and pepper

assorted fresh vegetables, to serve

S A U C E

14 oz can apricots, in natural juice

4 tbsp sweet sherry

1 Preheat the oven to 375°F. Wash the duck and trim away any excess fat. Place on a wire rack over a roasting pan and prick all over with a fork.

2 Brush the duck with the soy sauce. Sprinkle over the sugar and season with pepper. Cook in the oven, basting occasionally, for 50–60 minutes until the meat is cooked through—the juices should run clear when a skewer is inserted into the thickest part of the meat.

3 Meanwhile, core the apples and cut each into 6 wedges. Place in a small roasting pan and mix with the lemon juice and honey. Add a few bay leaves and season. Cook alongside the duck, basting occasionally, for 20–25 minutes until tender. Discard the bay leaves.

4 To make the sauce, place the apricots in a blender or food processor together with the juice from the can and the sherry. Process for a few seconds until smooth. Alternatively, mash the apricots with a fork until smooth and mix with the juice and sherry.

5 Just before serving, heat the apricot paste in a small pan. Remove the skin from the duck and pat the flesh with paper towels to absorb any fat. Serve the duck with the apple wedges, apricot sauce, and fresh vegetables.

VARIATION

Fruit complements duck perfectly. Use canned pineapple in natural juice for a delicious alternative.

Mexican Chicken

Chili, tomatoes, and corn are typical ingredients in a Mexican dish. This is a quick and easy meal for unexpected guests.

NUTRITIONAL INFORMATION

Calories	207	Sugars	.........8g
Protein	.......18g	Fat	..........9g
Carbohydrate	...13g	Saturates	......2g

5 MINS　　35 MINS

SERVES 4

INGREDIENTS

2 tbsp oil

8 chicken drumsticks

1 medium onion, finely chopped

1 tsp chili powder

1 tsp ground coriander

15 oz can chopped tomatoes

2 tbsp tomato paste

⅔ cup frozen corn kernels

salt and pepper

TO SERVE

boiled rice

mixed bell pepper salad

1 Heat the oil in a large frying pan, add the chicken drumsticks, and cook over a medium heat until lightly browned on all sides. Remove from the pan and set aside.

2 Add the onion to the pan and cook for 3–4 minutes until soft, then stir in the chili powder and coriander, and cook for a few seconds.

3 Add the chopped tomatoes with their juice and the tomato paste.

4 Return the chicken to the pan and simmer gently for 20 minutes until the chicken is tender and thoroughly cooked. Add the corn kernels and cook a further 3–4 minutes. Season to taste.

5 Serve with boiled rice and mixed bell pepper salad.

COOK'S TIP

If you dislike the heat of the chilies, just leave them out—the chicken will still taste delicious.

Barbecued Chicken

These chicken wings are brushed with a simple barbecue glaze, which can be made in minutes, but will be enjoyed by all.

NUTRITIONAL INFORMATION

Calories 143   Sugars 6g
Protein ....14g   Fat 7g
Carbohydrate ....6g   Saturates 1g

 5 MINS   20 MINS

SERVES 4

I N G R E D I E N T S

8 chicken wings or 1 chicken cut into
  8 portions

3 tbsp tomato paste

3 tbsp brown fruity sauce

1 tbsp white wine vinegar

1 tbsp clear honey

1 tbsp olive oil

1 clove garlic, crushed (optional)

salad leaves, to serve

1 Remove the skin from the chicken if you want to reduce the fat in the dish.

2 To make the barbecue glaze, place the tomato paste, brown fruity sauce, white wine vinegar, honey, oil, and garlic in a small bowl. Stir all of the ingredients together until they are thoroughly blended.

3 Brush the barbecue glaze over the chicken and barbecue over hot coals for 15–20 minutes. Turn the chicken portions over occasionally and baste frequently with the barbecue glaze.

4 If the chicken begins to blacken before it is cooked, raise the rack if possible or move the chicken to a cooler part of the barbecue to slow down the cooking.

5 Transfer the barbecued chicken to warm serving plates and serve with fresh salad leaves.

COOK'S TIP

When poultry is cooked over a very hot barbecue the heat immediately seals in all of the juices, leaving the meat succulent. For this reason make sure that the coals are hot enough before starting to barbecue.

Festive Apple Chicken

The stuffing in this recipe is cooked under the breast skin so all the flavor is sealed in, and the chicken stays really moist and succulent.

NUTRITIONAL INFORMATION

Calories 219   Sugars 7g
Protein . . . . .29g   Fat 8g
Carbohydrate . . . .9g   Saturates 4g

🍳 🍳 🍳

10 MINS   2¼ HOURS

SERVES 6

INGREDIENTS

1 chicken, weighing 4½ lb

2 dessert apples

1 tbsp butter

1 tbsp red currant jelly

parsley, to garnish

STUFFING

1 tbsp butter

1 small onion, chopped finely

2 oz mushrooms, chopped finely

2 oz lean smoked ham, chopped finely

½ cup fresh bread crumbs

1 tbsp chopped fresh parsley

1 crisp eating apple

1 tbsp lemon juice

oil, to brush

salt and pepper

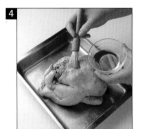

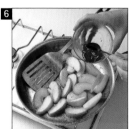

1 To make the stuffing, melt the butter and fry the onion gently, stirring until softened. Stir in the mushrooms and cook over a moderate heat for 2–3 minutes. Remove from the heat and stir in the ham, bread crumbs, and the chopped parsley.

2 Core the apple, leaving the skin on, and grate coarsely. Add the stuffing mixture to the apple with the lemon juice. Season to taste.

3 Loosen the breast skin of the chicken and carefully spoon the stuffing mixture under it, smoothing evenly with your hands.

4 Place the chicken in a roasting pan and brush lightly with oil.

5 Roast the chicken in a preheated oven, 375°F, for 25 minutes per 1 lb 2 oz plus 25 minutes, or until there is no trace of pink in the juices when the chicken is pierced through the thickest part with a skewer. If the breast starts to brown too much, cover with foil.

6 Core and slice the remaining apples and sauté in the butter until golden. Stir in the red currant jelly and warm through until melted. Serve the chicken garnished with the apple and parsley.

Citrus Duckling Skewers

The tartness of citrus fruit goes well with the rich meat of duckling. Duckling makes a change from chicken for the barbecue.

NUTRITIONAL INFORMATION

Calories 205   Sugars 5g
Protein ....24g   Fat 10g
Carbohydrate ....5g   Saturates 2g

45 MINS   20 MINS

SERVES 12

INGREDIENTS

3 duckling breasts, skinned, boned and cut into bite-size pieces

1 small red onion, cut into wedges

1 small eggplant, cut into cubes

lime and lemon wedges, to garnish (optional)

MARINADE

grated rind and juice of 1 lemon

grated rind and juice of 1 lime

grated rind and juice of 1 orange

1 clove garlic, crushed

1 tsp dried oregano

2 tbsp olive oil

dash of Tabasco sauce

1 Place the duckling pieces into a non-metallic bowl together with the prepared vegetables.

2 To make the marinade, place the lemon, lime and orange rinds and juices, garlic, oregano, oil, and Tabasco sauce in a screw-top jar and shake until well combined. Pour the marinade over the duckling and vegetables and toss to coat. Leave to marinate for 30 minutes.

3 Remove the duckling and vegetables from the marinade and thread them on to skewers, reserving the marinade.

4 Barbecue the skewers on an oiled rack over medium hot coals, turning and basting frequently with the reserved marinade, for 15-20 minutes until the meat is cooked through. Serve the kabobs garnished with lemon and lime wedges for squeezing (if using).

COOK'S TIP

For more zing add 1 teaspoon of chili sauce to the marinade. The meat can be marinated for several hours, but it is best to marinate the vegetables separately for only about 30 minutes.

Turkey with Red Currant

Prepare these steaks the day before they are needed and serve in toasted Italian bread, accompanied with crisp salad leaves.

NUTRITIONAL INFORMATION

Calories 219   Sugars 4g
Protein . . . . .28g   Fat 10g
Carbohydrate . . . .4g   Saturates 1g

  12 HOURS   15 MINS

SERVES 4

I N G R E D I E N T S

3½ oz red currant jelly

2 tbsp lime juice

3 tbsp olive oil

2 tbsp dry white wine

¼ tsp ground ginger

pinch grated nutmeg

4 turkey breast steaks

salt and pepper

T O   S E R V E

tossed salad leaves

vinaigrette dressing

1 Italian loaf

cherry tomatoes

1 Place the red currant jelly and lime juice in a saucepan and heat gently until the jelly melts. Add the oil, wine, ginger, and nutmeg.

2 Place the turkey steaks in a shallow, non-metallic dish and season with salt and pepper. Pour over the marinade, turning the meat so that it is well coated. Cover and refrigerate overnight.

3 Remove the turkey from the marinade, reserving the marinade for basting, and barbecue on an oiled rack over hot coals for about 4 minutes on each side. Baste the turkey steaks frequently with the reserved marinade.

4 Meanwhile, toss the salad leaves in the vinaigrette dressing. Cut the Italian loaf in half lengthwise and place, cut-side down, on the side of the barbecue. Barbecue until golden. Place each steak on top of a salad leaf, sandwich between 2 pieces of bread, and serve with cherry tomatoes.

COOK'S TIP

Turkey and chicken escalopes are also ideal for cooking on the barbecue. Because they are thin, they cook through without burning on the outside. Leave them overnight in a marinade of your choice and cook, basting with a little lemon juice and oil.

Crispy Stuffed Chicken

An attractive main course of chicken breasts filled with mixed bell peppers and set on a sea of red bell peppers and tomato sauce.

NUTRITIONAL INFORMATION

Calories	196	Sugars	.........4g
Protein	........29g	Fat	..........6g
Carbohydrate	....6g	Saturates	......2g

20 MINS   50 MINS

SERVES 4

INGREDIENTS

4 boneless chicken breasts, about 5½ oz each, skinned

4 sprigs fresh tarragon

½ small orange bell pepper, deseeded and sliced

½ small green bell pepper, deseeded and sliced

½ oz whole wheat bread crumbs

1 tbsp sesame seeds

4 tbsp lemon juice

1 small red bell pepper, halved and deseeded

7 oz can chopped tomatoes

1 small red chili, deseeded and chopped

¼ tsp celery salt

salt and pepper

fresh tarragon, to garnish

1 Preheat the oven to 400°F. Slit the chicken breasts with a small, sharp knife to create a pocket in each. Season inside each pocket.

2 Place a sprig of tarragon and a few slices of orange and green bell peppers in each pocket. Place the chicken breasts on a non-stick cookie sheet and sprinkle over the bread crumbs and sesame seeds.

3 Spoon 1 tablespoon of lemon juice over each chicken breast and bake in the oven for 35–40 minutes until the chicken is tender and cooked through.

4 Meanwhile, preheat the broiler to hot. Arrange the red bell pepper halves, skin side up, on the rack and cook for 5–6 minutes until the skin blisters. Leave to cool for 10 minutes, then peel off the skins.

5 Put the red bell pepper in a blender, add the tomatoes, chili, and celery salt, and process for a few seconds. Season to taste. Alternatively, finely chop the red bell pepper and press through a sieve with the tomatoes and chili.

6 When the chicken is cooked, heat the sauce, spoon a little on to a warm plate, and arrange a chicken breast in the center. Garnish with tarragon and serve.

Chicken with Whiskey Sauce

After cooking with stock and vegetables, chicken breasts are served with a velvety sauce made from whiskey and low-fat crème fraîche.

NUTRITIONAL INFORMATION

Calories 337   Sugars 6g
Protein . . . . .37g   Fat 15g
Carbohydrate . . . .6g   Saturates 8g

5 MINS   30 MINS

SERVES 4

I N G R E D I E N T S

2 tbsp butter

½ cup shredded leeks

⅓ cup diced carrot

¼ cup diced celery

4 shallots, sliced

2½ cups chicken stock

6 chicken breasts

¼ cup whiskey

1 cup low-fat crème fraîche

2 tbsp freshly grated horseradish

1 tsp honey, warmed

1 tsp chopped fresh parsley

salt and pepper

parsley, to garnish

T O   S E R V E

vegetable patty

mashed potato

fresh vegetables

1 Melt the butter in a large saucepan and add the leeks, carrot, celery, and shallots. Cook for 3 minutes, add half of the chicken stock, and cook for about 8 minutes.

2 Add the remaining chicken stock and bring to a boil. Add the chicken breasts and cook for about 10 minutes or until tender.

3 Remove the chicken with a perforated spoon and cut into thin slices. Place on a large, hot serving dish and keep warm.

4 In another saucepan, heat the whiskey until reduced by half. Strain the chicken stock through a fine sieve, add to the pan, and heat until the liquid is reduced by half.

5 Add the crème fraîche, the horseradish, and the honey. Heat gently and add the chopped fresh parsley and salt and pepper to taste.

6 Pour a little of the whiskey sauce around the chicken and pour the remaining sauce into a sauceboat to serve.

7 Serve with a vegetable patty made from the leftover vegetables, mashed potato, and fresh vegetables. Garnish with fresh parsley.

Sticky Chicken Drumsticks

These drumsticks are always popular—provide plenty of napkins for wiping sticky fingers or provide finger bowls with a slice of lemon.

NUTRITIONAL INFORMATION

Calories 213	Sugars 14g
Protein 27g	Fat 6g
Carbohydrate ...14g	Saturates 2g

   5 MINS   30 MINS

SERVES 4

INGREDIENTS

10 chicken drumsticks

4 tbsp fine-cut orange marmalade

1 tbsp Worcestershire sauce

grated rind and juice of ½ orange

salt and pepper

TO SERVE

cherry tomatoes

salad leaves

1 Using a sharp knife, make 2–3 slashes in the flesh of each chicken drumstick.

2 Bring a large saucepan of water to a boil and add the chicken drumsticks. Cover the pan, return to a boil, and cook for 5–10 minutes. Remove the chicken and drain thoroughly.

3 Meanwhile, make the baste. Place the orange marmalade, Worcestershire sauce, orange rind and juice, and salt and pepper to taste in a small saucepan. Heat gently, stirring continuously, until the marmalade melts and all of the ingredients are well combined.

4 Brush the baste over the par-cooked chicken drumsticks and transfer them to the barbecue to complete cooking. Barbecue over hot coals for about 10 minutes, turning and basting frequently with the remaining baste.

5 Carefully thread 3 cherry tomatoes on to a skewer and transfer to the barbecue for 1–2 minutes.

6 Transfer the chicken drumsticks to serving plates. Serve with the cherry tomato skewers and a selection of fresh salad leaves.

COOK'S TIP

Par-cooking the chicken is an ideal way of making sure that it is cooked through without becoming overcooked and burned on the outside.

Honeyed Citrus Chicken

This recipe is great when you are in a hurry. If you cut the chicken in half and press it flat, you can roast it in under an hour.

NUTRITIONAL INFORMATION

Calories	288	Sugars	.......32g
Protein	........30g	Fat	..........6g
Carbohydrate	...32g	Saturates	......1g

4¼ HOURS   55 MINS

SERVES 4

INGREDIENTS

4 lb 8 oz chicken

salt and pepper

tarragon sprigs, to garnish

MARINADE

1¼ cups orange juice

3 tbsp cider vinegar

3 tbsp clear honey

2 tbsp chopped fresh tarragon

2 oranges, cut into wedges

SAUCE

handful of chopped tarragon

1 cup fat-free plain yogurt

2 tbsp orange juice

1 tsp clear honey

½ cup stuffed olives, chopped

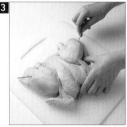

1 With the breast downwards, cut through the bottom part of the chicken using poultry shears or heavy kitchen scissors, making sure not to cut right through to the breast bone below.

2 Rinse the chicken with cold water, drain, and place on a board with the skin side uppermost. Press the chicken flat, then cut off the leg ends. Thread two long wooden skewers through the bird to keep it flat and season with salt and pepper.

3 Put all the marinade ingredients, except the orange wedges, in a shallow non-metallic dish, then add the chicken. Cover and chill for 4 hours. Turn the chicken several times.

4 Mix all the sauce ingredients. Season, spoon into a dish, cover, and chill.

5 Transfer the chicken and marinade to a roasting pan, open the chicken, and place skin-side downwards. Tuck the orange wedges around the chicken and roast in a preheated oven, 400°F, for 25 minutes.

6 Turn the chicken over and roast for another 20–30 minutes. Baste until the chicken is browned and the juices run clear when the thickest part of the leg is pierced with a skewer. Garnish with tarragon, slice, and serve with the sauce.

Springtime Roast Game Hens

This combination of baby vegetables and baby game hens with a tangy, low-fat sauce makes a healthy meal.

NUTRITIONAL INFORMATION

Calories	280	Sugars	.........7g
Protein	........32g	Fat	...........7g
Carbohydrate	...16g	Saturates	......2g

15 MINS   1 HOUR

SERVES 4

I N G R E D I E N T S

5 tbsp fresh brown bread crumbs

½ cup low-fat plain yogurt

5 tbsp chopped fresh parsley

5 tbsp chopped fresh chives

4 game hens

1 tbsp sunflower oil

1½ lb young spring vegetables, such as carrots, zucchini, sugar snap peas, corn cobs, and turnips, cut into small chunks

½ cup boiling chicken stock

2 tsp cornstarch

⅔ cup dry white wine

salt and pepper

1 Mix together the bread crumbs, one-third of the yogurt, and 2 tablespoons each of parsley and chives. Season well, then spoon into the neck ends of the game hens. Place the game hens on a rack in a roasting pan, brush with oil, and season well.

2 Roast in a preheated oven, 425°F, for 30–35 minutes or until the juices run clear, not pink, when the game hens are pierced with a skewer.

3 Place the vegetables in a shallow ovenproof dish in one layer and add half the remaining herbs with the stock.

4 Cover and bake for 25–30 minutes until tender. Lift the game hens on to a serving plate and skim any fat from the juices in the roasting pan. Add the vegetable juices.

5 Blend the cornstarch with the wine and whisk into the sauce with the remaining yogurt. Whisk until boiling, then add the remaining herbs. Season to taste. Spoon the sauce over the game hens and serve with the vegetables.

COOK'S TIP

Baby gamne hens are simple to prepare, quick to cook, and can be easily cut in half lengthways with a knife.

Duck with Berry Sauce

Duck is a rich meat and is best accompanied with fruit, as in this sophisticated dinner dish.

NUTRITIONAL INFORMATION

Calories	293	Sugars	........10g
Protein	........28g	Fat	..........8g
Carbohydrate	...13g	Saturates	......2g

1¼ HOURS   30 MINS

SERVES 4

I N G R E D I E N T S

1 lb boneless duck breasts, skin removed

2 tbsp raspberry vinegar

2 tbsp brandy

1 tbsp clear honey

1 tsp sunflower oil, to brush

salt and pepper

TO SERVE

2 kiwi fruit, peeled and sliced thinly

assorted vegetables

SAUCE

8 oz raspberries, thawed if frozen

1¼ cups rosé wine

2 tsp cornstarch blended with
    4 tsp cold water

1 Preheat the broiler to medium. Skin and trim the duck breasts to remove any excess fat. Using a sharp knife, score the flesh in diagonal lines and pound it with a meat mallet or a covered rolling pin until it is ¾ inch thick.

2 Place the duck breasts in a shallow dish. Mix together the vinegar, brandy, and honey in a small bowl and spoon it over the duck. Cover and leave to chill in the refrigerator for about 1 hour. Drain the duck, reserving the marinade,

and place on the grill (broiler) rack. Season and brush with a little oil. Cook for 10 minutes, turn over, season, and brush with oil again. Cook for 8–10 minutes until the meat is cooked through.

3 Meanwhile, make the sauce. Reserving about 2 oz raspberries, place the rest in a pan. Add the reserved marinade and the wine. Bring to the boil and simmer for 5 minutes until slightly reduced. Strain the

sauce through a sieve, pressing the raspberries with the back of a spoon. Return the liquid to the saucepan and add the cornstarch paste. Heat through, stirring, until thickened. Add the reserved raspberries and season to taste.

4 Thinly slice the duck breast and alternate with slices of kiwi fruit on warm serving plates. Spoon over the sauce and serve with a selection of vegetables.

Baked Chicken & Chips

Traditionally, this dish is deep-fried, but the low-fat version is just as mouthwatering. Serve with chunky potato wedge chips.

NUTRITIONAL INFORMATION

Calories 361	Sugars 2g	
Protein 24g	Fat 8g	
Carbohydrate . . .51g	Saturates 2g	

 10 MINS   🕐 35 MINS

SERVES 4

I N G R E D I E N T S

4 baking potatoes, each 8 oz

1 tbsp sunflower oil

2 tsp coarse sea salt

2 tbsp all-purpose flour

pinch of cayenne pepper

½ tsp paprika pepper

½ tsp dried thyme

8 chicken drumsticks, skin removed

1 medium egg, beaten

2 tbsp cold water

6 tbsp dry white bread crumbs

salt and pepper

T O   S E R V E

low-fat coleslaw salad

corn relish

1 Preheat the oven to 400°F. Wash and scrub the potatoes and cut each into 8 equal portions. Place in a clean plastic bag and add the oil. Seal and shake well to coat.

2 Arrange the potato wedges, skin side down, on a non-stick cookie sheet, sprinkle over the sea salt, and bake in the oven for 30–35 minutes until they are tender and golden.

3 Meanwhile, mix the flour, spices, thyme, and seasoning together on a plate. Press the chicken drumsticks into the seasoned flour to lightly coat.

4 On one plate, mix together the egg and water. On another plate sprinkle the bread crumbs. Dip the chicken drumsticks first in the egg and then in the breadcrumbs. Place on a non-stick cookie sheet.

5 Bake the chicken drumsticks along-side the potato wedges for 30 minutes, turning after 15 minutes, until both potatoes and chicken are tender and cooked through.

6 Drain the potato wedges thoroughly on absorbent paper towels to remove any excess fat and serve with the chicken, accompanied with low-fat coleslaw and corn relish.

Lime Fricassée of Chicken

The addition of lime juice and lime rind adds a delicious tangy flavor to this chicken stew.

NUTRITIONAL INFORMATION

Calories 235   Sugars 3g
Protein ....20g   Fat 6g
Carbohydrate ...26g   Saturates 1g

15 MINS   1³/₄ HOURS

SERVES 4

INGREDIENTS

2 tbsp oil

1 large chicken, cut into small portions

½ cup flour, seasoned

1 lb 2 oz baby onions or shallots, sliced

1 each green and red bell pepper, sliced thinly

⅔ cup chicken stock

juice and rind of 2 limes

2 chilies, chopped

2 tbsp oyster sauce

1 tsp Worcestershire sauce

salt and pepper

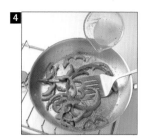

1 Heat the oil in a large frying pan. Coat the chicken pieces in the seasoned flour and cook for about 4 minutes until browned all over.

2 Transfer the chicken to a large casserole. Sprinkle with the onions.

3 Slowly fry the bell peppers in the juices in the frying pan.

4 Add the chicken stock, lime juice, and rind and cook for a further 5 minutes.

5 Add the chilies, oyster sauce, and Worcestershire sauce, mixing well.

6 Season to taste with salt and pepper, then pour the bell peppers and juices over the chicken and onions.

7 Cover the casserole with a lid or cooking foil.

8 Cook in the center of a preheated oven, 375°F, for 1½ hours until the chicken is very tender, then serve.

COOK'S TIP

Try this casserole with a cheese biscuit topping. About 30 minutes before the end of cooking time, simply top with rounds cut from cheese biscuit pastry.

Spicy Tomato Chicken

These low-fat, spicy skewers are cooked in a matter of minutes—assemble ahead of time and store in the fridge until you need them.

NUTRITIONAL INFORMATION

Calories	195	Sugars	........11g
Protein	........28g	Fat	...........4g
Carbohydrate	...12g	Saturates	......1g

 10 MINS 10 MINS

SERVES 4

I N G R E D I E N T S

1 lb 2 oz skinless, boneless chicken breasts

3 tbsp tomato paste

2 tbsp clear honey

2 tbsp Worcestershire sauce

1 tbsp chopped fresh rosemary

9 oz cherry tomatoes

sprigs of rosemary, to garnish

couscous or rice, to serve

1 Cut the chicken into 1 inch chunks and place in a bowl.

2 Mix together the tomato paste, honey, Worcestershire sauce, and rosemary. Add to the chicken, stirring to coat evenly.

3 Alternating the chicken pieces and cherry tomatoes, thread them onto eight wooden skewers.

4 Spoon over any remaining glaze. Cook under a preheated hot broiler for 8–10 minutes, turning occasionally, until the chicken is thoroughly cooked.

5 Serve on a bed of couscous or rice and garnish with sprigs of rosemary.

COOK'S TIP

Couscous is made from semolina that has been made into separate grains. It usually just needs moistening or steaming before serving.

Chicken & Plum Casserole

Full of the flavors of fall, this combination of lean chicken, shallots, garlic, and fresh, juicy plums is a very fruity blend.

NUTRITIONAL INFORMATION

Calories 270   Sugars 9g
Protein . . . . .27g   Fat 7g
Carbohydrate . . .16g   Saturates 2g

2¹/₄ HOURS   35 MINS

SERVES 4

INGREDIENTS

2 slices lean back bacon, rinds removed, trimmed and chopped

1 tbsp sunflower oil

1 lb skinless, boneless chicken thighs, cut into 4 equal strips

1 garlic clove, crushed

6 oz shallots, halved

8 oz plums, halved or quartered (if large) and pitted

1 tbsp brown sugar

²/₃ cup dry sherry

2 tbsp plum sauce

2 cups Fresh Chicken Stock (see page 30)

2 tsp cornstarch mixed with 4 tsp cold water

2 tbsp flat-leaf parsley, chopped, to garnish

crusty bread, to serve

1 In a large, non-stick frying pan, dry fry the bacon for 2–3 minutes until the juices run out. Remove the bacon from the pan with a slotted spoon, set aside, and keep warm.

2 In the same frying pan, heat the oil and fry the chicken with the garlic and shallots for 4–5 minutes, stirring occasionally, until well browned .

3 Return the bacon to the pan and stir in the plums, sugar, sherry, plum sauce, and stock.

4 Bring to a boil and simmer for 20 minutes until the plums are soft and the chicken is cooked through. Add the cornstarch mixture to the pan and cook, stirring, for a further 2–3 minutes until thickened.

5 Spoon the casserole on to warm serving plates and garnish with chopped parsley. Serve the casserole with chunks of bread.

Chicken Tikka

Traditionally, chicken tikka is cooked in a clay tandoori oven, but it works well on the barbecue, too.

NUTRITIONAL INFORMATION

Calories 173	Sugars 6g	
Protein 28g	Fat 4g	
Carbohydrate 6g	Saturates 2g	

2¼ HOURS   15 MINS

SERVES 4

INGREDIENTS

4 chicken breasts, skinned and boned

½ tsp salt

4 tbsp lemon or lime juice

oil, for brushing

MARINADE

⅔ cup low-fat plain yogurt

2 cloves garlic, crushed

1 inch piece fresh ginger, peeled and grated

1 tsp ground cumin

1 tsp chili powder

½ tsp ground coriander

½ tsp ground turmeric

SAUCE

⅔ cup low-fat plain yogurt

1 tsp mint sauce

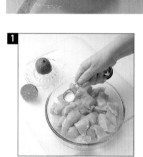  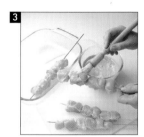

1 Cut the chicken into 1 inch cubes. Sprinkle with the salt and the citrus juice. Set aside for 10 minutes.

2 To make the marinade, combine all the ingredients together in a small bowl until well mixed.

3 Thread the cubes of chicken on to skewers. Brush the marinade over the

chicken. Cover and leave to marinate in the refrigerator for at least 2 hours, preferably overnight. Barbecue the chicken skewers over hot coals, brushing with oil and turning frequently, for 15 minutes or until cooked through.

4 Meanwhile, combine the yogurt and mint to make the sauce and serve with the chicken.

COOK'S TIP

Use the marinade to coat chicken portions, such as drumsticks, if you prefer. Barbecue over medium hot coals for 30–40 minutes, until the juices run clear when the chicken is pierced with a skewer.

Mediterranean Chicken

This recipe uses ingredients found in the Languedoc area of France, where cooking over hot embers is a way of life.

NUTRITIONAL INFORMATION

Calories 143   Sugars 4g
Protein ....13g   Fat 8g
Carbohydrate ....4g   Saturates 2g

 2³/₄ HOURS   40 MINS

SERVES 4

I N G R E D I E N T S

4 tbsp low-fat plain yogurt

3 tbsp sun-dried tomato paste

1 tbsp olive oil

¼ cup fresh basil leaves, lightly crushed

2 garlic cloves, chopped roughly

4 chicken quarters

green salad, to serve

1 Combine the yogurt, tomato paste, olive oil, basil leaves, and garlic in a small bowl and stir well to mix.

2 Put the marinade into a bowl large enough to hold the chicken quarters in a single layer. Add the chicken quarters. Make sure that the chicken pieces are thoroughly coated in the marinade.

3 Leave to marinate in the refrigerator for 2 hours. Remove and leave covered at room temperature for 30 minutes.

4 Place the chicken over a medium barbecue and cook for 30–40 minutes, turning frequently. Test for readiness by piercing the flesh at the

thickest part—usually at the top of the drumstick. If the juices that run out are clear, it is cooked through.

5 Serve hot with a green salad. It is also delicious eaten cold.

VARIATION

For a marinade with an extra zingy flavor combine 2 garlic cloves, coarsely chopped, the juice of 2 lemons and 3 tbsp olive oil, and cook in the same way.

Whiskey Roast Chicken

An unusual change from a plain roast, with a distinctly warming Scottish flavor and a delicious oatmeal stuffing.

NUTRITIONAL INFORMATION

Calories 254	Sugars 6g	
Protein 27g	Fat 8g	
Carbohydrate 11g	Saturates 2g	

5 MINS   1¹/₂ HOURS

SERVES 6

INGREDIENTS

1 chicken, weighing 4 lb 8 oz

1 tbsp honey

2 tbsp Scotch whiskey

2 tbsp all-purpose flour

1¼ cups chicken stock

vegetables and pan-fried potatoes,
  to serve

STUFFING

1 medium onion, finely chopped

1 stalk celery, sliced thinly

1 tbsp sunflower oil

1 tsp dried thyme

4 tbsp porridge oats

4 tbsp chicken stock

salt and pepper

1 To make the stuffing, fry the onion and celery in the sunflower oil, stirring over a moderate heat until softened and lightly browned.

2 Remove from the heat and stir in the thyme, oats, stock, salt and pepper.

3 Stuff the neck end of the chicken with the mixture and tuck the neck flap under. Place in a roasting pan, brush lightly with oil, and roast in a preheated oven, 375°F, for about 1 hour.

4 Mix the honey with 1 tablespoon whiskey and brush the mixture over the chicken. Return to the oven for a further 20 minutes, or until the chicken is golden brown and the juices run clear when pierced through the thickest part with a skewer.

5 Lift the chicken on to a serving plate. Skim the fat from the juices then stir in the flour. Stir over a moderate heat until the mixture bubbles, then gradually add the stock and remaining whiskey to the pan.

6 Bring to a boil, stirring, then simmer for 1 minute and serve the chicken with the sauce, green vegetables, and pan-fried potatoes.

Chicken with Vermouth

The aromatic flavors of vermouth make a good base for the sauce, and when partnered with refreshing grapes ensure a delicious meal.

NUTRITIONAL INFORMATION

Calories 271   Sugars 5g
Protein . . . . .31g   Fat 4g
Carbohydrate . . .22g   Saturates 1g

 2¹/₄ HOURS   45 MINS

SERVES 4

INGREDIENTS

4 × 6 oz "part-boned" chicken breasts, skinned

⅔ cup dry white vermouth

⅔ cup Fresh Chicken Stock (see page 30)

2 shallots, sliced thinly

13 oz can artichoke hearts, drained and halved

¾ cup seedless green grapes

1 tbsp cornstarch mixed with 2 tbsp cold water

salt and pepper

watercress sprigs to garnish

freshly cooked vegetables to serve

1 Cook the chicken in a heavy-based non-stick frying pan for 2–3 minutes on each side until sealed. Drain on paper towels.

2 Rinse out the pan, then add the dry vermouth and stock. Bring to a boil and add the shallots and chicken.

3 Cover and simmer for 35 minutes. Season to taste.

4 Stir in the artichokes and grapes and heat through for 2–3 minutes.

5 Stir in the cornstarch mixture until thickened. Garnish the chicken with watercress sprigs and serve with freshly cooked vegetables.

COOK'S TIP

Vermouth is a mixture of wines. It is fortified, and enriched with a secret blend of herbs and spices. It is available in sweet and dry forms. Dry white wine would make a suitable substitute in this recipe.

Chicken Tikka Masala

Try serving the chicken with mango chutney, lime pickle, and Cucumber Raita (see page 445). Add poppadoms and rice to make a delicious meal.

NUTRITIONAL INFORMATION

Calories	353	Sugars	.........8g
Protein	........44g	Fat	..........16g
Carbohydrate	....8g	Saturates	......2g

2¼ HOURS   50 MINS

SERVES 4

I N G R E D I E N T S

½ onion, chopped coarsely

3 tbsp tomato paste

1 tsp cumin seeds

1 inch piece fresh ginger, chopped

3 tbsp lemon juice

2 garlic cloves, crushed

2 tsp chili powder

1 lb 10 oz boneless chicken

salt and pepper

fresh mint sprigs, to garnish

M A S A L A   S A U C E

2 tbsp ghee or vegetable oil

1 onion, sliced

1 tbsp black onion seeds

3 garlic cloves, crushed

2 fresh green chilies, chopped

7 oz can tomatoes

½ cup low-fat plain yogurt

½ cup coconut milk

1 tbsp chopped fresh cilantro

1 tbsp chopped fresh mint

2 tbsp lemon or lime juice

½ tsp garam masala

sprigs of fresh mint, to garnish

1 Combine the first seven ingredients and seasoning in a food processor or blender and then transfer to a bowl. Cut chicken into 1½ inch cubes. Stir into the bowl and leave for 2 hours.

2 Make the masala sauce. Heat the ghee or oil in a saucepan, add the onion, and stir over a medium heat for 5 minutes. Add the spices and garlic. Add the tomatoes, yogurt, and coconut milk, bring to a boil, then simmer for 20 minutes.

3 Divide the chicken evenly between 8 oiled skewers and cook under a preheated very hot broiler for 15 minutes, turning frequently. Remove the chicken and add to the sauce. Stir in the herbs, lemon or lime juice, and garam masala. Serve garnished with mint sprigs.

Chicken & Lemon Skewers

A tangy lemon yogurt is served with these tasty lemon- and cilantro-flavored chicken skewers.

NUTRITIONAL INFORMATION

Calories 181   Sugars 6g
Protein . . . . .30g   Fat 4g
Carbohydrate . . . .6g   Saturates 2g

    2¼ HOURS   15 MINS

SERVES 4

I N G R E D I E N T S

4 chicken breasts, skinned and boned

1 tsp ground coriander

2 tsp lemon juice

1¼ cups low-fat plain yogurt

1 lemon

2 tbsp chopped, fresh cilantro

oil for brushing

salt and pepper

1 Cut the chicken into 1 inch pieces and place them in a shallow, non-metallic dish.

2 Add the coriander, lemon juice, salt and pepper to taste and 4 tbsp of the yogurt to the chicken and mix together until thoroughly combined. Cover and chill for at least 2 hours, preferably overnight.

3 To make the lemon yogurt, peel and finely chop the lemon, discarding any seeds. Stir the lemon into the yogurt together with the fresh cilantro. Refrigerate until required.

4 Thread the chicken pieces on to skewers. Brush the rack with oil and

barbecue the chicken over hot coals for about 15 minutes, basting with the oil.

5 Transfer the chicken kabobs to warm serving plates and garnish with a sprig of fresh cilantro, lemon wedges, and fresh salad leaves. Serve with the lemon yogurt.

COOK'S TIP

These kabobs are delicious served on a bed of blanched spinach, which has been seasoned with salt, pepper, and nutmeg.

Cheesy Baked Chicken

Cheese and mustard, and a simple, crispy coating, make a delicious combination for this healthy dish.

NUTRITIONAL INFORMATION

Calories	225	Sugars	.........1g
Protein	........32g	Fat	...........7g
Carbohydrate	....9g	Saturates	......3g

 5 MINS   35 MINS

SERVES 4

I N G R E D I E N T S

1 tbsp skim milk

2 tbsp prepared English mustard

1 cup grated low-fat sharp Cheddar cheese

3 tbsp all-purpose flour

2 tbsp chopped fresh chives

4 skinless, boneless chicken breasts

T O   S E R V E

jacket potatoes and fresh vegetables

crisp salad

1 Mix together the milk and mustard in a bowl. Mix the cheese with the flour and chives on a plate.

2 Dip the chicken into the milk and mustard mixture, brushing with a pastry brush to coat evenly.

3 Dip the chicken breasts into the cheese mixture, pressing to coat them evenly all over.

4 Place on a cookie sheet and spoon any spare cheese coating on top.

5 Bake the chicken in a preheated oven, 400°F, for 30–35 minutes, or until golden brown and the juices run clear, not pink, when pierced with a skewer.

6 Serve the chicken hot, with jacket potatoes and fresh vegetables, or serve cold, with a crisp salad.

COOK'S TIP

Part-boned chicken breasts are very suitable for pan-cooking and casseroling, as they stay moist and tender. Try using chicken quarters if part-boned breasts are unavailable.

Rich Chicken Casserole

Sun-dried tomatoes add a wonderful richness to this colorful casserole and you need very few to make this dish really special.

NUTRITIONAL INFORMATION

Calories 260	Sugars 8g	
Protein 32g	Fat 11g	
Carbohydrate 8g	Saturates 2g	

5 MINS   1¼ HOURS

SERVES 4

INGREDIENTS

8 chicken thighs

2 tbsp olive oil

1 medium red onion, sliced

2 garlic cloves, crushed

1 large red bell pepper, sliced thickly

thinly pared rind and juice of 1 small
   orange

½ cup chicken stock

14 oz can chopped tomatoes

½ cup sun-dried tomatoes, thinly sliced

1 tbsp chopped fresh thyme

½ cup pitted black olives

salt and pepper

thyme sprigs and orange rind, to garnish

1   In a heavy or non-stick large pan, fry the chicken without fat over a fairly high heat, turning occasionally until golden brown. Drain off any excess fat and transfer to a flameproof casserole.

2   Heat the olive oil in the pan and fry the onion, garlic, and bell pepper over a moderate heat for 3–4 minutes. Transfer to the casserole.

3   Add the orange rind and juice, stock, canned and sun-dried tomatoes.

4   Bring to a boil then cover with a lid and simmer very gently over a low heat for about 1 hour, stirring occasionally.

5   Add the thyme and olives, then adjust the seasoning to taste.

6   Scatter thyme sprigs and orange rind over the casserole to garnish and serve.

COOK'S TIP

Sun-dried tomatoes have a dense texture and concentrated taste, and add intense flavor to slow-cooking casseroles.

Spicy Sesame Chicken

This is a quick and easy recipe for the broiler, perfect for lunch or to eat outdoors on a picnic.

NUTRITIONAL INFORMATION

Calories	110	Sugars	.........3g
Protein	........15g	Fat	...........4g
Carbohydrate	....3g	Saturates	......1g

5 MINS   15 MINS

SERVES 4

INGREDIENTS

4 chicken quarters

½ cup low-fat plain yogurt

finely grated rind and juice of 1 small lemon

2 tsp medium-hot curry paste

1 tbsp sesame seeds

TO SERVE

salad

naan bread

lemon wedges

1 Remove the skin from the chicken and slash the flesh at intervals with a sharp knife.

2 Mix together the yogurt, lemon rind, lemon juice, and curry paste.

3 Spread the mixture over the chicken and arrange on a foil-lined broiler pan or cookie sheet.

4 Place under a preheated moderately hot broiler and broil for 12–15 minutes, turning once. Broil until golden brown and thoroughly cooked. Just before the end of the cooking time, sprinkle the chicken with the sesame seeds.

5 Serve with a salad, naan bread, and lemon wedges.

VARIATION

Poppy seeds, fennel seeds, or cumin seeds, or a mixture of all three, can also be used to sprinkle over the chicken.

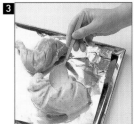

Marmalade Chicken

Marmalade lovers will enjoy this festive recipe. You can use any favorite marmalade, such as lemon or grapefruit.

NUTRITIONAL INFORMATION

Calories . . . . . . .304 Sugars 20g
Protein . . . . .29g Fat 7g
Carbohydrate . . .30g Saturates 2g

 10 MINS   2 HOURS

SERVES 6

I N G R E D I E N T S

1 chicken, weighing about 5 lb

bay leaves

2 tbsp marmalade

S T U F F I N G

1 stalk celery, chopped finely

1 small onion, chopped finely

1 tbsp sunflower oil

2 cups fresh whole wheat bread crumbs

4 tbsp marmalade

2 tbsp chopped fresh parsley

1 egg, beaten

salt and pepper

S A U C E

2 tsp cornstarch

2 tbsp orange juice

3 tbsp marmalade

⅔ cup chicken stock

1 medium orange

2 tbsp brandy

1 Lift the neck flap of the chicken and remove the wishbone. Place a sprig of bay leaves inside the body cavity.

2 To make the stuffing, sauté the celery and onion in the oil. Add the other ingredients. Season with salt and pepper to taste. Stuff the neck cavity of the chicken.

3 Place the chicken in a roasting pan and brush lightly with oil. Roast in a preheated oven, 375°F, for 20 minutes per 1 lb 2 oz plus 20 minutes or until the juices run clear when the chicken is pierced with a knife. Glaze the chicken with the remaining marmalade.

4 For the sauce, blend the cornstarch in a pan with the orange juice, then add the marmalade and stock. Heat gently, stirring, until thickened. Remove from the heat.

5 Cut the segments from the orange, discarding all white pith and membrane, add to the sauce with the brandy, and bring to a boil. Serve with the roast chicken.

Springtime Chicken Cobbler

Fresh spring vegetables are the basis of this colorful casserole, which is topped with hearty whole wheat dumplings.

NUTRITIONAL INFORMATION

Calories 560	Sugars 10g
Protein 39g	Fat 18g
Carbohydrate ...64g	Saturates 4g

  15 MINS   1½ HOURS

SERVES 4

I N G R E D I E N T S

8 skinless chicken drumsticks

1 tbsp oil

1 small onion, sliced

1½ cups baby carrots

2 baby turnips

1 cup broad beans or peas

1 tsp cornstarch

1¼ cups chicken stock

2 bay leaves

salt and pepper

C O B B L E R   T O P P I N G

2 cups whole wheat all-purpose flour

2 tsp baking powder

2 tbsp sunflower soft margarine

2 tsp dry wholegrain mustard

½ cup low-fat sharp Cheddar cheese, grated

skim milk, to mix

sesame seeds, to sprinkle

1 Fry the chicken in the oil, turning, until golden brown. Drain well and place in an ovenproof casserole. Sauté the onion for 2–3 minutes to soften.

2 Wash and trim the carrots and turnips and cut into equal-sized pieces. Add to the casserole with the onions and beans or peas.

3 Blend the cornstarch with a little of the stock, then stir in the rest, and heat gently, stirring until boiling. Pour into the casserole and add the bay leaves, salt and pepper.

4 Cover tightly and bake in a preheated oven, 400°F, for 50–60 minutes, or until the chicken juices run clear when pierced with a skewer.

5 For the topping, sift the flour and baking powder. Mix in the margarine with a fork. Stir in the mustard, the cheese, and enough milk to mix to a fairly soft dough.

6 Roll out and cut 16 rounds with a 4 cm/1½ inch cutter. Uncover the casserole, arrange the biscuit rounds on top, then brush with milk, and sprinkle with sesame seeds. Bake in the oven for 20 minutes or until the topping is golden and firm.

é82

é284

é82

2é884

é82

Chili Chicken Meatballs

These tender chicken and corn nuggets are served with a sweet and sour sauce.

NUTRITIONAL INFORMATION

Calories	196	Sugars	........12g
Protein	........26g	Fat	...........4g
Carbohydrate	...15g	Saturates	......1g

2½ HOURS   25 MINS

SERVES 4

INGREDIENTS

1 lb lean chicken, ground

4 green onions, trimmed and finely chopped, plus extra to garnish

1 small red chili, deseeded and finely chopped

1 inch piece fresh ginger, finely chopped

3½ oz can corn kernels (no added sugar or salt), drained

salt and white pepper

boiled jasmine rice, to serve

SAUCE

⅔ cup Fresh Chicken Stock (see page 30)

3½ oz cubed pineapple in natural juice, drained, with 4 tbsp reserved juice

1 medium carrot, cut into thin strips

1 small red bell pepper, deseeded and diced, plus extra to garnish

1 small green bell pepper, deseeded and diced

1 tbsp light soy sauce

2 tbsp rice vinegar

1 tbsp sugar

1 tbsp tomato paste

2 tsp cornstarch mixed to a paste with 4 tsp cold water

1 To make the meatballs, place the chicken in a bowl and mix with the green onions, chili, ginger, seasoning, and corn.

2 Divide into 16 portions and form each into a ball. Bring a saucepan of water to a boil. Arrange the meatballs on baking parchment in a steamer or large strainer, place over the water, cover, and steam for 10–12 minutes.

3 To make the sauce, pour the stock and pineapple juice into a pan and bring to a boil. Add the carrot and bell peppers, cover, and simmer for 5 minutes. Add the remaining ingredients stirring until thickened. Season and set aside.

4 Drain the meatballs and transfer to a serving plate. Garnish with snipped chives and serve with boiled rice and the sauce (re-heated if necessary).

Minty Lime Chicken

These tangy lime and honey-coated pieces have a matching sauce or dip based on creamy plain yogurt.

NUTRITIONAL INFORMATION

Calories 170   Sugars 12g
Protein . . . . .23g   Fat 3g
Carbohydrate . . .12g   Saturates 1g

35 MINS   15 MINS

SERVES 6

I N G R E D I E N T S

3 tbsp finely chopped mint

4 tbsp clear honey

4 tbsp lime juice

12 boneless chicken thighs

salt and pepper

salad, to serve

S A U C E

½ cup low-fat plain yogurt

1 tbsp finely chopped mint

2 tsp finely grated lime rind

1 Combine the mint, honey, and lime juice in a bowl and season with salt and pepper to taste.

2 Use toothpicks to keep the chicken thighs in neat shapes and add the chicken to the marinade, turning to coat evenly.

3 Leave the chicken to marinate for at least 30 minutes, longer if possible

4 Cook the chicken on a preheated moderately hot barbecue or broiler, turning frequently and basting with the marinade.

5 The chicken is cooked if the juices run clear when the chicken is pierced with a skewer.

6 Meanwhile, mix together the sauce ingredients.

7 Remove the toothpicks and serve the chicken with a salad and the sauce for dipping or pouring.

Tasmanian Duck

Some of the best cherries in the world are grown in Tasmania, hence the title for this recipe, though dried cherries from any country can be used.

NUTRITIONAL INFORMATION

Calories	259	Sugars	........12g
Protein	........24g	Fat	..........12g
Carbohydrate	...12g	Saturates	......2g

 5 MINS   35 MINS

SERVES 4

I N G R E D I E N T S

4 duck breasts

½ cup dried cherries

½ cup water

4 tbsp lemon juice

2 large leeks, quartered, or 8 baby leeks

2 tbsp olive oil

2 tbsp balsamic vinegar

2 tbsp port

2 tsp pink or black peppercorns

1 Using a sharp knife, make 3 slashes in the fat of the duck breasts in one direction, and 3 in the other.

2 Put the dried cherries, water, and lemon juice into a small saucepan. Bring to a boil. Remove from the heat and leave to cool.

3 Turn a large foil tray upside-down, make several holes in the bottom with a skewer, and put it over a hot barbecue. Put the duck into the tray. Cover with foil and cook for 20 minutes.

4 Brush the leeks with olive oil and cook on the open barbecue for 5–7 minutes, turning constantly.

5 Remove the duck from the tray and cook on the open barbecue for 5 minutes, skin-side down, while you make the sauce.

6 Stir the balsamic vinegar into the cooking sauces in the tray, scraping any bits from the bottom. Add to the cherries in the saucepan. Return to the

heat—either the stove top or barbecue—and stir in the port and pink peppercorns. Bring to a boil and cook for 5 minutes, until the sauce has thickened slightly.

7 Serve the duck piping hot, pour over the cherry sauce, and accompany with the leeks.

Chicken Fajitas

This spicy chicken filling, made up of mixed bell peppers, chilies, and mushrooms, is put into folded tortillas and topped with sour cream.

NUTRITIONAL INFORMATION

Calories 303   Sugars 8g
Protein ....23g   Fat 18g
Carbohydrate ...13g   Saturates 7g

 15 MINS   25 MINS

SERVES 4

I N G R E D I E N T S

2 red bell peppers

2 green bell peppers

2 tbsp olive oil

2 onions, chopped

3 garlic cloves, crushed

1 chili, deseeded and chopped finely

2 boneless chicken breasts (about 12 oz)

2 oz small white mushrooms, sliced

2 tsp freshly chopped cilantro

grated rind of ½ lime

2 tbsp lime juice

salt and pepper

4 wheat or corn tortillas

4–6 tbsp sour cream

TO GARNISH

Tomato Salsa (see page 444)

lime wedges

1 Halve the bell peppers, remove the seeds, and place skin-side upwards under a preheated moderate broiler until well charred. Leave to cool slightly and then peel off the skin; cut the flesh into thin slices.

2 Heat the oil in a pan, add the onions, garlic, and chili, and fry them for a few minutes just until the onion has softened.

3 Cut the chicken into narrow strips, add to the vegetable mixture in the pan, and fry for 4–5 minutes until almost cooked through, stirring occasionally.

4 Add the bell peppers, mushrooms, cilantro, lime rind, and juice, and continue to cook for 2–3 minutes. Season to taste.

5 Heat the tortillas, wrapped in foil, in a preheated oven at 350°F for a few minutes. Bend them in half and divide the chicken mixture between them.

6 Top the chicken filling in each tortilla with a spoonful of sour cream and serve garnished with tomato salsa and lime wedges.

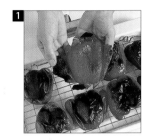

Curried Turkey with Apricots

An easy-to-prepare supper dish of lean turkey in a fruit curry sauce served on a bed of spicy rice.

NUTRITIONAL INFORMATION

Calories 377   Sugars 19g
Protein ....33g   Fat 6g
Carbohydrate ...51g   Saturates 1g

2½ HOURS   30 MINS

SERVES 4

INGREDIENTS

1 tbsp vegetable oil

1 large onion, chopped

1 lb skinless turkey breast, cut into 1 inch cubes

3 tbsp mild curry paste

1¼ cups Fresh Chicken Stock (see page 30)

6 oz frozen peas

14 oz can apricot halves in natural juice

⅓ cup golden raisins

6 cups Basmati rice, freshly cooked

1 tsp ground coriander

4 tbsp fresh cilantro, chopped

1 green chili, deseeded and sliced

salt and pepper

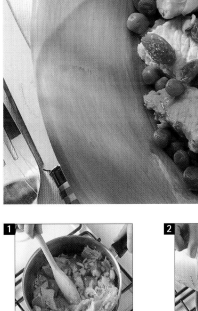

1 Heat the oil in a large saucepan and gently fry the onion and turkey for 4–5 minutes until the onion has softened but not browned and the turkey is a light golden color.

2 Stir in the curry paste. Pour in the stock, stirring, and bring to a boil. Cover and simmer for 15 minutes. Stir in the peas and bring back to a boil. Cover and simmer for 5 minutes.

3 Drain the apricots, reserving the juice, and cut into thick slices. Add to the curry, stirring in a little of the juice if the mixture is becoming dry. Add the raisins and cook for 2 minutes.

4 Mix the rice with the ground and fresh cilantro, stir in the sliced green chili, and season well. Transfer the rice to warm plates and top with the curry.

VARIATION

Peaches can be used instead of the apricots if you prefer. Cook in exactly the same way.

Golden Glazed Chicken

A glossy glaze with sweet and fruity flavors coats chicken breasts in this tasty recipe.

NUTRITIONAL INFORMATION

Calories	427	Sugars	........11g
Protein	........39g	Fat	.........12g
Carbohydrate	...42g	Saturates	.....3g

5 MINS   35 MINS

SERVES 4

INGREDIENTS

6 boneless chicken breasts

1 tsp turmeric

1 tbsp whole-grain mustard

1¼ cups orange juice

2 tbsp clear honey

2 tbsp sunflower oil

1½ cups long grain rice

1 orange

3 tbsp chopped mint

salt and pepper

mint sprigs, to garnish

1 With a sharp knife, mark the surface of the chicken breasts in a diamond pattern.

2 Mix together the turmeric, mustard, orange juice, and honey and pour over the chicken. Season with salt and pepper to taste. Chill until required.

3 Lift the chicken from the marinade and pat dry on paper towels.

4 Heat the oil in a wide pan, add the chicken, and sauté until golden, turning once. Drain off any excess oil. Pour over the marinade, cover, and simmer for 10–15 minutes until the chicken is tender.

5 Boil the rice in lightly salted water until tender and drain well. Finely grate the rind from the orange and stir into the rice with the mint.

6 Remove the peel and white pith from the orange and cut into segments.

7 Serve the chicken with the orange and mint rice, garnished with orange segments and mint sprigs.

COOK'S TIP

To make a slightly sharper sauce, use small grapefruit instead of the oranges.

Chicken with Lime Stuffing

A cheesy stuffing is tucked under the breast skin of the chicken to give added flavor and moistness to the meat.

NUTRITIONAL INFORMATION

Calories	236	Sugars	.........1g
Protein	........28g	Fat	..........12g
Carbohydrate	....3g	Saturates	......7g

 10 MINS   2 HOURS

SERVES 4

INGREDIENTS

1 chicken, weighing 5 lb

oil for brushing

1⅓ cups zucchini

2 tbsp butter

juice of 1 lime

lime slices and shreds of lime rind,
   to garnish

STUFFING

½ cup zucchini

¾ cup low-fat cream cheese

finely grated rind of 1 lime

2 tbsp fresh bread crumbs

salt and pepper

1 To make the stuffing, trim and coarsely grate the zucchini and mix with the cheese, lime rind, bread crumbs, salt and pepper.

2 Carefully ease the skin away from the breast of the chicken with the fingertips, taking care not to split it.

3 Push the stuffing under the skin, to cover the breast evenly.

4 Place in a baking pan, brush with oil, and roast in a preheated oven, 375°F, for 20 minutes per 1 lb 2 oz plus

  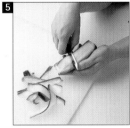

20 minutes, or until the chicken juices run clear when pierced with a skewer.

5 Meanwhile, trim the remaining zucchini and cut into long, thin strips with a potato peeler or sharp knife. Sauté in the butter and lime juice until just tender, then serve with the chicken. Garnish the chicken with lime slices and shreds of lime rind and serve immediately.

COOK'S TIP

For quicker cooking, finely grate the zucchini rather than cutting it into strips.

Garlicky Chicken Cushions

Stuffed with creamy ricotta, spinach, and garlic, then gently cooked in a rich tomato sauce, this is a suitable dish to make ahead of time.

NUTRITIONAL INFORMATION

Calories	316	Sugars	.........6g
Protein	........40g	Fat	..........13g
Carbohydrate	....6g	Saturates	......5g

  10 MINS · 40 MINS

SERVES 4

INGREDIENTS

4 part-boned chicken breasts

½ cup frozen spinach, defrosted

½ cup low-fat ricotta cheese

2 garlic cloves, crushed

1 tbsp olive oil

1 onion, chopped

1 red bell pepper, sliced

15 oz can chopped tomatoes

6 tbsp wine or chicken stock

10 stuffed olives, sliced

salt and pepper

flat-leaf parsley sprigs, to garnish

pasta, to serve

1 Make a slit between the skin and meat on one side of each chicken breast. Lift the skin to form a pocket, being careful to leave the skin attached to the other side.

2 Put the spinach into a sieve and press out the water with a spoon. Mix with the ricotta, half the garlic, and seasoning.

3 Spoon the spinach mixture under the skin of each chicken breast, then secure the edge of the skin with cocktail sticks.

4 Heat the oil in a frying pan, add the onion, and fry for 1 minute, stirring. Add the remaining garlic and red bell pepper and cook for 2 minutes. Stir in the tomatoes, wine or stock, olives, and seasoning. Set the sauce aside and chill the chicken if preparing in advance.

5 Bring the sauce to a boil, pour into an ovenproof dish, and arrange the chicken breasts on top in a single layer.

6 Cook, uncovered in a preheated oven, 400°F, for 35 minutes until the chicken is golden and cooked through. Test by making a slit in one of the chicken breasts with a skewer to make sure the juices run clear.

7 Spoon a little of the sauce over the chicken breasts then transfer to serving plates and garnish with parsley. Serve with pasta.

Rustic Chicken & Orange Pot

Low in fat and high in fiber, this colorful casserole makes a healthy and hearty meal.

NUTRITIONAL INFORMATION

Calories 345	Sugars 6g
Protein 29g	Fat 10g
Carbohydrate . . .39g	Saturates 2g

 5 MINS   1 HOUR

SERVES 4

INGREDIENTS

8 chicken drumsticks, skinned

1 tbsp whole wheat flour

1 tbsp olive oil

2 medium red onions

1 garlic clove, crushed

1 tsp fennel seeds

1 bay leaf

finely grated rind and juice of 1 small orange

14 oz can chopped tomatoes

14 oz can cannellini or flageolet beans, drained

salt and black pepper

TOPPING

3 thick slices whole wheat bread

2 tsp olive oil

1 Toss the chicken in the flour to coat evenly. Heat the oil in a non-stick pan and fry the chicken over a fairly high heat, turning often until golden brown. Transfer to a large ovenproof casserole.

2 Slice the red onions into thin wedges. Add to the pan and cook for a few minutes until lightly browned. Stir in the garlic, then add the onions and garlic to the casserole.

3 Add the fennel seeds, bay leaf, orange rind and juice, tomatoes, beans, and salt and pepper.

4 Cover tightly and cook in a preheated oven, 375°F, for 30–35 minutes until the chicken juices are clear and not pink when pierced through the thickest part with a skewer.

5 Cut the bread into small dice and toss in the oil. Remove the lid from the casserole and top with the bread cubes. Bake for a further 15–20 minutes until the bread is golden and crisp.

Marinated Chicken Kabobs

Pieces of chicken marinated in yogurt, chutney, and spices make meltingly tender kabobs, and are cooked quickly in the microwave.

NUTRITIONAL INFORMATION

Calories 180	Sugars 11g	
Protein 24g	Fat 5g	
Carbohydrate 11g	Saturates 1g	

1¼ HOURS   15 MINS

SERVES 4

I N G R E D I E N T S

1 tbsp peach chutney

3 tbsp low-fat plain yogurt

½ tsp ground cumin

pinch of apple pie spice

squeeze of lemon juice

3 chicken breast fillets, cut into even pieces

½ red bell pepper, cut into 16 even chunks

1 zucchini, cut into 16 slices

8 small white mushrooms

salt and pepper

C H I V E & M I N T D R E S S I N G

⅔ cup low-fat plain yogurt

2 tbsp low-fat mayonnaise

skim milk

1 tbsp chopped fresh chives

1 tbsp chopped fresh mint

tossed salad, to serve

TO GARNISH

sprigs of fresh mint

fresh chives

tossed salad, to serve

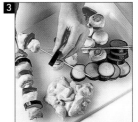

1 Mix the chutney, yogurt, spices, and lemon juice together in a bowl. Season to taste.

2 Add the chicken to the bowl. Mix well and leave in a cool place to marinate for 1 hour.

3 Thread the red bell pepper, zucchini, chicken, and mushrooms onto 8 long wooden skewers.

4 Arrange 4 skewers on a large plate or microwave rack. Cook on HIGH power for 6 minutes, turning over, and rearranging halfway through. Repeat with the remaining 4 kabobs.

5 To make the chive and mint dressing, mix together all the ingredients and season with salt and pepper to taste. Spoon the dressing over the kabobs and garnish with mint and chives. Serve with a tossed salad.

Chicken with Bramble Sauce

This autumnal recipe can be made with fresh-picked wild blackberries if you're lucky enough to live near a good supply.

NUTRITIONAL INFORMATION

Calories ....174 Sugars 5g
Protein ....27g Fat 4g
Carbohydrate ....5g Saturates 1g

 1¼ HOURS   20 MINS

SERVES 4

INGREDIENTS

4 chicken breasts or 8 thighs

4 tbsp dry white wine or cider

2 tbsp chopped fresh rosemary

pepper

rosemary sprigs and blackberries,
   to garnish

SAUCE

2 cups blackberries

1 tbsp cider vinegar

2 tbsp red currant jelly

¼ tsp grated nutmeg

1 Cut the chicken into 1 inch pieces and place in a bowl. Sprinkle over the wine or cider and rosemary, and season well with pepper. Cover and leave to marinate for at least 1 hour.

2 Drain the marinade from the chicken and thread the meat onto 8 metal or wooden skewers.

3 Cook under a preheated moderately hot broiler for 8–10 minutes, turning occasionally, until golden.

4 To make the sauce, place the marinade in a saucepan with the blackberries and simmer gently until soft. Press through a strainer.

5 Return the blackberry purée to the saucepan with the cider vinegar and red currant jelly and bring to a boil. Boil the sauce uncovered until it is reduced by about one-third.

6 Spoon a little bramble sauce onto each plate and place a chicken skewer on top. Sprinkle with nutmeg. Garnish each skewer with rosemary and blackberries.

COOK'S TIP

If you use canned fruit, omit the red currant jelly.

Chicken Jalfrezi

This is a quick and tasty way to use leftover roast chicken. The sauce can also be used for any cooked poultry, lamb, or beef.

NUTRITIONAL INFORMATION

Calories 270   Sugars 3g
Protein . . . . .36g   Fat 11g
Carbohydrate . . . .7g   Saturates 2g

 25 MINS   15 MINS

SERVES 4

I N G R E D I E N T S

1 tsp mustard oil

3 tbsp vegetable oil

1 large onion, chopped finely

3 garlic cloves, crushed

1 tbsp tomato paste

2 tomatoes, skinned and chopped

1 tsp ground turmeric

½ tsp cumin seeds, ground

½ tsp coriander seeds, ground

½ tsp chili powder

½ tsp garam masala

1 tsp red wine vinegar

1 small red bell pepper, chopped

1 cup frozen broad beans

1 lb 2 oz cooked chicken, cut into bite-sized
   pieces

salt

sprigs of fresh cilantro,
   to garnish

1 Heat the mustard oil in a large frying pan set over a high heat for about 1 minute until it begins to smoke.

2 Add the vegetable oil, reduce the heat, and then add the onion and the garlic. Fry the garlic and onion until they are golden.

3 Add the tomato paste, chopped tomatoes, turmeric, ground cumin and coriander seeds, chili powder, garam masala, and wine vinegar to the frying pan. Stir the mixture until fragrant.

4 Add the red bell pepper and broad beans and stir for 2 minutes until the bell pepper is softened. Stir in the chicken and salt to taste.

5 Simmer gently for 6–8 minutes until the chicken is heated through and the beans are tender.

6 Serve garnished with sprigs of cilantro.

Jamaican Hot Pot

A tasty way to make chicken joints go a long way, this hearty casserole is spiced with the warm, subtle flavor of ginger.

NUTRITIONAL INFORMATION

Calories 277	Sugars 6g
Protein 33g	Fat 7g
Carbohydrate . . .22g	Saturates 1g

 5 MINS   1¼ HOURS

SERVES 4

INGREDIENTS

2 tsp sunflower oil

4 chicken drumsticks

4 chicken thighs

1 medium onion

1 lb 10 oz piece squash or pumpkin, peeled

1 green bell pepper

1 inch piece fresh ginger, chopped finely

15 oz can chopped tomatoes

1¼ cups chicken stock

¼ cup split lentils

garlic salt and cayenne pepper

12 oz can corn kernels

1 Heat the oil in a large flameproof casserole and fry the chicken joints, turning frequently, until they are golden all over.

2 Peel and slice the onion.

3 Using a sharp knife, cut the squash or pumpkin into dice.

4 Deseed and slice the green bell pepper.

5 Drain any excess fat from the pan and add the onion, pumpkin, and bell pepper. Gently fry for a few minutes. Add the ginger, tomatoes, stock, and lentils. Season with garlic salt and cayenne.

6 Cover and place in a preheated oven, 375°F, for about 1 hour, until the vegetables are tender and the juices from the chicken run clear.

7 Add the drained corn and cook for a further 5 minutes. Season to taste and serve with crusty bread.

Spanish Chicken Casserole

Tomatoes, olives, bell peppers, and potatoes, with a splash of Spanish red wine, make this a marvellous peasant-style dish.

NUTRITIONAL INFORMATION

Calories	293	Sugar	.........6g
Protein	........15g	Fats	..........12g
Carbohydrates	...26g	Saturates	......2g

10 MINS   1¼ HOURS

SERVES 4

INGREDIENTS

¼ cup all-purpose flour

1 tsp salt

pepper

1 tbsp paprika

4 chicken portions

3 tbsp olive oil

1 large onion, chopped

2 garlic cloves, crushed

6 tomatoes, chopped, or 15 oz can chopped tomatoes

1 green bell pepper, cored, deseeded and chopped

⅔ cup Spanish red wine

1¼ cups chicken stock

3 medium potatoes, peeled and quartered

12 pitted black olives

1 bay leaf

crusty bread, to serve

1 Put the all-purpose flour, salt, pepper, and paprika into a large polythene bag.

2 Rinse the chicken and pat dry with paper towels. Put them into the bag and shake to coat in the seasoned flour.

3 Heat the oil in a large flameproof casserole dish. Add the chicken portions and cook over a medium–high heat for 5–8 minutes until well-browned on each side. Lift out of the casserole with a perforated spoon and set aside.

4 Add the onion and garlic to the casserole and cook for a few minutes until browned. Add the tomatoes and bell pepper and cook for 2–3 minutes.

5 Return the chicken to the casserole. Add the wine, stock, and potatoes, and then the olives and bay leaf. Cover and bake in a preheated oven at 375°F for 1 hour until the chicken is tender.

6 Check the seasoning, adding more salt and pepper if necessary. Serve the chicken casserole hot with chunks of crusty bread.

Indian Charred Chicken

An Indian-influenced dish that is delicious served with naan bread and a cucumber raita.

20 MINS   10 MINS

SERVES 4

I N G R E D I E N T S

4 chicken breasts, skinned and boned

2 tbsp curry paste

1 tbsp sunflower oil

1 tbsp brown sugar

1 tsp ground ginger

½ tsp ground cumin

TO SERVE

naan bread

green salad leaves

CUCUMBER RAITA

¼ cucumber

salt

⅔ cup low-fat plain yogurt

¼ tsp chili powder

1 Place the chicken breasts between 2 sheets of baking parchment or plastic wrap. Pound them with the flat side of a meat mallet or rolling pin to flatten them.

2 Mix together the curry paste, oil, sugar, ginger, and cumin in a small bowl. Spread the mixture over both sides of the chicken and set aside until required.

3 To make the raita, peel the cucumber and scoop out the seeds with a spoon. Grate the cucumber flesh, sprinkle with salt, place in a sieve, and leave to stand for 10 minutes. Rinse off the salt and squeeze out any moisture by pressing the cucumber with the base of a glass or back of a spoon.

4 Mix the cucumber with the yogurt and stir in the chili powder. Leave to chill until required.

5 Transfer the chicken to an oiled rack and barbecue over hot coals for 10 minutes, turning once.

6 Warm the naan bread at the side of the barbecue.

7 Serve the chicken with the naan bread and raita and accompanied with fresh green salad leaves.

Fish & Seafood

Naturally low in fat yet rich in minerals and proteins, white fish and shellfish are ideal to include in a low fat diet. There are so many different textures and flavors

available that they lend themselves to a wide range of cooking methods, as you will see from the recipes that follow. White fish such as cod, haddock, halibut, swordfish, and snapper are readily available and easy to cook. Shellfish, such as shrimp, oysters, crab, and lobster may take a little longer to prepare, but are well worth the effort. Oily fish—like salmon, trout, tuna, and mackerel—are high in fat and should be eaten in moderation.

Piquant Fish Cakes

The combination of pink- and white-fleshed fish, with a tasty tomato sauce, transforms the humble fish into something a bit special.

NUTRITIONAL INFORMATION

Calories	334	Sugars	.........7g
Protein	........31g	Fat	...........7g
Carbohydrate	...37g	Saturates	......1g

2 HOURS   55 MINS

SERVES 4

I N G R E D I E N T S

1 lb potatoes, diced

8 oz each trout and haddock fillet

1 bay leaf

1¾ cups Fresh Fish Stock
   (see page 30)

2 tbsp low-fat plain yogurt

4 tbsp fresh snipped chives

2¾ oz dry white bread crumbs

1 tbsp sunflower oil

salt and pepper

freshly snipped chives, to garnish

lemon wedges and salad leaves,
   to serve

PIQUANT TOMATO SAUCE

¾ cup strained tomatoes

4 tbsp dry white wine

4 tbsp low-fat plain yogurt

chili powder

1 Place the potatoes in a saucepan and cover with water. Bring to a boil and cook for about 10 minutes or until the potatoes are tender. Drain well and mash.

2 Meanwhile, place the fish in a pan with the bay leaf and fish stock. Bring to a boil and simmer for 7–8 minutes until tender.

3 Remove the fish with a slotted spoon and flake the flesh away from the skin. Gently mix the cooked fish with the potato, plain yogurt, chives, and seasoning. Leave to cool, then cover, and leave to chill for 1 hour.

4 Sprinkle the bread crumbs on to a plate. Divide the fish mixture into 8 and form each portion into a patty, about 3 inches in diameter. Press each fish cake into the bread crumbs, coating all over.

5 Brush a frying pan with oil and fry the fish cakes for 6 minutes. Turn the fish cakes over and cook for a further 5–6 minutes until golden. Drain on paper towels and keep warm.

6 To make the sauce, heat the strained tomatoes and wine. Season, remove from the heat, and stir in the yogurt. Return briefly to the heat, then transfer to a small serving bowl, and sprinkle with chilli powder. Garnish the fish cakes with chives and serve with lemon wedges, salad leaves, and the sauce.

Charred Tuna Steaks

Tuna has a firm flesh, which is ideal for barbecuing, but it can be a little dry unless it is marinated first.

NUTRITIONAL INFORMATION

Calories ....153 Sugars 1g
Protein ....29g Fat 3g
Carbohydrate ....1g Saturates 1g

 2 HOURS   15 MINS

SERVES 4

INGREDIENTS

4 tuna steaks

3 tbsp soy sauce

1 tbsp Worcestershire sauce

1 tsp whole-grain mustard

1 tsp sugar

1 tbsp sunflower oil

green salad, to serve

TO GARNISH

flat-leaf parsley

lemon wedges

1 Place the tuna steaks in a shallow dish.

2 Mix together the soy sauce, Worcestershire sauce, mustard, sugar, and oil in a small bowl.

3 Pour the marinade over the tuna steaks.

4 Gently turn over the tuna steaks, using your fingers or a fork. Make sure that the fish steaks are well coated with the marinade.

5 Cover and place the tuna steaks in the refrigerator. Leave to chill for between 30 minutes and 2 hours.

6 Barbecue the marinated fish over hot coals for 10–15 minutes, turning once.

7 Baste frequently with any of the marinade that is left in the dish.

8 Garnish with flat-leaf parsley and lemon wedges. Serve with a fresh green salad.

COOK'S TIP

If a marinade contains soy sauce, the marinating time should be limited, usually to 2 hours. If allowed to marinate for too long, the fish will dry out and become tough.

Pineapple & Fish Curry

This is a fiery hot Thai curry dish all the better for serving with refreshing (and cooling) fresh pineapple pieces.

NUTRITIONAL INFORMATION

Calories .... .249	Sugars 4g	
Protein .... .29g	Fat 9g	
Carbohydrate ...15g	Saturates 1g	

15 MINS | 15 MINS

SERVES 4

INGREDIENTS

2 pineapples

3 inch piece galangal, sliced

2 blades of lemon grass, bruised then chopped

5 sprigs fresh basil

1 lb firm white fish fillets (swordfish, halibut, or cod, for example), cubed

4½ oz peeled shrimp

2 tbsp vegetable oil

2 tbsp red curry paste

½ cup thick coconut milk or cream

2 tbsp fish sauce

2 tsp brown sugar

2-3 red chilies, seeded and cut into thin julienne strips

6 kaffir lime leaves, torn into pieces

cilantro sprigs, to garnish

1 Cut the pineapples in half lengthways. Remove the flesh, reserving the shells if using (see right). Remove the core from the pineapple flesh, then dice into bite-sized pieces.

2 Place the galangal in a large shallow pan with the lemon grass and basil. Add the fish cubes and just enough water to cover. Bring to a boil, reduce the heat, and simmer for about 2 minutes.

3 Add the shrimp and cook for a further 1 minute or until the fish is just cooked. Remove from the flavored stock with a slotted spoon and keep warm.

4 Heat the oil in a heavy-based pan or wok. Add the curry paste and cook for 1 minute. Stir in the coconut milk or cream, fish sauce, brown sugar, chilies, and lime leaves.

5 Add the pineapple and cook until just heated through. Add the cooked fish and mix gently to combine.

6 Spoon into the reserved pineapple shells, if liked, and serve immediately, garnished with sprigs of cilantro.

COOK'S TIP

Sole goes well with many different types of sauces—cream, tomato, or hollandaise—and is delicious served cold with fresh mayonnaise.

Oriental Shellfish Kabobs

These shellfish and vegetable kabobs are ideal for serving at parties. They are quick and easy to prepare and take next to no time to cook.

NUTRITIONAL INFORMATION

Calories 93   Sugars 1g
Protein . . . . .15g   Fat 2g
Carbohydrate . . . .2g   Saturates 0.3g

2½ HOURS   5 MINS

MAKES 12

I N G R E D I E N T S

12 oz raw jumbo shrimp, peeled leaving tails intact

12 oz scallops, cleaned, trimmed, and halved (quartered if large)

1 bunch green onions, sliced into 1 inch pieces

1 medium red bell pepper, deseeded and cubed

3½ oz baby corn-on-the-cobs, trimmed and sliced into ½ inch pieces

3 tbsp dark soy sauce

½ tsp hot chili powder

½ tsp ground ginger

1 tbsp sunflower oil

1 red chili, deseeded and sliced, to garnish

D I P

4 tbsp dark soy sauce

4 tbsp dry sherry

2 tsp clear honey

1 inch piece fresh ginger, peeled and grated

1 green onion, trimmed and sliced very finely

1 Divide the shrimp, scallops, green onions, bell pepper, and baby corn into 12 portions and thread onto the skewers (soaked for 10 minutes in water to prevent them from burning). Cover the ends with foil so that they do not burn and place in a shallow dish.

2 Mix the soy sauce, chili powder, and ground ginger and coat the kabobs. Cover and chill for about 2 hours.

3 Preheat the broiler to hot. Arrange the kabobs on the rack, brush with oil, and cook for 2–3 minutes on each side until the shrimp turn pink, the scallops become opaque, and the vegetables soften.

4 Mix together the dip ingredients.

5 Remove the foil and transfer the kabobs to a warm serving platter. Garnish with sliced chili and serve with the dip.

Poached Salmon

Salmon steaks, poached in a well-flavored stock and served with a piquant sauce, make a delicious summer lunch or supper dish.

NUTRITIONAL INFORMATION

Calories 712	Sugars 5g
Protein 66g	Fat 47g
Carbohydrate 6g	Saturates 9g

🍲 10 MINS   🕐 30 MINS

SERVES 4

I N G R E D I E N T S

1 small onion, sliced

1 small carrot, sliced

1 stick celery, sliced

1 bay leaf

pared rind and juice of ½ orange

a few stalks of parsley

salt

5-6 black peppercorns

3 cups water

4 salmon steaks, about 12 oz each

salad leaves, to serve

lemon twists, to garnish

S A U C E

1 large avocado, peeled, halved and pitted

½ cup low-fat plain yogurt

grated zest and juice of ½ orange

black pepper

a few drops of hot red pepper sauce

1 Put the onion, carrot, celery, bay leaf, orange rind, orange juice, parsley stalks, salt, and peppercorns in a pan just large enough to take the salmon steaks in a single layer. Pour on the water, cover the pan, and bring to a boil. Simmer the stock for 20 minutes.

2 Arrange the salmon steaks in the pan, return the stock to a boil, and simmer for 3 minutes. Cover the pan, remove from the heat, and leave the salmon to cool in the stock.

3 Roughly chop the avocado and place it in a blender or food processor with the yogurt, orange zest, and orange juice. Process until smooth, then season to taste with salt, pepper, and hot pepper sauce.

4 Remove the salmon steaks from the stock (reserve it to make fish soup or a sauce), skin them, and pat dry with paper towels.

5 Cover the serving dish with salad leaves, arrange the salmon steaks on top, and spoon a little of the sauce into the center of each one. Garnish the fish with lemon twists, and serve the remaining sauce separately.

Scallop Skewers

As the scallops are marinated, it is not essential that they are fresh; frozen shellfish are fine for a barbecue.

NUTRITIONAL INFORMATION

Calories 182   Sugars 0g
Protein ....29g   Fat 7g
Carbohydrate ....0g   Saturates 1g

 30 MINS   10 MINS

SERVES 4

I N G R E D I E N T S

grated zest and juice of 2 limes

2 tbsp finely chopped lemon grass or 1 tbsp lemon juice

2 garlic cloves, crushed

1 green chili, deseeded and chopped

16 scallops, with corals

2 limes, each cut into 8 segments

2 tbsp sunflower oil

1 tbsp lemon juice

salt and pepper

TO SERVE

1 cup arugula salad

3 cups tossed salad leaves

1 Soak 8 skewers in warm water for at least 10 minutes before you use them to prevent the food from sticking.

2 Combine the lime juice and zest, lemon grass, garlic, and chili together in a pestle and mortar or spice grinder to make a paste.

3 Thread 2 scallops on to each of the soaked skewers. Cover the ends with foil to prevent them from burning.

4 Alternate the scallops with the lime segments.

5 Whisk together the oil, lemon juice, salt, and pepper to make the dressing.

6 Coat the scallops with the spice paste and place over a medium barbecue, basting occasionally.

7 Cook for 10 minutes, turning once.

8 Toss the arugula, tossed salad leaves, and dressing together well. Put into a serving bowl.

9 Serve the scallops piping hot, 2 skewers on each plate, with the salad.

Mackerel with Lime

The secret of this dish lies in the simple, fresh flavors which perfectly complement the fish.

NUTRITIONAL INFORMATION

Calories 302	Sugars 0g	
Protein 21g	Fat 24g	
Carbohydrate 0g	Saturates 4g	

10 MINS　　10 MINS

SERVES 4

INGREDIENTS

4 small mackerel

¼ tsp ground coriander

¼ tsp ground cumin

4 sprigs fresh cilantro

3 tbsp chopped, fresh cilantro

1 red chili, deseeded and chopped

grated rind and juice of 1 lime

2 tbsp sunflower oil

salt and pepper

1 lime, sliced, to garnish

chili flowers (optional), to garnish

salad leaves, to serve

1 To make the chili flowers (if using), cut the tip of a small chili lengthways into thin strips, leaving the chili intact at the stem end. Remove the seeds and place in iced water until curled.

 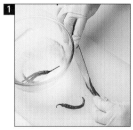 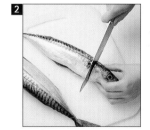 

2 Clean and gut the mackerel, removing the heads if preferred. Transfer the mackerel to a chopping board.

3 Sprinkle the fish with the ground spices and salt and pepper to taste. Sprinkle 1 teaspoon of chopped cilantro inside the cavity of each fish.

4 Mix together the chopped cilantro, chili, lime rind and juice, and the oil in a small bowl. Brush the mixture liberally over the fish.

5 Place the fish in a hinged rack if you have one. Barbecue the fish over hot coals for 3–4 minutes on each side, turning once. Brush the fish frequently with the remaining basting mixture. Transfer to plates.

6 Garnish with lime slices and chili flowers, if using, and serve with salad leaves.

COOK'S TIP

This recipe is suitable for other oily fish, such as trout, herring, or sardines.

Salmon Yakitori

The Japanese sauce used here complements the salmon, although it is usually served with chicken.

NUTRITIONAL INFORMATION

Calories	247	Sugars	........10g
Protein	........19g	Fat	...........11g
Carbohydrate	...12g	Saturates	......2g

20 MINS   15 MINS

SERVES 4

INGREDIENTS

12 oz chunky salmon fillet

8 baby leeks

YAKITORI SAUCE

5 tbsp light soy sauce

5 tbsp fish stock

2 tbsp sugar

5 tbsp dry white wine

3 tbsp sweet sherry

1 clove garlic, crushed

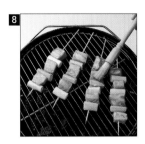

1 Skin the salmon and cut the flesh into 2 inch chunks. Trim the leeks and cut them into 2 inch lengths.

2 Thread the salmon and leeks alternately on to 8 pre-soaked wooden skewers. Leave to chill in the refrigerator until required.

3 To make the sauce, place all of the ingredients in a small pan and heat gently, stirring, until the sugar has dissolved.

4 Bring to a boil, then reduce the heat, and simmer for 2 minutes. Strain the sauce through a fine strainer and leave to cool until it is required.

5 Pour about one-third of the sauce into a small dish and set aside to serve with the kabobs.

6 Brush plenty of the remaining sauce over the skewers and cook directly on the rack.

7 If preferred, place a sheet of oiled kitchen foil on the rack and cook the salmon on that.

8 Barbecue the salmon and leek kabobs over hot coals for about 10 minutes or until cooked through, turning once.

9 Use a brush to baste frequently during cooking with the remaining sauce in order to prevent the fish and vegetables from drying out. Transfer the kabobs to a large serving platter and serve with a small bowl of the reserved sauce for dipping.

Smoky Fish Pie

This flavorsome and colorful fish pie is perfect for a light supper. The addition of smoked salmon gives it a touch of luxury.

NUTRITIONAL INFORMATION

Calories ....523 Sugars 15g
Protein ....58g Fat 6g
Carbohydrate ...63g Saturates 2g

 15 MINS   1 HOUR

SERVES 4

INGREDIENTS

2 lb smoked haddock or
  cod fillets

2½ cups skimmed milk

2 bay leaves

4 oz button mushrooms, quartered

4 oz frozen English peas

4 oz frozen corn kernels

1½ lb potatoes, diced

5 tbsp low-fat unsweetened yogurt

4 tbsp chopped fresh parsley

2 oz smoked salmon, sliced into
  thin strips

3 tbsp cornstarch

1 oz smoked cheese, grated

salt and pepper

1 Preheat the oven to 400°F. Place the fish in a pan and add the milk and bay leaves. Bring to a boil, cover, and then simmer for 5 minutes.

2 Add the mushrooms, peas, and corn, bring back to a simmer, cover, and cook for 5–7 minutes. Leave to cool.

3 Place the potatoes in a saucepan, cover with water, boil and cook for 8 minutes. Drain well and mash with a fork or a potato masher. Stir in the yogurt, parsley, and seasoning. Set aside.

4 Using a draining spoon, remove the fish from the pan. Flake the cooked fish away from the skin and place in an ovenproof gratin dish. Reserve the cooking liquid.

5 Drain the vegetables, reserving the cooking liquid, and gently stir into the fish with the salmon strips.

6 Blend a little cooking liquid into the cornstarch to make a paste. Transfer the rest of the liquid to a saucepan and add the paste. Heat through, stirring, until thickened. Discard the bay leaves and season to taste. Pour the sauce over the fish and vegetables and mix. Spoon over the mashed potato so that the fish is covered, sprinkle with cheese, and bake for 25–30 minutes.

COOK'S TIP

If possible, use smoked haddock or cod that has not been dyed bright yellow or artificially flavored to give the illusion of having been smoked.

Salmon Fillet with Herbs

This is a great party dish, as the salmon is cooked in one piece. The combination of the herbs and barbecue give a great flavor.

NUTRITIONAL INFORMATION

Calories 507   Sugars 0.4g
Protein . . . . .46g   Fat 35g
Carbohydrate . . .0.5g   Saturates 6g

5 MINS   30 MINS

SERVES 4

I N G R E D I E N T S

½ large bunch dried thyme

5 fresh rosemary branches, 6–8 inches long

8 bay leaves

2 lb salmon fillet

1 bulb fennel, cut into 8 pieces

2 tbsp lemon juice

2 tbsp olive oil

TO SERVE

crusty bread

green salad

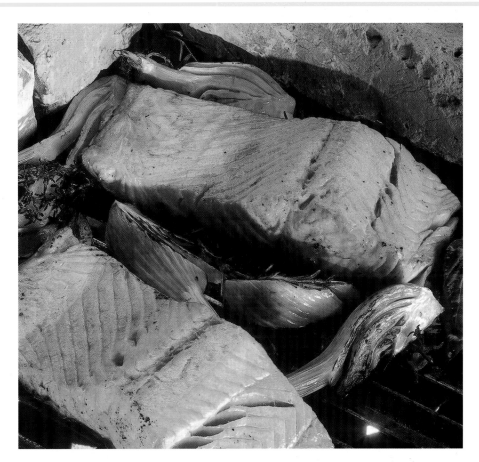

1 Make a base on a hot broiler with the dried thyme, rosemary branches, and bay leaves, overlapping them so that they cover a slightly bigger area than the salmon.

2 Carefully place the salmon on top of the herbs.

3 Arrange the fennel around the edge of the fish.

4 Combine the lemon juice and oil and brush the salmon with it.

5 Cover the salmon loosely with a piece of foil, to keep it moist.

6 Cook for about 20–30 minutes, basting frequently with the lemon juice mixture.

7 Remove the salmon from the barbecue, cut it into slices, and serve with the fennel.

8 Serve with slices of crusty bread and a green salad.

VARIATION

Use whatever combination of herbs you may have available—but avoid the stronger tasting herbs, such as sage and marjoram, which are unsuitable for fish.

Balti Scallops

This is a wonderful recipe for a special occasion dish. Cooked with cilantro and tomatoes, the scallops have a spicy flavor.

NUTRITIONAL INFORMATION

Calories	258	Sugars	.........2g
Protein	........44g	Fat	...........8g
Carbohydrate	....3g	Saturates	......1g

1¼ HOURS   15 MINS

SERVES 4

INGREDIENTS

1 lb 10 oz shelled scallops

2 tbsp oil

2 onions, chopped

3 tomatoes, quartered

2 fresh green chilies, sliced

4 lime wedges, to garnish

MARINADE

3 tbsp chopped fresh cilantro

1 inch piece ginger root, grated

1 tsp ground coriander

3 tbsp lemon juice

grated rind of 1 lemon

¼ tsp ground black pepper

½ tsp salt

½ tsp ground cumin

1 garlic clove, crushed

1 To make the marinade, mix all the ingredients together in a bowl.

2 Put the scallops into a bowl. Add the marinade and turn the scallops until they are well coated.

3 Then cover and leave to marinate for 1 hour or overnight in the fridge.

4 Heat the oil in a wok, add the onions, and stir-fry until softened.

5 Add the tomatoes and chilies and stir-fry for 1 minute.

6 Add the scallops and stir-fry for 6–8 minutes until the scallops are cooked through, but still succulent inside.

7 Serve garnished with lime wedges.

COOK'S TIP

It is best to buy the scallops fresh in the shell with the roe—you will need 3 lb 5 oz—a fish store will clean them and remove the shell for you.

Spicy Shrimp

Basil and tomatoes are ideal flavorings for shrimp, spiced with cumin seeds and garlic.

NUTRITIONAL INFORMATION

Calories	208	Sugars	.........8g
Protein	........27g	Fat	..........8g
Carbohydrate	....8g	Saturates	......1g

5 MINS   20 MINS

SERVES 4

INGREDIENTS

2 tbsp corn oil

1 onion

2 cloves garlic, crushed

1 tsp cumin seeds

1 tbsp sugar

14 oz can chopped tomatoes

1 tbsp sundried tomato paste

1 tbsp chopped fresh basil

1 lb peeled jumbo shrimp

salt and pepper

1 Heat the corn oil in a large preheated wok.

2 Using a sharp knife, finely chop the onion. Add the onion and crushed garlic to the wok and stir-fry for 2–3 minutes, or until softened.

3 Stir in the cumin seeds and stir-fry for 1 minute.

4 Add the sugar, chopped tomatoes, and tomato paste to the wok.

5 Bring the mixture to a boil, then reduce the heat, and leave the sauce to simmer for 10 minutes.

6 Add the basil and shrimp to the mixture in the wok. Season to taste with salt and pepper.

7 Increase the heat and cook for a further 2–3 minutes or until the shrimp are completely cooked through. Transfer to a warm serving dish and serve immediately.

COOK'S TIP

Sundried tomato paste has a much more intense flavor than that of normal tomato paste. It adds a distinctive intensity to any tomato-based dish.

Seafood Stir Fry

This combination of assorted seafood and tender vegetables flavored with ginger makes an ideal light meal served with thread noodles.

NUTRITIONAL INFORMATION

Calories 226	Sugars 5g	
Protein 35g	Fat 7g	
Carbohydrate 6g	Saturates 1g	

 5 MINS   15 MINS

SERVES 4

INGREDIENTS

3½ oz small, thin asparagus, trimmed

1 tbsp sunflower oil

1 inch piece fresh ginger, cut into thin strips

1 medium leek, shredded

2 medium carrots, julienned

3½ oz baby corn cobs, quartered lengthwise

2 tbsp light soy sauce

1 tbsp oyster sauce

1 tsp clear honey

1 lb cooked, assorted shellfish, thawed if frozen

freshly cooked egg noodles, to serve

TO GARNISH

4 large cooked prawns

small bunch fresh chives, freshly snipped

1 Bring a small saucepan of water to a boil and blanch the asparagus for 1–2 minutes.

2 Drain the asparagus, set aside, and keep warm.

3 Heat the oil in a wok or large frying pan and stir-fry the ginger, leek, carrot, and corn for about 3 minutes. Do not allow the vegetables to brown.

4 Add the soy sauce, oyster sauce, and honey to the wok or frying pan.

5 Stir in the cooked shellfish and continue to stir-fry for 2–3 minutes until the vegetables are just tender and the shellfish are thoroughly heated through. Add the blanched asparagus and stir-fry for about 2 minutes.

6 To serve, pile the cooked noodles on to 4 warm serving plates and spoon the seafood and vegetable stir fry over them.

7 Garnish with the cooked shrimp and freshly snipped chives and serve immediately.

Delicately Spiced Trout

The firm, sweet flesh of the trout is enhanced by the sweet-spicy flavor of the marinade and cooking juices.

NUTRITIONAL INFORMATION

Calories 374	Sugars 13g
Protein 38g	Fat 19g
Carbohydrate . . .14g	Saturates 3g

45 MINS   20 MINS

SERVES 4

INGREDIENTS

4 trout, each weighing 6–9 oz, cleaned

3 tbsp oil

1 tsp fennel seeds

1 tsp onion seeds

1 garlic clove, crushed

⅔ cup coconut milk or fish stock

3 tbsp tomato paste

⅓ cup golden raisins

½ tsp garam masala (see page 78)

TO GARNISH

¼ cup chopped cashew nuts

lemon wedges

sprigs of fresh cilantro

MARINADE

4 tbsp lemon juice

2 tbsp chopped fresh cilantro

1 tsp ground cumin

½ tsp salt

½ tsp ground black pepper

1 Slash the trout skin in several places on both sides with a sharp knife.

2 To make the marinade, mix all the ingredients together in a bowl.

3 Put the trout in a shallow dish and pour over the marinade. Marinate for 30–40 minutes; turn the fish occasionally.

4 Heat the oil in a wok and fry the fennel seeds and onion seeds until they start popping.

5 Add the crushed garlic, coconut milk or fish stock, and tomato paste and bring the mixture in the wok to a boil.

6 Add the golden raisins, garam masala, and trout with the juices from the marinade. Cover and simmer for 5 minutes. Turn the trout over and simmer for a further 10 minutes.

7 Serve garnished with the nuts, lemon, and cilantro sprigs.

Szechuan White Fish

Szechuan pepper is quite hot and should be used sparingly to avoid making the dish unbearably spicy.

NUTRITIONAL INFORMATION

Calories . . . . . . .225 Sugars 3g
Protein . . . . .20g Fat 8g
Carbohydrate . . .17g Saturates 1g

 5 MINS   20 MINS

SERVES 4

INGREDIENTS

12 oz white fish fillets

1 small egg, beaten

3 tbsp all-purpose flour

4 tbsp dry white wine

3 tbsp light soy sauce

vegetable oil, for frying

1 garlic clove, cut into slivers

½-inch piece fresh ginger, finely chopped

1 onion, finely chopped

1 celery stalk, chopped

1 fresh red chili, chopped

3 green onions, chopped

1 tsp rice wine vinegar

½ tsp ground Szechuan pepper

¾ cup fish stock

1 tsp sugar

1 tsp cornstarch

2 tsp water

1 Cut the fish into 1½ inch cubes. Beat together the egg, flour, wine, and 1 tablespoon of soy sauce to make a batter. Dip the cubes of fish into the batter to coat well.

2 Heat the oil in a wok, reduce the heat slightly and cook the fish, in batches, for 2–3 minutes, until golden brown. Remove with a slotted spoon, drain on paper towels, set aside, and keep warm.

3 Pour all but 1 tablespoon of oil from the wok and return to the heat. Add the garlic, ginger, onion, celery, chili, and green onions and stir-fry for 1–2 minutes. Stir in the remaining soy sauce and the vinegar.

4 Add the Szechuan pepper, fish stock, and sugar to the wok. Mix the cornstarch with the water to form a smooth paste and stir it into the stock. Bring to a boil and cook, stirring, for 1 minute, until the sauce thickens and clears.

5 Return the fish cubes to the wok and cook for 1–2 minutes. Serve immediately.

Spiced Balti Seafood

Although shrimp are not a traditional ingredient of Balti cooking, they work well with Balti spices and cooking methods.

NUTRITIONAL INFORMATION

Calories	194	Sugars	.........2g
Protein	.......29g	Fat	...........8g
Carbohydrate	....2g	Saturates	......1g

2¼ HOURS   15 MINS

SERVES 4

INGREDIENTS

1 garlic clove, crushed

2 tsp freshly grated fresh ginger

2 tsp ground coriander

2 tsp ground cumin

½ tsp ground cardamom

¼ tsp chili powder

2 tbsp tomato paste

5 tbsp water

3 tbsp chopped fresh cilantro

1 lb 2 oz peeled cooked jumbo shrimp

2 tbsp oil

2 small onions, sliced

1 fresh green chili, chopped

salt

1 Put the garlic, ginger, ground coriander, cumin, cardamom, chili powder, tomato paste, 4 tablespoons of the water, and 2 tablespoons of the fresh cilantro into a bowl. Mix all the ingredients together.

2 Add the shrimp to the bowl and leave to marinate for 2 hours.

3 Heat the oil in a karahi or wok, add the onions, and stir-fry until golden brown.

4 Add the shrimp, marinade, and the chili and stir-fry over a medium heat for 5 minutes. Add salt and the remaining tablespoon of water if the mixture is very dry. Stir-fry over a medium heat for a further 5 minutes.

5 Serve the shrimp immediately, garnished with the remaining fresh chopped cilantro.

COOK'S TIP

Shrimp lose less flavor if they are put without water in a tightly covered pan and set over a high heat to cook in their own juice.

Butterfly Shrimp

These shrimp look stunning when presented on the skewers, and they will certainly be an impressive prelude to the main meal.

NUTRITIONAL INFORMATION

Calories 183	Sugars 0g	
Protein 28g	Fat 8g	
Carbohydrate 0g	Saturates 1g	

4¹/₂ HOURS   10 MINS

SERVES 2–4

INGREDIENTS

1 lb 2 oz or 16 raw tiger shrimp, shelled, leaving tails intact

juice of 2 limes

1 tsp cardamom seeds

2 tsp cumin seeds, ground

2 tsp coriander seeds, ground

½ tsp ground cinnamon

1 tsp ground turmeric

1 garlic clove, crushed

1 tsp cayenne pepper

2 tbsp oil

cucumber slices, to garnish

1 Soak 8 wooden skewers in water for 20 minutes. Cut the shrimp lengthways in half down to the tail and flatten out to a symmetrical shape.

2 Thread a shrimp onto 2 wooden skewers, with the tail between them, so that, when laid flat, the skewers hold the shrimp in shape. Thread another 3 shrimp onto these 2 skewers in the same way.

3 Repeat until you have 4 sets of 4 shrimp each.

4 Lay the skewered shrimp in a non-porous, non-metallic dish and sprinkle over the lime juice.

5 Combine the spices and the oil, and coat the shrimp well in the mixture. Cover the shrimp and chill for 4 hours.

6 Cook over a hot barbecue or in a broiler pan lined with foil under a preheated broiler for 6 minutes, turning once.

7 Serve immediately, garnished with cucumber, and accompanied by a sweet chutney—walnut chutney is ideal.

Seafood Pizza

Make a change from the standard pizza toppings—this dish is piled high with seafood baked with a red bell pepper and tomato sauce.

NUTRITIONAL INFORMATION

Calories 248	Sugars 7g	
Protein 27g	Fat 6g	
Carbohydrate . . .22g	Saturates 2g	

25 MINS   55 MINS

SERVES 4

INGREDIENTS

5 oz standard pizza base mix

4 tbsp chopped fresh dill or 2 tbsp dried dill

fresh dill, to garnish

SAUCE

1 large red bell pepper

14 oz can chopped tomatoes with onion and herbs

3 tbsp tomato paste

salt and pepper

TOPPING

12 oz assorted cooked seafood, thawed if frozen

1 tbsp capers in brine, drained

1 oz pitted black olives in brine, drained

1 oz low-fat Mozzarella cheese, grated

1 tbsp grated, fresh Parmesan cheese

1 Preheat the oven to 400°F. Place the pizza base mix in a bowl and stir in the dill. Make the dough according to the instructions on the package.

2 Press the dough into a round measuring 10 inches across on a cookie sheet lined with baking parchment. Set aside to rise.

3 Preheat the broiler to hot. To make the sauce, halve and deseed the bell pepper and arrange on a broiler rack. Cook for 8–10 minutes until softened and charred. Leave to cool slightly, peel off the skin, and chop the flesh.

4 Place the tomatoes and bell pepper in a pan. Bring to a boil and simmer for 10 minutes. Stir in the tomato paste and season.

5 Spread the sauce over the pizza base and top with the seafood. Sprinkle over the capers and olives, top with the cheeses, and bake for 25–30 minutes.

6 Garnish with sprigs of dill and serve hot.

Swordfish with Coconut

This is a tasty kabob with a mild marinade. Allow the skewers to marinate for at least an hour before cooking.

NUTRITIONAL INFORMATION

Calories	193	Sugars	.........2g
Protein	........39g	Fat	...........3g
Carbohydrate	....2g	Saturates	......1g

4 HOURS   30 MINS

SERVES 4

INGREDIENTS

1 lb swordfish tails

8 oz uncooked peeled shrimp

shredded coconut, toasted, to garnish (optional)

MARINADE

1 tsp sunflower oil

½ small onion, finely grated

1 tsp fresh ginger, grated

⅔ cup canned coconut milk

2 tbsp chopped, fresh cilantro

1 To make the marinade, heat the oil in a wok or saucepan and fry the onion and ginger for 5 minutes until just softened but not browned.

COOK'S TIP

Look out for uncooked shrimp in the freezer cabinet in large supermarkets. If you cannot obtain them, you can use cooked shrimp, but remember they only need heating through.

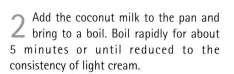

2 Add the coconut milk to the pan and bring to a boil. Boil rapidly for about 5 minutes or until reduced to the consistency of light cream.

3 Remove the pan from the heat and allow to cool completely.

4 When cooled, stir the cilantro into the coconut milk and pour into a shallow dish.

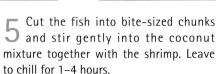

5 Cut the fish into bite-sized chunks and stir gently into the coconut mixture together with the shrimp. Leave to chill for 1–4 hours.

6 Thread the fish and shrimp onto skewers and discard any remaining marinade. Barbecue the skewers over hot coals for 10–15 minutes, turning frequently. Garnish with toasted coconut (if using).

Baked Seabass

Seabass is often paired with subtle oriental flavors. For a special occasion, you may like to bone the fish.

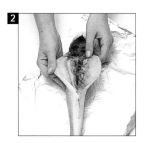
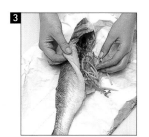
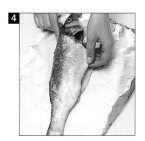

NUTRITIONAL INFORMATION

Calories 140   Sugars 0.1g
Protein ....29g   Fat 1g
Carbohydrate ...0.1g   Saturates 0.2g

10 MINS   15 MINS

SERVES 4–6

INGREDIENTS

2 seabass, about 2 lb 4 oz each, cleaned and scaled

2 green onions, green part only, cut into strips

2 inch piece ginger, peeled and cut into strips

2 garlic cloves, unpeeled, crushed lightly

2 tbsp mirin or dry sherry

salt and pepper

TO SERVE

pickled sushi ginger (optional)

soy sauce

1 For each fish lay out a double thickness of foil and oil the top piece well, or lay a piece of silicon paper over the foil.

2 Place the fish in the middle and expose the cavity.

3 Divide the green onion and ginger between each cavity. Put a garlic clove in each cavity.

4 Pour over the mirin or dry sherry. Season the fish well.

5 Close the cavities and lay each fish on its side. Bring over the foil and fold the edges together to seal securely. Fold each end neatly.

6 Cook over a medium barbecue for 15 minutes, turning once.

7 To serve, remove the foil and cut each fish into 2 or 3 pieces.

8 Serve with the pickled ginger (if using) accompanied by soy sauce.

COOK'S TIP

Fresh seabass is just as delicious when cooked very simply. Stuff the fish with garlic and chopped herbs, brush with olive oil, and bake in the oven.

Indonesian-style Spicy Cod

A delicious aromatic coating makes this dish rather special. Serve it with a crisp salad and crusty bread.

NUTRITIONAL INFORMATION

Calories	146	Sugars	.........2g
Protein	........19g	Fat	..........7g
Carbohydrate	....2g	Saturates	......4g

10 MINS   15 MINS

SERVES 4

INGREDIENTS

4 cod steaks

1 stalk lemon grass

1 small red onion, chopped

3 cloves garlic, chopped

2 fresh red chilies, deseeded and chopped

1 tsp grated fresh ginger

¼ tsp turmeric

2 tbsp butter, cut into small cubes

8 tbsp canned coconut milk

2 tbsp lemon juice

salt and pepper

red chilies, to garnish (optional)

1 Rinse the cod steaks and pat them dry on absorbent paper towels.

2 Remove and discard the outer leaves from the lemon grass and thinly slice the inner section.

3 Place the lemon grass, onion, garlic, chilies, ginger, and turmeric in a food processor and blend until the ingredients are finely chopped. Season with salt and pepper to taste.

4 With the processor running, add the butter, coconut milk, and lemon juice and process until well blended.

5 Place the fish in a shallow, non-metallic dish. Pour over the coconut mixture and turn the fish until well coated.

6 If you have one, place the fish steaks in a hinged basket, which will make them easier to turn. Barbecue over hot coals for 15 minutes or until the fish is cooked through, turning once. Serve garnished with red chilies (if using).

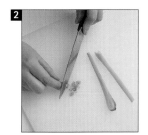

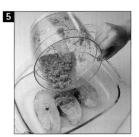

COOK'S TIP

If you prefer a milder flavor, omit the chilies altogether. For a hotter flavor do not remove the seeds from the chilies.

Provençale-style Mussels

These delicious large mussels are served hot with a tasty tomato and vegetable sauce. Mop up the delicious sauce with some crusty bread.

NUTRITIONAL INFORMATION

Calories ....253 Sugars 8g
Protein ....31g Fat 8g
Carbohydrate ....9g Saturates 1g

 5 MINS   50 MINS

SERVES 4

INGREDIENTS

1 tbsp olive oil

1 large onion, finely chopped

1 garlic clove, finely chopped

1 small red bell pepper, deseeded and finely chopped

sprig of rosemary

2 bay leaves

14 oz can chopped tomatoes

⅔ cup white wine

1 zucchini, diced finely

2 tbsp tomato paste

1 tsp sugar

1¾ oz pitted black olives in brine, drained and chopped

1½ lb cooked New Zealand mussels in their shells

1 tsp orange rind

salt and pepper

crusty bread, to serve

2 tbsp chopped, fresh parsley, to garnish

1 Heat the olive oil in a large saucepan and gently fry the chopped onion, garlic, and bell pepper for 3–4 minutes until just softened.

2 Add the rosemary and bay leaves to the saucepan with the tomatoes and ⅓ cup wine. Season to taste, then bring to a boil, and simmer for 15 minutes.

3 Stir in the zucchini, tomato paste, sugar, and olives. Simmer for 10 minutes.

4 Meanwhile, bring a pan of water to a boil. Arrange the mussels in a steamer or a large strainer and place over the water. Sprinkle with the remaining wine and the orange rind. Cover and steam until the mussels open (discard any that remain closed).

5 Remove the mussels with a slotted spoon and arrange on a serving plate. Discard the herbs and spoon the sauce over the mussels. Garnish with chopped parsley and serve with crusty bread.

Yucatan Fish

Herbs, onion, green bell pepper, and pumpkin seeds are used to flavor this baked fish dish, which is first marinated in lime juice.

NUTRITIONAL INFORMATION

Calories	248	Sugars	.........2g
Protein	........33g	Fat	...........11g
Carbohydrate	....3g	Saturates	......1g

 40 MINS   35 MINS

SERVES 4

I N G R E D I E N T S

4 cod cutlets or steaks or halibut fillets
  (about 6 oz each)

2 tbsp lime juice

salt and pepper

1 green bell pepper

1 tbsp olive oil

1 onion, chopped finely

1–2 garlic cloves, crushed

1½ oz green pumpkin seeds

grated rind of ½ lime

1 tbsp chopped fresh cilantro
  or parsley

1 tbsp chopped fresh mixed herbs

2 oz small, white mushrooms,
  sliced thinly

2–3 tbsp fresh orange juice or
  white wine

T O   G A R N I S H

lime wedges

fresh mixed herbs

1 Wipe the fish, place in a shallow ovenproof dish, and pour the lime juice over. Turn the fish in the juice, season with salt and pepper, cover, and leave in a cool place for 15–30 minutes.

2 Halve the bell pepper, remove the seeds, and place under a preheated moderate broiler, skin-side upwards, until the skin burns and splits. Leave to cool slightly, then peel off the skin, and chop the flesh.

3 Heat the oil in a pan and fry the onion, garlic, bell pepper, and pumpkin seeds gently for a few minutes until the onion is soft.

4 Stir in the lime rind, cilantro or parsley, mixed herbs, mushrooms, and seasoning and spoon over the fish.

5 Spoon or pour the orange juice or wine over the fish, cover with foil or a lid, and place in a preheated oven at 350°F for about 30 minutes, or until the fish is just tender.

6 Garnish the fish with lime wedges and fresh herbs and serve.

Fish & Yogurt Quenelles

These quenelles, made from a thick purée of fish and yogurt, can be prepared well in advance and stored in the refrigerator before poaching.

NUTRITIONAL INFORMATION

Calories 228   Sugars 7g
Protein . . . . .39g   Fat 2g
Carbohydrate . . .14g   Saturates 1g

45 MINS   15 MINS

SERVES 4

INGREDIENTS

1 lb 10 oz white fish fillets, such as cod, sole, or halibut

2 small egg whites

½ tsp ground coriander

1 tsp ground mace

⅔ cup low-fat plain yogurt

1 small onion, sliced

salt and pepper

mixture of boiled Basmati rice and wild rice, to serve

SAUCE

1 bunch watercress, trimmed

1¼ cups chicken stock

2 tbsp cornstarch

⅔ cup low-fat plain yogurt

2 tbsp low-fat crème fraîche

1 Cut the fish into pieces and process it in a food processor for about 30 seconds. Add the egg whites to the fish and process for a further 30 seconds until the mixture forms a stiff paste. Add the coriander, mace, seasoning, and the yogurt and process until smooth. Cover and chill for at least 30 minutes.

2 Spoon the mixture into a pastry bag, and pipe into sausage shapes about 4 inches long. Alternatively, take rounded dessertspoons of the mixture and shape into ovals, using 2 spoons.

3 Bring about 2 inches of water to a boil in a frying pan and add the onion for flavoring. Lower the quenelles into the water, using a fish slice or spoon. Cover the pan, keep the water at a gentle boil, and poach the quenelles for 8 minutes, turning them once. Remove with a slotted spoon and drain.

4 Roughly chop the watercress, reserving a few sprigs for garnish. Process the remainder with the chicken stock until well blended, then pour into a small pan. Stir the cornstarch into the yogurt and pour the mixture into the pan. Bring to a boil, stirring.

5 Stir in the crème fraîche, season, and remove from the heat. Garnish with the watercress sprigs. Serve with the rice.

Seafood in Red Curry Sauce

For something very quick and simple that sets your tastebuds alight, try this inspired dish of shrimp in a wonderfully spicy sauce.

NUTRITIONAL INFORMATION

Calories 175	Sugars 3g
Protein 29g	Fat 5g
Carbohydrate 3g	Saturates 1g

 10 MINS   10 MINS

SERVES 4

I N G R E D I E N T S

1 tbsp vegetable oil

6 green onions, trimmed and sliced

1 stalk lemon grass

½ inch piece of fresh ginger

1 cup coconut milk

2 tbsp Thai red curry paste

1 tbsp fish sauce

3 cups uncooked jumbo shrimp

1 tbsp chopped fresh cilantro

fresh chilies, to garnish

1 Heat the vegetable oil in a wok or large frying pan and fry the green onions gently until softened, about 2 minutes.

VARIATION

Try this recipe using Thai green curry sauce instead of red. Both varieties are obtainable from many supermarkets—look for them in the oriental foods section.

2 Bruise the stalk of lemon grass using a meat mallet or rolling pin.

3 Peel and finely grate the piece of fresh ginger.

4 Add the bruised lemon grass and grated ginger to the wok or frying pan with the coconut milk, Thai red curry paste, and fish sauce. Heat the coconut milk until almost boiling.

5 Peel the shrimp, leaving the tails intact. Remove the black vein along the back of each shrimp.

6 Add the shrimp to the wok or frying pan with the chopped cilantro and cook gently for 5 minutes.

7 Serve the shrimp with the sauce, garnished with fresh chilies.

Swordfish & Okra Balti

Okra is known as bindi or ladies' fingers. It can be found both in large supermarkets and Asian food stores.

NUTRITIONAL INFORMATION

Calories ....266 Sugars 4g
Protein ....46g Fat 7g
Carbohydrate ....5g Saturates 1g

1¹/₄ HOURS   25 MINS

SERVES 4

INGREDIENTS

1 lb 10 oz swordfish, cut into 1¼ inch cubes

9 oz okra

2 tbsp oil

1 onion, sliced

1 garlic clove, crushed

1 inch piece ginger, sliced

²/₃ cup coconut milk or fish stock

2 tsp garam masala

MARINADE

3 tbsp lemon juice

grated rind of 1 lemon

¼ tsp aniseed

½ tsp salt

½ tsp ground black pepper

TO GARNISH

4 lime wedges

sprigs of fresh cilantro

1 To make the marinade, mix the ingredients together in a bowl. Stir the swordfish into the bowl and leave to marinate for 1 hour.

2 Bring a saucepan of water to a boil, add the okra, and boil for 4–5 minutes. Drain and cut into ¹/₂ inch slices.

3 Heat the oil in a wok, add the onion, and stir-fry until golden brown. Add the garlic and ginger and fry for 1 minute. Add the fish with the marinade and stir-fry for 2 minutes.

4 Stir in the okra, coconut milk or stock, and the garam masala and simmer for 10 minutes. Serve garnished with lime wedges and fresh cilantro.

VARIATION
Swordfish is a very meaty fish, resembling lobster, which could be used instead of swordfish for a special occasion.

Green Fish Curry

This dish has a wonderful fresh, hot, exotic taste resulting from the generous amount of fresh herbs, sharp fresh chilies, and coconut milk.

NUTRITIONAL INFORMATION

Calories	223	Sugars	.........2g
Protein	........44g	Fat	..........5g
Carbohydrate	....2g	Saturates	......1g

5 MINS   20 MINS

SERVES 4

I N G R E D I E N T S

1 tbsp oil

2 green onions, sliced

1 tsp cumin seeds, ground

2 fresh green chilies, chopped

1 tsp coriander seeds, ground

4 tbsp chopped fresh cilantro

4 tbsp chopped fresh mint

1 tbsp chopped chives

⅔ cup coconut milk

4 white fish fillets, about 8 oz each

salt and pepper

Basmati rice, to serve

1 mint sprig, to garnish

1 Heat the oil in a large frying pan or shallow saucepan and add the green onions.

2 Stir-fry the green onions over a medium heat until they are softened but not colored.

3 Stir in the cumin, chilies, and ground coriander, and cook until fragrant.

4 Add the fresh cilantro, mint, chives, and coconut milk and season liberally.

5 Carefully place the fish in the pan and poach for 10–15 minutes until the flesh flakes when tested with a fork.

6 Serve the fish fillets in the sauce with the rice. Garnish with a mint sprig.

COOK'S TIP

Never overcook fish—it is surprising how little time it takes compared to meat. It will continue to cook slightly while keeping warm in the oven and while being dished up and brought to the table.

Japanese Flounder

The marinade for this dish has a distinctly Japanese flavor. Its subtle flavor goes well with any white fish.

NUTRITIONAL INFORMATION

Calories 207	Sugars 9g	
Protein 22g	Fat 8g	
Carbohydrate . . .10g	Saturates 1g	

6 HOURS   10 MINS

SERVES 4

INGREDIENTS

4 small flounders

6 tbsp soy sauce

2 tbsp sake or dry white wine

2 tbsp sesame oil

1 tbsp lemon juice

2 tbsp brown sugar

1 tsp fresh ginger, grated

1 clove garlic, crushed

TO GARNISH

1 small carrot

4 green onions

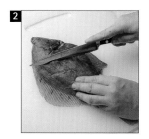

1 Rinse the fish and pat them dry on paper towels.

2 Cut a few slashes into the sides of the fish so that they absorb the marinade.

3 Mix together the soy sauce, sake or wine, oil, lemon juice, sugar, ginger, and garlic in a large, shallow dish.

4 Place the fish in the marinade and turn so they are well coated. Leave to stand in the refrigerator for 1–6 hours.

5 Meanwhile, prepare the garnish. Cut the carrot into evenly sized thin sticks, and clean and shred the green onions.

6 Barbecue the fish over hot coals for about 10 minutes, turning once.

7 Scatter the chopped green onions and carrot over the fish and transfer the fish to a serving dish. Serve immediately.

VARIATION

Use sole instead of the flounders and scatter over some toasted sesame seeds instead of the carrot and green onions, if you prefer.

Mediterranean Fish Stew

Popular in fishing ports around Europe, gentle stewing is an excellent way to maintain the flavor and succulent texture of fish and shellfish.

NUTRITIONAL INFORMATION

Calories 533   Sugars 11g
Protein ....71g   Fat 10g
Carbohydrate ...30g   Saturates 2g

   1¼ HOURS   25 MINS

SERVES 4

I N G R E D I E N T S

2 tsp olive oil

2 red onions, sliced

2 garlic cloves, crushed

2 tbsp red wine vinegar

2 tsp sugar

1¼ cups Fresh Fish Stock (see page 30)

1¼ cups dry red wine

2 × 14 oz cans chopped tomatoes

8 oz baby eggplant, quartered

8 oz yellow zucchini, quartered or sliced

1 green bell pepper, sliced

1 tbsp chopped fresh rosemary

1 lb 2 oz halibut fillet, skinned and cut into
    1 inch cubes

1 lb 10 oz fresh mussels, prepared

8 oz baby squid, cleaned, trimmed and
    sliced into rings

8 oz fresh tiger shrimp, peeled and
    deveined

salt and pepper

4 slices toasted French bread rubbed with a
    cut garlic clove

lemon wedges, to serve

1 Heat the oil in a large non-stick saucepan and fry the onions and garlic gently for 3 minutes.

2 Stir in the vinegar and sugar and cook for a further 2 minutes.

3 Stir in the stock, wine, canned tomatoes, eggplant, zucchini, bell pepper, and rosemary. Bring to a boil and simmer, uncovered, for 10 minutes.

4 Add the halibut, mussels, and squid. Mix well and simmer, covered, for 5 minutes until the fish is opaque.

5 Stir in the shrimp and continue to simmer, covered, for a further 2–3 minutes until the shrimp are pink and cooked through.

6 Discard any mussels which haven't opened and season to taste.

7 To serve, put a slice of the prepared garlic bread in the base of each warmed serving bowl and ladle the stew over the top. Serve with lemon wedges.

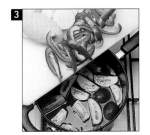

Herrings with Tarragon

The fish are filled with an orange-flavored stuffing and are wrapped in kitchen foil before being baked on the barbecue.

NUTRITIONAL INFORMATION

Calories ....332 Sugars 4g
Protein ....21g Fat 24g
Carbohydrate ....9g Saturates 6g

15 MINS   35 MINS

SERVES 4

INGREDIENTS

1 orange

4 green onions

1¾ oz fresh whole wheat bread crumbs

1 tbsp fresh tarragon, chopped

4 herrings, cleaned and gutted

salt and pepper

green salad, to serve

TO GARNISH

2 oranges

1 tbsp light brown sugar

1 tbsp olive oil

sprigs of fresh tarragon

1 To make the stuffing, grate the rind from half of the orange, using a zester.

2 Peel and chop all of the orange flesh on a plate in order to catch all of the juice.

3 Mix together the orange flesh, juice, rind, green onions, bread crumbs, and tarragon in a bowl. Season with salt and pepper to taste.

4 Divide the stuffing into 4 equal portions and use it to fill the body cavities of the fish.

5 Place each fish onto a square of lightly greased kitchen foil and wrap the foil around the fish so that it is completely enclosed. Barbecue over hot coals for 20–30 minutes until the fish are cooked through—the flesh should be white and firm to the touch.

6 Meanwhile, make the garnish. Peel and thickly slice the 2 oranges and sprinkle over the sugar.

7 Just before the fish is cooked, drizzle a little oil over the orange slices and place them on the barbecue for about 5 minutes to heat through.

8 Transfer the fish to serving plates and garnish with the barbecued orange slices and sprigs of fresh tarragon.

9 Serve the fish with a fresh green salad.

Shrimp Bhuna

This is a fiery recipe with subtle undertones. As the flavor of the shrimps should be noticeable, the spices should not take over this dish.

NUTRITIONAL INFORMATION

Calories	141	Sugars	.......0.4g
Protein	........19g	Fat	..........7g
Carbohydrate	....1g	Saturates	......1g

15 MINS   20 MINS

SERVES 4–6

I N G R E D I E N T S

2 dried red chilies, deseeded if liked

3 fresh green chilies, finely chopped

1 tsp ground turmeric

3 garlic cloves, crushed

½ tsp pepper

1 tsp paprika

2 tsp white wine vinegar

½ tsp salt

1 lb 2 oz uncooked peeled jumbo shrimp

3 tbsp oil

1 onion, chopped very finely

¾ cup water

2 tbsp lemon juice

2 tsp garam masala

sprigs of fresh cilantro,
    to garnish

COOK'S TIP

Garam masala should be used sparingly and is generally added to foods towards the end of their cooking time. It is also used sprinkled over cooked meats, vegetables, and beans and peas as a garnish.

1 Combine the chilies, spices, vinegar, and salt in a non-metallic bowl. Stir in the shrimp and leave for 10 minutes.

2 Heat the oil in a large frying pan or wok, add the onion, and fry for 3–4 minutes until soft.

3 Add the shrimp and the contents of the bowl to the pan and stir-fry over a high heat for 2 minutes. Reduce the heat, add the water, and boil for 10 minutes, stirring occasionally, until the water is evaporated and the curry is fragrant.

4 Stir in the lemon juice and garam masala, then transfer the mixture to a warm serving dish, and garnish with fresh cilantro sprigs.

Scallops With Mushrooms

Scallops have a rich but delicate flavor. When sautéed with mushrooms and bathed in brandy and cream, they make a really special meal.

NUTRITIONAL INFORMATION

Calories 390	Sugars 1g	
Protein 31g	Fat 28g	
Carbohydrate 1g	Saturates 4g	

5 MINS   10 MINS

SERVES 2

I N G R E D I E N T S

1 tbsp butter

8 oz shelled queen scallops

1 tbsp olive oil

1¾ oz oyster mushrooms, sliced

1¾ oz shiitake mushrooms, sliced

1 garlic clove, chopped

4 green onions, white and green parts
  sliced

3 tbsp heavy cream

1 tbsp brandy

salt and pepper

sprigs of fresh dill, to garnish

Basmati rice to serve

1 Heat the butter in a heavy-based frying pan and fry the scallops for about 1 minute, turning occasionally.

2 Remove the scallops from the frying pan with a perforated spoon and keep warm.

3 Add the olive oil to the pan and heat. Add the mushrooms, garlic, and green onions and cook for 2 minutes, stirring constantly.

4 Return the scallops to the pan. Add the heavy cream and brandy, stirring well to mix.

5 Season with salt and pepper to taste and heat to warm through.

6 Garnish with fresh dill sprigs and serve with rice.

COOK'S TIP

Scallops, which consist of a large, round white muscle with bright orange roe, are the most delicious seafood in the prettiest of shells. The rounded half of the shell can be used as a dish in which to serve the scallops.

Salmon with Caper Sauce

The richness of salmon is beautifully balanced by the tangy capers in this creamy herb sauce.

NUTRITIONAL INFORMATION

Calories	302	Sugars	.........0g
Protein	........21g	Fat	..........24g
Carbohydrate	....1g	Saturates	......9g

5 MINS   25 MINS

SERVES 4

INGREDIENTS

4 salmon fillets, skinned

1 fresh bay leaf

few black peppercorns

1 tsp white wine vinegar

⅔ cup fish stock

3 tbsp heavy cream

1 tbsp capers

1 tbsp chopped fresh dill

1 tbsp chopped fresh chives

1 tsp cornstarch

2 tbsp skim milk

salt and pepper

new potatoes, to serve

TO GARNISH

fresh dill sprigs

chive flowers

1 Lay the salmon fillets in a shallow ovenproof dish. Add the bay leaf, peppercorns, vinegar, and stock.

2 Cover with foil and bake in a preheated oven at 350°F for 15–20 minutes until the flesh is opaque and flakes easily when tested with a fork.

3 Transfer the fish to warmed serving plates, cover, and keep warm.

4 Strain the cooking liquid into a saucepan. Stir in the cream, capers, dill, and chives and seasoning to taste.

5 Blend the cornstarch with the milk. Add to the saucepan and heat, stirring, until thickened slightly. Boil for 1 minute.

6 Spoon the sauce over the salmon, garnish with dill sprigs and chive flowers.

7 Serve with new potatoes.

COOK'S TIP

Ask the fish store to skin the fillets for you. The cooking time for the salmon will depend on the thickness of the fish: the thin tail end of the salmon takes the least time to cook.

Fish with Black Bean Sauce

Any firm and delicate fish steaks, such as salmon or salmon trout, can be cooked by the same method.

NUTRITIONAL INFORMATION

Calories	194	Sugars	.......0.2g
Protein	........27g	Fat	...........9g
Carbohydrate	....1g	Saturates	......1g

5 MINS   20 MINS

SERVES 6

INGREDIENTS

1 sea bass or trout, weighing about 1 lb 9 oz, cleaned

1 tsp salt

1 tbsp sesame oil

2-3 green onions, cut in half lengthways

1 tbsp light soy sauce

1 tbsp Chinese rice wine or dry sherry

1 tbsp finely shredded fresh ginger

1 tbsp oil

2 tbsp crushed black bean sauce

2 finely shredded green onions

fresh cilantro leaves, to garnish (optional)

lemon slices, to garnish

1 Score both sides of the fish with diagonal cuts at 1 inch intervals. Rub both the inside and outside of the fish with salt and sesame oil.

2 Place the fish on top of the green onions on a heat-proof platter. Blend the soy sauce and wine with the ginger shreds and pour evenly all over the fish.

3 Place the fish on the platter in a very hot steamer (or inside a wok on a rack), cover, and steam vigorously for 12-15 minutes.

  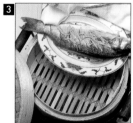

4 Heat the oil until hot, then blend in the black bean sauce. Remove the fish from the steamer and place on a serving dish.

5 Pour the hot black bean sauce over the whole length of the fish and place the shredded green onions on top. Place the fish on a platter and serve garnished with cilantro leaves (if using) and lemon slices.

COOK'S TIP

If using fish steaks, rub them with the salt and sesame oil, but do not score with a knife. The fish may require less cooking, depending on the thickness of the steaks—test with a skewer after about 8 minutes to check whether they are done.

Sole Fillets with Grapes

Fish is ideal for a quick meal, especially when cut into strips as in this recipe—it takes only minutes to cook.

1 Cut the fish into strips about 1¾ inches long and put into a frying pan with the onions, wine, and seasoning.

2 Bring to a boil, cover, and simmer for 4 minutes. Carefully transfer the fish to a warm serving dish. Cover and keep warm.

3 Mix the cornstarch and milk, then add to the pan with the dill and cream. Bring to a boil, and boil, stirring, for 2 minutes until thickened.

4 Add the grapes and lemon juice and heat through gently for 1–2 minutes, then pour over the fish. Garnish with dill and serve with rice and zucchini ribbons.

NUTRITIONAL INFORMATION

Calories 226   Sugars 6g
Protein ....23g   Fat 9g
Carbohydrate ....9g   Saturates 4g

5 MINS   10 MINS

SERVES 4

INGREDIENTS

1 lb 2 oz sole fillets

4 green onions, white and green parts, sliced diagonally

½ cup dry white wine

1 tbsp cornstarch

2 tbsp skim milk

2 tbsp chopped fresh dill

¼ cup heavy cream

4½ oz seedless green grapes

1 tsp lemon juice

salt and pepper

fresh dill sprigs, to garnish

TO SERVE

Basmati rice

zucchini ribbons

COOK'S TIP

Dill has a fairly strong aniseed flavor that goes very well with fish. The feathery leaves are particularly attractive when used as a garnish.

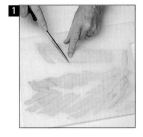  

Caribbean Shrimp

This is an ideal recipe for cooks who have difficulty in finding raw shrimp.

NUTRITIONAL INFORMATION

Calories 110   Sugars 15g
Protein . . . . .5g   Fat 4g
Carbohydrate . . .15g   Saturates 3g

🐷 🐷 🐷

40 MINS   15 MINS

SERVES 4

INGREDIENTS

16 cooked jumbo shrimp

1 small pineapple

flaked coconut, to garnish (optional)

MARINADE

⅔ cup pineapple juice

2 tbsp white wine vinegar

2 tbsp brown sugar

2 tbsp shredded coconut

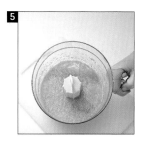

1 If they are unpeeled, peel the shrimp, leaving the tails attached if preferred.

2 Peel the pineapple and cut it in half lengthways. Cut one pineapple half into wedges then into chunks.

3 To make the marinade, mix together half of the pineapple juice and the vinegar, sugar, and coconut in a shallow, non-metallic dish. Add the peeled shrimp and pineapple chunks and toss until well coated. Leave the shrimp and pineapple to marinate for at least 30 minutes.

4 Remove the pineapple and shrimp from the marinade and thread them onto skewers. Reserve the marinade.

5 Strain the marinade and place in a food processor. Roughly chop the remaining pineapple and add to the processor with the remaining pineapple juice. Process the pineapple for a few seconds to produce a thick sauce.

6 Pour the sauce into a small saucepan. Bring to a boil, then simmer for about 5 minutes. If you prefer, you can heat up the sauce by the side of the barbecue.

7 Transfer the kabobs to the barbecue and brush with some of the sauce. Barbecue for about 5 minutes until the kabobs are piping hot. Turn the kabobs, brushing occasionally with the sauce.

8 Serve the kabobs with extra sauce, sprinkled with flaked coconut (if using).

Curried Crab

If you can buy fresh crab, clean the shell and brush lightly with oil and use as a container for the crab meat.

NUTRITIONAL INFORMATION

Calories 272	Sugars 5g
Protein 27g	Fat 16g
Carbohydrate 5g	Saturates 2g

5 MINS   15 MINS

SERVES 4

INGREDIENTS

2 tbsp mustard oil

1 tbsp ghee or vegetable oil

1 onion, chopped finely

2 inch piece fresh ginger, grated

2 garlic cloves, peeled but left whole

1 tsp ground turmeric

1 tsp salt

1 tsp chili powder

2 fresh green chilies, chopped

1 tsp paprika

½ cup brown crab meat

1½ cups white crab meat

1 cup low-fat plain yogurt

1 tsp garam masala

Basmati rice, to serve

fresh cilantro, to garnish

1 Heat the mustard oil in a large, preferably non-stick frying pan, wok, or saucepan.

2 When it starts to smoke, add the ghee or oil and onion. Stir for 3 minutes over a medium heat until the onion is soft.

3 Stir in the ginger and whole garlic cloves.

4 Add the turmeric, salt, chili powder, chilies, and paprika. Mix thoroughly.

5 Increase the heat and add the crab meat and yogurt. Simmer, stirring occasionally, for 10 minutes until the sauce is thickened slightly.

6 Add garam masala to taste.

7 Serve hot, over plain Basmati rice, with the fresh cilantro either chopped or in sprigs.

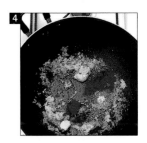

COOK'S TIP

For an unusual combination of flavors, mix the crabmeat with segments of grapefruit in a mayonnaise. Sprinkle with slivers of almonds.

Spicy Fish & Potato Fritters

You need nice, floury-textured main crop potatoes for making these tasty fritters. Any white fish of your choice may be used.

NUTRITIONAL INFORMATION

Calories	349	Sugars	........4g
Protein	........31g	Fat	..........8g
Carbohydrate	...41g	Saturates	......1g

 15 MINS   25 MINS

SERVES 4

I N G R E D I E N T S

1 lb 2 oz potatoes, peeled and cut into even-sized pieces

1 lb 2 oz white fish fillets, such as cod or haddock, skinned and boned

6 green onions, sliced

1 fresh green chili, seeded

2 garlic cloves, peeled

1 tsp salt

1 tbsp medium or hot curry paste

2 eggs, beaten

2½ cups fresh white bread crumbs

vegetable oil, for shallow frying

mango chutney, to serve

lime wedges and cilantro sprigs, to garnish

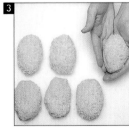

1 Cook the potatoes in a pan of boiling, salted water until tender. Drain well, return the potatoes to the pan, and place over a moderate heat for a few moments to dry off. Cool slightly, then place in a food processor with the fish, onions, chili, garlic, salt, and curry paste. Process until the ingredients are very finely chopped and blended.

2 Turn the potato mixture into a bowl and mix in 2 tablespoons of beaten egg and 1 cup of bread crumbs. Place the remaining beaten egg and bread crumbs in separate dishes.

3 Divide the fish mixture into 8 and, using a spoon to help you (the mixture is quite soft), dip first in the beaten egg, then coat in the bread crumbs, and then carefully shape the mixture into ovals.

4 Heat enough oil in a large frying pan for shallow frying and fry the fritters over moderate heat for 3-4 minutes, turning frequently, until golden brown and cooked through.

5 Drain on absorbent paper towels and garnish with lime wedges and cilantro sprigs. Serve hot, with mango chutney.

Five-Spice Salmon

Five-spice powder is a blend of star anise, fennel, cinnamon, cloves, and Szechuan peppercorns (farchiew) that is often used in Chinese dishes.

NUTRITIONAL INFORMATION

Calories 267	Sugars 3g	
Protein 24g	Fat 17g	
Carbohydrate 4g	Saturates 3g	

 15 MINS 15 MINS

SERVES 4

I N G R E D I E N T S

4 salmon fillets, skinned, 4½ oz each

2 tsp five-spice powder

1 large leek

1 large carrot

4 oz snow peas

1 inch piece fresh ginger

2 tbsp ginger wine

2 tbsp light soy sauce

1 tbsp vegetable oil

salt and pepper

TO GARNISH

shredded leek

fresh ginger, shredded

carrot, shredded

1 Wash the salmon and pat dry on paper towels. Rub the five-spice powder into both sides of the fish and season with salt and pepper. Set aside until required.

2 Trim the leek, slice it down the center, and rinse under cold water to remove any dirt. Finely shred the leek. Peel the carrot and cut it into very thin strips. Top and tail the snow peas and cut them into shreds. Peel the ginger and slice thinly into strips.

3 Place all of the vegetables into a large bowl and toss in the ginger wine and 1 tablespoon of soy sauce.

4 Preheat the broiler to medium. Place the salmon fillets on the rack and brush with the remaining soy sauce. Cook for 2–3 minutes on each side until cooked through.

5 While the salmon is cooking, heat the oil in a non-stick wok or large frying pan and stir-fry the vegetables for 5 minutes until just tender. Take care that you do not overcook the vegetables—they should still have "bite". Transfer to serving plates. Drain the salmon on kitchen paper and serve on a bed of stir-fried vegetables. Garnish with shredded leek, ginger, and carrot.

COOK'S TIP

Five-spice powder is strong and pungent and should be used sparingly.

Flounder with Mushrooms

The moist texture of broiled fish is complemented by the texture of the mushrooms.

NUTRITIONAL INFORMATION

Calories 243   Sugars 2g
Protein ....30g   Fat 13g
Carbohydrate ....2g   Saturates 3g

10 MINS   20 MINS

SERVES 4

INGREDIENTS

4 × 5½ oz white-skinned flounder fillets

2 tbsp lime juice

celery salt and pepper

⅓ cup low-fat spread

2½ cups mixed small mushrooms such as button, oyster, shiitake, chanterelle, or morel, sliced or quartered

4 tomatoes, skinned (see page 18), seeded, and chopped

basil leaves, to garnish

tossed salad, to serve

1 Line a broiler rack with baking parchment and place the fish on top.

2 Sprinkle over the lime juice and season with celery salt and pepper.

3 Place under a preheated moderate broiler and cook for 7–8 minutes without turning, until just cooked. Keep warm.

4 Meanwhile, gently melt the low fat spread in a non-stick frying pan, add the mushrooms, and fry for 4–5 minutes over a low heat until cooked through.

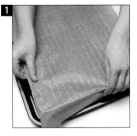

5 Gently heat the tomatoes in a small saucepan.

6 Spoon the mushrooms, with any pan juices, and the tomatoes over the fish.

7 Garnish the broiled fish with the basil leaves and serve with a tossed salad.

COOK'S TIP

Mushrooms are ideal in a low-fat diet, as they are packed full of flavor and contain no fat. More "meaty" types of mushroom, such as crimini, will take slightly longer to cook.

Indian Cod with Tomatoes

Quick and easy—cod steaks are cooked in a rich tomato and coconut sauce to produce tender, succulent results.

NUTRITIONAL INFORMATION

Calories	194	Sugars	.........6g
Protein	........21g	Fat	...........9g
Carbohydrate	....7g	Saturates	......1g

5 MINS   25 MINS

SERVES 4

I N G R E D I E N T S

3 tbsp vegetable oil

4 cod steaks, about 1 inch thick

salt and freshly ground black pepper

1 onion, peeled and finely chopped

2 garlic cloves, peeled and crushed

1 red bell pepper, seeded and chopped

1 tsp ground coriander

1 tsp ground cumin

1 tsp ground turmeric

½ tsp garam masala

1 x 14 oz can chopped tomatoes

⅔ cup coconut milk

1-2 tbsp chopped fresh cilantro or parsley

VARIATION

The mixture may be flavored with a tablespoonful of curry powder or curry paste (mild, medium, or hot, according to personal preference) instead of the mixture of spices in step 2, if wished.

1 Heat the oil in a frying pan, add the fish steaks, season with salt and pepper, and fry until browned on both sides (but not cooked through). Remove from the pan and reserve.

2 Add the onion, garlic, red bell pepper, and spices and cook very gently for 2 minutes, stirring frequently. Add the tomatoes, bring to a boil, and simmer for 5 minutes.

3 Add the fish steaks to the pan and simmer gently for 8 minutes or until the fish is cooked through.

4 Remove from the pan and keep warm on a serving dish. Add the coconut milk and cilantro or parsley to the pan and reheat gently.

5 Spoon the sauce over the cod steaks and serve immediately.

Steamed Stuffed Snapper

Red mullet may be used instead of the snapper, although they are a little more difficult to stuff because of their size. Use one mullet per person.

NUTRITIONAL INFORMATION

Calories	406	Sugar	.........4g
Protein	........68g	Fat	...........9g
Carbohydrate	....9g	Saturates	.......0g

20 MINS   10 MINS

SERVES 4

I N G R E D I E N T S

3 lb whole snapper, cleaned and scaled

16 oz spinach

orange slices and shredded green onion, to garnish

S T U F F I N G

2 cups cooked long-grain rice

1 tsp grated fresh ginger

2 green onions, finely chopped

2 tsp light soy sauce

1 tsp sesame oil

½ tsp ground star anise

1 orange, segmented and chopped

1 Rinse the fish inside and out under cold running water and pat dry with paper towels.

2 Blanch the spinach for 40 seconds, rinse in cold water and drain well, pressing out as much moisture as possible.

3 Arrange the spinach on a heatproof plate and place the fish on top.

4 To make the stuffing, mix together the cooked rice, grated ginger, green onions, soy sauce, sesame oil, star anise, and orange in a bowl.

5 Spoon the stuffing into the body cavity of the fish, pressing it in well with a spoon.

6 Cover the plate and cook in a steamer for 10 minutes, or until the fish is cooked through.

7 Transfer the fish to a warmed serving dish, garnish with orange slices and shredded green onion, and serve.

COOK'S TIP

The name snapper covers a family of tropical and subtropical fish that vary in color. They may be red, orange, pink, grey or blue-green. Some are striped or spotted and they range in size from about 6 inches to 3 ft.

Smoky Fish Skewers

The combination of fresh and smoked fish gives these kabobs a special flavor. Choose thick fish fillets to get good-sized pieces.

NUTRITIONAL INFORMATION

Calories 221	Sugars 0g
Protein 33g	Fat 10g
Carbohydrate 0g	Saturates 1g

4 HOURS   10 MINS

SERVES 4

I N G R E D I E N T S

12 oz smoked cod fillet

12 oz cod fillet

8 large raw shrimp

8 bay leaves

fresh dill, to garnish (optional)

M A R I N A D E

4 tbsp sunflower oil, plus a little for brushing

2 tbsp lemon or lime juice

rind of ½ lemon or lime, grated

¼ tsp dried dill

salt and pepper

1 Skin both types of cod and cut the flesh into bite-size pieces. Peel the shrimp, leaving just the tail.

2 To make the marinade, combine the oil, lemon or lime juice and rind, dill, and salt and pepper to taste in a shallow, non-metallic dish.

3 Place the prepared fish in the marinade and stir together until the fish is well coated on all sides. Leave the fish to marinate for 1–4 hours.

4 Thread the fish on to 4 skewers, alternating the 2 types of cod with the shrimp and bay leaves.

5 Cover the rack with lightly oiled kitchen foil and place the fish skewers on top of the foil.

6 Barbecue the fish skewers over hot coals for 5-10 minutes, basting with any remaining marinade, turning once.

7 Garnish the skewers with fresh dill (if using) and serve immediately.

COOK'S TIP

Cod fillet can be rather flaky, so choose the thicker end which is easier to cut into chunky pieces. Cook the fish on kitchen foil rather than directly on the rack, so that if the fish breaks away from the skewer, it is not wasted.

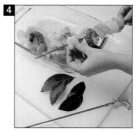

Crab-Stuffed Red Snapper

This popular fish is pinkish-red in color and has moist, tender flesh. For this recipe it is steamed, but it can also be baked or braised.

NUTRITIONAL INFORMATION

Calories 205	Sugars 0.1g
Protein 36g	Fat 6g
Carbohydrate . . .0.1g	Saturates 1g

10 MINS   25 MINS

SERVES 4

I N G R E D I E N T S

4 red snappers, cleaned and scaled, about
   6 oz each

2 tbsp dry sherry

salt and pepper

wedges of lime, to garnish

red chili strips, to garnish

stir-fried shredded vegetables, to serve

S T U F F I N G

1 small red chili

1 garlic clove

1 green onion

½ tsp finely grated lime rind

1 tbsp lime juice

3½ oz white crab meat, flaked

1 Rinse the fish and pat dry on paper towels. Season inside and out and place in a shallow dish. Spoon over the sherry and set aside.

2 Meanwhile, make the stuffing. Carefully halve, deseed, and finely chop the chili. Place in a small bowl.

3 Peel and finely chop the garlic. Trim and finely chop the green onion. Add to the chili together with the grated lime rind, lime juice, and the flaked crab meat.

4 Season with salt and pepper to taste and combine.

5 Spoon some of the stuffing into the cavity of each fish.

6 Bring a large saucepan of water to a boil. Arrange the fish in a steamer lined with baking parchment or in a large strainer and place over the boiling water.

7 Cover and steam for 10 minutes. Turn the fish over and steam for a further 10 minutes or until the fish is cooked through.

8 Drain the fish and transfer to serving plates.

9 Garnish with wedges of lime and strips of chili, and serve the fish on a bed of stir-fried vegetables.

Lemony Swordfish Skewers

A simple basting sauce is brushed over these tasty kabobs. When served with crusty bread, they make a perfect light meal.

NUTRITIONAL INFORMATION

Calories 191	Sugars 2g	
Protein 21g	Fat 11g	
Carbohydrate 1g	Saturates 1g	

10 MINS   15 MINS

SERVES 4

INGREDIENTS

1 lb swordfish tail

2 zucchini

1 lemon

12 cherry tomatoes

8 bay leaves

SAUCE

3 tbsp olive oil

2 tbsp lemon juice

1 tsp chopped, fresh thyme

½ tsp lemon pepper

salt

TO SERVE

green salad leaves

fresh, crusty bread

1 Cut the swordfish into 2 inch chunks.

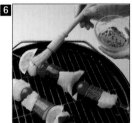

2 Cut the zucchini into thick slices and the lemon into wedges.

3 Thread the swordfish, zucchini, lemon, tomatoes, and bay leaves on to 4 skewers.

4 To make the basting sauce, combine the oil, lemon juice, thyme, lemon pepper, and salt to taste in a small bowl.

5 Brush the basting sauce liberally all over the fish, lemon, tomatoes, and bay leaves on the skewers.

6 Cook the skewers on the barbecue for about 15 minutes over medium-hot coals, basting them frequently with the sauce, until the fish is cooked through. Transfer the skewers to plates and serve with green salad leaves and wedges of crusty bread.

VARIATION

Use flounder fillets instead of the swordfish, if you prefer. Allow two fillets per person, and skin and cut each fillet lengthways into two. Roll up each piece and thread them on to the skewers.

Ocean Pie

A tasty fish pie combining a mixture of fish and shellfish. You can use a wide variety of fish—whatever is available.

NUTRITIONAL INFORMATION

Calories 599   Sugars 8g
Protein ....45g   Fat 21g
Carbohydrate ...58g   Saturates 4g

 15 MINS   1 HOUR

SERVES 4

I N G R E D I E N T S

1 lb 2 oz cod or haddock fillet, skinned

8 oz salmon steak

2 cups skim milk

1 bay leaf

2 lb potatoes

⅓ cup peeled shrimp, thawed if frozen

¼ cup margarine

4 tbsp all-purpose flour

2–4 tbsp white wine

1 tsp chopped fresh dill or ½ tsp dried dill

2 tbsp drained capers

salt and pepper

few whole shrimp in their shells,
   to garnish

1 Put the fish into a saucepan with 1¼ cups of the milk, the bay leaf, and seasoning. Bring to a boil, cover, and simmer gently for 10–15 minutes until tender.

2 Coarsely chop the potatoes and cook in boiling salted water until tender.

3 Drain the fish, reserving 1¼ cups of the cooking liquid (make up with more milk if necessary). Flake the fish, discarding any bones, and place in a shallow ovenproof dish. Add the shrimp.

4 Melt half of the margarine in a saucepan, add the flour, and cook, stirring, for a minute or so. Gradually stir in the reserved stock and the wine and bring to a boil. Add the dill, capers, and seasoning to taste and simmer until thickened. Pour over the fish and mix well.

5 Drain the potatoes and mash, adding the remaining margarine, seasoning, and sufficient milk to give a piping consistency.

6 Put the mashed potato into a pastry bag. Use a large star tip and pipe over the fish. Cook in a preheated oven at 400°F for about 25 minutes until piping hot and browned. Serve garnished with shrimp.

Sole & Smoked Salmon Rolls

In this elegant dish, the delicate flavor of sole and salmon blend together perfectly with a light, citrus filling.

NUTRITIONAL INFORMATION

Calories 191   Sugars 3g
Protein . . . . .31g   Fat 4g
Carbohydrate . . . .9g   Saturates 1g

1 HOUR   20 MINS

SERVES 4

I N G R E D I E N T S

1 cup fresh whole wheat bread crumbs

½ tsp grated lime rind

1 tbsp lime juice

¼ cup low-fat cream cheese

4 × 4½ oz sole fillets

2 oz smoked salmon

⅔ cup Fresh Fish Stock (see page 30)

⅔ cup low-fat plain yogurt

1 tbsp chopped fresh chervil

salt and pepper

fresh chervil, to garnish

T O   S E R V E

selection of freshly steamed vegetables

lime wedges

COOK'S TIP

When buying fresh fish, choose fish with a bright eye and red gills. The fish should be firm to the touch, with just a slight "fishy" smell.

1 In a mixing bowl, combine the bread crumbs, lime rind and juice, cream cheese, and seasoning to form a soft stuffing mixture.

2 Skin the sole fillets by inserting a sharp knife in between the skin and flesh at the tail end. Holding the skin in your fingers and keeping it taut, strip the flesh away from the skin.

3 Halve the sole fillets lengthways. Place strips of smoked salmon over the skinned side of each fillet, trimming the salmon as necessary.

4 Spoon one-eighth of the stuffing on to each fish fillet and press down along the fish with the back of a spoon. Carefully roll up from the head to the tail end. Place, seam-side down, in an ovenproof dish and pour in the stock. Bake in a preheated oven at 375°F for 15 minutes.

5 Using a fish slice, transfer the fish to a warm serving plate, cover, and keep warm. Pour the cooking juices into a saucepan and add the yogurt and chopped chervil. Season to taste and heat gently without boiling. Garnish the fish rolls with chervil and serve with the yogurt sauce, and the steamed vegetables and lime wedges.

Citrus Fish Kabobs

Use your favorite fish for this dish as long as it is firm enough to thread on to skewers. The tang of orange makes this a refreshing meal.

NUTRITIONAL INFORMATION

Calories 333   Sugars 10g
Protein . . . . .31g   Fat 14g
Carbohydrate . . .10g   Saturates 3g

2½ HOURS   10 MINS

SERVES 4

INGREDIENTS

1 lb firm white fish fillets (such as cod or swordfish)

1 lb thick salmon fillet

2 large oranges

1 pink grapefruit

1 bunch fresh bay leaves

1 tsp finely grated lemon rind

3 tbsp lemon juice

2 tsp clear honey

2 garlic cloves, crushed

salt and pepper

TO SERVE

crusty bread

tossed salad

1 Skin the white fish and the salmon, rinse, and pat dry on paper towels. Cut each fillet into 16 pieces.

2 Using a sharp knife, remove the skin and pith from the oranges and grapefruit. Cut out the segments of flesh, removing all remaining traces of the pith and dividing membrane.

3 Thread the pieces of fish alternately with the orange and grapefruit segments and the bay leaves on to 8 skewers. Place the kabobs in a shallow dish.

4 In a small bowl, mix together the lemon rind and juice, the honey, and garlic.

5 Pour over the fish kabobs and season well. Cover and chill for 2 hours, turning occasionally.

6 Preheat the broiler to medium. Remove the fish kabobs from the marinade and place on the rack.

7 Cook for 7–8 minutes, turning once, until cooked through.

8 Drain, transfer to serving plates, and serve with crusty bread and a fresh tossed salad.

Shrimp Curry & Fruit Sauce

Serve this lightly-spiced dish as part of a buffet meal, or as a refreshingly different lunch dish, with a bowl of rice.

NUTRITIONAL INFORMATION

Calories	538	Sugars	........28g
Protein	........40g	Fat	.........28g
Carbohydrate	...33g	Saturates	.....15g

  30 MINS 20 MINS

SERVES 4

INGREDIENTS

2 tbsp vegetable oil

2 tbsp butter

2 onions, finely chopped

2 garlic cloves, finely chopped

1 tsp cumin seeds, lightly crushed

1 tsp ground turmeric

1 tsp paprika

½ tsp chili powder, or to taste

2 oz creamed coconut

1 x 14 oz can chopped tomatoes

1 tbsp tomato paste

1 lb 2 oz frozen cooked shrimps, defrosted

½ cucumber, thinly diced

⅔ cup low-fat plain yogurt

2 hard-boiled eggs, quartered

salt

cilantro and onion rings, to garnish

FRUIT SAUCE

1¼ cups low-fat plain yogurt

¼ tsp salt

1 garlic clove, crushed

2 tbsp chopped mint

4 tbsp seedless raisins

1 small pomegranate

1 Heat the oil and butter in a frying pan. Add the chopped onions and fry until translucent. Add the garlic and fry for a further minute, until softened but not browned.

2 Stir in the spices and cook for 2 minutes, stirring. Stir in the creamed coconut, chopped tomatoes, and tomato paste and bring to a boil. Simmer for 10 minutes, or until the sauce has thickened slightly. It should not be at all runny.

3 Remove the pan from the heat and set aside to cool. Stir in the shrimps, cucumber, and yogurt. Taste the sauce and adjust the seasoning if necessary. Cover and chill until ready to serve.

4 To make the fruit sauce, place everything except the pomegrantes into a bowl. Cut the pomegranate in half, scoop out the seeds, discarding the white membrane, and stir into the fruit mixture, reserving a few for garnish.

5 Transfer the curry to a serving dish and arrange the hard-boiled egg, cilantro, and onion rings on top. Serve the sauce separately, sprinkled with the reserved pomegranate seeds.

Bajan Fish

Bajan seasoning comes from Barbados and can be used with all kinds of meat, fish, poultry, and game. Add more chili if you like it really hot.

NUTRITIONAL INFORMATION

Calories ....247 Sugars 4g
Protein ....27g Fat 12g
Carbohydrate ....5g Saturates 1g

45 MINS 15 MINS

SERVES 4

INGREDIENTS

1 lb 2 oz–1 lb 6 oz swordfish, boned and cubed

2 large carrots

6-8 oz baby corn cobs

3 tbsp sunflower oil

1 yellow bell pepper, cored, seeded, and thinly sliced

1 tbsp wine vinegar

⅔ cup fish or vegetable stock

1 tbsp lemon juice

2 tbsp sherry

1 tsp cornstarch

salt and pepper

fresh herbs and lemon slices, to garnish

BAJAN SEASONING

1 small onion, quartered

2 shallots

3-4 garlic cloves, crushed

4-6 large green onions, sliced

small handful of fresh parsley

2-3 sprigs of fresh thyme

small strip of green chili pepper, seeds removed, or ½–¼ tsp chili powder

½ tsp salt

¼ tsp freshly ground black pepper

2 tbsp brown rum or red wine vinegar

1 Process the ingredients for the Bajan seasoning very finely. Put the fish in a dish, spread with the seasoning to coat evenly. Cover and chill for 30 minutes.

2 Cut the carrots into narrow 1½ inch slices. Slice the baby corn diagonally. Heat 2 tbsp of oil in the wok, swirling it around until really hot. Add the fish and stir-fry for 3-4 minutes. Remove to a bowl and keep warm.

3 Add the remaining oil and stir-fry the carrots and corn for 2 minutes. Add the bell pepper and stir-fry for another minute. Return the fish and juices to the wok and stir-fry for 1-2 minutes.

4 Blend the vinegar, stock, lemon juice, sherry, and seasoning with the cornstarch. Stir into the wok and boil until thickened. Serve garnished with herbs and lemon.

Shrimp Dansak

The spicy lentil purée sauce in this recipe is of Parsi origin and is popular throughout the Indian continent.

NUTRITIONAL INFORMATION

Calories	379	Sugars	........5g
Protein	........45g	Fat	..........12g
Carbohydrate	...25g	Saturates	......2g

1¼ HOURS   1¼ HOURS

SERVES 4

INGREDIENTS

1 lb 9 oz uncooked jumbo shrimp in their shells, or 1 lb 7 oz peeled jumbo shrimp, or cooked, peeled Atlantic shrimp

1 tsp salt

1 dried bay leaf

3 garlic cloves, crushed

⅓ cup split yellow peas, soaked for 1 hour in cold water and drained

¼ cup red lentils

1 carrot, chopped

1 potato, cut into large dice

3 tbsp drained canned corn kernels

3 tbsp oil

2 onions, chopped

½ tsp yellow mustard seeds

1½ tsp coriander seeds, ground

½ tsp cumin seeds, ground

½ tsp fenugreek seeds, ground

1½ tsp ground turmeric

1 dried red chili

15 oz can tomatoes

½ tsp garam masala

3 tbsp chopped fresh cilantro

2 tbsp chopped fresh mint

1 Reserve 4 shrimp for garnish and peel the rest. Cook those for the garnish in boiling water for 3–5 minutes.

2 Fill a pan with water and add the salt, bay leaf, ⅓ of the garlic, and the split peas. Bring to a boil and cook for 15 minutes. Add the lentils, carrot, and potato and cook for a further 15 minutes. Drain, discarding the garlic and bay leaf, and blend with the corn until smooth.

3 Heat the oil in a large saucepan and cook the remaining garlic and onion for 3–4 minutes. Add the mustard seeds and when they start to pop, stir in the other spices. Add the peeled shrimp and stir for 1–2 minutes. Add the tomatoes and lentil purée, and simmer, uncovered, for 30–40 minutes. Stir in the garam masala and season. Serve sprinkled with cilantro and mint and garnished with the shrimp.

Baked Red Snapper

You can substitute other whole fish for the snapper, or use cutlets of cod or halibut.

NUTRITIONAL INFORMATION

Calories 519	Sugars 12g
Protein 61g	Fat 23g
Carbohydrate . . .18g	Saturates 3g

20 MINS 50 MINS

SERVES 4

INGREDIENTS

1 red snapper, about 2 lb 12 oz, cleaned

juice of 2 limes, or 1 lemon

4-5 sprigs of thyme or parsley

3 tbsp olive oil

1 large onion, chopped

2 garlic cloves, finely chopped

1 x 15 oz can chopped tomatoes

2 tbsp tomato paste

2 tbsp red wine vinegar

5 tbsp low-fat plain yogurt

2 tbsp chopped parsley

2 tsp dried oregano

6 tbsp dry breadcrumbs

¼ cup low-fat yogurt cheese, crumbled

salt and pepper

SALAD

1 small lettuce, thickly sliced

10-12 young spinach leaves, torn

½ small cucumber, sliced and quartered

4 green onions, thickly sliced

3 tbsp chopped parsley

2 tbsp olive oil

2 tbsp plain low-fat yogurt

1 tbsp red wine vinegar

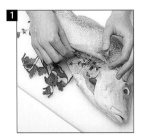

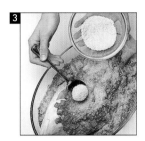

1 Sprinkle the lime or lemon juice inside and over the fish and season. Place the herbs inside the fish.

2 Heat the oil in a pan and fry the onion until translucent. Stir in the garlic and cook for 1 minute, then add the chopped tomatoes, tomato paste, and vinegar. Simmer, uncovered, for 5 minutes. Allow the sauce to cool, then stir in the yogurt, parsley, and oregano.

3 Pour half of the sauce into an ovenproof dish just large enough for the fish. Add the fish, pour the remainder of the sauce over it, and sprinkle with bread crumbs. Bake uncovered for 30-35 minutes. Sprinkle the cheese over the fish and serve with lime wedges and dill sprigs.

4 Arrange the salad ingredients in a bowl. Whisk the oil, yogurt, and vinegar and pour over the salad.

Pan-Seared Halibut

Liven up firm steaks of white fish with a spicy, colorful relish. Use red onions for a slightly sweeter flavor.

NUTRITIONAL INFORMATION

Calories 197	Sugars 1g	
Protein 31g	Fat 7g	
Carbohydrate 2g	Saturates 1g	

 55 MINS   30 MINS

SERVES 4

I N G R E D I E N T S

1 tsp olive oil

4 halibut steaks, skinned, 6 oz each

½ tsp cornstarch mixed with
  2 tsp cold water

salt and pepper

2 tbsp fresh chives, snipped, to garnish

R E D   O N I O N   R E L I S H

2 tsp olive oil

2 medium red onions

6 shallots

1 tbsp lemon juice

2 tbsp red wine vinegar

2 tsp sugar

⅔ cup Fresh Fish Stock (see page 30)

1 To make the relish, peel and thinly shred the onions and shallots. Place in a small bowl and toss in the lemon juice.

2 Heat the oil in a pan and fry the onions and shallots for 3–4 minutes until just softened.

3 Add the vinegar and sugar and continue to cook for a further 2 minutes over a high heat. Pour in the stock and season well. Bring to a boil and simmer gently for a further 8–9 minutes until the sauce has thickened and is slightly reduced.

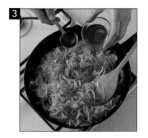

4 Brush a non-stick, ridged frying pan with oil and heat until hot. Press the fish steaks into the pan to seal, lower the heat, and cook for 4 minutes. Turn the fish over and cook for 4–5 minutes until cooked through. Drain on paper towels and keep warm.

5 Stir the cornstarch paste into the onion sauce and heat through, stirring, until thickened. Season to taste.

6 Pile the relish on to 4 warm serving plates and place a halibut steak on top of each. Garnish with chives.

COOK'S TIP

If raw onions make your eyes water, try peeling them under a tap of cold, running water. Alternatively, stand or sit well back from the onion so that your face isn't hanging over it.

Fish & Seafood Chowder

Served with warm crusty bread and a salad, this tasty soup makes a substantial lunch or supper dish.

NUTRITIONAL INFORMATION

Calories	286	Sugars	.........6g
Protein	........30g	Fat	..........3g
Carbohydrate	...31g	Saturates	......1g

20 MINS   25 MINS

SERVES 4

I N G R E D I E N T S

2 lb 4 oz mussels in their shells

1 large onion, thinly sliced

2 garlic cloves, chopped

3 bay leaves

a few stalks of parsley

a few stalks of thyme

1¼ cups water

8 oz smoked haddock fillets

1 lb 2 oz potatoes, peeled and diced

4 celery stalks, thickly sliced

9 oz can corn kernels, drained and rinsed

⅔ cup low-fat plain yogurt

1 tsp cornstarch

⅔ cup dry white wine, or dry cider

½ tsp cayenne pepper, or to taste

black pepper

2 tbsp chopped parsley

1 Scrub the mussels, pull off the "beards" and rinse thoroughly. Discard any shells that remain open when tapped.

2 Put the onion, garlic, herbs, water, and the mussels in a large pan. Cover and cook over high heat for 5 minutes, shaking the pan once or twice.

3 Line a colander with cheesecloth and strain the mussel liquid into a bowl. Shell the mussels and discard the rest. Reserve the liquid.

4 Put the haddock and vegetables into a pan, add 2½ cups of cold water, cover, and simmer for 10 minutes. Remove the fish and skin, bone, and flake it. Strain the liquid into the seafood liquid. Reserve the vegetables.

5 Return the cooking liquid to the rinsed pan, add the corn, and bring to a boil. Stir together the yogurt and cornstarch. Stir in a little of the fish liquid, then pour it into the pan. Stir the yogurt in well, then add the reserved fish and vegetables. Add the white wine, season with cayenne and black pepper, and heat the soup gently, without boiling. Season, transfer to a platter, and sprinkle with the parsley.

Fragrant Tuna Steaks

Fresh tuna steaks are very meaty—they have a firm texture, yet the flesh is succulent. Steaks from the belly are best of all.

NUTRITIONAL INFORMATION

Calories	239	Sugars	.......0.1g
Protein	........42g	Fat	..........8g
Carbohydrate	...0.5g	Saturates	......2g

 15 MINS   15 MINS

SERVES 4

INGREDIENTS

4 tuna steaks, 6 oz each

½ tsp finely grated lime rind

1 garlic clove, crushed

2 tsp olive oil

1 tsp ground cumin

1 tsp ground coriander

pepper

1 tbsp lime juice

fresh cilantro, to garnish

TO SERVE

avocado relish (see Cook's Tip, below)

lime wedges

tomato wedges

COOK'S TIP

For the avocado relish, peel and chop a small, ripe avocado. Mix in 1 tbsp lime juice, 1 tbsp freshly chopped cilantro, 1 small finely chopped red onion, and some chopped fresh mango or tomato. Season to taste.

1 Trim the skin from the tuna steaks, rinse, and pat dry on absorbent paper towels.

2 In a small bowl, mix together the lime rind, garlic, olive oil, cumin, ground coriander, and pepper to make a paste.

3 Spread the paste thinly on both sides of the tuna. Heat a non-stick, ridged frying pan until hot and press the tuna steaks into the pan to seal them. Lower the heat and cook for 5 minutes. Turn the fish over and cook for a further 4–5 minutes until the fish is cooked through. Drain on paper towels and transfer to a serving plate.

4 Sprinkle the lime juice and chopped cilantro over the fish. Serve with avocado relish (see Cook's Tip), and tomato and lime wedges.

Sole Paupiettes

A delicate dish of sole fillets rolled up with spinach and shrimp, and served in a creamy ginger sauce.

NUTRITIONAL INFORMATION

Calories . . . . . . .253 Sugars 7g
Protein . . . . .24g Fat 14g
Carbohydrate . . . .9g Saturates 5g

 10 MINS   45 MINS

SERVES 4

INGREDIENTS

4½ oz fresh young spinach leaves

2 soles or large lemon soles or plaice, filleted

4½ oz peeled shrimp, defrosted if frozen

2 tsp sunflower oil

2-4 green onions, finely sliced diagonally

2 thin slices fresh ginger, finely chopped

⅔ cup fish stock or water

2 tsp cornstarch

4 tbsp light cream

6 tbsp low-fat plain yogurt

salt and pepper

whole shrimp, to garnish (optional)

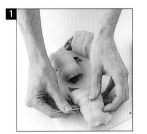

1 Strip the stalks off the spinach, wash, and dry on paper towels. Divide the spinach between the seasoned fish fillets, laying the leaves on the skin side. Divide half the shrimp between them. Roll up the fillets from head to tail and secure with wooden cocktail sticks. Arrange the rolls on a plate in the base of a bamboo steamer.

2 Stand a low metal trivet in the wok and add enough water to come almost to the top of it. Bring to a boil.

Place the bamboo steamer on the trivet, cover with the steamer lid, and then the wok lid, or cover tightly with a domed piece of foil. Steam gently for 30 minutes until the fish is tender and cooked through.

3 Remove the fish rolls and keep warm. Empty the wok and wipe dry with paper towels. Heat the oil in the wok, swirling it around until really hot. Add the green onions and ginger and stir-fry for 1-2 minutes.

4 Add the stock to the wok and bring to a boil. Blend the cornstarch with the cream. Add the yogurt and remaining shrimp to the wok and heat gently until boiling. Add a little sauce to the blended cream and return it all to the wok. Heat gently until thickened and season to taste. Serve the paupiettes with the sauce spooned over and garnished with whole shrimp, if using.

Baked Trout Mexican-Style

Make this dish as hot or as mild as you like by adjusting the amount of red chili. The green chilies are milder and add a pungency to the dish.

NUTRITIONAL INFORMATION

Calories 329	Sugars 5g	
Protein 53g	Fat 10g	
Carbohydrate 6g	Saturates 2g	

10 MINS   30 MINS

SERVES 4

INGREDIENTS

4 trout, 8 oz each

1 small bunch fresh cilantro

4 shallots, shredded finely

1 small yellow bell pepper, deseeded and very finely chopped

1 small red bell pepper, deseeded and very finely chopped

2 green chilies, deseeded and finely chopped

1–2 red chilies, deseeded and finely chopped

1 tbsp lemon juice

1 tbsp white wine vinegar

2 tsp sugar

salt and pepper

fresh cilantro, to garnish

salad leaves, to serve

COOK'S TIP

For the chili bean rice, cook 1¼ cup long-grain white rice. Drain and rinse a 14 oz can kidney beans and stir into the rice with 1 tsp each of ground cumin and coriander. Stir in 4 tbsp chopped fresh cilantro and season.

1 Preheat the oven to 350°F. Wash the trout and pat dry with paper towels. Season and stuff with cilantro leaves.

2 Place the fish side by side in a shallow ovenproof dish. Sprinkle over the shallots, bell peppers, and chilies.

3 Mix together the lemon juice, vinegar, and sugar in a bowl. Spoon over the trout and season with salt and pepper.

Cover the dish and bake for 30 minutes or until the fish is tender and the flesh is opaque.

4 Remove the the fish with a fish slice and drain. Transfer to warm serving plates and spoon the cooking juices over the fish. Garnish with fresh cilantro and serve with salad and chili bean rice (see Cook's Tip).

Soused Trout

In this recipe, fillets of trout are gently poached in a spiced vinegar, left to marinate for 24 hours and served cold with a potato salad.

NUTRITIONAL INFORMATION

Calories 521	Sugars 3g
Protein 61g	Fat 20g
Carbohydrate . . .27g	Saturates 4g

🕐 5 HOURS   ⏱ 35 MINS

SERVES 4

I N G R E D I E N T S

4 trout, about 8–12 oz each, filleted

1 onion, sliced very thinly

2 bay leaves, preferably fresh

sprigs of fresh parsley and dill, or other fresh herbs

10–12 black peppercorns

4–6 cloves

pinch of salt

⅔ cup red wine vinegar

salad leaves, to garnish

P O T A T O   S A L A D

1 lb 2 oz small new potatoes

2 tbsp French dressing

4 tbsp thick low-fat mayonnaise

3–4 green onions, sliced

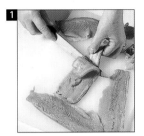

1 Trim the trout fillets, cutting off any pieces of fin. If preferred, remove the skin—use a sharp knife and, beginning at the tail end, carefully cut the flesh from the skin, pressing the knife down firmly as you go.

2 Lightly grease a shallow ovenproof dish and lay the fillets in it, packing them fairly tightly together but keeping them in a single layer. Arrange the sliced onion, bay leaves, and herbs over the fish.

3 Put the peppercorns, cloves, salt, and vinegar into a saucepan and bring almost to a boil. Remove from the heat and pour evenly over the fish. Cover with foil and cook in a preheated oven at 325°F for 15 minutes. Leave until cold, and then chill thoroughly.

4 Cook the potatoes in boiling salted water for 10–15 minutes until just tender. Drain. While still warm, cut into large dice and place in a bowl. Combine the French dressing and mayonnaise, add to the potatoes while warm, and toss evenly. Leave until cold, then sprinkle the potato salad with chopped green onions.

5 Pour a little of the juices over each portion of fish. Garnish with salad leaves and serve with the potato salad.

Char-broiled Mackerel

The sharpness of the apricot glaze complements the oiliness of the fish and has a delicious hint of ginger.

NUTRITIONAL INFORMATION

Calories	343	Sugars	.......21g
Protein	........23g	Fat	..........18g
Carbohydrate	...22g	Saturates	......4g

 5 MINS   10 MINS

SERVES 4

I N G R E D I E N T S

4 mackerel, about 8 oz each

14 oz can apricots in natural juice

3 tbsp brown sugar

3 tbsp Worcestershire sauce

3 tbsp soy sauce

2 tbsp tomato paste

1 tsp ground ginger

dash Tabasco sauce

1 clove garlic, crushed (optional)

salt and pepper

1 Clean and gut the mackerel, removing the heads if preferred. Place the fish in a shallow dish.

2 Drain the apricots, reserving the juice. Roughly chop half of the apricots and set aside. Place the remaining apricots in a food processor with the sugar, Worcestershire sauce, soy sauce, tomato paste, ginger, Tabasco sauce, and garlic (if using) and process until smooth. Alternatively, chop the apricots and mix with the other ingredients. Season to taste.

3 Pour the sauce over the fish, turning them so that they are well coated on both sides. Leave to chill in the refrigerator until required.

4 Transfer the mackerel to the barbecue either directly on the rack or on a piece of greased kitchen foil. Barbecue the mackerel over hot coals for 5–7 minutes, turning once.

5 Spoon any remaining marinade into a saucepan. Add the reserved chopped apricots and about half of the reserved apricot juice and bring to a boil. Reduce the heat and simmer for 2 minutes. Transfer the mackerel to a serving plate and serve with the apricot sauce.

COOK'S TIP

Use a hinged rack if you have one as it will make it much easier to turn the fish during barbecuing.

Ginger Shrimp

Quick and easy to prepare, this dish is also extremely good to eat. Use the larger jumbo shrimp for special occasions, if you prefer.

NUTRITIONAL INFORMATION

Calories ....196 Sugars 5g
Protein ....21g Fat 10g
Carbohydrate ....6g Saturates 1g

15 MINS   25 MINS

SERVES 4

INGREDIENTS

3 medium onions

1 green bell pepper

1 tsp fresh ginger, finely chopped

1 tsp fresh garlic, crushed

1 tsp salt

1 tsp chili powder

2 tbsp lemon juice

12 oz frozen shrimp

3 tbsp oil

14 oz can tomatoes

fresh cilantro leaves, to garnish

TO SERVE

boiled rice

crisp green salad

1 Using a sharp knife, slice the onions and the green bell pepper.

2 Place the ginger, garlic, salt, and chili powder in a small bowl and mix to combine. Add the lemon juice and mix to form a paste.

3 Place the shrimp in a bowl of cold water and set aside to defrost. Drain thoroughly.

4 Heat the oil in a saucepan. Add the onions and fry until golden brown.

5 Add the spice paste to the onions, reduce the heat to low, and cook, stirring and mixing well, for about 3 minutes. Add the tomatoes and the green bell pepper and cook for 5-7 minutes, stirring occasionally.

6 Add the shrimp to the pan and cook for 10 minutes, stirring occasionally. Garnish with fresh cilantro and serve with rice and salad.

COOK'S TIP

Fresh ginger looks like a knobbly potato. The skin should be peeled, then the flesh either grated, finely chopped, or sliced. You can use ground ginger as a substitute, but fresh ginger is far superior.

Vegetarian Dishes

There is more to the vegetarian diet than lentil roast and nut cutlets. For those of you who have cut out meat and fish completely from your diet or if you just want to

reduce your intake of these ingredients, this chapter offers an exciting assortment of vegetarian dishes, ranging from pizzas, to curries, and bakes. The advantage of vegetable dishes is that very often the ingredients can be varied according to personal preference or seasonal availability, but always remember to buy the freshest vegetables available to ensure maximum flavor.

Sweet Potato & Leek Patties

Sweet potatoes have very dense flesh and a delicious, sweet, earthy taste, which contrasts well with the pungent flavor of the ginger.

NUTRITIONAL INFORMATION

Calories 403   Sugars 34g
Protein . . . . .8g   Fat 12g
Carbohydrate . . .67g   Saturates 2g

    2 HOURS   40 MINS

SERVES 4

I N G R E D I E N T S

2 lb sweet potato

4 tsp sunflower oil

2 medium leeks, trimmed and finely
   chopped

1 garlic clove, crushed

1 inch piece fresh ginger, finely chopped

7 oz can corn kernels, drained

2 tbsp low-fat plain yogurt

2 oz whole wheat flour

salt and pepper

GINGER SAUCE

2 tbsp white wine vinegar

2 tsp sugar

1 red chili, deseeded and chopped

1 inch piece fresh ginger, cut into thin strips

2 tbsp ginger wine

4 tbsp Fresh Vegetable Stock (see page 31)

1 tsp cornstarch

TO SERVE

lettuce leaves

green onions, shredded

1 Peel the potatoes, cut into thick cubes, and boil for 10–15 minutes. Drain well and mash. Leave to cool.

2 Heat 2 tsp of oil and fry the leeks, garlic, and ginger for 2–3 minutes. Stir into the potato with the corn, seasoning, and plain yogurt. Form into 8 patties and toss in flour. Chill for 30 minutes. Place the patties on a preheated broiler rack and lightly brush with oil.

Broil for 5 minutes, then turn over, brush with oil, and broil for a further 5 minutes.

3 Place the vinegar, sugar, chili, and ginger in a pan and simmer for 5 minutes. Stir in the wine. Blend the stock and cornstarch and add to the sauce, stirring, until thickened. Serve the patties with lettuce and green onions, and the sauce.

Mixed Vegetable Balti

Any combination of vegetables or beans can be used in this recipe. It would make a good dish to serve to vegetarians.

NUTRITIONAL INFORMATION

Calories 207   Sugars 6g
Protein . . . . .8g   Fat 9g
Carbohydrate . . .24g   Saturates 1g

10 MINS   1 HOUR

SERVES 4

INGREDIENTS

1 cup split yellow peas, washed

3 tbsp oil

1 tsp onion seeds

2 onions, sliced

4½ oz zucchini, sliced

4½ oz potatoes, cut into ½ inch cubes

4½ oz carrots, sliced

1 small eggplant, sliced

8 oz tomatoes, chopped

1¼ cups water

3 garlic cloves, chopped

1 tsp ground cumin

1 tsp ground coriander

1 tsp salt

2 fresh green chilies, sliced

½ tsp garam masala

2 tbsp chopped fresh cilantro

1 Put the split peas into a saucepan and cover with salted water. Bring to a boil and simmer for 30 minutes. Drain the peas and keep warm.

2 Heat the oil in a wok, add the onion seeds, and fry until they start popping.

3 Add the onions and stir-fry until golden brown.

4 Add the zucchini, potatoes, carrots, and eggplant to the pan.

5 Stir-fry the vegetables for about 2 minutes, stirring with a wooden spoon.

6 Stir in the tomatoes, water, garlic, cumin, ground coriander, salt, chilies, garam masala, and reserved split peas.

7 Bring to a boil, then simmer for 15 minutes until all the vegetables are tender.

8 Stir the fresh cilantro into the vegetables and serve.

Tofu Skewers

Altough tofu is rather bland on its own, it develops a fabulous flavor when it is marinated in garlic and herbs.

NUTRITIONAL INFORMATION

Calories 149	Sugars 5g
Protein 13g	Fat 9g
Carbohydrate 5g	Saturates 1g

40 MINS   15 MINS

SERVES 4

INGREDIENTS

12 oz tofu

1 red bell pepper

1 yellow bell pepper

2 zucchini

8 small white mushrooms

slices of lemon, to garnish

MARINADE

grated rind and juice of ½ lemon

1 clove garlic, crushed

½ tsp fresh rosemary, chopped

½ tsp chopped, fresh thyme

1 tbsp walnut oil

1 To make the marinade, combine the lemon rind and juice, garlic, rosemary, thyme, and oil in a shallow dish.

2 Drain the tofu, pat it dry on paper towels, and cut it into squares. Add to the marinade and toss to coat. Leave to marinate for 20–30 minutes.

3 Meanwhile, deseed and cut the bell peppers into 1 inch pieces. Blanch in boiling water for 4 minutes, refresh in cold water, and drain.

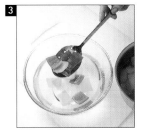

4 Using a canelle knife (or potato peeler), remove strips of peel from the zucchini. Cut the zucchini into 1 inch chunks.

5 Remove the tofu from the marinade, reserving the liquid for basting. Thread the tofu onto 8 skewers, alternating with the bell peppers, zucchini, and mushrooms.

6 Barbecue the skewers over medium hot coals for about 6 minutes, turning and basting with the marinade. Transfer the skewers to warm serving plates, garnish with slices of lemon, and serve.

Stuffed Tomatoes

These barbecued tomato cups are filled with a delicious Greek-style combination of herbs, nuts, and raisins.

NUTRITIONAL INFORMATION

Calories	156	Sugars	........10g
Protein	.........3g	Fat	...........7g
Carbohydrate	...22g	Saturates	.....0.7g

 25 MINS   🕐 10 MINS

SERVES 4

I N G R E D I E N T S

4 large tomatoes

4½ cups cooked rice

8 green onions, chopped

3 tbsp chopped, fresh mint

2 tbsp chopped, fresh parsley

3 tbsp pine nuts

3 tbsp raisins

2 tsp olive oil

salt and pepper

1 Cut the tomatoes in half, then scoop out the seeds, and discard.

2 Stand the tomatoes upside down on absorbent paper towels for a few moments in order for the juices to drain out.

3 Turn the tomatoes the right way up and sprinkle the insides with salt and pepper.

4 Mix together the rice, green onions, mint, parsley, pine nuts, and raisins.

5 Spoon the mixture into the tomato cups.

6 Drizzle over a little olive oil, then barbecue the tomatoes on an oiled rack over medium hot coals for about 10 minutes until they are tender and cooked through.

7 Transfer the tomatoes to serving plates and serve immediately while still hot.

COOK'S TIP

Tomatoes are a popular barbecue vegetable. Try broiling slices of tomato and slices of onion, brushed with a little oil and topped with sprigs of fresh herbs. Or thread cherry tomatoes onto skewers and barbecue for 5–10 minutes.

Mexican-Style Pizzas

Ready-made pizza bases are topped with a chili-flavored tomato sauce and topped with kidney beans, cheese, and jalapeño chilies.

NUTRITIONAL INFORMATION

Calories	350	Sugars	.........8g
Protein	.........18g	Fat	..........10g
Carbohydrate	...49g	Saturates	......3g

10 MINS   20 MINS

SERVES 4

INGREDIENTS

4 x ready-made individual pizza bases

1 tbsp olive oil

7 oz can chopped tomatoes with garlic and herbs

2 tbsp tomato paste

7 oz can kidney beans, drained and rinsed

4 oz corn kernels, thawed if frozen

1–2 tsp chili sauce

1 large red onion, shredded

3½ oz reduced-fat sharp Cheddar cheese, grated

1 large green chili, sliced into rings

salt and pepper

1 Preheat the oven to 425°F. Arrange the pizza bases on a cookie sheet and brush them lightly with the oil.

2 In a bowl, mix together the chopped tomatoes, tomato paste, kidney beans, and corn, and add chili sauce to taste. Season with salt and pepper.

3 Spread the tomato and kidney bean mixture evenly over each pizza base to cover.

4 Top each pizza with shredded onion and sprinkle with some grated cheese and a few slices of green chili to taste.

5 Bake in the oven for about 20 minutes until the vegetables are tender, the cheese has melted, and the base is crisp and golden.

6 Remove the pizzas from the cookie sheet and transfer to serving plates. Serve immediately.

COOK'S TIP

Serve a Mexican-style salad with this pizza. Arrange sliced tomatoes, fresh cilantro leaves, and a few slices of a small, ripe avocado on a platter. Sprinkle with fresh lime juice and coarse sea salt.

Quick Vegetable Curry

This vegetable curry is quick and easy to prepare, and it tastes superb.
A colorful Indian salad and a mint raita make perfect accompaniments.

NUTRITIONAL INFORMATION

Calories 473	Sugars 18g
Protein 19g	Fat 9g
Carbohydrate ...84g	Saturates 1g

 1 HOUR 50 MINS

SERVES 4

I N G R E D I E N T S

1 tbsp vegetable oil

2 garlic cloves, crushed

1 onion, chopped

3 celery stalks, sliced

1 apple, chopped

1 tbsp medium-strength curry powder

1 tsp ground ginger

14 oz can garbanzo beans

4½ oz dwarf green beans, sliced

8 oz cauliflower, broken into florets

8 oz potatoes, cut into cubes

2 cups mushrooms, sliced

2½ cups Fresh Vegetable Stock (see page 31)

1 tbsp tomato paste

1 oz golden raisins

1 cup Basmati rice

1 tbsp garam masala

mint raita and salad, to serve

1 Heat the oil in a large saucepan and fry the garlic, onion, celery, and apple gently for 3–4 minutes. Add the curry powder and ginger. Cook for 1 minute.

2 Drain the gabanzo beans and add to the onion mixture with the remaining ingredients except for the rice and garam masala.Bring to a boil, then reduce the heat. Cover the bean mixture and simmer for 35–40 minutes.

3 To make the raita mix the yogurt and mint together. Cover and chill.

4 Cook the rice in boiling, lightly salted water according to the instructions on the package. Drain thoroughly.

5 Just before serving, stir the garam masala into the curry. Divide between four warmed serving plates, and serve with the rice, a mint raita, and salad.

Ratatouille Vegetable Broil

Ratatouille is a classic dish of vegetables cooked in a tomato and herb sauce. Here it is topped with diced potatoes and cheese.

NUTRITIONAL INFORMATION

Calories 287	Sugars 13g
Protein 14g	Fat 4g
Carbohydrate . . .53g	Saturates 2g

 15 MINS   45 MINS

SERVES 4

INGREDIENTS

2 medium onions

1 garlic clove

1 medium red bell pepper

1 medium green bell pepper

1 medium eggplant

2 medium zucchini

2 x 14 oz cans chopped tomatoes

1 bouquet garni

2 tbsp tomato paste

2 lb potatoes

2¾ oz reduced-fat sharp Cheddar cheese, grated

salt and pepper

2 tbsp snipped fresh chives, to garnish

VARIATION

You can vary the vegetables in this dish depending on seasonal availability and personal preference. Try broccoli, carrots, or corn, if you prefer.

1 Peel and finely chop the onions and garlic. Rinse, deseed, and slice the bell peppers. Rinse, trim, and cut the eggplant into small dice. Rinse, trim, and thinly slice the zucchini.

2 Place the onion, garlic, and bell peppers into a large saucepan. Add the tomatoes and stir in the bouquet garni, tomato paste, and salt and pepper to taste. Bring to a boil, cover, and simmer for 10 minutes, stirring half-way through. Stir in the prepared eggplant and zucchini and cook, uncovered, for a further 10 minutes, stirring occasionally.

3 Meanwhile, peel the potatoes and cut into 1 inch cubes. Place the potatoes into another saucepan and cover with water. Bring to a boil and cook for 10–12 minutes until tender. Drain and set aside.

4 Transfer the vegetables to a heatproof gratin dish. Arrange the cooked potatoes evenly over the vegetables.

5 Preheat the broiler to medium. Sprinkle grated cheese over the potatoes and place under the broiler for 5 minutes until golden, bubbling, and hot. Serve garnished with snipped chives.

Potato Hash

This is a variation of the American dish, beef hash, which was made with salt beef and leftovers, and served to seagoing New Englanders.

NUTRITIONAL INFORMATION

Calories 302	Sugars 5g	
Protein 15g	Fat 10g	
Carbohydrate ...40g	Saturates 4g	

 5 MINS   30 MINS

SERVES 4

INGREDIENTS

2 tbsp butter

1 red onion, halved and sliced

1 carrot, diced

1 oz green beans, halved

3 large new potatoes, diced

2 tbsp all-purpose flour

1¼ cups vegetable stock

8 oz tofu, diced

salt and pepper

chopped fresh parsley, to garnish

1 Melt the butter in a frying pan.

2 Add the onion, carrot, green beans, and potatoes and fry gently, stirring, for 5–7 minutes or until the vegetables begin to brown.

3 Add the flour to the frying pan and cook for 1 minute, stirring constantly.

4 Gradually pour in the stock.

5 Reduce the heat and leave the mixture to simmer for 15 minutes or until the potatoes are tender.

6 Add the diced tofu to the mixture and cook for a further 5 minutes.

7 Season to taste with salt and pepper.

8 Sprinkle the chopped parsley over the top of the potato hash to garnish, then serve hot from the pan.

COOK'S TIP

Hash is an American term meaning to chop food into small pieces. Therefore a traditional hash dish is made from chopped fresh ingredients, such as roast beef or corned beef, bell peppers, onion, and celery, often served with gravy.

Chinese Vegetable Pancakes

Chinese pancakes are made with hardly any fat—they are simply flattened white flour dough.

NUTRITIONAL INFORMATION

Calories	312	Sugars	5g
Protein	13g	Fat	19g
Carbohydrate	25g	Saturates	7g

5 MINS   10 MINS

SERVES 4

INGREDIENTS

1 tbsp vegetable oil

1 garlic clove, crushed

1 inch piece fresh ginger, grated

1 bunch green onions, trimmed and shredded lengthwise

3½ oz snow peas, topped, tailed, and shredded

8 oz tofu, drained and cut into ½ inch pieces

2 tbsp dark soy sauce, plus extra to serve

2 tbsp hoisin sauce, plus extra to serve

2 oz canned bamboo shoots, drained

2 oz canned water chestnuts, drained and sliced

3½ oz bean sprouts

1 small red chili, deseeded and sliced thinly

1 small bunch fresh chives

12 soft Chinese pancakes

TO SERVE

shredded Chinese cabbage

1 cucumber, sliced

strips of red chili

1 Heat the oil in a non-stick wok or a large frying pan and stir-fry the garlic and ginger for 1 minute.

2 Add the green onions, snow peas, tofu, soy, and hoisin sauces. Stir-fry for 2 minutes.

3 Add the bamboo shoots, water chestnuts, bean sprouts, and sliced red chili to the pan.

4 Stir-fry gently for a further 2 minutes until the vegetables are just tender.

5 Snip the chives into 1 inch lengths and stir into the mixture.

6 Heat the pancakes according to the package instructions and keep warm.

7 Divide the vegetables and tofu among the pancakes. Roll up and serve with the Chinese cabbage, cucumber, chili, and extra sauce for dipping.

Layered Vegetable Gratin

In this tasty recipe an assortment of vegetables are cooked in a light nutmeg sauce with a potato and cheese topping.

NUTRITIONAL INFORMATION

Calories . . . . . . .236 Sugars 9g
Protein . . . . .9g Fat 9g
Carbohydrate . . .31g Saturates 3g

25 MINS   1 1/2 HOURS

SERVES 6

I N G R E D I E N T S

2 large carrots

8 oz baby parsnips

1 fennel bulb

3 potatoes

1/3 cup low-fat spread

1/4 cup all-purpose flour

1 1/4 cups skim milk

1/2 tsp ground nutmeg

1 egg, beaten

1/4 cup freshly grated Parmesan cheese

salt and pepper

T O   S E R V E

crusty bread

tomato salad

1 Cut the carrots and parsnips into thin strips lengthways. Cook in boiling water for 5 minutes. Drain well and transfer to an ovenproof baking dish.

2 Thinly slice the fennel and cook in boiling water for 2–3 minutes. Drain well and add to the carrots and parsnips. Season.

3 Peel and dice the potatoes into 3/4 inch cubes. Cook in boiling water for 6 minutes. Drain well.

4 Gently melt half of the low-fat spread and stir in the flour. Remove from the heat and gradually mix in the milk.

5 Return to the heat and stir until thickened. Season and stir in the nutmeg. Cool for 10 minutes.

6 Beat in the egg and spoon over the vegetables. Arrange the potatoes on top and sprinkle over the cheese.

7 Dot the cheesy potatoes with the remaining low-fat spread. Bake in a preheated oven at 350°F for 1 hour until the vegetables are tender.

8 Serve the vegetable gratin as a light meal with wedges of crusty bread and a tomato salad, or as an accompaniment to a light main course, such as steamed fish or broiled chicken.

Baked Potatoes with Salsa

This is a great way to eat a baked potato! Once cooked, the flesh is flavored with avocado and served with a hot tomato salsa.

NUTRITIONAL INFORMATION

Calories	274	Sugars	.........4g
Protein	........10g	Fat	...........8g
Carbohydrate	...43g	Saturates	......2g

  15 MINS   1 HOUR

SERVES 4

INGREDIENTS

4 baking potatoes, about 8 oz each

1 large ripe avocado

1 tsp lemon juice

6 oz smoked tofu, diced

2 garlic cloves, crushed

1 onion, chopped finely

1 tomato, chopped finely

4½ oz tossed salad leaves

fresh cilantro sprigs, to garnish

SALSA

2 ripe tomatoes, seeded and diced

1 tbsp chopped cilantro

1 shallot, diced finely

1 green chili, diced

1 tbsp lemon juice

salt and pepper

1 Scrub the potatoes and prick the skins with a fork. Rub a little salt into the skins and place them on a cookie sheet.

2 Cook in a preheated oven, 375°F, for 1 hour or until cooked through and the skins are crisp.

3 Cut the potatoes in half lengthways and scoop the flesh into a bowl, leaving a thin layer of potato inside the shells.

4 Halve and pit the avocado. Using a spoon, scoop out the avocado flesh and add to the bowl containing the potato. Stir in the lemon juice and mash the mixture together with a fork. Mix in the tofu, garlic, onion, and tomato. Spoon the mixture into one half of the potato shells.

5 Arrange the tossed salad leaves on top of the guacamole mixture and place the other half of the potato shell on top.

6 To make the salsa, mix the tomatoes, cilantro, shallots, chili, lemon juice, and salt and pepper to taste in a bowl. Garnish the potatoes with sprigs of fresh cilantro and serve with the salsa.

Char-Broiled Vegetables

This medley of bell peppers, zucchini, eggplant, and red onion can be served on its own or as an unusual side dish.

NUTRITIONAL INFORMATION

Calories 66   Sugars 7g
Protein . . . . .2g   Fat 3g
Carbohydrate . . . .7g   Saturates 0.5g

15 MINS   15 MINS

SERVES 4

I N G R E D I E N T S

1 large red bell pepper

1 large green bell pepper

1 large orange bell pepper

1 large zucchini

4 baby eggplant

2 medium red onions

2 tbsp lemon juice

1 tbsp olive oil

1 garlic clove, crushed

1 tbsp chopped, fresh rosemary or 1 tsp
   dried rosemary

salt and pepper

T O S E R V E

cracked wheat, cooked

tomato and olive relish

1 Halve and deseed the bell peppers and cut into even sized pieces, about 1 inch wide.

2 Trim the zucchini, cut in half lengthways, and slice into 1 inch pieces. Place the bell peppers and zucchini in a large bowl.

3 Trim the eggplant and quarter them lengthways. Peel both the onions, then cut each one into 8 even-sized wedges.

4 Add the pieces of eggplant and onions to the bowl containing the wedges of bell peppers and zucchini.

5 In a small bowl, whisk together the lemon juice, olive oil, garlic, rosemary, and seasoning.

6 Pour the mixture over the vegetables and stir to coat evenly.

7 Preheat the broiler to medium. Thread the vegetables onto 8 metal or pre-soaked wooden skewers. Arrange the kabobs on the rack and cook for 10–12 minutes, turning frequently, until the vegetables are lightly charred and just softened.

8 Drain the vegetables and serve on a bed of cracked wheat accompanied with a tomato and olive relish.

Potato & Tomato Calzone

These pizza dough Italian pasties are best served hot with a salad for a delicious lunch or supper dish.

NUTRITIONAL INFORMATION

Calories . . . . . . .524 Sugars 8g
Protein . . . . .17g Fat 8g
Carbohydrate . .103g Saturates 2g

1½ HOURS   35 MINS

SERVES 4

I N G R E D I E N T S

DOUGH

4 cups white bread flour

1 tsp easy blend dried yeast

1¼ cups vegetable stock

1 tbsp clear honey

1 tsp caraway seeds

skim milk, for glazing

FILLING

1 tbsp vegetable oil

8 oz new potatoes, diced

1 onion, halved and sliced

2 garlic cloves, crushed

1½ oz sun-dried tomatoes

2 tbsp chopped fresh basil

2 tbsp tomato paste

2 celery sticks, sliced

1¾ oz Mozzarella cheese, grated

1 To make the dough, sift the flour into a large mixing bowl and stir in the yeast. Make a well in the center of the mixture. Stir in the vegetable stock, honey, and caraway seeds and bring the mixture together to form a dough.

2 Turn the dough out onto a lightly floured surface and knead for 8 minutes until smooth. Place the dough in a lightly oiled mixing bowl, cover, and leave to rise in a warm place for 1 hour or until it has doubled in size.

3 Meanwhile, make the filling. Heat the oil in a frying pan and add all the remaining ingredients except for the cheese. Cook for about 5 minutes, stirring.

4 Divide the risen dough into 4 pieces. On a lightly floured surface, roll them out to form four 7 inch circles. Spoon equal amounts of the filling onto one half of each circle. Sprinkle the cheese over the filling. Brush the edge of the dough with milk and fold the dough over to form 4 semi-circles, pressing to seal the edges.

5 Place on a non-stick cookie sheet and brush with milk. Cook in a preheated oven, 425°F, for 30 minutes until golden and risen.

Coconut Vegetable Curry

A mildly spiced, but richly flavored Indian-style dish full of different textures and flavors. Serve with naan bread to soak up the tasty sauce.

NUTRITIONAL INFORMATION

Calories ....159 Sugars 8g
Protein ....8g Fat 6g
Carbohydrate ...19g Saturates 1g

1¾ HOURS   35 MINS

SERVES 4

INGREDIENTS

1 large eggplant, cut into
   1 inch cubes

2 tbsp salt

2 tbsp vegetable oil

2 garlic cloves, crushed

1 fresh green chili, deseeded and chopped
   finely

1 tsp grated fresh ginger

1 onion, chopped finely

2 tsp garam masala

8 cardamom pods

1 tsp ground turmeric

1 tbsp tomato paste

3 cups Fresh Vegetable Stock (see page 31)

1 tbsp lemon juice

8 oz potatoes, diced

9 oz small cauliflower florets

8 oz okra, trimmed

8 oz frozen peas

⅔ cups coconut milk

salt and pepper

flaked coconut, to garnish

naan bread, to serve

1 Layer the eggplant in a bowl, sprinkling with salt as you go. Set aside for 30 minutes. Rinse well under running water. Drain and pat dry. Set aside.

2 Heat the oil in a large saucepan and gently fry the garlic, chili, ginger, onion, and spices for 4–5 minutes.

3 Stir in the tomato paste, stock, lemon juice, potatoes, and cauliflower and mix well. Bring to a boil, cover, and simmer for 15 minutes.

4 Stir in the eggplant, okra, peas, and coconut milk and season with salt and pepper to taste. Continue to simmer, uncovered, for a further 10 minutes until tender. Discard the cardamom pods. Pile the curry onto a warmed serving platter, garnish with flaked coconut and serve with naan bread.

Stuffed Vegetables

You can fill your favorite vegetables with this nutty-tasting combination of cracked wheat, tomatoes, and cucumber.

NUTRITIONAL INFORMATION

Calories	194	Sugars	.........7g
Protein	.........5g	Fat	...........4g
Carbohydrate	...36g	Saturates	.....0.5g

40 MINS   25 MINS

SERVES 4

INGREDIENTS

4 large tomatoes

4 medium zucchini

2 orange bell peppers

salt and pepper

FILLING

1¼ cups cracked wheat

¼ cucumber

1 medium red onion

2 tbsp lemon juice

2 tbsp chopped fresh cilantro

2 tbsp chopped fresh mint

1 tbsp olive oil

2 tsp cumin seeds

TO SERVE

warm pita bread and low-fat hummus

COOK'S TIP

It is a good idea to blanch vegetables (except for tomatoes) before stuffing. Blanch bell peppers, zucchini, and eggplant for 5 minutes.

1 Preheat the oven to 400°F. Cut off the tops of the tomatoes and reserve. Using a teaspoon, scoop out the tomato pulp, chop, and place in a bowl. Season the tomato shells, then turn them upside down on absorbent paper towels.

2 Trim the zucchini and cut a V-shaped groove lengthwise down each one. Finely chop the cut-out zucchini flesh and add to the tomato pulp. Season the zucchini shells and set aside. Halve the bell peppers. Leaving the stalks intact, cut out the seeds and discard. Season the bell pepper shells and set aside.

3 To make the filling, soak the cracked wheat according to the instructions on the package. Finely chop the cucumber and add to the reserved tomato pulp and zucchini mixture. Finely chop the red onion, add to the vegetable mixture with the lemon juice, herbs, olive oil, cumin, and seasoning, and mix together well.

4 When the wheat has soaked, mix with the vegetables and stuff into the tomato, zucchini, and bell pepper shells. Place the tops on the tomatoes, transfer to a roasting pan, and bake for 20–25 minutes until cooked through. Drain and serve pita bread and hummus.

Oriental Vegetable Noodles

This dish has a mild, nutty flavor from the peanut butter and dry-roasted peanuts.

NUTRITIONAL INFORMATION

Calories	193	Sugars	5g
Protein	7g	Fat	12g
Carbohydrate	14g	Saturates	2g

10 MINS   15 MINS

SERVES 4

INGREDIENTS

1½ cups green thread noodles or multi-colored spaghetti

1 tsp sesame oil

2 tbsp crunchy peanut butter

2 tbsp light soy sauce

1 tbsp white wine vinegar

1 tsp clear honey

4½ oz mooli, grated

1 large carrot, grated

4½ oz cucumber, shredded finely

1 bunch green onions, shredded finely

1 tbsp dry-roasted peanuts, crushed

TO GARNISH

carrot flowers

green onion tassels

1 Bring a large saucepan of water to a boil, add the noodles or spaghetti, and cook according to the package instructions. Drain well and rinse in cold water. Leave in a bowl of cold water until required.

2 To make the peanut butter sauce, put the sesame oil, peanut butter, soy sauce, vinegar, honey, and seasoning into a small screw-top jar. Seal and shake well to mix thoroughly.

3 Drain the noodles or spaghetti well, place in a large serving bowl, and mix in half of the peanut sauce.

4 Using 2 forks, toss in the mooli, carrot, cucumber, and green onions. Sprinkle with crushed peanuts and garnish with carrot flowers and green onion tassels. Serve the noodles with the remaining peanut sauce.

COOK'S TIP

There are many varieties of noodles available from oriental markets, delicatessens, and supermarkets. Try rice noodles, which contain very little fat and require little cooking; usually soaking in boiling water is sufficient.

Curried Vegetable Kabobs

Warmed Indian bread is served with barbecued vegetable kabobs, which are brushed with a curry-spiced yogurt baste.

NUTRITIONAL INFORMATION

Calories	396	Sugars	........11g
Protein	........13g	Fat	..........13g
Carbohydrate	...60g	Saturates	.....0.3g

 25 MINS   20 MINS

SERVES 4

I N G R E D I E N T S

warm naan bread, to serve

sprigs of fresh mint, to garnish

Y O G U R T   B A S T E

⅔ cup low-fat plain yogurt

1 tbsp chopped fresh mint or 1 tsp dried mint

1 tsp ground cumin

1 tsp ground coriander

½ tsp chili powder

pinch of turmeric

pinch of ground ginger

salt and pepper

K A B O B S

8 small new potatoes

1 small eggplant

1 zucchini, cut into chunks

8 large whole cup mushrooms

8 small tomatoes

1 To make the spiced yogurt baste, mix together the yogurt and the spices. Season to taste with salt and pepper. Cover and chill.

2 Boil the potatoes until just tender. Meanwhile, chop the eggplant into chunks and sprinkle them liberally with salt. Leave for 10–15 minutes to extract the bitter juices. Rinse and drain them well. Drain the potatoes.

3 Thread the vegetables on to 4 metal or wooden skewers, alternating the different types. If using wooden skewers, soak in warm water for 10 minutes.

4 Place the skewers in a shallow dish and evenly coat with the yogurt baste. Cover and chill until required. Wrap the naan bread in foil and place towards one side of the barbecue to warm through.

5 Cook the kabobs over the barbecue basting with any remaining spiced yogurt, until they just begin to char slightly. Serve the kabobs with the warmed naan bread, garnished with sprigs of fresh mint.

Lemony Spaghetti

Steaming vegetables helps to preserve their nutritional content and allows them to retain their bright, natural colors and crunchy texture.

NUTRITIONAL INFORMATION

Calories ....133 Sugars 8g
Protein ....8g Fat 1g
Carbohydrate ...25g Saturates 0.2g

10 MINS   25 MINS

SERVES 4

INGREDIENTS

8 oz celeriac

2 medium carrots

2 medium leeks

1 small red bell pepper

1 small yellow bell pepper

2 garlic cloves

1 tsp celery seeds

1 tbsp lemon juice

10½ oz spaghetti

celery leaves, chopped, to garnish

LEMON DRESSING

1 tsp finely grated lemon rind

1 tbsp lemon juice

4 tbsp low-fat plain yogurt

salt and pepper

2 tbsp snipped fresh chives

1 Peel the celeriac and carrots, cut into thin matchsticks, and place in a bowl. Trim and slice the leeks, rinse under running water to flush out any trapped dirt, then shred finely. Halve, deseed, and slice the bell peppers. Peel and thinly slice the garlic.

2 Add all of the vegetables to the bowl with the celeriac and the carrots. Toss the vegetables with the celery seeds and lemon juice.

3 Bring a large saucepan of water to a boil and cook the spaghetti according to the instructions on the package. Drain and keep warm.

4 Meanwhile, bring another large saucepan of water to a boil, put the vegetables in a steamer or strainer, and place over the boiling water. Cover and steam for 6–7 minutes or until tender.

5 While the spaghetti and vegetables are cooking, mix the ingredients for the lemon dressing together.

6 Transfer the spaghetti and vegetables to a warm serving bowl and mix with the dressing. Garnish with chopped celery leaves and serve.

Eggplant Gratin

Similar to a simple moussaka, this recipe is made up of layers of tomatoes, eggplant, and potatoes.

NUTRITIONAL INFORMATION

Calories	409	Sugars	........17g
Protein	.......28g	Fat	.........14g
Carbohydrate	...45g	Saturates	......3g

15 MINS   1¼ HOURS

SERVES 4

INGREDIENTS

1 lb new potatoes, sliced

1 tbsp vegetable oil

1 onion, chopped

2 garlic cloves, crushed

1 lb tofu, diced

2 tbsp tomato paste

2 tbsp all-purpose flour

1¼ cups vegetable stock

2 large tomatoes, sliced

1 eggplant, sliced

2 tbsp chopped fresh thyme

1 lb low-fat plain yogurt

2 eggs, beaten

salt and pepper

1 Cook the sliced potatoes in a saucepan of boiling water for 10 minutes until tender but not breaking up. Drain and set aside.

2 Heat the oil in a pan and fry the onion and garlic for 2-3 minutes.

3 Add the diced tofu, tomato purée, and flour and cook for 1 minute. Gradually stir in the vegetable stock and bring to a boil, stirring constantly. Reduce the heat and leave to simmer for 10 minutes.

4 Arrange a layer of the potato slices in the base of a deep ovenproof dish. Spoon the tofu mixture on top.

5 Layer the tomatoes, then the eggplant, and then the remaining potato slices on top of the tofu mixture, so that it is completely covered.

6 Mix the yogurt and beaten eggs together in a bowl and season well with salt and pepper. Spoon the yogurt topping over the sliced potatoes.

7 Cook the gratin in a preheated oven, 375°F, for 35-45 minutes or until the topping is browned, and serve hot.

Vegetable Curry

Vegetables are cooked in a mildly spiced curry sauce with yogurt and fresh cilantro stirred in just before serving.

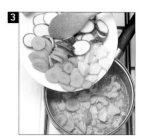

NUTRITIONAL INFORMATION

Calories 423	Sugars 24g	
Protein 16g	Fat 19g	
Carbohydrate . . .50g	Saturates 7g	

10 MINS   30 MINS

SERVES 4

I N G R E D I E N T S

2 tbsp sunflower oil

1 onion, sliced

2 tsp cumin seeds

2 tbsp ground coriander

1 tsp ground turmeric

2 tsp ground ginger

1 tsp chopped fresh red chili

2 garlic cloves, chopped

14 oz can chopped tomatoes

3 tbsp powdered coconut mixed with
1¼ cups boiling water

1 small cauliflower, broken into florets

2 zucchini, sliced

2 carrots, sliced

1 potato, diced

14 oz can garbanzo beans, drained and
rinsed

⅔ cup thick yogurt

2 tbsp mango chutney

3 tbsp chopped fresh cilantro

salt and pepper

fresh cilantro sprigs, to garnish

T O   S E R V E

onion relish

banana raita

Basmati rice and naan bread

1 Heat the oil in a saucepan and fry the onion until softened. Add the cumin, ground coriander, turmeric, ginger, chili, and garlic and fry for 1 minute.

2 Add the tomatoes and coconut mixture and mix well.

3 Add the cauliflower, zucchini, carrots, potato, garbanzo beans, and salt and pepper to taste. Cover and simmer for 20 minutes or until the vegetables are tender.

4 Stir in the yogurt, mango chutney, and fresh cilantro and heat through gently, but do not boil.

5 Garnish the curry with cilantro sprigs and serve with onion relish, banana raita, Basmati rice, and naan bread.

Pasta & Grains, Beans

Pasta, grains, and beans are ideal ingredients to include in a low fat diet because they make you feel satisfyingly full without having consumed lots of fat. They are also cheap,

highly nutritious, and versatile and form a substantial base to which other ingredients can be added. Pasta lends itself to virtually any ingredient. In this chapter, it is combined with eggplants in Eggplant Cake, seafood in Mussel & Scallop Spaghetti, and mushrooms in Mushroom Cannelloni. Although they take longer to cook, grains and beans add fiber to the diet and are a useful household ingredient as they keep for a long time.

Eggplant Cake

This dish would make a stunning dinner party dish, yet it contains simple ingredients and is easy to make.

NUTRITIONAL INFORMATION

Calories 201   Sugars 4g
Protein . . . . .14g   Fat 7g
Carbohydrate . . .22g   Saturates 4g

55 MINS   35 MINS

SERVES 4

INGREDIENTS

1 medium eggplant

10½ oz tricolor pasta shapes

4½ oz low-fat cream cheese with garlic and herbs

1⅓ cups strained tomatoes

4 tbsp grated Parmesan cheese

1½ tsp dried oregano

2 tbsp dry white bread crumbs

salt and pepper

1 Preheat the oven to 375°F. Grease and line a 8 inch round spring-form cake pan.

2 Trim the eggplant and slice lengthwise into slices about ¼ inch thick. Place in a bowl, sprinkle with salt, and set aside for 30 minutes to remove any bitter juices. Rinse well under cold running water and drain.

3 Bring a saucepan of water to a boil and blanch the eggplant slices for 1 minute. Drain and pat dry with paper towels. Set aside.

4 Cook the pasta shapes according to the instructions on the package; for best results, the pasta should be slightly undercooked. Drain well and return to the

saucepan. Add the cream cheese and allow it to melt over the pasta.

5 Stir in the strained tomatoes, Parmesan cheese, oregano, and salt and pepper. Set aside.

6 Arrange the eggplant over the base and sides of the pan, overlapping the slices and making sure there are no gaps.

7 Pile the pasta mixture into the pan, packing down well, and sprinkle with the bread crumbs. Bake for 20 minutes and leave to stand for 15 minutes.

8 Loosen the cake round the edge with a spatula and release from the pan. Turn out the pasta cake, eggplant-side uppermost, and serve hot.

Sage Chicken & Rice

Cooking in a single pot means that all of the flavors are retained. This is a substantial meal that needs only a salad and some crusty bread.

NUTRITIONAL INFORMATION

Calories 247	Sugars 5g
Protein 26g	Fat 5g
Carbohydrate ...25g	Saturates 2g

10 MINS   50 MINS

SERVES 4

I N G R E D I E N T S

1 large onion, chopped

1 garlic clove, crushed

2 sticks celery, sliced

2 carrots, diced

2 sprigs fresh sage

1¼ cups chicken stock

12 oz boneless, skinless chicken breasts

1⅓ cups mixed brown and wild rice

14 oz can chopped tomatoes

dash of Tabasco sauce

2 medium courgettes (zucchini), trimmed and thinly sliced

3½ oz lean ham, diced

salt and pepper

fresh sage, to garnish

TO SERVE

salad leaves

crusty bread

1 Place the pieces of onion, garlic, celery, carrots, and sprigs of fresh sage in a large saucepan and pour in the chicken stock.

2 Bring to a boil, cover the pan, and simmer for 5 minutes.

3 Cut the chicken into 1 inch cubes and stir into the pan with the vegetables. Cover the pan and continue to cook for a further 5 minutes.

4 Stir in the mixed brown and wild rice and chopped tomatoes.

5 Add a dash of Tabasco sauce to taste and season well. Bring to a boil, cover, and simmer for 25 minutes.

6 Stir in the sliced zucchini and diced ham and continue to cook, uncovered, for a further 10 minutes, stirring occasionally, until the rice is just tender.

7 Remove and discard the sprigs of sage.

8 Garnish with sage leaves and serve with a salad and fresh crusty bread.

Spicy Mexican Beans

These stewed beans form the basis of many Mexican recipes. Don't add salt until the beans are tender—it prevents them from softening.

NUTRITIONAL INFORMATION

Calories 234	Sugars 6g	
Protein 11g	Fat 13g	
Carbohydrate ...20g	Saturates 2g	

12 HOURS   4 HOURS

SERVES 4

INGREDIENTS

8 oz pinto beans or cannellini beans

1 large onion, sliced

2 garlic cloves, crushed

1¾ pints water

salt

chopped fresh cilantro or parsley, to garnish

BEAN STEW

1 large onion, sliced

2 garlic cloves, crushed

8 slices lean streaky bacon, diced

2 tbsp oil

14 oz can chopped tomatoes

1 tsp ground cumin

1 tbsp sweet chili sauce

REFRIED BEANS

1 onion, chopped

2 garlic cloves, crushed

2 tbsp oil

1 Soak the beans in a saucepan of cold water overnight. Drain the beans and put into a saucepan with the onion, garlic, and water, bring to a boil, cover, and simmer gently for 1½ hours. Stir well, add more boiling water if necessary, and simmer, covered, for a further 1–1½ hours, or until the beans are tender.

2 When the beans are tender, add salt to taste (about 1 tsp) and continue to cook, uncovered, for about 15 minutes to allow most of the liquid to evaporate to form a thick sauce. Serve the beans hot sprinkled with chopped cilantro or parsley; or cool then store in the refrigerator for up to 1 week.

3 To make a bean stew, fry the onion, garlic, and bacon for 3–4 minutes in the oil, add the other ingredients, and bring to a boil. Cover and simmer very gently for 30 minutes, then season.

4 To make refried beans, fry the onion and garlic in the oil until golden brown. Add a quarter' of the beans with a little of their liquid and mash. Continue adding and mashing the beans, while simmering gently until thick. Adjust the seasoning and serve hot.

Vermicelli with Clam Sauce

Another cook-in-a-hurry recipe that transforms pantry ingredients into a dish with style.

NUTRITIONAL INFORMATION

Calories ....392 Sugars 2g
Protein ....23g Fat 15g
Carbohydrate ...37g Saturates 6g

 5 MINS   20 MINS

SERVES 4

I N G R E D I E N T S

14 oz vermicelli, spaghetti, or other long pasta

1 tbsp olive oil

2 tbsp butter

2 tbsp flaked Parmesan, to garnish

sprig of basil, to garnish

S A U C E

1 tbsp olive oil

2 onions, chopped

2 garlic cloves, chopped

2 x 7 oz cans clams in brine

½ cup white wine

4 tbsp chopped parsley

½ tsp dried oregano

pinch of grated nutmeg

salt and pepper

1 Cook the pasta in a large saucepan of boiling salted water, adding the olive oil.

2 When the pasta is almost tender, drain in a colander, return to the pan, and add the butter. Cover the pan. Shake it and keep it warm.

3 To make the clam sauce, heat the oil in a pan over a medium heat and fry the onion until it is translucent but not browned. Stir in the garlic and cook for 1 further minute.

4 Strain the liquid from one can of clams, pour into the pan, and add the wine.

5 Stir well, bring to simmering point, and simmer for 3 minutes. Drain the brine from the second can of clams and discard.

6 Add the shellfish and herbs to the pan and season with pepper and nutmeg. Lower the heat and cook until the sauce is heated through.

7 Transfer the pasta to a warmed serving platter and pour on the sauce.

8 Sprinkle on the Parmesan and garnish with the basil. Serve hot.

Garlic Chicken Cassoulet

This is a cassoulet with a twist—it is made with chicken instead of duck and lamb. If you use canned beans, the result will be just as tasty.

NUTRITIONAL INFORMATION

Calories 550	Sugars 2g
Protein 60g	Fat 19g
Carbohydrate . . .26g	Saturates 4g

5 MINS   2¼ HOURS

SERVES 4

INGREDIENTS

4 tbsp sunflower oil

2 lb chicken meat, chopped

3 cups mushrooms, sliced

16 shallots

6 garlic cloves, crushed

1 tbsp all-purpose flour

1 cup white wine

1 cup chicken stock

1 bouquet garni (1 bay leaf, sprig thyme, celery, parsley, & sage tied with string)

14 oz can borlotti beans

salt and pepper

1 Heat the sunflower oil in an ovenproof casserole and fry the chicken until browned all over. Remove from the casserole with a slotted spoon.

2 Add the mushrooms, shallots, and garlic to the oil in the casserole and cook for 4 minutes.

3 Return the chicken to the casserole and sprinkle with the flour, then cook for a further 2 minutes.

4 Add the wine and stock, stir until boiling, then add the bouquet garni. Season well with salt and pepper.

5 Stir in the borlotti beans.

6 Cover and place in the center of a preheated oven, 300°F, for 2 hours.

7 Remove the bouquet garni and serve piping hot.

COOK'S TIP

Add chunks of potatoes and other vegetables, such as carrots and celery, for a delicious one-pot meal.

Chicken Pasta Bake

Tender, lean chicken is baked with pasta in a creamy low-fat sauce which contrasts well with the fennel and the sweetness of the raisins.

NUTRITIONAL INFORMATION

Calories	380	Sugars	........15g
Protein	........39g	Fat	..........14g
Carbohydrate	...27g	Saturates	......6g

15 MINS   45 MINS

SERVES 4

I N G R E D I E N T S

2 bulbs fennel

2 medium red onions, finely shredded

1 tbsp lemon juice

4½ oz small white mushrooms

1 tbsp olive oil

8 oz penne (pasta quills)

⅓ cup raisins

8 oz lean, boneless cooked chicken, skinned and shredded

13 oz low-fat cream cheese with garlic and herbs

4½ oz low-fat Mozzarella cheese, thinly sliced

2 tbsp Parmesan cheese, grated

salt and pepper

chopped fennel fronds, to garnish

1 Preheat the oven to 400°F. Trim the fennel, reserving the green fronds, and slice the bulbs thinly.

2 Generously coat the onions in the lemon juice. Quarter the mushrooms.

3 Heat the oil in a large frying pan and fry the fennel, onion, and mushrooms for 4–5 minutes, stirring, until just softened. Season well, transfer the mixture to a large bowl, and set aside.

4 Bring a pan of lightly salted water to a boil and cook the penne (pasta quills) according to the instructions on the package until just cooked. Drain and mix the pasta with the vegetables.

5 Stir the raisins and chicken into the pasta mixture. Soften the cream cheese by beating it, then mix into the pasta and chicken—the heat from the pasta should make the cheese melt slightly.

6 Put the mixture into an ovenproof baking dish and transfer to a cookie sheet. Arrange slices of Mozzarella cheese over the top and sprinkle with the grated Parmesan.

7 Bake in the oven for 20–25 minutes until golden-brown.

8 Garnish with chopped fennel fronds and serve hot.

Aromatic Seafood Rice

One of those easy, delicious meals where the rice and fish are cooked together in one pan. Remove the whole spices before serving.

NUTRITIONAL INFORMATION

Calories 380   Sugar 2g
Protein . . . . .40g   Fats 13g
Carbohydrates . . .26g   Saturates 5g

20 MINS   25 MINS

SERVES 4

INGREDIENTS

1¼ cups Basmati rice

2 tbsp ghee or vegetable oil

1 onion, peeled and chopped

1 garlic clove, peeled and crushed

1 tsp cumin seeds

½-1 tsp chili powder

4 cloves

1 cinnamon stick

2 tsp curry paste

8 oz peeled shrimp

1 lb 2 oz white fish fillets (such as swordfish, cod, or haddock), skinned and boned and cut into bite-sized pieces

salt and freshly ground black pepper

2½ cups boiling water

⅓ cup frozen peas

⅓ cup frozen corn kernels

1-2 tbsp lime juice

2 tbsp toasted shredded coconut

cilantro sprigs and lime slices, to garnish

1 Place the rice in a sieve and wash well under cold running water until the water runs clear, then drain well.

2 Heat the ghee or oil in a saucepan, add the onion, garlic, spices, and curry paste, and fry very gently for 1 minute.

3 Stir in the rice and mix well until coated in the spiced oil. Add the shrimp and white fish and season well with salt and pepper. Stir lightly, then pour in the boiling water.

4 Cover and cook gently for 10 minutes, without uncovering the pan. Add the peas and corn, cover, and continue cooking for a further 8 minutes. Remove from the heat and allow to stand for 10 minutes.

5 Uncover the pan, fluff up the rice with a fork, and transfer to a warm serving platter.

6 Sprinkle the dish with the lime juice and toasted coconut and serve garnished with cilantro sprigs and lime slices.

Basil & Tomato Pasta

Roasting the tomatoes gives a sweeter and smoother flavor to this sauce. Italian tomatoes, such as plum or flavia, have the best flavor.

NUTRITIONAL INFORMATION

Calories	177	Sugars	.........4g
Protein	.........5g	Fat	..........4g
Carbohydrate	...31g	Saturates	......1g

10 MINS   35 MINS

SERVES 4

INGREDIENTS

1 tbsp olive oil

2 sprigs rosemary

2 cloves garlic, unpeeled

1 lb tomatoes, halved

1 tbsp sun-dried tomato paste

12 fresh basil leaves, plus extra to garnish

salt and pepper

1½ lb fresh farfalle or 12 oz dried farfalle

1 Place the oil, rosemary, garlic, and tomatoes, skin side up, in a shallow roasting pan.

2 Drizzle with a little oil and cook under a preheated broiler for 20 minutes or until the tomato skins are slightly charred.

3 Peel the skin from the tomatoes. Roughly chop the tomato flesh and place in a pan.

4 Squeeze the pulp from the garlic cloves and mix with the tomato flesh and sun-dried tomato paste.

5 Roughly tear the fresh basil leaves into smaller pieces and then stir them into the sauce. Season with a little salt and pepper to taste.

6 Cook the farfalle in a saucepan of boiling water according to the instructions on the package or until it is just cooked through. Drain.

7 Gently heat the tomato and basil sauce.

8 Transfer the farfalle to serving plates and garnish with the basil. Serve with the tomato sauce.

COOK'S TIP

This sauce tastes just as good when mixed in with the pasta and served cold as a salad. Sprinkle some chopped parsley on top for added flavor and color.

Balti Cod & Red Lentils

The aniseed in this recipe gives a very delicate aroma to the fish and really enhances the flavor. Serve with whole wheat bread.

NUTRITIONAL INFORMATION

Calories 236	Sugars 3g
Protein 29g	Fat 7g
Carbohydrate ...15g	Saturates 1g

5 MINS   1 HOUR

SERVES 4

INGREDIENTS

2 tbsp oil

¼ tsp ground asafoetida (optional)

1 tbsp crushed aniseed

1 tsp ground ginger

1 tsp chili powder

¼ tsp ground turmeric

1 cup split red lentils, washed

1 tsp salt

1 lb 2 oz cod, skinned, filleted, and cut into 1 inch cubes

1 fresh red chili, chopped

3 tbsp low-fat plain yogurt

2 tbsp chopped fresh cilantro

whole wheat bread, to serve

COOK'S TIP

Ground asafoetida is easier to use than the type that comes on a block. It should only be used in small quantities. Do not be put off by the smell, which is very pungent.

 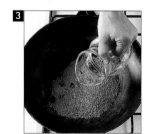 

1 Heat the oil in a wok, add the asafoetida (if using), and fry for about 10 seconds to burn off the smell of the asafoetida.

2 Add the aniseed, ginger, chili powder, and turmeric and fry for 30 seconds.

3 Wash the lentils thoroughly, then add to the pan with the salt and enough water to cover.

4 Bring to a boil, then simmer gently for 45 minutes, until the lentils are soft but not mushy.

5 Add the cod and red chili, bring to a boil, and simmer for a further 10 minutes.

6 Stir the yogurt and fresh cilantro into the fish mixture and serve with warm bread.

Pesto Pasta

Italian pesto is usually laden with fat. This version has just as much flavor but is much healthier.

NUTRITIONAL INFORMATION

Calories 283   Sugars 5g
Protein . . . . .14g   Fat 3g
Carbohydrate . . .37g   Saturates 1g

1 HOUR   30 MINS

SERVES 4

INGREDIENTS

8 oz chestnut mushrooms, sliced

¾ cup fresh vegetable stock

6 oz asparagus, trimmed and cut into 2 inch lengths

10½ oz green and white tagliatelle

14 oz canned artichoke hearts, drained and halved

bread sticks, to serve

TO GARNISH

basil leaves, shredded

Parmesan shavings

PESTO

2 large garlic cloves, crushed

½ oz fresh basil leaves, washed

6 tbsp low-fat plain yogurt

2 tbsp freshly grated Parmesan cheese

salt and pepper

1 Place the mushrooms in a saucepan with the stock. Bring to a boil, cover, and simmer for 3–4 minutes until just tender. Drain and set aside, reserving the liquid to use in soups if wished.

2 Bring a small saucepan of water to a boil and cook the asparagus for 3–4 minutes until just tender. Drain and set aside until required.

3 Bring a large pan of lightly salted water to a boil and cook the tagliatelle according to the instructions on the package. Drain, return to the pan, and keep warm.

4 Meanwhile, make the pesto. Place all of the ingredients in a blender or food processor and process for a few seconds until smooth. Alternatively, finely chop the basil and mix all the ingredients together.

5 Add the mushrooms, asparagus, and artichoke hearts to the pasta and cook, stirring, over a low heat for 2–3 minutes.

6 Remove from the heat and mix with the pesto.

7 Transfer to a warm bowl. Garnish with shredded basil leaves and Parmesan shavings and serve.

Mussel & Scallop Spaghetti

Juicy mussels and scallops poached gently in white wine are the perfect accompaniment to pasta to make a sophisticated meal.

NUTRITIONAL INFORMATION

Calories	301	Sugars	1g
Protein	42g	Fat	5g
Carbohydrate	17g	Saturates	1g

55 MINS   30 MINS

SERVES 4

INGREDIENTS

8 oz dried whole wheat spaghetti

2 slices rindless lean back bacon, chopped

2 shallots, chopped finely

2 celery stalks, chopped finely

⅔ cup dry white wine

⅔ cup Fresh Fish Stock
(see page 30)

1 lb 2 oz fresh mussels, prepared

8 oz shelled queen or China bay scallops

1 tbsp chopped fresh parsley

salt and pepper

1 Cook the spaghetti in a saucepan of boiling water according to the package instructions, or until the pasta is cooked but "al dente", still firm to the bite—about 10 minutes.

2 Meanwhile, gently dry-fry the bacon in a large non-stick frying pan for 2–3 minutes. Stir in the shallots, celery, and wine. Simmer gently, uncovered, for 5 minutes until softened.

3 Add the stock, mussels, and scallops, cover, and cook for a further 6–7 minutes. Discard any mussels that remain unopened.

4 Drain the spaghetti and add to the frying pan. Add the parsley, season to taste, and toss together. Continue to cook for 1–2 minutes to heat through. Pile onto warmed serving plates, spooning over the cooking juices.

COOK'S TIP

Whole wheat pasta doesn't have any egg added to the dough, so it is low in fat, and higher in fiber than other pastas.

Orange Turkey with Rice

This is a good way to use up left-over rice. Use fresh or canned sweet pink grapefruit for an interesting alternative to the orange.

NUTRITIONAL INFORMATION

Calories 337	Sugars 12g	
Protein 32g	Fat 7g	
Carbohydrate ...40g	Saturates 1g	

 30 MINS   40 MINS

SERVES 4

I N G R E D I E N T S

1 tbsp olive oil

1 medium onion, chopped

1 lb skinless lean turkey (such as fillet), cut into thin strips

1¼ cups unsweetened orange juice

1 bay leaf

8 oz small broccoli florets

1 large zucchini, diced

1 large orange

6 cups cooked brown rice

salt and pepper

tomato and onion salad, to serve

TO GARNISH

1 oz pitted black olives in brine, drained and quartered

shredded basil leaves

1 Heat the oil in a large frying pan and fry the onion and turkey, stirring, for 4–5 minutes until lightly browned.

2 Pour in the orange juice and add the bay leaf and seasoning. Bring to a boil and simmer for 10 minutes.

3 Meanwhile, bring a large saucepan of water to a boil and cook the broccoli florets, covered, for 2 minutes. Add the diced zucchini, bring back to a boil, cover, and cook for a further 3 minutes (do not overcook). Drain and set aside.

4 Using a sharp knife, peel off the skin and white pith from the orange.

5 Thinly slice down the orange to make round slices, then halve each slice.

6 Stir the broccoli, zucchini, rice, and orange slices into the turkey mixture. Gently mix together and season, then heat through for a further 3–4 minutes until piping hot.

7 Transfer the turkey rice to warm serving plates and garnish with black olives and shredded basil leaves. Serve the turkey with a fresh tomato and onion salad.

Mixed Bean Stir-Fry

Any type of canned beans can be used—lima beans, black-eyed beans, etc.—but rinse under cold water and drain well before use.

NUTRITIONAL INFORMATION

Calories 326   Sugars 16g
Protein . . . . .18g   Fat 7g
Carbohydrate . . .51g   Saturates 1g

10 MINS   10 MINS

SERVES 4

INGREDIENTS

1 x 14 oz can red kidney beans

1 x 14 oz can cannellini beans

6 green onions

1 x 7 oz can pineapple rings or pieces in natural juice, chopped

2 tbsp pineapple juice

3-4 pieces stem ginger

2 tbsp ginger syrup from the jar

thinly pared rind of ½ lime or lemon, cut into julienne strips

2 tbsp lime or lemon juice

2 tbsp soy sauce

1 tsp cornstarch

1 tbsp sesame oil

4½ oz green beans, cut into 1½ inch lengths

1 x 8 oz can bamboo shoots

salt and pepper

COOK'S TIP

Be sure to drain and rinse the beans before using, as they are usually canned in salty water, which will spoil the flavor of the finished dish.

1 Drain all the beans, rinse under cold water, and drain again very thoroughly.

2 Cut 4 green onions into narrow slanting slices. Thinly slice the remainder and reserve for garnish.

3 Combine the pineapple and juice, ginger and syrup, lime rind and juice, soy sauce, and cornstarch in a bowl.

4 Heat the oil in the wok, swirling it around until really hot. Add the green onions and stir-fry for about 1 minute, then add the green beans. Drain and thinly slice the bamboo shoots, add to the pan, and continue to stir-fry for 2 minutes.

5 Add the pineapple and ginger mixture and bring just to a boil. Add the canned beans and stir until very hot—for about 1 minute.

6 Season to taste, sprinkled with the reserved chopped green onions; or serve as a vegetable accompaniment.

Biryani with Onions

An assortment of vegetables cooked with tender rice is flavored and colored with bright yellow turmeric and other warming Indian spices.

NUTRITIONAL INFORMATION

Calories	223	Sugars	18g
Protein	8g	Fat	4g
Carbohydrate	42g	Saturates	1g

1¼ HOURS   25 MINS

SERVES 4

INGREDIENTS

1 cup Basmati rice, rinsed

⅓ cup red lentils, rinsed

1 bay leaf

6 cardamom pods, split

1 tsp ground turmeric

6 cloves

1 tsp cumin seeds

1 cinnamon stick, broken

1 onion, chopped

8 oz cauliflower, broken into small florets

1 large carrot, diced

3½ oz frozen peas

2 oz golden raisins

2½ cups Fresh Vegetable Stock (see page 31)

salt and pepper

naan bread, to serve

CARAMELIZED ONIONS

2 tsp vegetable oil

1 medium red onion, shredded

1 medium onion, shredded

2 tsp sugar

1 Place the rice, lentils, bay leaf, spices, onion, cauliflower, carrot, peas, and golden raisins in a large saucepan. Season with salt and pepper and mix well.

2 Pour in the stock, bring to a boil, cover, and simmer for 15 minutes, stirring occasionally, until the rice is tender. Remove from the heat and leave to stand, covered, for 10 minutes to allow the stock to be absorbed. Discard the bay leaf, cardamom pods, cloves, and cinnamon stick.

3 Heat the oil in a frying pan and fry the onions over a medium heat for 3-4 minutes until just softened. Add the sugar, raise the heat, and cook, stirring, for a further 2-3 minutes until the onions are golden.

4 Gently mix the rice and vegetables and transfer to warm serving plates. Spoon over the caramelized onions and serve with plain, warmed naan bread.

Egg & Garbanzo Bean Curry

This quick and easy vegetarian curry is a great favorite. Double the quantities if you're cooking for a crowd.

NUTRITIONAL INFORMATION

Calories 403   Sugars 19g
Protein ....19g   Fat 15g
Carbohydrate ...31g   Saturates 3g

1¼ HOURS   45 MINS

SERVES 4

INGREDIENTS

2 tbsp vegetable oil

2 garlic cloves, crushed

1 large onion, chopped

1 large carrot, sliced

1 apple, cored and chopped

2 tbsp medium-hot curry powder

1 tsp finely grated fresh ginger

2 tsp paprika

3½ cups Fresh Vegetable Stock (see page 31)

2 tbsp tomato paste

½ small cauliflower, broken into florets

15 oz can garbanzo beans, rinsed and drained

2 tbsp golden raisins

2 tbsp cornstarch

2 tbsp water

4 hard-boiled eggs, quartered

salt and pepper

paprika, to garnish

CUCUMBER DIP

3 inch piece cucumber, chopped

1 tbsp chopped fresh mint

⅔ cup low-fat plain yogurt

sprigs of fresh mint, to garnish

1 Heat the oil in a large saucepan and fry the garlic, onion, carrot, and apple for 4–5 minutes. Add the curry powder, ginger, and paprika and fry for 1 minute. Stir in the stock and tomato paste.

2 Add the cauliflower, garbanzo beans, and golden raisins. Bring to a boil, then reduce the heat, and simmer, covered, for 25–30 minutes until tender.

3 Blend the cornstarch with the water and add to the curry, stirring until thickened. Cook gently for 2 minutes. Season to taste.

4 Mix together the cucumber, mint, and yogurt in a small serving bowl. Ladle the curry onto serving plates and arrange the eggs on top. Sprinkle with a little paprika. Garnish the cucumber and mint dip with mint and serve with the curry.

Chicken & Beans

Beans are a valuable source of nourishment. You could use any variety of beans in this recipe, but adjust the cooking times accordingly.

NUTRITIONAL INFORMATION

Calories 291   Sugars 3g
Protein . . . . .33g   Fat 10g
Carbohydrate . . .18g   Saturates 2g

  12 HOURS   1HOUR

SERVES 4

I N G R E D I E N T S

1 cup dried black-eye peas, soaked
    overnight and drained

1 tsp salt

2 onions, chopped

2 garlic cloves, crushed

1 tsp ground turmeric

1 tsp ground cumin

2 lb 12 oz chicken, jointed into 8 pieces

1 green bell pepper, chopped

2 tbsp oil

1 inch piece fresh ginger, grated

2 tsp coriander seeds

½ tsp fennel seeds

2 tsp garam masala

1 tbsp chopped fresh cilantro,
    to garnish

1 Put the dried black-eye peas into a wok with the salt, onions, garlic, turmeric, and cumin. Cover the beans with water, bring to a boil, and cook for 15 minutes.

2 Add the chicken and green bell pepper to the pan and bring to a boil. Lower the heat and simmer gently for 30 minutes until the beans are tender and the chicken juices run clear when the thickest parts of the pieces are pierced with a sharp knife or skewer.

3 Heat the oil in a wok and fry the ginger, coriander seeds, and fennel seeds for 30 seconds.

4 Stir the spices into the chicken and add the garam masala. Simmer for a further 5 minutes, garnish, and serve.

COOK'S TIP

For convenience, use a 15 oz can of black-eye peas instead of dried peas. Add in step 2.

Mushroom Cannelloni

Thick pasta tubes are filled with a mixture of seasoned chopped mushrooms, and baked in a rich fragrant tomato sauce.

NUTRITIONAL INFORMATION

Calories 156   Sugar 8g
Protein . . . . .6g   Fats 1g
Carbohydrates . . .21g   Saturates 0.2g

35 MINS   1¹/₂ HOURS

SERVES 4

INGREDIENTS

12 oz cremini mushrooms

1 medium onion, chopped finely

1 garlic clove, minced

1 tbsp chopped fresh thyme

½ tsp ground nutmeg

4 tbsp dry white wine

4 tbsp fresh white bread crumbs

12 dried "quick-cook" cannelloni

Parmesan shavings, to garnish (optional)

TOMATO SAUCE

1 large red bell pepper

¾ cup dry white wine

2 cups sieved tomatoes

2 tbsp tomato paste

2 bay leaves

1 tsp superfine sugar

1 Preheat the oven to 400°F. Finely chop the mushrooms and place in a pan with the onion and garlic. Stir in the thyme, nutmeg, and 4 tbsp wine. Bring to a boil, cover, and simmer for 10 minutes.

2 Stir in the bread crumbs to bind the mixture together and season. Cool for 10 minutes.

3 Preheat the broiler to hot. To make the sauce, halve and seed the bell pepper, place on the broiler rack, and cook for 8–10 minutes until charred. Leave to cool for 10 minutes.

4 Once the bell pepper has cooled, peel off the charred skin. Chop the flesh and place in a food processor with the wine. Blend until smooth, and pour into a pan.

5 Mix the remaining sauce ingredients with the bell pepper and wine. Bring to a boil and simmer for 10 minutes. Discard the bay leaves.

6 Cover the base of an ovenproof dish with a thin layer of sauce. Fill the cannelloni with the mushroom mixture and place in the dish. Spoon over the remaining sauce, cover with foil, and bake for 35–40 minutes.

COOK'S TIP

For a more filling meal, add some flaked tuna or diced cooked chicken or ham to the stuffing mixture.

Fragrant Spiced Chicken

The combination of chicken and garbanzo beans is particlarly good. Use the canned variety for a quick meal.

NUTRITIONAL INFORMATION

Calories . . . . . . .343 Sugars 5g
Protein . . . . .28g Fat 16g
Carbohydrate . . .24g Saturates 3g

🍲 5 MINS   🕐 30 MINS

SERVES 4

I N G R E D I E N T S

3 tbsp ghee or vegetable oil

8 small chicken portions, such as thighs or drumsticks

1 large onion, peeled and chopped

2 garlic cloves, peeled and minced

1-2 fresh green chilies, seeded and chopped, or use 1-2 tsp minced chili (from a jar)

2 tsp ground cumin

2 tsp ground coriander

1 tsp garam masala

1 tsp ground turmeric

1 x 14 oz can chopped tomatoes

⅔ cup water

1 tbsp chopped fresh mint

1 x 14 oz can garbanzo beans, drained

salt

1 tbsp chopped fresh cilantro

low-fat unsweetened yogurt, to serve (optional)

1 Heat the ghee or oil in a large saucepan and fry the chicken until sealed all over and lightly golden.

2 Remove from the pan. Add the onion, garlic, chili, and spices and cook very gently for 2 minutes, stirring frequently.

3 Stir in the tomatoes, water, mint, and garbanzo beans. Mix well, return the chicken portions to the pan, season with salt, cover, and simmer gently for about 20 minutes or until the chicken is tender.

4 Taste and adjust the seasoning, then sprinkle with the cilantro and serve hot with yogurt (if using)

VARIATION

Canned black-eyed peas and red kidney beans also make delicious additions to this spicy chicken dish. Be sure to drain and rinse canned beans before adding to the pan.

Fish & Rice with Dark Rum

Based on a traditional Cuban recipe, this dish is similar to Spanish paella, but it has the added kick of dark rum.

NUTRITIONAL INFORMATION

Calories	547	Sugars	.........9g
Protein	........27g	Fat	...........4g
Carbohydrate	...85g	Saturates	......1g

2¼ HOURS   35 MINS

SERVES 4

INGREDIENTS

1 lb firm white fish fillets (such as cod or swordfish), skinned and cut into 1 inch cubes

2 tsp ground cumin

2 tsp dried oregano

2 tbsp lime juice

⅔ cup dark rum

1 tbsp brown sugar

3 garlic cloves, chopped finely

1 large onion, chopped

1 medium red bell pepper, deseeded and sliced into rings

1 medium green (bell) pepper, deseeded and sliced into rings

1 medium yellow bell pepper, deseeded and sliced into rings

5 cups fish stock

2 cups long-grain rice

salt and pepper

crusty bread, to serve

TO GARNISH

fresh oregano leaves

lime wedges

1 Place the cubes of fish in a bowl and add the cumin, oregano, salt and pepper, lime juice, rum, and sugar. Mix everything together well, cover, and leave to chill for 2 hours.

2 Meanwhile, place the garlic, onion, and bell peppers in a large saucepan. Pour over the stock and stir in the rice. Bring to a boil, cover, and leave to cook for 15 minutes.

3 Gently add the fish and the marinade juices to the pan. Bring back to a boil and simmer, uncovered, stirring occasionally, but taking care not to break up the fish, for 10 minutes until the fish is cooked and the rice is tender.

4 Season to taste and transfer to a warm serving plate. Garnish with fresh oregano and lime wedges and serve with crusty bread.

Balti Dal

Chang dal is the husked, split, black garbanzo bean, which is yellow on the inside and has a nutty taste.

NUTRITIONAL INFORMATION

Calories 132	Sugars 2g
Protein 6g	Fat 6g
Carbohydrate ...15g	Saturates 1g

5 MINS   1¼ HOURS

SERVES 4

INGREDIENTS

1 cup chang dal or yellow split peas, washed

½ tsp ground turmeric

1 tsp ground coriander

1 tsp salt

4 curry leaves

2 tbsp oil

½ tsp asafoetida powder (optional)

1 tsp cumin seeds

2 onions, chopped

2 garlic cloves, crushed

½ inch piece fresh ginger, grated

½ tsp garam masala

1 Put the chang dal in a large saucepan. Pour in enough water to cover by 1 inch.

2 Bring to a boil and use a spoon to remove the scum that has formed.

3 Add the turmeric, ground coriander, salt, and curry leaves. Simmer for 1 hour. The chang dal should be tender, but not mushy.

4 Heat the oil in a wok. Add the asafoetida (if using) and fry for 30 seconds.

5 Add the cumin seeds and fry until they start popping.

6 Add the onions and stir-fry until golden brown.

7 Add the garlic, ginger, garam masala, and chang dal to the pan or wok and stir-fry for 2 minutes. Serve the balti hot as a side dish with a curry meal or store in the refrigerator for later use.

COOK'S TIP

Dal reheats and keeps well so it is a good idea to make a large amount and store it in the refrigerator or freezer in small portions.

Red Bean Stew & Dumplings

There's nothing better on a cold day than a hearty dish topped with dumplings. This recipe is quick and easy to prepare.

NUTRITIONAL INFORMATION

Calories 508   Sugars 15g
Protein . . . . .22g   Fat 12g
Carbohydrate . . .83g   Saturates 4g

   1¼ HOURS   35 MINS

SERVES 4

INGREDIENTS

1 tbsp vegetable oil

1 red onion, sliced

2 celery stalks, chopped

3½ cups Fresh Vegetable Stock (see page 31)

8 oz carrots, diced

8 oz potatoes, diced

8 oz zucchini, diced

4 tomatoes, peeled and chopped

½ cup red lentils

14 oz can kidney beans, rinsed and drained

1 tsp paprika

salt and pepper

DUMPLINGS

1 cup all-purpose flour

½ tsp salt

2 tsp baking powder

1 tsp paprika

1 tsp dried mixed herbs

2 tbsp vegetable suet

7 tbsp water

sprigs of fresh flat-leaf parsley, to garnish

1 Heat the oil in a flameproof casserole or a large saucepan and gently fry the onion and celery for 3–4 minutes until just softened. Pour in the stock and stir in the carrots and potatoes. Bring to a boil, cover, and cook for 5 minutes.

2 Stir in the zucchini, tomatoes, lentils, kidney beans, paprika, and seasoning. Bring to a boil, cover, and cook for 5 minutes.

3 To make the dumplings, sift the flour, salt, baking powder, and paprika into a bowl. Stir in the herbs and suet. Bind together with the water to form a soft dough. Divide into eight and roll into balls.

4 Add the dumplings to the stew, pushing them slightly into the stew. Cover and simmer for 15 minutes until the dumplings have risen and are cooked through. Garnish with flat-leaf parsley.

Tofu (Bean Curd) Burgers

Flavored with spices and served with a sesame-flavored relish, these delicious burgers are perfect for vegetarians.

NUTRITIONAL INFORMATION

Calories 471	Sugars 7g	
Protein 22g	Fat 12g	
Carbohydrate . . .74g	Saturates 2g	

15 MINS   20 MINS

SERVES 4

INGREDIENTS

1 small red onion, chopped finely

1 garlic clove, minced

1 tsp ground cumin

1 tsp ground coriander

2 tbsp lemon juice

14 oz can garbanzo beans, drained and rinsed

2¾ oz soft silken tofu (bean curd), drained

4 oz cooked potato, diced

4 tbsp freshly chopped cilantro

2¾ oz dry brown bread crumbs

1 tbsp vegetable oil

burger buns

2 medium tomatoes, sliced

1 large carrot, grated

salt and pepper

RELISH

1 tsp sesame seed paste

4 tbsp low-fat unsweetened yogurt

1 inch piece cucumber, finely chopped

1 tbsp chopped, fresh cilantro

garlic salt, to season

1 Place the onion, garlic, spices, and lemon juice in a pan, bring to a boil, cover, and simmer for 5 minutes until softened.

2 Place the garbanzo beans, tofu (bean curd), and potato in a bowl and mash well. Stir in the onion mixture, cilantro, and seasoning, and mix together. Divide into 4 and form into patties 4 inches across. Sprinkle the bread crumbs on to a plate and press the burgers into the crumbs to coat both sides.

3 Heat the oil in a large skillet and fry the burgers for 5 minutes on each side until golden. Mix the relish ingredients together in a bowl and leave to chill. Place sliced tomato and grated carrot on the buns and top with a burger. Serve with the relish.

Risotto Verde

Risotto is an Italian dish which is easy to make and uses arborio rice, onion, and garlic as a base for a range of savory recipes.

NUTRITIONAL INFORMATION

Calories 374   Sugars 5g
Protein ....10g   Fat 9g
Carbohydrate ...55g   Saturates 2g

 5 MINS   45 MINS

SERVES 4

INGREDIENTS

7½ cups vegetable stock

2 tbsp olive oil

2 garlic cloves, crushed

2 leeks, shredded

1¼ cups arborio rice

1¼ cups dry white wine

4 tbsp chopped mixed herbs

8 oz baby spinach

3 tbsp low-fat plain yogurt

salt and pepper

shredded leek, to garnish

1 Pour the stock into a large saucepan and bring to a boil. Reduce the heat to a simmer.

2 Meanwhile, heat the oil in a separate pan and sauté the garlic and leeks for 2–3 minutes until softened.

3 Stir in the rice and cook for 2 minutes, stirring, until well coated.

4 Pour in half of the wine and a little of the hot stock. Cook over a gentle heat until all of the liquid has been absorbed.

5 Add the remaining stock and wine and cook over a low heat for 25 minutes or until the rice is creamy.

6 Stir in the chopped mixed herbs and baby spinach, season well with salt and pepper, and cook for 2 minutes.

7 Stir in the plain yogurt, garnish with the shredded leek, and serve immediately.

COOK'S TIP

Do not hurry the process of cooking the risotto as the rice must absorb the liquid slowly in order for it to reach the correct consistency.

Chicken with Rice & Peas

The secret of this dish is that it must be brown in color, which is achieved by caramelizing the chicken first.

NUTRITIONAL INFORMATION

Calories	335	Sugars	........11g
Protein	........20g	Fat	..........12g
Carbohydrate	...38g	Saturates	......6g

10 MINS 1 HOUR

SERVES 6

INGREDIENTS

1 onion, chopped

2 garlic cloves

1 tbsp chopped fresh chives

1 tbsp chopped fresh thyme

2 celery stalks with leaves, chopped

1½ cups water

½ fresh coconut, chopped

liquid from 1 fresh coconut

1 lb 2 oz can kidney beans, drained

1 red chili, deseeded and sliced thinly

2 tbsp walnut oil

2 tbsp sugar

3 lb 5 oz chicken pieces

1¼ cups white long-grain rice, rinsed and drained

salt and pepper

celery leaves, to garnish

1 Put the onion, garlic, chives, thyme, celery, and 4 tablespoons of the water into a food processor. Blend until smooth.

2 Alternatively, chop the onion and celery very finely, then grind with the garlic and herbs in a pestle and mortar, gradually mixing in the water. Pour into a saucepan and set aside.

3 Put the coconut and liquid into the food processor and mix to form a thick milk, adding water if necessary. Alternatively, finely grate the coconut and mix with the liquid. Add to the onion and celery mixture. Stir in the drained or kidney beans and chili. Cook over a low heat for 15 minutes, then season.

4 Put the oil and sugar in a heavy-based casserole and cook over a moderate heat until the sugar begins to caramelize. Add the chicken and cook for 15–20 minutes, turning frequently, until browned all over.

5 Stir in the coconut mixture, the rice, and remaining water. Bring to a boil, then reduce the heat, cover, and simmer for 20 minutes until the chicken and rice are tender and the liquid has been absorbed. Garnish with celery leaves.

Lamb Biryani

In India, this elaborate, beautifully colored dish is usually served on festive occasions. This simpler version can be made anytime.

NUTRITIONAL INFORMATION

Calories	448	Sugars	.........9g
Protein	........32g	Fat	..........22g
Carbohydrate	...32g	Saturates	......7g

2¼ HOURS   45 MINS

SERVES 4

INGREDIENTS

generous 1 cup basmati rice, washed and drained

½ tsp salt

2 garlic cloves, peeled and left whole

1 inch piece gingerroot, grated

4 cloves

½ tsp black peppercorns

2 green cardamom pods

1 tsp cumin seeds

1 tsp coriander seeds

1 inch piece cinnamon stick

¼ tsp grated nutmeg

1 tsp saffron strands

4 tbsp tepid water

2 tbsp ghee

2 shallots, sliced

¼ tsp chili powder

1 lb boneless lean leg of lamb, cut into 1 inch cubes

¾ cup low-fat unsweetened yogurt

2 tbsp golden raisins

¼ cup slivered almonds, toasted

1   Add the rice to a saucepan of boiling water and boil for 6 minutes, then drain. Grind the garlic and the spices. Mix the saffron and water. Heat the ghee in a saucepan, add the shallots and fry until golden brown, then add the spices, nutmeg, and chili. Stir for 1 minute and add the lamb. Cook until browned. Add the yogurt and golden raisins and simmer for 40 minutes. Pile the rice on top of the sauce and trickle over the saffron water.

2   Cover the pan with a clean dish cloth and place the lid on top. Reduce the heat and cook for 10 minutes.

3   Remove the lid and cloth, and quickly make 3 holes in the rice with a wooden spoon handle, to the level of the sauce, but not touching it. Replace the cloth and the lid and leave for 5 minutes, then lightly fork the rice. Serve with toasted almonds.

Chicken & Spinach Lasagne

A delicious pasta bake with all the colors of the Italian flag – red tomatoes, green spinach, and pasta, and white chicken and sauce.

NUTRITIONAL INFORMATION

Calories 358   Sugars 12g
Protein ....42g   Fat 9g
Carbohydrate ...22g   Saturates 4g

 25 MINS   50 MINS

SERVES 4

I N G R E D I E N T S

12 oz frozen chopped spinach, thawed and drained

½ tsp ground nutmeg

1 lb lean, cooked chicken meat, skinned and diced

4 sheets no-pre-cook lasagne verde

1½ tbsp cornstarch

1¾ cups skimmed milk

4 tbsp Parmesan cheese, freshly grated

salt and pepper

T O M A T O   S A U C E

14 oz can chopped tomatoes

1 medium onion, finely chopped

1 garlic clove, minced

⅔ cup white wine

3 tbsp tomato paste

1 tsp dried oregano

green salad, to serve

1 Preheat the oven to 400°F. For the tomato sauce, place the tomatoes in a saucepan and stir in the onion, garlic, wine, tomato paste, and oregano. Bring to a boil and simmer for 20 minutes until thick. Season well.

2 Drain the spinach again and spread it out on paper towels to make sure that as much water as possible is removed. Layer the spinach in the base of an ovenproof baking dish. Sprinkle with nutmeg and season.

3 Arrange the diced chicken over the spinach and spoon over the tomato sauce. Arrange the sheets of lasagne over the tomato sauce.

4 Blend the cornstarch with a little of the milk to make a paste. Pour the remaining milk into a saucepan and stir in the cornstarch paste. Heat for 2–3 minutes, stirring, until the sauce thickens. Season well.

5 Spoon the sauce over the lasagne and transfer the dish to a baking sheet. Sprinkle the grated cheese over the sauce and bake in the oven for 25 minutes until golden-brown. Serve with a green salad.

Fragrant Asparagus Risotto

Soft, creamy rice combines with the flavors of citrus and light aniseed to make this a delicious supper for four or a substantial starter for six.

NUTRITIONAL INFORMATION

Calories . . . . .223 Sugars 9g
Protein . . . . .6g Fat 6g
Carbohydrate . . .40g Saturates 1g

10 MINS   45 MINS

SERVES 4

I N G R E D I E N T S

4 oz fine asparagus, trimmed

5 cups vegetable stock

2 bulbs fennel

1 oz low-fat spread

1 tsp olive oil

2 sticks celery, trimmed and chopped

2 medium leeks, trimmed and shredded

2 cups arborio rice

3 medium oranges

salt and pepper

1 Bring a small saucepan of water to a boil and cook the asparagus for 1 minute. Drain the asparagus and set aside until required.

2 Pour the stock into a saucepan and bring to a boil. Reduce the heat to maintain a gentle simmer.

3 Meanwhile, trim the fennel, reserving the fronds. Use a sharp knife to cut into thin slices.

4 Carefully melt the low-fat spread with the oil in a large saucepan, taking care that the water in the low-fat spread does not evaporate, and gently fry the fennel, celery, and leeks for 3–4 minutes until just softened. Add the rice

and cook, stirring, for a further 2 minutes until mixed.

5 Add a ladleful of stock to the pan and cook gently, stirring, until absorbed.

6 Continue ladling the stock into the rice until the rice becomes creamy, thick, and tender. This process will take about 25 minutes and should not be hurried.

7 Finely grate the rind and extract the juice from 1 orange and mix into the rice. Carefully remove the peel and pith from the remaining oranges. Holding the fruit over the saucepan, cut out the orange segments and add to the rice, along with any juice that falls.

8 Stir the orange into the rice along with the asparagus. Season to taste and garnish with the fennel fronds.

Shrimp Pasta Bake

This dish is ideal for a substantial supper. You can use whatever pasta you like, but the tricolor varieties will give the most colorful results.

NUTRITIONAL INFORMATION

Calories	723	Sugars	.........9g
Protein	........56g	Fat	...........8g
Carbohydrate	...114g	Saturates	......2g

10 MINS   50 MINS

SERVES 4

INGREDIENTS

8 oz tricolor pasta shapes

1 tbsp vegetable oil

6 oz small white mushrooms, sliced

1 bunch green onions, trimmed and chopped

14 oz can tuna in water, drained and flaked

6 oz peeled shrimp, thawed if frozen

2 tbsp cornstarch

1¾ cups skim milk

4 medium tomatoes, sliced thinly

1 oz fresh bread crumbs

1 oz reduced-fat Cheddar cheese, grated

salt and pepper

TO SERVE

whole wheat bread

fresh salad

1 Preheat the oven to 375°F. Bring a large saucepan of water to a boil and cook the pasta according to the instructions on the package. Drain well.

2 Meanwhile, heat the vegetable oil in a frying pan and fry the mushrooms and all but a handful of the green onions for 4–5 minutes until softened.

3 Place the cooked pasta in a bowl and mix in the green onions, mushrooms, tuna, and shrimp.

4 Blend the cornstarch with a little milk to make a paste. Pour the remaining milk into a saucepan and stir in the paste. Heat, stirring, until the sauce begins to thicken. Season well. Add the sauce to the pasta mixture and mix well. Transfer to an ovenproof gratin dish and place on a cookie sheet.

5 Arrange the tomato slices over the pasta and sprinkle with the bread crumbs and cheese. Bake for 25–30 minutes until golden. Serve sprinkled with the reserved green onions and accompanied with bread and salad.

Lamb Couscous

Couscous is a North African speciality and is usually accompanied by a spicy mixture of meat or sausage and fruit.

NUTRITIONAL INFORMATION

Calories	647	Sugars	........22g
Protein	........41g	Fat	..........21g
Carbohydrate	...79g	Saturates	......6g

🥘 15 MINS   🕐 20 MINS

SERVES 4

INGREDIENTS

2 tbsp olive oil

1 lb 2 oz lean lamb tenderloin, sliced thinly

2 onions, sliced

2 garlic cloves, chopped

1 cinnamon stick

1 tsp ground ginger

1 tsp paprika

½ tsp chili powder

2½ cups hot chicken stock

3 carrots, sliced thinly

2 turnips, halved and sliced

14 oz can chopped tomatoes

2 tbsp raisins

15 oz can garbanzo beans, drained and rinsed

3 zucchini, sliced

4½ oz fresh dates, halved and pitted or 4½ oz dried apricots

1¾ cups couscous

2½ cups boiling water

salt

1 Heat the oil in a frying pan and fry the lamb briskly for 3 minutes until browned. Remove the meat from the pan with a perforated spoon or fish slice and set aside.

2 Add the onions to the pan and cook, stirring, until soft. Add the garlic and spices and cook for 1 minute.

3 Add the stock, carrots, turnips, tomatoes, raisins, garbanzo beans, and lamb. Cover, bring to a boil, and simmer for 12 minutes.

4 Add the zucchini, dates or apricots, and season with salt. Cover again and cook for 8 minutes.

5 Meanwhile, put the couscous in a bowl with 1 teaspoon of salt and pour over the boiling water. Leave to soak for 5 minutes, then fluff with a fork.

6 To serve, pile the couscous onto a warmed serving platter and make a hollow in the center. Put the meat and vegetables in the hollow and pour over some of the sauce. Serve the rest of the sauce separately.

Italian Chicken Spirals

Steaming allows you to cook without fat, and these little foil parcels retain all the natural juices of the chicken.

NUTRITIONAL INFORMATION

Calories	Sugar ....
Protein	Fats ....
Carbohydrates	Saturates ....

🐑 🐑 🐑

🍲 MINS   🕐 MINS

SERVES 4

I N G R E D I E N T S

4 skinless, boneless, chicken breasts

1 cup fresh basil leaves

2 tbsp hazelnuts

1 garlic clove, crushed

2 cups whole wheat pasta spirals

2 sun-dried tomatoes or fresh tomatoes

1 tbsp lemon juice

1 tbsp olive oil

1 tbsp capers

½ cup black olives

salt and pepper

sprigs of basil, to garnish

1 Place the chicken breasts between pieces of plastic wrap and beat with a rolling pin to flatten evenly.

2 Place the basil and hazelnuts in a food processor and process until finely chopped. Mix with the garlic, salt and pepper.

3 Spread the basil mixture over the chicken breasts and roll up from one short end to enclose the filling. Wrap the chicken roll tightly in foil so that they hold their shape, then seal the ends well.

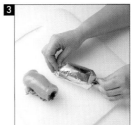

4 Add the pasta to a large pan of lightly salted, boiling water. Place the chicken parcels in a steamer basket or colander set over the pan, cover tightly, and steam for 10 minutes. Meanwhile, dice the tomatoes.

5 Drain the pasta and return to the pan with the lemon juice, olive oil, tomatoes, capers, and olives. Heat until warmed through.

6 Pierce the chicken with a skewer to make sure that the juices run clear and not pink, then slice the chicken and arrange over the pasta. Garnish with sprigs of basil and serve with a tomato salad.

Rice-Stuffed Mushrooms

Flat mushrooms are ideal for baking. They are filled with more strongly flavored wild mushrooms although you can use the ordinary varieties.

NUTRITIONAL INFORMATION

Calories 168	Sugars 1g
Protein 7g	Fat 3g
Carbohydrate . . .23g	Saturates 1g

25 MINS   35 MINS

SERVES 4

I N G R E D I E N T S

4 large flat mushrooms

3½ oz assorted wild mushrooms, sliced

4 dry-pack, sun-dried tomatoes, shredded

⅔ cup dry red wine

4 green onions, trimmed and finely chopped

1½ cups cooked red rice

2 tbsp freshly grated Parmesan cheese

4 thick slices multigrain bread

salt and pepper

green onion, shredded, to garnish

1 Preheat the oven to 375°F. Peel the flat mushrooms, pull out the stalks, and set aside. Finely chop the stalks and place in a saucepan.

2 Add the wild mushrooms to the saucepan along with the tomatoes and red wine.

3 Bring to a boil, cover, and gently simmer the tomatoes and mushrooms for 2–3 minutes until just tender. Drain, reserving the cooking liquid, and place in a small bowl.

4 Gently stir in the chopped green onions and cooked rice. Season well

and spoon into the flat mushrooms, pressing the mixture down gently. Sprinkle with the grated Parmesan.

5 Arrange the mushrooms in an ovenproof baking dish and pour the reserved cooking juices around them. Bake in the oven for 20–25 minutes until they are just cooked.

6 Meanwhile, preheat the broiler to hot. Trim the crusts from the bread and toast on each side until lightly browned.

7 Drain the mushrooms and place each one onto a piece of toasted bread. Garnish with green onions and serve.

Masala Lamb & Lentils

This recipe makes a good warming winter curry. Gram lentils are used here but you could use split yellow peas instead, if you prefer.

NUTRITIONAL INFORMATION

Calories	397	Sugars	.........1g
Protein	........42g	Fat	..........22g
Carbohydrate	....8g	Saturates	......9g

🐻 🐻

🥔 6¼ HOURS   🕐 1½ HOURS

SERVES 4

INGREDIENTS

2 tbsp oil

1 tsp cumin seeds

2 bay leaves

1 inch piece cinnamon stick

1 onion, chopped

1 lb 10 oz lean, boneless lamb, cut into
   1 inch cubes

½ cup split gram lentils or split yellow peas,
   soaked for 6 hours and drained

1 tsp salt

1 fresh green chili, sliced

5 cups water

1 garlic clove, crushed

¼ tsp ground turmeric

1 tsp chili powder

½ tsp garam masala or curry powder
   (optional)

1 tbsp chopped fresh cilantro (optional)

1 Heat the oil in a wok and add the cumin seeds, bay leaves, and cinnamon and fry until the seeds start popping.

2 Add the onion to the pan and stir-fry until golden brown. Stir the lamb into the wok and stir-fry until browned.

3 Add the lentils, salt, chili, water, garlic, turmeric, and chili powder and stir well. Bring the mixture to a boil and simmer for 1 hour.

4 Taste and stir the garam masala into the pan (if using) and cook for a further 5 minutes.

5 Stir in the cilantro, if using, and serve.

COOK'S TIP
To save time on soaking, use a 14 oz can of lentils. These should be added at the end of stage 4 and cooked for 15 minutes. The meat still needs the same cooking time.

Cajun Chicken Gumbo

This complete main course is cooked in one saucepan. If you're cooking for one, halve the ingredients—the cooking time should stay the same.

NUTRITIONAL INFORMATION

Calories	425	Sugars	.........8g
Protein	........34g	Fat	..........12g
Carbohydrate	...48g	Saturates	......3g

5 MINS   25 MINS

SERVES 2

I N G R E D I E N T S

1 tbsp sunflower oil

4 chicken thighs

1 small onion, diced

2 stalks celery, diced

1 small green bell pepper, diced

½ cup long grain rice

1¼ cups chicken stock

1 small red chili

8 oz okra

1 tbsp tomato paste

salt and pepper

COOK'S TIP

The whole chili makes the dish hot and spicy—if you prefer a milder flavor, discard the seeds of the chili.

1 Heat the oil in a wide pan and fry the chicken until golden. Remove the chicken from the pan.

2 Stir in the onion, celery, and bell pepper and fry for 1 minute. Pour off any excess oil.

3 Add the rice and fry, stirring for a further minute. Add the stock and heat until boiling. Thinly slice the chili and trim the okra. Add to the pan with the tomato paste. Season to taste.

4 Return the chicken to the pan and stir. Cover tightly and simmer gently for 15 minutes, or until the rice is tender, the chicken is thoroughly cooked, and the liquid absorbed. Stir occasionally and if it becomes too dry, add a little extra stock.

Chicken & Chili Bean Pot

This aromatic chicken dish has a spicy Mexican kick. Chicken thighs have a wonderful flavor when cooked in this way.

NUTRITIONAL INFORMATION

Calories 333	Sugars 10g
Protein 25g	Fat 13g
Carbohydrate ...32g	Saturates 2g

 10 MINS   40 MINS

SERVES 4

INGREDIENTS

2 tbsp all-purpose flour

1 tsp chili powder

8 chicken thighs or 4 chicken legs

3 tbsp vegetable oil

2 garlic cloves, crushed

1 large onion, chopped

1 green or red bell pepper, deseeded and chopped

1¼ cups chicken stock

12 oz tomatoes, chopped

14 oz can red kidney beans, rinsed and drained

2 tbsp tomato paste

salt and pepper

1 Mix together the flour, chili powder, and seasoning in a shallow dish. Rinse the chicken, but do not dry. Dip the chicken into the seasoned flour, turning to coat it on all sides.

2 Heat the oil in a large, deep frying pan or saucepan and add the chicken. Cook over a high heat for 3–4 minutes, turning the pieces to brown them all over.

3 Lift the chicken out of the pan with a perforated spoon and drain well on paper towels.

4 Add the garlic, onion, and bell pepper to the pan and cook for 2–3 minutes until softened.

5 Add the stock, tomatoes, kidney beans, and tomato paste, stirring well. Bring to a boil, then return the chicken to the pan. Reduce the heat and simmer, covered, for about 30 minutes, until the chicken is tender. Season to taste and serve at once.

COOK'S TIP

For extra intensity of flavor, use sun-dried tomato paste instead of ordinary tomato paste.

Seafood Spaghetti

You can use whatever combination of shellfish you like in this recipe – it is poached in a savory stock and served with freshly cooked spaghetti.

NUTRITIONAL INFORMATION

Calories 341	Sugars 1g	
Protein 50g	Fat 7g	
Carbohydrate . . .15g	Saturates 1g	

1¼ HOURS   35 MINS

SERVES 4

INGREDIENTS

2 tsp olive oil

1 small red onion, chopped finely

1 tbsp lemon juice

1 garlic clove, crushed

2 sticks celery, chopped finely

⅔ cup Fresh Fish Stock (see page 30)

⅔ cup dry white wine

small bunch fresh tarragon

1 lb fresh mussels, prepared

8 oz fresh shrimp, peeled and deveined

8 oz baby squid, cleaned, trimmed, and sliced into rings

8 small cooked crab claws, cracked and peeled

8 oz spaghetti

salt and pepper

2 tbsp chopped fresh tarragon, to garnish

1 Heat the oil in a large saucepan and fry the onion with the lemon juice, garlic, and celery for 3–4 minutes until just softened.

2 Pour in the stock and wine. Bring to a boil and add the tarragon and mussels. Cover and simmer for 5 minutes.

3 Add the shrimp, squid, and crab claws to the pan, mix together, and cook for 3–4 minutes until the mussels have opened, the shrimp are pink, and the squid is opaque. Discard any mussels that have not opened and the tarragon.

4 Meanwhile, cook the spaghetti in a saucepan of boiling water according to the directions on the package. Drain well.

5 Add the spaghetti to the shellfish mixture and toss together. Season with salt and pepper to taste.

6 Transfer to warm serving plates and spoon over the cooking juices. Serve garnished with freshly chopped tarragon.

Shrimp Biryani

The flavors are more subtle than those of Lamb Biryani (see page 366), so it is a lighter dish and more suitable for every day.

NUTRITIONAL INFORMATION

Calories 177   Sugars 6g
Protein ....15g   Fat 6g
Carbohydrate ...18g   Saturates 0.5g

2½ HOURS   45 MINS

SERVES 8

INGREDIENTS

1 tsp saffron strands

4 tbsp tepid water

2 shallots, chopped coarsely

3 garlic cloves, crushed

1 tsp chopped fresh ginger

2 tsp coriander seeds

½ tsp black peppercorns

2 cloves

2 green cardamom pods

1 inch piece cinnamon stick

1 tsp ground turmeric

1 fresh green chili, chopped

½ tsp salt

2 tbsp ghee or vegetable oil

1 tsp whole black mustard seeds

1 lb 2 oz uncooked tiger shrimp in their
   shells, or 14 oz uncooked and peeled

1¼ cups coconut milk

1¼ cups low-fat plain yogurt

1 cup Basmati rice, soaked for
   2 hours and drained

1 tbsp golden raisins

slivered almonds, toasted and 1 green
   onion, sliced, to garnish

1 Soak the saffron in the tepid water for 10 minutes. Put the shallots, garlic, spices, and salt into a spice grinder or pestle and mortar and grind to a paste.

2 Heat the ghee in a saucepan and add the mustard seeds. When they start to pop, add the shrimp and stir over a high heat for 1 minute. Stir in the spice mix, then the coconut milk, and yogurt. Simmer for 20 minutes.

3 Bring a large saucepan of salted water to a boil. Add the rice to the pan. Boil for 12 minutes. Drain. Pile the rice on the shrimp. Spoon over the golden raisins and trickle the saffron water over the rice in lines. Cover the pan with a clean cloth and put the lid on tightly. Remove the pan from heat and leave to stand for 5 minutes. Serve, garnished with the almonds and sliced green onion.

Cannelloni

Traditionally a rich dish of meat, cheese, and sauces, this lighter version is equally delicious and satisfying.

NUTRITIONAL INFORMATION

Calories	233	Sugars	.........9g
Protein	........20g	Fat	...........6g
Carbohydrate	...17g	Saturates	......3g

20 MINS   1½ HOURS

SERVES 4

INGREDIENTS

2½ cups small white mushrooms

1 cup lean ground beef

1 large red onion, chopped finely

1 garlic clove, crushed

½ tsp ground nutmeg

1 tsp dried mixed herbs

2 tbsp tomato paste

4 tbsp dry red wine

12 dried "quick cook" cannelloni tubes

salt and pepper

tossed salad, to serve

TOMATO SAUCE

1 red onion, chopped finely

1 large carrot, grated

1 celery stick, chopped finely

1 dried bay leaf

⅔ cup dry red wine

14 oz can chopped tomatoes

2 tbsp tomato paste

1 tsp sugar

salt and pepper

TO GARNISH

1 oz Parmesan cheese shavings

p

sprig

1 Chop the mushrooms. In a non-stick frying pan, dry-fry the ground beef, onion, mushrooms, and garlic for 3–4 minutes. Stir in the nutmeg, herbs, seasoning, tomato paste, and wine. Simmer for 15–20 minutes. Cool for 10 minutes.

2 Place the onion, carrot, celery, bay leaf, and wine in a saucepan. Bring to a boil and simmer for 5 minutes. Add the other sauce ingredients and simmer for 15 minutes. Discard the bay leaf.

3 Spoon a quarter of the sauce into an ovenproof dish. Fill the cannelloni with the meat mixture and place on the sauce. Spoon over the remaining sauce. Cover and bake in a preheated oven at 400°F for 35–40 minutes. Garnish with the Parmesan cheese, the plum tomato, and basil sprig.

Spicy Black Eye Peas

A hearty casserole of black eye peas in a rich, sweet tomato sauce flavored with molasses and mustard.

NUTRITIONAL INFORMATION

Calories	.233	Sugars	.21g
Protein	.11g	Fat	.4g
Carbohydrate	.42g	Saturates	.1g

12 HOURS   2¹/₂ HOURS

SERVES 4

INGREDIENTS

2 cups black eye peas, soaked overnight in cold water

1 tbsp vegetable oil

2 medium onions, chopped

1 tbsp clear honey

2 tbsp molasses

4 tbsp dark soy sauce

1 tsp dry mustard powder

4 tbsp tomato paste

2 cups Fresh Vegetable Stock (see page 31)

1 bay leaf

1 sprig each of rosemary, thyme and sage

1 small orange

pepper

1 tbsp cornstarch

2 medium red bell peppers, deseeded and diced

2 tbsp chopped fresh flat-leaf parsley, to garnish

crusty bread, to serve

1 Preheat the oven to 300°F. Rinse the peas and place in a saucepan. Cover with water, bring to a boil, and boil rapidly for 10 minutes. Drain and place in an ovenproof casserole dish.

2 Meanwhile, heat the oil in a frying pan and fry the onions for 5 minutes. Stir in the honey, molasses, soy sauce, mustard, and tomato paste. Pour in the stock, bring to a boil, and pour over the peas.

3 Tie the bay leaf and herbs together with a clean piece of string and add to the pan containing the peas. Using a vegetable peeler, pare off 3 pieces of orange rind and mix into the peas, along with plenty of pepper. Cover and cook for 1 hour.

4 Extract the juice from the orange and blend with the cornstarch to form a paste. Stir into the peas along with the red bell peppers. Cover and cook for 1 hour, until the sauce is rich and thick and the peas are tender. Discard the herbs and orange rind.

5 Garnish with chopped parsley and serve with fresh, crusty bread.

Salads

Too frequently, salads are nothing more than a dismal leaf or two of pale green lettuce with a slice of tomato and a dry ring of onion. Make the most of the wonderful range of fresh fruit and vegetables that are now available from our shops and markets. In this chapter, there is a sumptuous selection of hot and cold salads which can be

eaten as side dishes or as meals in themselves. In some salads, sweet and savory flavours are mixed, for example Hot & Spicy Rice Salad, while in others, spices and rich flavors from other countries give an interesting twist to traditional vegetables, for example Indian Potato Salad. Remember that although salad ingredients may not contain fat, the dressings often do, so use oil sparingly or use a low-fat dressing containing yogurt instead.

Beetroot & Orange Salad

Use freshly cooked beetroot in this unusual combination of colors and flavors, as beetroot soaked in vinegar will spoil the delicate balance.

NUTRITIONAL INFORMATION

Calories 240	Sugars 29g
Protein 10g	Fat 2g
Carbohydrate . . .49g	Saturates 0.3g

2¼ HOURS   1 HOUR

SERVES 4

INGREDIENTS

1⅓ cups long-grain and wild rices

4 large oranges

1 lb cooked beetroot, peeled and drained (if necessary)

2 heads of chicory

salt and pepper

fresh snipped chives, to garnish

DRESSING

4 tbsp low-fat plain yogurt

1 garlic clove, crushed

1 tbsp whole-grain mustard

½ tsp finely grated orange rind

2 tsp clear honey

1 Cook the rices according to the package instructions. Drain and set aside to cool.

2 Meanwhile, slice the top and bottom off each orange. Using a sharp knife, remove the skin and pith. Holding the orange over a bowl to catch the juice, carefully slice between each segment. Place the segments in a separate bowl. Cover the juice and leave to chill.

3 Dice the beetroot into small cubes. Mix with the orange segments, cover, and chill.

4 When the rice has cooled, mix in the reserved orange juice until thoroughly incorporated and season with salt and pepper to taste.

5 Line 4 bowls or plates with the chicory leaves. Spoon over the rice and top with the beetroot and orange.

6 Mix all the dressing ingredients together and spoon over the salad, or serve separately in a bowl, if preferred. Garnish with fresh snipped chives.

Sweet & Sour Fruit

This mixture of fresh and canned fruit, which has a sweet and sour flavor, is very cooling, especially in the summer.

NUTRITIONAL INFORMATION

Calories .... .240	Sugars 58g
Protein 2g	Fat 0.4g
Carbohydrate ...60g	Saturates 0g

 5 MINS   0 MINS

SERVES 4

I N G R E D I E N T S

14 oz can mixed fruit cocktail

14 oz can guavas

2 large bananas

3 apples (optional)

1 tsp ground black pepper

1 tsp salt

½ tsp ground ginger

2 tbsp lemon juice

fresh mint leaves, to garnish

1 Drain the can of mixed fruit cocktail and place the fruit in a deep mixing bowl.

2 Mix the drained fruit cocktail with the guavas and their syrup so that the fruit is well coated.

3 Peel the bananas and cut into thick slices.

4 Peel the apples (optional) and cut into dice.

5 Add the fresh fruit to the bowl containing the canned fruit and mix together.

6 Add the ground black pepper, salt, and ginger and stir to mix. Add the lemon juice to prevent the banana and apple from turning brown and mix again.

7 Serve the sweet and sour fruit as a snack garnished with a few fresh mint leaves.

COOK'S TIP

Guavas are tropical fruits with a powerful, exotic smell. You may find fresh guavas in speciality food shops and large supermarkets, but the canned variety is more widely available. Surprisingly, they have a higher vitamin C content than many citrus fruits.

Mexican Potato Salad

This dish is full of Mexican flavors, where potato slices are topped with tomatoes, chilies, and ham, and served with a guacamole dressing.

NUTRITIONAL INFORMATION

Calories	260	Sugars	.........6g
Protein	.........6g	Fat	...........9g
Carbohydrate	...41g	Saturates	......2g

10 MINS   15 MINS

SERVES 4

INGREDIENTS

4 large new potatoes, sliced

1 ripe avocado

1 tsp olive oil

1 tsp lemon juice

1 garlic clove, crushed

1 onion, chopped

2 large tomatoes, sliced

1 green chili, chopped

1 yellow bell pepper, sliced

2 tbsp chopped fresh cilantro

salt and pepper

lemon wedges, to garnish

1 Cook the potato slices in a saucepan of boiling water for 10-15 minutes or until tender. Drain and leave to cool.

2 Meanwhile, cut the avocado in half and carefully remove the pit. Using a spoon, scoop the avocado flesh from the 2 halves and place in a mixing bowl.

3 Mash the avocado flesh with a fork and stir in the olive oil, lemon juice, garlic, and chopped onion. Cover the bowl and set aside.

4 Mix the tomatoes, chili, and yellow bell pepper together. Then transfer to a salad bowl with the potato slices.

5 Spoon the avocado mixture on top and sprinkle with the cilantro. Season to taste and serve garnished with lemon wedges.

COOK'S TIP

Mixing the avocado flesh with lemon juice prevents it from turning brown once exposed to the air.

Mussel Salad

A colorful combination of cooked mussels tossed together with char-broiled red bell peppers and salad leaves in a lemon dressing.

NUTRITIONAL INFORMATION

Calories 124	Sugars 5g
Protein 16g	Fat 5g
Carbohydrate 5g	Saturates 1g

40 MINS   10 MINS

SERVES 4

INGREDIENTS

2 large red bell peppers

12 oz cooked shelled mussels, thawed if frozen

1 head of radicchio

1 oz arugula leaves

8 cooked New Zealand mussels in their shells

TO SERVE

lemon wedges

crusty bread

DRESSING

1 tbsp olive oil

1 tbsp lemon juice

1 tsp finely grated lemon rind

2 tsp clear honey

1 tsp French mustard

1 tbsp snipped fresh chives

salt and pepper

1 Preheat the broiler to hot. Halve and deseed the bell peppers and place them skin-side up on the rack.

2 Cook for 8–10 minutes until the skin is charred and blistered and the flesh is soft. Leave to cool for 10 minutes, then peel off the skin.

3 Slice the bell pepper flesh into thin strips and place in a bowl. Gently mix in the shelled mussels and set aside until required.

4 To make the dressing, mix all of the ingredients until well blended.

5 Mix into the bell pepper and mussel mixture until coated.

6 Remove the central core of the radicchio and shred the leaves. Place in a serving bowl with the arugula leaves and toss together.

7 Pile the mussel mixture into the center of the leaves and arrange the large mussels in their shells round the edge of the dish. Serve with lemon wedges and crusty bread.

Grapefruit & Coconut Salad

This salad is deceptively light—although it is, in fact, quite filling.
Reserve the grapefruit juices and add to the coconut dressing.

NUTRITIONAL INFORMATION

Calories 201	Sugars 13g
Protein 3g	Fat 15g
Carbohydrate . . .14g	Saturates 9g

15 MINS   5 MINS

SERVES 4

INGREDIENTS

1 cup grated coconut

2 tsp light soy sauce

2 tbsp lime juice

2 tbsp water

2 tsp sunflower oil

1 garlic clove, halved

1 onion, chopped finely

2 large ruby grapefruits

1½ cups alfalfa sprouts

1 Toast the coconut in a dry frying pan, stirring constantly, until golden brown, about 3 minutes. Transfer to a bowl.

2 Add the light soy sauce, lime juice, and water and mix together well..

3 Heat the oil in a saucepan and fry the garlic and onion until soft. Then remove the garlic. Stir the onion into the coconut mixture.

4 Peel the ruby grapefruits, and then segment them carefully. Divide the segments between 4 plates.

5 Sprinkle each plate with a quarter of the alfalfa sprouts, and spoon over a quarter of the coconut mixture.

VARIATION

Try replacing the grapefruit with other citrus fruits belonging to the grapefruit family, such as pomelos, ugli fruit, and mineolas.

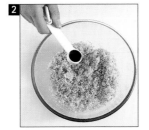

Potato & Radish Salad

The radishes and the herb and mustard dressing give this colorful salad a mild mustard flavor which complements the potatoes perfectly.

NUTRITIONAL INFORMATION

Calories 140	Sugars 3g
Protein 3g	Fat 6g
Carbohydrate ...20g	Saturates 1g

1³/₄ HOURS   20 MINS

SERVES 4

INGREDIENTS

1 lb new potatoes, scrubbed and halved

½ cucumber, sliced thinly

2 tsp salt

1 bunch radishes, sliced thinly

DRESSING

1 tbsp Dijon mustard

2 tbsp olive oil

1 tbsp white wine vinegar

2 tbsp mixed chopped herbs

1 Cook the potatoes in a saucepan of boiling water for 10–15 minutes or until tender. Drain and leave to cool.

2 Spread out the cucumber slices on a plate and sprinkle with the salt. Leave to stand for 30 minutes, then rinse under cold running water and pat dry with paper towels.

3 Arrange the cucumber and radish slices on a serving plate in a decorative pattern.

4 Pile the cooked potatoes in the center of the cucumber and radish slices.

5 Pour all the dressing ingredients in a screw-top jar and shake vigorously to combine all the ingredients. Pour the dressing over the salad, tossing well to coat all of the salad ingredients.

6 Leave the salad to chill in the refrigerator before serving.

COOK'S TIP

Dijon mustard has a mild clean taste which is perfect for this salad as it does not overpower the other flavors. If unavailable, use another mild mustard—English mustard is too strong for this salad.

Hot & Spicy Rice Salad

Serve this spicy Indian-style dish with a low-fat plain yogurt salad for a refreshing contrast.

NUTRITIONAL INFORMATION

Calories	329	Sugars	........27g
Protein	.........8g	Fat	...........8g
Carbohydrate	...59g	Saturates	......1g

30 MINS   25 MINS

SERVES 4

INGREDIENTS

2 tsp vegetable oil

1 onion, chopped finely

1 fresh red chili, deseeded and chopped finely

8 cardamom pods

1 tsp ground turmeric

1 tsp garam masala

1¾ cups Basmati rice, rinsed

3 cups boiling water

1 orange bell pepper, chopped

8 oz cauliflower florets, divided into small sprigs

4 ripe tomatoes, skinned, deseeded, and chopped

¾ cup seedless raisins

¼ cup toasted slivered almonds

salt and pepper

salad of low-fat plain yogurt, onion, cucumber, and mint, to serve

1 Heat the oil in a large non-stick saucepan, add the onion, chili, cardamom pods, turmeric, and garam masala, and fry gently for 2–3 minutes until the vegetables are just softened.

2 Stir in the rice, boiling water, seasoning, bell pepper, and cauliflower.

3 Cover with a tight-fitting lid, bring to a boil, then cook over a low heat for 15 minutes without lifting the lid.

4 Uncover, fork through, and stir in the tomatoes and raisins.

5 Cover again, turn off the heat, and leave for 15 minutes. Discard the cardamom pods.

6 Pile on to a warmed serving platter and sprinkle over the toasted slivered almonds.

7 Serve the rice salad with the yogurt salad.

Layered Chicken Salad

This layered main course salad has lively tastes and textures. For an interesting variation, substitute canned tuna for the chicken.

NUTRITIONAL INFORMATION

Calories	352	Sugars	.........9g
Protein	........29g	Fat	...........9g
Carbohydrate	...43g	Saturates	......2g

1 HOUR   40 MINS

SERVES 4

INGREDIENTS

1 lb 10 oz new potatoes, scrubbed

1 red bell pepper, halved, cored, and deseeded

1 green bell pepper, halved, cored, and deseeded

2 small zucchini, sliced

1 small onion, thinly sliced

3 tomatoes, sliced

12 oz cooked chicken, sliced

snipped fresh chives, to garnish

YOGURT DRESSING

⅔ cup low-fat plain yogurt

3 tbsp low-fat mayonnaise

1 tbsp snipped fresh chives

salt and pepper

1 Put the potatoes into a large saucepan of cold water. Bring to a boil, then reduce the heat. Cover and simmer for 15–20 minutes until tender.

2 Meanwhile place the bell pepper halves, cut side down, under a preheated hot broiler and broil until the skins blacken and begin to char.

3 Remove the bell peppers and leave to cool, then peel off the skins, and slice the flesh. Set aside.

4 Cook the zucchini in a small amount of lightly salted boiling water for 3 minutes.

5 Rinse the zucchini with cold water to cool quickly and set aside.

6 To make the dressing, mix the yogurt, mayonnaise, and snipped chives together in a small bowl. Season well with salt and pepper.

7 Drain, cool, and slice the potatoes. Add them to the dressing and mix well to coat evenly. Divide between 4 serving plates.

8 Top each plate with one quarter of the bell pepper slices and cooked zucchini. Layer one quarter of the onion and tomato slices, then the sliced chicken, on top of each serving. Garnish with snipped fresh chives and serve.

Melon & Mango Salad

A little grated fresh ginger mixed with creamy yogurt and clear honey makes a perfect dressing for this refreshing salad.

NUTRITIONAL INFORMATION

Calories	189	Sugars	........30g
Protein	.........5g	Fat	...........7g
Carbohydrate	...30g	Saturates	......1g

 15 MINS 0 MINS

SERVES 4

I N G R E D I E N T S

1 cantaloupe melon

½ cup black grapes, halved and deseeded

½ cup green grapes

1 large mango

1 bunch of watercress, trimmed

iceberg lettuce leaves, shredded

2 tbsp olive oil

1 tbsp cider vinegar

1 passion fruit

salt and pepper

D R E S S I N G

⅔ cup low-fat thick plain yogurt

1 tbsp clear honey

1 tsp grated fresh root ginger

1 To make the dressing for the melon, mix together the yogurt, honey, and ginger.

2 Halve the melon and scoop out the seeds. Slice, peel, and cut into chunks. Mix with the grapes.

3 Slice the mango on each side of its large flat pit. On each mango half, slash the flesh into a criss-cross pattern down to, but not through, the skin. Push

the skin from underneath to turn the mango halves inside out. Now remove the flesh and add to the melon mixture.

4 Arrange the watercress and lettuce on 4 serving plates.

5 Make the dressing for the salad leaves by mixing the olive oil and cider vinegar with a little salt and pepper. Drizzle over the watercress and lettuce.

6 Divide the melon mixture between the 4 plates and spoon over the yogurt dressing.

7 Scoop the seeds out of the passion fruit and sprinkle them over the salads. Serve immediately or chill in the refrigerator until required.

Cool Cucumber Salad

This cooling salad is another good foil for a highly spiced meal. Omit the green chili, if preferred.

NUTRITIONAL INFORMATION

Calories 11   Sugars 2g
Protein . . . . .0.4g   Fat 0g
Carbohydrate . . . .2g   Saturates 0g

1¼ HOURS   0 MINS

SERVES 4

I N G R E D I E N T S

8 oz cucumber

1 green chili (optional)

fresh cilantro leaves, finely chopped

2 tbsp lemon juice

½ tsp salt

1 tsp sugar

fresh mint leaves and red bell pepper
   strips, to garnish

1 Using a sharp knife, slice the cucumber thinly. Arrange the cucumber slices on a round serving plate.

2 Using a sharp knife, chop the green chili (if using). Scatter the chopped chili over the cucumber.

3 To make the dressing, mix together the cilantro, lemon juice, salt, and sugar.

4 Place the cucumber in the refrigerator and leave to chill for at least 1 hour, or until required.

5 When ready to serve, transfer the cucumber to a serving dish. Pour the salad dressing over the cucumber just before serving and garnish with mint and red bell pepper.

Sweet & Sour Fish Salad

This refreshing blend of pink and white fish mixed with fresh pineapple and bell peppers makes an interesting starter or a light meal.

NUTRITIONAL INFORMATION

Calories	168	Sugars	.........5g
Protein	........24g	Fat	...........6g
Carbohydrate	....5g	Saturates	......1g

  35 MINS   10 MINS

SERVES 4

I N G R E D I E N T S

8 oz trout fillets

8 oz white fish fillets (such as haddock or cod)

1¼ cups water

1 stalk lemon grass

2 lime leaves

1 large red chili

1 bunch green onions, trimmed and shredded

4 oz fresh pineapple flesh, diced

1 small red bell pepper, deseeded and diced

1 bunch watercress, washed and trimmed

fresh snipped chives, to garnish

D R E S S I N G

1 tbsp sunflower oil

1 tbsp rice wine vinegar

pinch of chili powder

1 tsp clear honey

salt and pepper

1 Rinse the fish, place in a frying pan, and pour over the water. Bend the lemon grass in half to bruise it and add to the pan with the lime leaves. Prick the chili with a fork and add to the pan. Bring to a boil and simmer for 7–8 minutes. Let cool.

2 Drain the fish fillet thoroughly, flake the flesh away from the skin, and place in a bowl. Gently stir in the green onions, pineapple, and bell pepper.

3 Arrange the washed watercress on 4 serving plates and spoon the cooked fish mixture on top.

4 To make the dressing, mix all the ingredients together and season well. Spoon over the fish and serve garnished with chives.

Mixed Bean Salad

Any canned beans can be used in this salad—there are a wide variety available. For a light lunch, add some spicy garlic sausage or flaked tuna.

NUTRITIONAL INFORMATION

Calories 213   Sugars 4g
Protein . . . . .13g   Fat 5g
Carbohydrate . . .30g   Saturates 1g

20 MINS   20 MINS

SERVES 8

INGREDIENTS

14 oz can of small navy beans, drained

14 oz can of red kidney beans, drained

14 oz can of pinto beans, drained

½ red onion, sliced finely

6 oz green beans, topped and tailed

1 red bell pepper, cut in half

2 tbsp chopped fresh cilantro

sprig of fresh cilantro,
    to garnish

SOY DRESSING

½ inch piece fresh ginger

1 garlic clove

3 tbsp olive oil

2 tsp red wine vinegar

½ tbsp soy sauce

1 tsp chili sauce

1 tsp sesame oil

1 Put the small navy, red kidney, and pinto beans into a bowl. Add the sliced onion to the beans.

2 Cut the green beans into 1 inch lengths and cook in boiling salted water for 10 minutes until just tender.

Drain the beans and add to the bowl with the other beans.

3 Lay the red bell pepper cut-side down on a broiler pan and cook gently until blackened.

4 Put in a plastic bag to cool. Carefully peel off the skin and chop the bell pepper roughly.

5 To make the dressing, chop the fresh ginger finely, crush the garlic, and place in a screw-top jar with the olive oil, vinegar, soy sauce, chili sauce, and sesame oil. Shake vigorously.

6 Add the dressing to the salad with the red bell pepper and cilantro and mix well. Transfer to a serving dish, garnish, and serve.

Moroccan Couscous Salad

Couscous is a type of semolina made from durum wheat. It is wonderful in salads as it readily takes up the flavor of the dressing.

NUTRITIONAL INFORMATION

Calories 195	Sugars 15g	
Protein 8g	Fat 2g	
Carbohydrate . . .40g	Saturates 0.3g	

15 MINS   15 MINS

SERVES 6

INGREDIENTS

2 cups couscous

1 bunch green onions, trimmed and chopped finely

1 small green bell pepper, cored,deseeded, and chopped

4 inch piece cucumber, chopped

7 oz can garbanzo beans, rinsed and drained

⅔ cup golden raisins

2 oranges

salt and pepper

lettuce leaves, to serve

sprigs of fresh mint, to garnish

DRESSING

finely grated rind of 1 orange

1 tbsp chopped fresh mint

⅔ cup low-fat plain yogurt

1 Put the couscous into a bowl and cover with boiling water. Leave it to soak for about 15 minutes to swell the grains, then stir with a fork to separate them.

2 Add the green onions, green bell pepper, cucumber, garbanzo beans, and golden raisins to the couscous, stirring to combine. Season well with salt and pepper.

3 To make the dressing, mix the orange rind, mint, and yogurt. Pour over the couscous mixture and stir well.

4 Using a sharp serrated knife, remove the peel and pith from the oranges. Cut the flesh into segments, removing all the membrane.

5 Arrange the lettuce leaves on serving plates. Divide the couscous mixture between the plates and arrange the orange segments on top.

6 Garnish with sprigs of fresh mint and serve.

VARIATION

As an alternative, use cracked wheat instead of the couscous. Rinse thoroughly until the water runs clear, then soak in boiling water for 1 hour. Strain if necessary.

Quick Bean Salad

This attractive-looking salad served with meat from the barbecue makes a delicious light meal in summer.

NUTRITIONAL INFORMATION

Calories ....139 Sugars 5g
Protein ....8g Fat 3g
Carbohydrate ...21g Saturates 0.4g

10 MINS   0 MINS

SERVES 4

INGREDIENTS

14 oz can garbanzo beans

4 carrots

1 bunch green onions

1 medium cucumber

½ tsp salt

½ tsp pepper

3 tbsp lemon juice

1 red bell pepper

1 Drain the garbanzo beans and place in a salad bowl.

2 Using a sharp knife, peel and slice the carrots.

3 Cut the green onions into small pieces.

4 Cut the cucumber into thick quarters.

5 Add the carrots, green onions, and cucumber to the garbanzo beans and mix. Season with the salt and pepper and sprinkle with the lemon juice.

6 Toss the salad ingredients together gently using 2 serving spoons.

7 Using a sharp knife, slice the red bell pepper thinly.

8 Arrange the slices of red bell pepper on top of the garbanzo bean salad.

9 Serve the salad immediately or leave to chill in the refrigerator and serve when required.

COOK'S TIP

Using canned garbanzo beans rather than the dried ones speeds up the cooking time.

Pasta Niçoise Salad

Based on the classic French salad niçoise, this recipe has a light olive oil dressing with the tang of capers and the fragrance of fresh basil.

NUTRITIONAL INFORMATION

Calories	.214	Sugars	.2g
Protein	.26g	Fat	.7g
Carbohydrate	.14g	Saturates	.1g

🍲 15 MINS   🕐 35 MINS

SERVES 4

INGREDIENTS

8 oz farfalle (pasta bows)

6 oz green beans, topped and tailed

12 oz fresh tuna steaks

4 oz baby plum tomatoes, halved

8 anchovy fillets, drained on absorbent paper towels

2 tbsp capers in brine, drained

1 oz pitted black olives in brine, drained

fresh basil leaves, to garnish

salt and pepper

DRESSING

1 tbsp olive oil

1 garlic clove, crushed

1 tbsp lemon juice

½ tsp finely grated lemon rind

1 tbsp shredded fresh basil leaves

1 Cook the pasta in lightly salted boiling water according to the instructions on the package until just cooked. Drain well, set aside, and keep warm.

2 Bring a small saucepan of lightly salted water to a boil and cook the green beans for 5–6 minutes until just tender. Drain well and toss into the pasta. Set aside and keep warm.

3 Preheat the broiler to medium. Rinse and pat the tuna steaks dry on absorbent paper towels. Season on both sides with black pepper. Place the tuna steaks on the broiler rack and cook for 4–5 minutes on each side until cooked through.

4 Drain the tuna on absorbent paper towels and flake into bite-sized pieces. Toss the tuna into the pasta along with the tomatoes, anchovies, capers, and olives. Set aside and keep warm.

5 Meanwhile, prepare the dressing. Mix all the ingredients together and season well. Pour the dressing over the pasta mixture and mix carefully. Transfer to a warmed serving bowl and serve sprinkled with fresh basil leaves.

VARIATION

Any pasta shape is suitable for this salad—to make it even more colorful, use different colored pasta.

Indian Potato Salad

There are many hot Indian-flavored potato dishes which are served with curry, but this fruity salad is delicious chilled.

NUTRITIONAL INFORMATION

Calories ....175 Sugars 8g
Protein ....6g Fat 1g
Carbohydrate ...38g Saturates 0.3g

25 MINS   20 MINS

SERVES 4

INGREDIENTS

4 medium russet or Idaho potatoes, diced

2¾ oz small broccoli florets

1 small mango, diced

4 green onions, sliced

salt and pepper

small cooked spiced poppadoms, to serve

DRESSING

½ tsp ground cumin

½ tsp ground coriander

1 tbsp mango chutney

⅔ cup low-fat plain yogurt

1 tsp fresh ginger, chopped

2 tbsp chopped fresh cilantro

1 Cook the potatoes in a saucepan of boiling water for 10 minutes or until tender. Drain and place in a mixing bowl.

2 Meanwhile, blanch the broccoli florets in a separate saucepan of boiling water for 2 minutes. Drain the broccoli well and add to the potatoes in the bowl.

3 When the potatoes and broccoli have cooled, add the diced mango and sliced green onions. Season to taste with salt and pepper and mix well to combine.

4 In a small bowl, stir all of the dressing ingredients together.

5 Spoon the dressing over the potato mixture and mix together carefully, taking care not to break up the potatoes and broccoli.

6 Serve the salad immediately, accompanied by small cooked spiced poppadoms.

COOK'S TIP

Mix the dressing ingredients together in advance and leave to chill in the refrigerator for a few hours in order for a stronger flavor to develop.

Coleslaw

Home-made coleslaw tastes far superior to any that you can buy. If you make it in advance, add the sunflower seeds just before serving.

NUTRITIONAL INFORMATION

Calories	224	Sugars	.........8g
Protein	.........3g	Fat	..........20g
Carbohydrate	....8g	Saturates	......3g

🥗 10 MINS   🕐 5 MINS

SERVES 4

INGREDIENTS

⅔ cup low-fat mayonnaise

⅔ cup low-fat plain yogurt

dash of Tabasco sauce

1 medium head white cabbage

4 carrots

1 green bell pepper

2 tbsp sunflower seeds

salt and pepper

1 To make the dressing, combine the mayonnaise, yogurt, Tabasco sauce, and salt and pepper to taste in a small bowl. Leave to chill until required.

2 Cut the cabbage in half and then into quarters. Remove and discard the tough center stalk. Shred the cabbage leaves finely. Wash the leaves and dry them thoroughly.

VARIATION

For a slightly different taste, add one or more of the following ingredients to the coleslaw: raisins, grapes, grated apple, chopped walnuts, cubes of cheese, or roasted peanuts.

3 Peel the carrots and shred using a food processor. Alternatively, coarsely grate the carrot.

4 Quarter and deseed the bell pepper and cut the flesh into thin strips.

5 Combine the vegetables in a large mixing bowl and toss to mix. Pour over the dressing and toss until the

vegetables are well coated. Leave to chill in the refrigerator until required.

6 Just before serving, place the sunflower seeds on a cookie sheet and toast them in the oven or under the broiler until golden brown. Transfer the salad to a large serving dish, scatter with sunflower seeds, and serve.

Mango & Wild Rice Salad

Wild rice is, in fact, an aquatic grass that is native to North America. It has a delicious nutty flavor and a slightly chewy texture.

NUTRITIONAL INFORMATION

Calories	320	Sugars	........10g
Protein	.........6g	Fat	..........20g
Carbohydrate	...30g	Saturates	......2g

   15 MINS   1¼ HOURS

SERVES 4

INGREDIENTS

½ cup wild rice

1 cup Basmati rice

3 tbsp hazelnut oil

1 tbsp sherry vinegar

1 ripe mango

3 sticks celery

2¾ oz ready-to-eat dried apricots, chopped

2¾ oz slivered almonds, toasted

2 tbsp chopped, fresh cilantro or mint

salt and pepper

sprigs of fresh cilantro or mint, to garnish

1 Cook the rice in separate saucepans in lightly salted boiling water. Cook the wild rice for 45–50 minutes and the Basmati rice for 10–12 minutes. Drain, rinse well, and drain again. Place the rice in a large bowl.

2 Mix the oil, vinegar, and seasoning. Pour over the rice and toss well.

3 Cut the mango in half lengthwise, as close to the pit as possible. Remove and discard the pit.

4 Peel the skin from the mango and cut the flesh into slices.

5 Slice the celery thinly and add to the cooled rice with the mango, apricots, almonds, and chopped herbs. Toss together and transfer to a serving dish.

6 Garnish the salad with sprigs of fresh herbs.

COOK'S TIP

To toast almonds, place them on a cookie sheet in a preheated oven, 350°F, for 5–10 minutes. Alternatively, toast them under the broiler, turning frequently and keeping a close eye on them because they will quickly burn.

Eggplant Salad

This tasty Middle Eastern-style salad, with tomatoes and garbanzo beans is perfect to serve with lamb or chicken dishes.

NUTRITIONAL INFORMATION

Calories	206	Sugars	........11g
Protein	........10g	Fat	...........7g
Carbohydrate	...28g	Saturates	......1g

2½ HOURS   25 MINS

SERVES 4

INGREDIENTS

1 lb 2 oz eggplant

4 tbsp salt

1 tbsp olive oil

1 large onion, chopped

1 garlic clove, crushed

⅔ cup Fresh Vegetable Stock (see page 31)

14 oz can chopped tomatoes

2 tbsp tomato paste

1 tsp ground cinnamon

2 tsp sugar

freshly ground black pepper

1 tbsp chopped fresh cilantro

1 tbsp lemon juice

15 oz can garbanzo beans, drained

fresh cilantro sprigs to garnish

TO SERVE

warmed pita bread

lemon wedges

1 Cut the eggplant into ½ inch thick slices and then into cubes. Layer in a bowl, sprinkling well with salt as you go. Set aside for 30 minutes for the bitter juices to drain out.

2 Transfer to a colander and rinse well under running cold water to remove the salt. Drain well and pat dry with paper towels.

3 Heat the oil in a large non-stick frying pan, add the onion and garlic, and fry gently for 2–3 minutes until slightly softened.

4 Pour in the stock and bring to a boil. Add the eggplant, canned tomatoes, tomato paste, cinnamon, sugar, and pepper. Mix together well and simmer gently, uncovered, for 20 minutes until softened. Then set aside to cool completely.

5 Stir in the fresh cilantro, lemon juice, and garbanzo beans Cover the mixture and chill for about 1 hour.

6 Garnish with the cilantro sprigs, and serve with warmed pita bread and lemon wedges.

Green Bean & Carrot Salad

This colorful salad of crisp vegetables is tossed in a delicious sun-dried tomato dressing.

NUTRITIONAL INFORMATION

Calories 104   Sugars 9g
Protein . . . . .2g   Fat 6g
Carbohydrate . . .10g   Saturates 1g

 10 MINS   5 MINS

SERVES 4

INGREDIENTS

12 oz green beans

8 oz carrots

1 red bell pepper

1 red onion

DRESSING

2 tbsp extra virgin olive oil

1 tbsp red wine vinegar

2 tsp sun-dried tomato paste

¼ tsp sugar

salt and pepper

1 Top and tail the green beans and blanch them in boiling water for 4 minutes, until just tender. Drain the beans and rinse them under cold water until they are cool. Drain again thoroughly.

2 Transfer the beans to a large salad bowl.

3 Peel the carrots and cut them into thin matchsticks.

4 Halve and deseed the bell pepper and cut the flesh into thin strips.

5 Peel the onion and cut it into thin slices.

6 Add the carrot, bell pepper, and onion to the beans and toss to mix.

7 To make the dressing, place the oil, wine vinegar, sun-dried tomato paste, sugar, and salt and pepper to taste in a small screw-top jar and shake well.

8 Pour the dressing over the vegetables and serve immediately or leave to chill in the refrigerator until required.

COOK'S TIP

Use canned beans if fresh ones are unavailable. Rinse off the salty liquid and drain well. There is no need to blanch canned beans.

Mixed Leaf Salad

Make this green leafy salad made from as many varieties of salad leaves and flowers as you can find to give an unusual effect.

NUTRITIONAL INFORMATION

Calories	51	Sugars	0.1g
Protein	0.1g	Fat	.6g
Carbohydrate	1g	Saturates	1g

5 MINS   0 MINS

SERVES 4

INGREDIENTS

½ head chicory and of leaf lettuce

few leaves of radiccio

1 head endive

½ cup arugula leaves

few sprigs fresh basil or flat-leaf parsley

6 tbsp French Dressing (see page 420)

flowers of your choice (see Cook's Tip)

FRENCH DRESSING

3 tbsp olive oil

1 tbsp wine vinegar

1 small garlic clove, crushed

½ tsp Dijon or Meaux mustard

1 tsp clear honey

salt and pepper

1 Tear the chicory, oak leaf lettuce, and radiccio into manageable pieces.

2 Place the salad leaves into a large serving bowl, or individual bowls if you prefer.

3 Cut the endive into diagonal slices and add to the bowl with the arugula leaves, basil, or parsley.

4 To make the French dressing, put all the ingredients into a screw-top jar and shake vigorously.

5 Pour the dressing over the salad and toss thoroughly. Scatter a mixture of flowers over the top.

COOK'S TIP

Violas, rock geraniums, nasturtiums, chive flowers, and pot marigolds add vibrant colors and a sweet flavor to any salad. Use as a centerpiece at a dinner party, or to liven up a simple everyday meal.

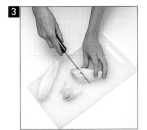

Spinach & Orange Salad

This is a refreshing and very nutritious salad. Add the dressing just before serving so that the leaves do not become soggy.

NUTRITIONAL INFORMATION

Calories ....126 Sugars 10g
Protein ....3g Fat 9g
Carbohydrate ...10g Saturates 1g

 10 MINS   0 MINS

SERVES 4

INGREDIENTS

8 oz baby spinach leaves

2 large oranges

½ red onion

DRESSING

3 tbsp extra virgin olive oil

2 tbsp freshly squeezed orange juice

2 tsp lemon juice

1 tsp clear honey

½ tsp wholegrain mustard

salt and pepper

1 Wash the spinach leaves under cold running water and then dry them thoroughly on absorbent paper towels. Remove any tough stalks and tear the larger leaves into smaller pieces.

2 Slice the top and bottom off each orange with a sharp knife, then remove the peel. Carefully slice between the membranes of the orange to remove the segments. Reserve any juices for the salad dressing.

3 Using a sharp knife, finely chop the onion.

4 Mix together the salad leaves and orange segments and arrange in a serving dish.

5 Scatter the chopped onion over the salad.

6 To make the dressing, whisk together the olive oil, orange juice, lemon juice, honey, mustard, and salt and pepper to taste in a small bowl.

7 Pour the dressing over the salad just before serving. Toss the salad well to coat the leaves with the dressing.

VARIATION
Use a mixture of spinach and watercress leaves, if you prefer a slightly more peppery flavor.

Potato & Tuna Salad

This colorful dish is a variation of the classic Salade Niçoise. Packed with tuna and vegetables, it is both filling and delicious.

NUTRITIONAL INFORMATION

Calories ....225 Sugars 5g
Protein ....21g Fat 5g
Carbohydrate ...27g Saturates 2g

40 MINS   20 MINS

SERVES 4

I N G R E D I E N T S

1 lb new potatoes, scrubbed and quartered

1 green bell pepper, sliced

1¾ oz canned corn kernels, drained

1 red onion, sliced

10½ oz canned tuna in water, drained and flaked

2 tbsp chopped pitted black olives

salt and pepper

lime wedges, to garnish

D R E S S I N G

2 tbsp low-fat mayonnaise

2 tbsp sour cream

1 tbsp lime juice

2 garlic cloves, crushed

finely grated rind of 1 lime

1 Cook the potatoes in a saucepan of boiling water for 15 minutes until tender. Drain and leave to cool in a mixing bowl.

2 Gently stir in the sliced green bell pepper, corn, and sliced red onion.

3 Spoon the potato mixture into a large serving bowl and arrange the flaked tuna and chopped black olives over the top.

4 Season the salad generously with salt and pepper.

5 To make the dressing, mix together the mayonnaise, sour cream, lime juice, garlic, and lime rind in a bowl.

6 Spoon the dressing over the tuna and olives, garnish with lime wedges, and serve.

COOK'S TIP

Green beans and hard-boiled egg slices can be added to the salad for a more traditional Salade Niçoise.

Chicken & Spinach Salad

Slices of lean chicken with fresh young spinach leaves and a few fresh raspberries are served with a refreshing yogurt and honey dressing.

NUTRITIONAL INFORMATION

Calories	235	Sugars	.........9g
Protein	........37g	Fat	..........6g
Carbohydrate	....9g	Saturates	......2g

 3¹/₂ HOURS 🕐 25 MINS

SERVES 4

INGREDIENTS

4 boneless, skinless chicken breasts, 5½ oz each

2 cups Fresh Chicken Stock (see page 30)

1 bay leaf

8 oz fresh young spinach leaves

1 small red onion, shredded

4 oz fresh raspberries

salt and freshly ground pink or black peppercorns

fresh toasted croutons, to garnish

DRESSING

4 tbsp low-fat plain yogurt

1 tbsp raspberry vinegar

2 tsp clear honey

1 Place the chicken breasts in a frying pan. Pour over the stock and add the bay leaf. Bring to a boil, cover, and simmer for 15–20 minutes, turning half-way through, until the chicken is cooked. Leave to cool in the liquid.

2 Arrange the spinach on 4 serving plates and top with the onion. Cover and leave to chill.

3 Drain the cooked chicken and pat dry on absorbent paper towels. Slice the chicken breasts thinly and arrange, fanned

out, over the spinach and onion, on a large platter. Sprinkle the salad with the raspberries.

4 To make the dressing, mix all the ingredients together in a small bowl. Drizzle a spoonful of dressing over each chicken breast and season with salt and ground pink peppercorns to taste. Serve the salad with freshly toasted croutons.

VARIATION

This recipe is delicious with smoked chicken, but it will be more expensive and richer, so use slightly less. It would make an impressive starter for a dinner party.

Three-Bean Salad

Fresh, thin, green beans are combined with soybeans and red kidney beans in a chive and tomato dressing, to make a tasty salad.

NUTRITIONAL INFORMATION

Calories 276	Sugars 7g	
Protein 18g	Fat 15g	
Carbohydrate ...18g	Saturates 4g	

10 MINS   5 MINS

SERVES 6

I N G R E D I E N T S

3 tbsp olive oil

1 tbsp lemon juice

1 tbsp tomato paste

1 tbsp light malt vinegar

1 tbsp chopped fresh chives

6 oz thin green beans

14 oz can soybeans, rinsed and drained

14 oz can red kidney beans, rinsed and drained

2 tomatoes, chopped

4 green onions, trimmed and chopped

4½ oz Feta cheese, cut into cubes

salt and pepper

tossed salad greens, to serve

chopped fresh chives, to garnish

COOK'S TIP

For a more substantial light meal, top the salad with 2–3 sliced hard-boiled eggs and serve with crusty bread to mop up the juices.

1 Put the olive oil, lemon juice, tomato paste, light malt vinegar, and chopped fresh chives into a large bowl and mix thoroughly. Set aside until required.

2 Cook the thin green beans in a little boiling, lightly salted water for 4–5 minutes. Drain, refresh under cold water, and drain again. Dry with paper towels.

3 Add all the beans to the dressing, stirring well to mix.

4 Add the tomatoes, green onions, and Feta cheese to the bean mixture, tossing gently to coat in the dressing. Season well with salt and pepper.

5 Arrange the salad greens on 4–6 serving plates. Pile the bean salad on top, garnish with chives, and serve.

Smoked Trout & Apple Salad

Smoked trout and horseradish are natural partners, but with apple and watercress this makes a wonderful first course.

NUTRITIONAL INFORMATION

Calories	133	Sugars	........11g
Protein	........12g	Fat	...........5g
Carbohydrate	....11g	Saturates	......1g

 10 MINS   0 MINS

SERVES 4

INGREDIENTS

2 orange-red apples, such as Cox's Orange

2 tbsp French Dressing (see page 8)

½ bunch watercress

1 smoked trout, about 6 oz

HORSERADISH DRESSING

½ cup low-fat plain yogurt

½–1 tsp lemon juice

1 tbsp horseradish sauce

milk (optional)

salt and pepper

TO GARNISH

1 tbsp chopped chives

chive flowers (optional)

1 Leaving the skin on, cut the apples into quarters and remove the core. Slice the apples into a bowl and toss in the French dressing to prevent them from browning.

2 Break the watercress into sprigs and arrange on 4 serving plates.

3 Skin the trout and take out the bone. Carefully remove any fine bones that remain. Flake the trout into fairly large pieces and arrange between the watercress with the apple.

4 To make the horseradish dressing, whisk all the ingredients together, adding a little milk if too thick, then drizzle over the trout. Sprinkle the chopped chives and flowers (if using) over the trout, then serve.

COOK'S TIP

To make Melba toast, toast thinly sliced bread then cut off the crusts and carefully slice in half horizontally, using a sharp knife. Cut in half diagonally and place, toasted side down, in a warm oven for 15–20 minutes until the edges start to curl and the toast is crisp.

Potato Salad

You can use left-over cold potatoes, cut into bite-size pieces, for this salad, but tiny new potatoes are best for maximum flavor.

NUTRITIONAL INFORMATION

Calories 275	Sugars 8g	
Protein 5g	Fat 13g	
Carbohydrate ...38g	Saturates 2g	

20 MINS   20 MINS

SERVES 4

INGREDIENTS

1 lb 9 oz tiny new potatoes

8 green onions

1 hard-boiled egg (optional)

1 cup low-fat mayonnaise

1 tsp paprika

salt and pepper

TO GARNISH

2 tbsp chives, snipped

pinch of paprika

1 Bring a large pan of lightly salted water to a boil. Add the potatoes to the pan and cook for 10–15 minutes or until they are just tender.

2 Drain the potatoes in a colander and rinse them under cold running water until they are completely cold. Drain them again thoroughly. Transfer the potatoes to a mixing bowl and set aside until required.

3 Trim and slice the green onions thinly on the diagonal.

4 Chop the hard-boiled egg (if using).

5 Mix together the mayonnaise, paprika, and salt and pepper to taste in a bowl until well blended. Pour the mixture over the potatoes.

6 Add the sliced green onions and egg (if using) to the potatoes and toss together.

7 Transfer the potato salad to a serving bowl and sprinkle with snipped chives and a pinch of paprika. Cover and leave to chill in the refrigerator until required.

COOK'S TIP

To make a lighter dressing, use a mixture of half mayonnaise and half plain yogurt.

Coconut Couscous Salad

The nutty taste of toasted coconut really stands out in this delicious dish. Serve it hot, without the dressing, to accompany a rich lamb stew.

NUTRITIONAL INFORMATION

Calories 330	Sugars 18g	
Protein 7g	Fat 7g	
Carbohydrate . . .63g	Saturates 3g	

1½ HOURS   15 MINS

SERVES 4

I N G R E D I E N T S

12 oz precooked couscous

6 oz no-need-to-soak dried apricots

1 small bunch fresh chives

2 tbsp unsweetened shredded coconut

1 tsp ground cinnamon

salt and pepper

shredded mint leaves, to garnish

D R E S S I N G

1 tbsp olive oil

2 tbsp unsweetened orange juice

½ tsp finely grated orange rind

1 tsp wholegrain mustard

1 tsp clear honey

2 tbsp chopped fresh mint leaves

1 Soak the couscous according to the instructions on the package. Bring a large saucepan of water to a boil. Transfer the couscous to a steamer or large strainer lined with cheesecloth and place over the water. Cover and steam as directed. Remove from the heat, place in heatproof bowl, and set aside to cool.

2 Slice the apricots into thin strips and place in a small bowl. Using scissors, snip the chives over the apricots.

3 When the couscous is cool, mix in the apricots, chives, coconut, and cinnamon. Season well.

4 To make the dressing, mix all the ingredients together and season. Pour over the couscous and mix until well combined. Cover and leave to chill for 1 hour to allow the flavors to develop. Serve the salad garnished with shredded mint leaves.

VARIATION

To serve this salad hot, when the couscous has been steamed, mix in the apricots, chives, coconut, cinnamon, and seasoning along with 1 tbsp olive oil. Transfer to a warmed serving bowl and serve.

Beef & Peanut Salad

Although peanuts are very high in fat, they do have a strong flavor, so you can make a little go a long way.

NUTRITIONAL INFORMATION

Calories	194	Sugars	........3g
Protein	........21g	Fat	..........10g
Carbohydrate	....5g	Saturates	......3g

 10 MINS   10 MINS

SERVES 4

INGREDIENTS

½ head Chinese cabbage

1 large carrot

4½ oz radishes

3½ oz baby corn-on-the-cobs

1 tbsp walnut oil

1 red chili, deseeded and chopped finely

1 clove garlic, chopped finely

12 oz lean beef

1 tbsp dark soy sauce

1 oz fresh peanuts (optional)

red chili, sliced, to garnish

DRESSING

1 tbsp smooth peanut butter

1 tsp sugar

2 tbsp light soy sauce

1 tbsp sherry vinegar

salt and pepper

1 Finely shred the Chinese cabbage and arrange on a platter. Peel the carrot and cut into thin, matchstick-like strips.

2 Wash, trim, and quarter the radishes and halve the baby corn lengthwise. Arrange these ingredients around the edge of the dish and set aside.

3 Trim the beef and slice into fine strips. Heat the oil in a non-stick wok or large frying pan and stir-fry the chili, garlic, and beef for 5 minutes. Add the dark soy sauce and stir-fry for a further 1–2 minutes until tender and cooked through.

4 Meanwhile, make the dressing. Place all of the ingredients in a small bowl and blend them together until smooth.

5 Place the hot cooked beef in the center of the salad ingredients. Spoon over the dressing and sprinkle with a few peanuts (if using).

6 Garnish the salad with slices of red chili and serve immediately.

VARIATION

If preferred, use chicken, turkey, lean pork, or even strips of venison instead of beef in this recipe. Cut off all visible fat before you begin.

Red Hot Slaw

As well as being an exciting side dish, this colorful salad makes an unusual filling for baked potatoes.

NUTRITIONAL INFORMATION

Calories 169	Sugars 16g	
Protein 11g	Fat 7g	
Carbohydrate . . .17g	Saturates 3g	

1 HOUR   0 MINS

SERVES 4

INGREDIENTS

½ small red cabbage

1 large carrot

2 red-skinned apples

1 tbsp lemon juice

1 medium red onion

3½ oz reduced-fat Cheddar cheese, grated

TO GARNISH

red chili strips

carrot strips

DRESSING

3 tbsp reduced-calorie mayonnaise

3 tbsp low-fat plain yogurt

1 garlic clove, crushed

1 tsp paprika

1–2 tsp chili powder

pinch cayenne pepper (optional)

salt and pepper

1 Cut the red cabbage in half and remove the central core. Finely shred the leaves and place in a large bowl. Peel and coarsely grate or finely shred the carrot and mix into the cabbage.

2 Core the apples and finely dice, leaving on the skins. Place in another bowl and toss in the lemon juice to help prevent the apple from browning. Mix the apple into the cabbage and carrot.

3 Peel and finely shred or grate the onion. Stir into the other vegetables along with the cheese and mix together.

4 To make the dressing, mix together the mayonnaise, yogurt, garlic, and paprika in a small bowl. Add chili powder according to taste and the cayenne pepper (if using)—remember this will add more spice to the dressing. Season to taste.

5 Toss the dressing into the vegetables and mix well. Cover and leave to chill in the refrigerator for 1 hour to allow the flavors to develop.

6 Serve garnished with strips of red chili and carrot.

Hot Potato & Ham Salad

With potatoes as a base you can vary the other ingredients, using egg, pickled herring, or beetroot in place of the smoked ham.

NUTRITIONAL INFORMATION

Calories	224	Sugars	.........6g
Protein	........14g	Fat	...........7g
Carbohydrate	...28g	Saturates	......2g

  10 MINS 10 MINS

SERVES 4

INGREDIENTS

6 oz lean smoked ham

1 lb 2 oz salad potatoes

6 green onions, white and
　green parts, sliced

3 pickled dill cucumbers, halved and
　sliced

4 tbsp low-fat mayonnaise

4 tbsp low-fat thick plain yogurt

2 tbsp chopped fresh dill

salt and pepper

COOK'S TIP

The feathery green leaves of fresh dill are used to flavor many dishes for example salads, soups, sauces, and vegetables. The distinctive flavor of fresh dill is far superior to the dried form and should therefore not be substituted.

1 Cut the ham into 1½ inch long strips.

2 Cut the potatoes into ½ inch pieces. Cook the potatoes in boiling, salted water for about 8 minutes until tender.

3 Drain the potatoes and return to the pan with the green onions, ham, and cucumber.

4 To make the dressing, combine the mayonnaise, yogurt, chopped fresh dill, and seasoning in a small bowl. Add the dressing to the pan with the ham and vegetables.

5 Stir until the potatoes are coated with the dressing.

6 Transfer the salad to a warm dish and serve.

Minted Fennel Salad

This is a very refreshing salad. The subtle licorice flavor of fennel combines well with the cucumber and mint.

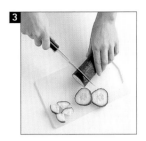

NUTRITIONAL INFORMATION

Calories 90	Sugars 7g
Protein 4g	Fat 5g
Carbohydrate 7g	Saturates 1g

  25 MINS   0 MINS

SERVES 4

INGREDIENTS

1 bulb fennel

2 small oranges

1 small or ½ a large cucumber

1 tablespoon chopped mint

1 tablespoon virgin olive oil

2 eggs, hard-cooked

1 Using a sharp knife, trim the outer leaves from the fennel. Slice the fennel bulb thinly into a bowl of water and sprinkle with lemon juice (see Cook's Tip).

2 Grate the rind of the oranges over a bowl. Using a sharp knife, pare away the orange peel, then segment the orange by carefully slicing between each line of membrane. Do this over the bowl in order to retain the juice.

3 Using a sharp knife, cut the cucumber into ½-inch rounds and then cut each round into quarters.

4 Add the cucumber to the fennel and orange mixture, together with the mint.

5 Pour the olive oil over the fennel and cucumber salad and toss well.

6 Peel and quarter the eggs and use these to decorate the top of the salad. Serve at once.

COOK'S TIP

Fennel will discolor if it is left for any length of time without a dressing. To prevent any discoloration, place it in a bowl of water and sprinkle with lemon juice.

Root Vegetable Salad

This salad of grated vegetables is perfect for a light starter. The peppery flavors of the white radish and radishes are refreshingly pungent.

NUTRITIONAL INFORMATION

Calories 132	Sugars 9g
Protein 4g	Fat 8g
Carbohydrate ...12g	Saturates 1g

20 MINS   0 MINS

SERVES 4

I N G R E D I E N T S

12 oz carrots

8 oz white radish

4 oz radishes

12 oz celery root

1 tbsp orange juice

2 sticks celery with leaves, washed and trimmed

3½ oz assorted salad leaves

1 oz walnuts, chopped

D R E S S I N G

1 tbsp walnut oil

1 tbsp white wine vinegar

1 tsp wholegrain mustard

½ tsp finely grated orange rind

1 tsp celery seeds

salt and pepper

1 Peel and coarsely grate or very finely shred the carrots, white radish, and radishes. Set aside in separate bowls.

2 Peel and coarsely grate or finely shred the celery root and mix with the orange juice.

3 Remove the celery leaves and reserve. Finely chop the celery sticks.

4 Divide the salad leaves among 4 serving plates and arrange the vegetables in small piles on top. Set aside while you make the dressing.

5 Mix all of the dressing ingredients together and season well. Drizzle a little over each salad.

6 Shred the reserved celery leaves and sprinkle over the salad with the chopped walnuts.

COOK'S TIP

Also known as mooli and daikon, white radish resembles a large white parsnip. It has crisp, slightly pungent flesh, which can be eaten raw or cooked. It is a useful ingredient in stir-fries.

Salad with Garlic Dressing

This is a very quick and refreshing salad using a whole range of colorful ingredients which make it look as good as it tastes.

NUTRITIONAL INFORMATION

Calories	82	Sugars	.........5g
Protein	.........2g	Fat	..........6g
Carbohydrate	....5g	Saturates	......1g

10 MINS   0 MINS

SERVES 4

INGREDIENTS

2¾ oz cucumber, cut into sticks

6 green onions, halved

2 tomatoes, seeded and cut into eight

1 yellow bell pepper, cut into strips

2 celery sticks, cut into strips

4 radishes, quartered

2¾ oz arugula

1 tbsp chopped mint, to serve

DRESSING

2 tbsp lemon juice

1 garlic clove, crushed

⅔ cup low-fat plain yogurt

2 tbsp olive oil

salt and pepper

1 To make the salad, mix the cucumber, green onions, tomatoes, bell pepper, celery, radishes, and arugula together in a large serving bowl.

2 To make the dressing, stir the lemon juice, garlic, plain yogurt, and olive oil together.

3 Season well with salt and pepper to taste.

4 Spoon the dressing over the salad and toss to mix. Sprinkle the salad with chopped mint and serve.

COOK'S TIP

Arugula has a distinct warm, peppery flavor which is ideal in green salads. If arugula is unavailable, corn salad makes a good substitute.

Chicken & Grape Salad

Tender chicken breast, sweet grapes, and crisp celery coated in a mild curry mayonnaise make a wonderful al fresco lunch.

NUTRITIONAL INFORMATION

Calories 413	Sugars 20g
Protein 39g	Fat 20g
Carbohydrate . . .20g	Saturates 3g

25 MINS   0 MINS

SERVES 4

I N G R E D I E N T S

1 lb 2 oz cooked skinless, boneless chicken
   breasts

2 celery stalks, sliced finely

2 cups black grapes

½ cup split almonds, toasted

pinch of paprika

sprigs of fresh cilantro or
   flat-leafed parsley, to garnish

C U R R Y   S A U C E

½ cup lean mayonnaise

½ cup natural low-fat fromage frais

1 tbsp clear honey

1 tbsp curry paste

1 Cut the chicken into fairly large pieces and transfer to a bowl with the sliced celery.

2 Halve the grapes, remove the seeds, and add to the bowl.

3 To make the curry sauce, mix the mayonnaise, fromage frais, honey, and curry paste together until blended.

4 Pour the curry sauce over the salad and mix together carefully until well coated.

5 Transfer to a shallow serving dish and sprinkle with the almonds and paprika.

6 Garnish the salad with the cilantro or parsley.

COOK'S TIP

To save time, use seedless grapes, now widely available in supermarkets, and add them whole to the salad.

Carrot & Orange Salad

A crunchy and colorful, sweet and savory dish which would also make an excellent appetizer.

 20 MINS   0 MINS

SERVES 4

INGREDIENTS

1 lb 2 oz celery root

2 tbsp orange juice

4 carrots, sliced finely

2 celery sticks, chopped finely

1 cup celery leaves

4 oranges

¼ cup walnut pieces

DRESSING

1 tbsp walnut oil

½ tsp grated orange rind

3 tbsp orange juice

1 tbsp white wine vinegar

1 tsp clear honey

salt and pepper

1   Trim and peel the celery root and slice or grate finely into a bowl. Add the orange juice and toss together.

2   Mix in the carrots, celery, and celery leaves. Cover and chill while preparing the oranges.

3   Slice off the tops and bottoms from the oranges. Using a sharp knife, slice off the skin, taking the pith away at the same time. Cut out the orange flesh by slicing along the side of the membranes dividing the segments. Gently mix the segments into the celery root mixture.

4   To make the dressing, place all the ingredients in a small screw-top jar. Seal and shake well to mix.

5   Pile the vegetable mixture onto a plate. Sprinkle over the walnut pieces and serve with the dressing.

COOK'S TIP

Celery root is a variety of celery with a bulbous, knobbly root. It has a rough, light brown skin and creamy white flesh and is delicious raw or cooked.

Char-grilled Chicken Salad

This is a quick starter to serve at a barbecue—if the bread is bent in half, the chicken salad can be put in the middle and eaten as finger-food.

NUTRITIONAL INFORMATION

Calories . . . . . . .225 Sugars 5g
Protein . . . . .16g Fat 12g
Carbohydrate . . .15g Saturates 2g

🍳 10 MINS   🕐 15 MINS

SERVES 4

INGREDIENTS

2 skinless, boneless chicken breasts

1 red onion

oil for brushing

1 avocado, peeled and pitted

1 tbsp lemon juice

½ cup low-fat mayonnaise

¼ tsp chili powder

½ tsp pepper

¼ tsp salt

4 tomatoes, quartered

½ loaf sun-dried tomato-flavored focaccia
  bread

green salad, to serve

1 Using a sharp knife, cut the chicken breasts into ½ inch strips.

VARIATION

Instead of focaccia, serve the salad in pita bread which have been warmed through on the barbecue.

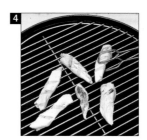 

2 Cut the onion into eight pieces, held together at the root. Rinse under cold running water and then brush with oil.

3 Purée or mash the avocado and lemon juice together. Whisk in the mayonnaise. Add the chili powder, pepper, and salt.

4 Put the chicken and onion over a hot barbecue and broil for 3–4 minutes

on each side. Combine the chicken, onion, tomatoes, and avocado mixture together.

5 Cut the bread in half twice, so that you have quarter-circle-shaped pieces, then in half horizontally. Toast on the hot barbecue for about 2 minutes on each side.

6 Spoon the chicken mixture on to the toasts and serve with a green salad.

Pear & Roquefort Salad

The sweetness of the pear is a perfect partner to the "bite" of the radicchio.

NUTRITIONAL INFORMATION

Calories	94	Sugars	........10g
Protein	.........5g	Fat	..........4g
Carbohydrate	...10g	Saturates	......3g

 10 MINS   0 MINS

SERVES 4

INGREDIENTS

1¾ oz Roquefort cheese

⅔ cup low-fat plain yogurt

2 tbsp snipped chives

few leaves of leaf lettuce

few leaves of radicchio

few leaves of corn salad

2 ripe pears

pepper

whole chives, to garnish

1 Place the cheese in a bowl and mash with a fork. Gradually blend the yogurt into the cheese to make a smooth dressing. Add the chives and season with pepper to taste.

2 Tear the lollo rosso, radicchio, and corn salad leaves into manageable pieces. Arrange the salad leaves on a serving platter or on individual serving plates.

3 Quarter and core the pears and then cut them into slices.

4 Arrange the pear slices over the salad leaves.

5 Drizzle the dressing over the pears and garnish with a few whole chives.

COOK'S TIP

Look out for bags of tossed salad leaves as these are generally more economical than buying lots of different leaves separately.

Endive Salad

The contrast of the pink grapefruit, creamy endive, and bright green corn salad make this a stunning accompaniment.

NUTRITIONAL INFORMATION

Calories 137	Sugars 4g
Protein 1g	Fat 13g
Carbohydrate 4g	Saturates 2g

 10 MINS   0 MINS

SERVES 4

INGREDIENTS

1 pink grapefruit

1 avocado

1 package corn salad, washed thoroughly

2 heads endive, sliced diagonally

1 tbsp chopped fresh mint

FRENCH DRESSING

3 tbsp olive oil

1 tbsp wine vinegar

1 small garlic clove, crushed

½ tsp Dijon or Meaux mustard

1 tsp clear honey

salt and pepper

1 Peel the grapefruit with a serrated-edge knife.

2 Cut the grapefruit into segments by cutting between the membranes.

3 To make the French dressing, put all the ingredients into a screw-top jar and shake vigorously.

4 Halve the avocado and remove the pit by stabbing the pit with a sharp knife and twisting to loosen. Remove the skin.

5 Cut the avocado into small slices, put into a bowl, and toss in the French dressing.

6 Remove any stalks from the corn salad and put into a bowl with the grapefruit, endive, and mint.

7 Add the avocado and 2 tablespoons of the French dressing. Toss well and transfer to serving plates.

1

2

5

COOK'S TIP

Corn salad is also known as lamb's lettuce because the shape of its dark green leaves resembles a lamb's tongue. It is easy to grow in the garden and will withstand the frost.

Spicy Chicken Salad

This is an excellent recipe for leftover roast chicken. Add the dressing just before serving, so that the spinach retains its crispness.

NUTRITIONAL INFORMATION

Calories . . . . .225 Sugars 4g
Protein . . . . .25g Fat 12g
Carbohydrate . . . .4g Saturates 2g

 10 MINS   0 MINS

SERVES 4

INGREDIENTS

8 oz young spinach leaves

3 stalks celery, sliced thinly

½ cucumber, sliced thinly

2 green onions, sliced thinly

3 tbsp chopped fresh parsley

12 oz boneless, lean roast chicken, sliced thinly

DRESSING

1 inch piece fresh ginger, grated finely

3 tbsp olive oil

1 tbsp white wine vinegar

1 tbsp clear honey

½ tsp ground cinnamon

salt and pepper

toasted almonds, to garnish (optional)

1 Thoroughly wash and dry the spinach leaves.

2 Toss the celery, cucumber, and green onions with the spinach and parsley in a large bowl.

3 Transfer the salad ingredients to serving plates and arrange the chicken over the salad.

4 To make the dressing, combine the grated ginger, olive oil, wine vinegar, honey, and cinnamon in a screw-topped jar and shake well to mix. Season with salt and pepper to taste.

5 Pour the dressing over the salad. Scatter a few toasted almonds over the salad to garnish (if using).

COOK'S TIP

For extra color, add some cherry tomatoes and some thin strips of red and yellow bell peppers and garnish with a little grated carrot.

Potato, Apple, & Bean Salad

Use any mixture of beans you have available in this recipe, but the wider the variety, the more colorful the salad.

NUTRITIONAL INFORMATION

Calories	183	Sugars	.........8g
Protein	.........6g	Fat	...........7g
Carbohydrate	...26g	Saturates	......1g

10 MINS   15 MINS

SERVES 4

INGREDIENTS

8 oz new potatoes, scrubbed and quartered

8 oz mixed canned beans, such as red kidney beans, small navy, and borlotti beans, drained and rinsed

1 red eating apple, diced and tossed in 1 tbsp lemon juice

1 small yellow bell pepper, diced

1 shallot, sliced

½ head fennel, sliced

oak leaf lettuce leaves

DRESSING

1 tbsp red wine vinegar

2 tbsp olive oil

½ tbsp mustard

1 garlic clove, crushed

2 tsp chopped fresh thyme

1 Cook the quartered potatoes in a saucepan of boiling water for 15 minutes until tender. Drain and transfer to a mixing bowl.

2 Add the potatoes to the mixed beans with the diced apple, yellow bell pepper, the sliced shallots, and fennel. Mix well, taking care not to break up the cooked potatoes.

3 In a bowl, whisk all the dressing ingredients together.

4 Pour the dressing over the potato salad.

5 Line a plate or salad bowl with the oak leaf and spoon the potato mixture into the center. Serve the salad immediately.

COOK'S TIP

Canned beans are used here for convenience, but dried beans may be used instead. Soak for 8 hours or overnight, drain, and place in a saucepan. Cover with water, bring to a boil, and boil for 10 minutes, then simmer until tender.

Waldorf Chicken Salad

This colorful and healthy dish is a variation of a classic salad. You can use a selection of tossed salad leaves, if preferred.

NUTRITIONAL INFORMATION

Calories	.471	Sugars	19g
Protein	.38g	Fat	27g
Carbohydrate	.20g	Saturates	.4g

30 MINS   0 MINS

SERVES 4

INGREDIENTS

1 lb 2 oz red apples, diced

3 tbsp fresh lemon juice

⅔ cup low-fat mayonnaise

1 head of celery

4 shallots, sliced

1 garlic clove, crushed

¾ cup walnuts, chopped

1 lb 2 oz lean cooked chicken, cubed

1 romaine lettuce

pepper

sliced apple and walnuts, to garnish

1 Place the apples in a bowl with the lemon juice and 1 tablespoon of mayonnaise. Leave for 40 minutes or until required.

2 Slice the celery very thinly. Add the celery, shallots, garlic, and walnuts to the apple, mix, and then add the remaining mayonnaise and blend thoroughly.

3 Add the chicken and mix with the other ingredients.

4 Line a glass salad bowl or serving dish with the lettuce.

5 Pile the chicken salad into the center, sprinkle with pepper, and garnish with apple slices and walnuts.

VARIATION

Instead of the shallots, use green onions for a milder flavor. Trim the green onions and slice finely.

Potato & Beetroot Salad

The beetroot adds a rich color to this dish. The dill dressing with the potato salad is a classic combination.

NUTRITIONAL INFORMATION

Calories	174	Sugars 8g
Protein	.........4g	Fat 6g
Carbohydrate	...27g	Saturates 1g

 25 MINS 15 MINS

SERVES 4

INGREDIENTS

1 lb new potatoes, diced

4 small cooked beetroot, sliced

½ small cucumber, sliced thinly

2 large dill pickles, sliced

1 red onion, halved and sliced

dill sprigs, to garnish

DRESSING

1 garlic clove, crushed

2 tbsp olive oil

2 tbsp red wine vinegar

2 tbsp chopped fresh dill

salt and pepper

COOK'S TIP

If making the salad in advance, do not mix the beetroot and potatoes until just before serving, as the beetroot will bleed its color.

1 Cook the potatoes in a saucepan of boiling water for 15 minutes or until tender. Drain and leave to cool.

2 When cool, mix the potato and beetroot together in a bowl and set aside.

3 Line a salad platter with the slices of cucumber, dill pickles, and red onion.

4 Spoon the potato and beetroot mixture into the center of the platter.

5 In a small bowl, whisk all the dressing ingredients together, then pour it over the salad.

6 Serve the potato and beetroot salad immediately, (see Cook's Tip, left), garnished with dill sprigs.

Coronation Salad

This dish is based on Coronation Chicken which was invented to celebrate Queen Victoria's coronation as a symbol of Anglo-Indian links.

NUTRITIONAL INFORMATION

Calories 236   Sugars 24g
Protein ....7g   Fat 5g
Carbohydrate ...43g   Saturates 1g

25 MINS   0 MINS

SERVES 4

INGREDIENTS

1 red bell pepper

⅓ cup golden raisins

1 celery stick, sliced

¾ cup corn kernels

1 Granny Smith apple, diced

1 cup green seedless grapes, washed and halved

1½ cups cooked Basmati rice

½ cup cooked, peeled shrimp (optional)

1 romaine lettuce, washed and drained

1 tsp paprika to garnish

DRESSING

4 tbsp low-fat mayonnaise

2 tsp mild curry powder

1 tsp lemon juice

1 tsp paprika

pinch of salt

1 Deseed and chop the red bell pepper.

2 Combine the golden raisins, red bell pepper, celery, corn, apple, and grapes in a large bowl. Stir in the rice, and shrimp, if using.

3 For the dressing, put the mayonnaise, curry powder, lemon juice, paprika, and salt into a small bowl and mix well.

4 Pour the dressing over the salad and gently mix until evenly coated.

5 Line the serving plate with romaine lettuce leaves and spoon on the salad. Sprinkle over the paprika and serve.

COOK'S TIP

Mayonnaise can be bought in varying thicknesses, from the type that you spoon out of the jar to the pouring variety. If you need to thin down mayonnaise for a dressing, simply add water little by little until the desired consistency is reached.

Sweet & Sour Tuna Salad

Small navy beans, zucchini, and tomatoes are briefly cooked in a sweet and sour sauce, before being mixed with tuna.

NUTRITIONAL INFORMATION

Calories	245	Sugars	.........5g
Protein	........22g	Fat	...........8g
Carbohydrate	...24g	Saturates	......1g

15 MINS   10 MINS

SERVES 4

INGREDIENTS

2 tbsp olive oil

1 onion, chopped

2 garlic cloves, chopped

2 zucchini, sliced

4 tomatoes, skinned

14 oz can small navy beans, drained and rinsed

10 black olives, halved and pitted

1 tbsp capers

1 tsp sugar

1 tbsp wholegrain mustard

1 tbsp white wine vinegar

7 oz can tuna fish, drained

2 tbsp chopped fresh parsley

chopped fresh parsley, to garnish

crusty bread, to serve

1 Heat the oil in a frying pan and fry the onion and garlic for 5 minutes until soft.

2 Add the zucchini and cook for 3 minutes, stirring occasionally.

3 Cut the tomatoes in half, then into thin wedges.

4 Add the tomatoes to the pan with the beans, olives, capers, sugar, mustard, and vinegar.

5 Simmer for 2 minutes, stirring gently, then allow to cool slightly.

6 Flake the tuna fish and stir into the bean mixture with the parsley.

7 Garnish with parsley and serve lukewarm with crusty bread.

COOK'S TIP

Capers are the flower buds of the caper bush, which is native to the Mediterranean region. Capers are preserved in vinegar and salt and give a distinctive flavor to this salad. They are much used in Italian and Provençale cooking.

Cool Bean Salad

This salad is ideal for serving at a barbecue, to accompany one of the hotter Indian curries, or served as part of a salad buffet at parties.

NUTRITIONAL INFORMATION

Calories	98	Sugars	.........5g
Protein	.........9g	Fat	...........1g
Carbohydrate	...14g	Saturates	.....0.3g

 15 MINS 15 MINS

SERVES 4

INGREDIENTS

1 red onion, finely sliced

3 cups broad beans, fresh or frozen

⅔ cup low-fat plain yogurt

1 tbsp chopped fresh mint

½ tbsp lemon juice

1 garlic clove, halved

salt and ground white pepper

½ cucumber, peeled, halved and sliced

1 Rinse the red onion slices briefly under cold running water, and drain thoroughly.

2 Put the broad beans into a pan of boiling water and cook until tender, 8–10 minutes for fresh, 5–6 minutes for frozen.

3 Drain, rinse under cold running water, and drain again.

4 If you wish, shell the beans from their white outer shell to leave the sweet green bean.

5 Combine the yogurt, mint, lemon juice, garlic, and seasoning in a bowl.

6 Combine the onion, cucumber, and broad beans.

7 Toss them in the yogurt dressing. Remove the garlic halves.

8 Spoon the salad onto the serving plate and serve immediately.

COOK'S TIP

Rinsing the raw onion under cold running water takes the edge off the raw taste, as it washes away some of the juices. The same technique can be used on other pungent vegetables and salads, such as green onions, bitter cucumbers, and chilies.

Side Dishes

An ideal acompaniment should complement the main dish, both visually and nutritionally. This chapter contains a range of exciting side dishes which add a new twist to traditional vegetables, for example, Casseroled Potatoes in which potatoes are baked with a mixture of leeks, white

wine, lemon juice, and herbs, or Carrot & Poppy Seed Bake in which carrots are flavored in an orange, honey, and thyme sauce, baked, and then sprinkled with poppy seeds. Although these may take slightly longer to prepare than simpler side dishes, they are well worth it for appearance and flavor. There are also some traditional accompaniments for specific dishes, for example Raitas and Sesame Seed Chutney for curries, and Tomato Salsa to serve alongside fajitas.

Vegetable Medley

Serve this as a crisp and colorful vegetarian dish, with pita bread, chapatis, or naan, or as an accompaniment to roast or broiled meats.

NUTRITIONAL INFORMATION

Calories ....190 Sugars 17g
Protein ....7g Fat 7g
Carbohydrate ...27g Saturates 1g

10 MINS   20 MINS

SERVES 4

I N G R E D I E N T S

5½ oz young, tender green beans

8 baby carrots

6 baby turnips

½ small cauliflower

2 tbsp vegetable oil

2 large onions, sliced

2 garlic cloves, finely chopped

1¼ cups low-fat plain yogurt

1 tbsp cornstarch

2 tbsp tomato paste

large pinch of chili powder

salt

1 Top and tail the beans and snap them in half. Cut the carrots in half and the turnips in quarters. Divide the cauliflower into florets, discarding the thickest part of the stalk. Steam the vegetables over boiling, salted water for 3 minutes, then turn them into a colander, and plunge them at once in a large bowl of cold water to prevent further cooking.

2 Heat the vegetable oil in a frying pan and fry the onions until they are translucent. Stir in the garlic and cook for 1 further minute.

3 Mix together the yogurt, cornstarch, and tomato paste to form a smooth paste. Stir this paste into the onions in the pan and cook for 1-2 minutes until the sauce is well blended.

4 Drain the vegetables well, then gradually stir them into the sauce, taking care not to break them up. Season with salt and chili powder to taste, cover, and simmer gently for 5 minutes, until the vegetables are just tender. Taste and adjust the seasoning if necessary. Serve immediately.

Corn-on-the-Cob

Corn-on-the-cob is available nearly all the year round, and it can be barbecued with the husk on or off.

NUTRITIONAL INFORMATION

Calories	79	Sugars	.........2g
Protein	.........3g	Fat	...........2g
Carbohydrate	...14g	Saturates	.....0.2g

  25 MINS   30 MINS

SERVES 6

I N G R E D I E N T S

4–6 corn-on-the-cobs

vegetable oil for brushing

T O S E R V E

butter (optional)

salt (optional)

1 Soak the corn cobs in hand-hot water for 20 minutes. Drain them thoroughly and pat dry with paper towels.

2 If the cobs have no husks, brush with oil and cook over a hot barbecue for 30 minutes, brushing occasionally with the oil and turning often.

3 If your cobs have husks, tear off all but the last two layers and brush with oil.

4 Cook over a hot barbecue for 40 minutes, brushing with oil once or twice and turning occasionally.

5 Serve the corn-on-the-cobs hot, without the husks. If you like, add a knob of butter and salt to taste.

Vegetable Stir-Fry

A range of delicious flavors are captured in this simple recipe which is ideal if you are in a hurry.

NUTRITIONAL INFORMATION

Calories 127	Sugars 7g
Protein 4g	Fat 9g
Carbohydrate 8g	Saturates 1g

5 MINS   25 MINS

SERVES 4

I N G R E D I E N T S

3 tbsp olive oil

8 baby onions, halved

1 eggplant, cubed

8 oz zucchini, sliced

8 oz open-cap mushrooms, halved

2 cloves garlic, crushed

14 oz can chopped tomatoes

2 tbsp sun-dried tomato paste

freshly ground black pepper

fresh basil leaves, to garnish

1 Heat the olive oil in a large preheated wok or frying pan.

2 Add the baby onions and eggplant to the wok and stir-fry for 5 minutes, or until the vegetables are golden and just beginning to soften.

3 Add the zucchini, mushrooms, garlic, tomatoes, and tomato paste to the wok and stir-fry for about 5 minutes.

4 Reduce the heat and leave to simmer for 10 minutes, or until the vegetables are tender.

5 Season with freshly ground black pepper and scatter with fresh basil leaves. Serve immediately.

COOK'S TIP

Wok cooking is an excellent means of cooking for vegetarians as it is a quick and easy way of serving up delicious dishes of crisp, tasty vegetables. All ingredients should be cut into uniform sizes with as many cut surfaces exposed as possible for quick cooking.

Eggplant Curry

This is a rich vegetable dish, ideal served with tandoori chicken and naan bread. It is also delicious served as a vegetarian dish with rice.

NUTRITIONAL INFORMATION

Calories 73	Sugars 6g
Protein 3g	Fat 4g
Carbohydrate 6g	Saturates 1g

 15 MINS   🕐 15 MINS

SERVES 6

INGREDIENTS

2 whole eggplants

1 cup low-fat plain yogurt

2 cardamom pods

½ tsp ground turmeric

1 dried red chili

½ tsp coriander seeds

½ tsp ground black pepper

1 tsp garam masala

1 clove

2 tbsp sunflower oil

1 onion, sliced lengthways

2 garlic cloves, crushed

1 tbsp grated fresh ginger

6 ripe tomatoes, peeled, deseeded, and quartered

fresh cilantro, to garnish

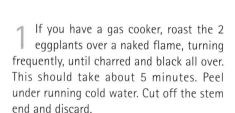  

1 If you have a gas cooker, roast the 2 eggplants over a naked flame, turning frequently, until charred and black all over. This should take about 5 minutes. Peel under running cold water. Cut off the stem end and discard.

2 Put the peeled eggplants into a large bowl and mash lightly with a fork. Stir in the yogurt.

3 Grind together the cardamom pods, turmeric, red chili, coriander seeds, black pepper, garam masala, and clove in a large pestle and mortar or spice grinder.

4 Heat the oil in a wok or heavy frying pan over a moderate heat and cook the onion, garlic, and fresh ginger until soft. Add the tomatoes and ground spices, and stir well.

5 Add the eggplant mixture to the pan and stir well. Cook for 5 minutes over a gentle heat, stirring constantly, until all the flavors are combined, and some of the liquid has evaporated.

6 Serve the eggplant immediately, garnished with cilantro.

Casseroled Potatoes

This potato dish is cooked in the oven with leeks and wine. It is very quick and simple to make.

NUTRITIONAL INFORMATION

Calories	187	Sugars	.........2g
Protein	.........4g	Fat	...........3g
Carbohydrate	...31g	Saturates	......2g

10 MINS   50 MINS

SERVES 4

INGREDIENTS

1½ lb new potatoes, cut into chunks

1 tbsp butter

2 leeks, sliced

⅔ cup dry white wine

⅔ cup vegetable stock

1 tbsp lemon juice

2 tbsp chopped mixed fresh herbs

salt and pepper

TO GARNISH

grated lemon rind

mixed fresh herbs (optional)

1 Cook the potato chunks in a saucepan of boiling water for 5 minutes. Drain thoroughly.

2 Meanwhile, melt the butter in a frying pan and sauté the leeks for 5 minutes or until they have softened.

3 Spoon the partly cooked potatoes and leeks into an ovenproof dish.

4 In a measuring jug, mix together the wine, vegetable stock, lemon juice, and chopped mixed herbs. Season to taste with salt and pepper, then pour the mixture over the potatoes.

5 Cook in a preheated oven, 375°F, for 35 minutes or until the potatoes are tender.

6 Garnish the potato casserole with lemon rind and fresh herbs (if using) and serve as an accompaniment to meat casseroles or roast meat.

COOK'S TIP

Cover the ovenproof dish halfway through cooking if the leeks start to brown on the top.

Vegetables with Vermouth

Serve these vegetables in their paper parcels to retain the juices. The result is truly delicious.

NUTRITIONAL INFORMATION

Calories ....62 Sugars 9g
Protein ....2g Fat 0.5g
Carbohydrate ...12g Saturates 0.1g

 10 MINS   20 MINS

SERVES 4

INGREDIENTS

1 carrot, cut into sticks

1 fennel bulb, sliced

3½ oz zucchini, sliced

1 red bell pepper, sliced

4 small onions, halved

8 tbsp vermouth

4 tbsp lime juice

zest of 1 lime

pinch of paprika

4 sprigs tarragon

salt and pepper

fresh tarragon sprigs, to garnish

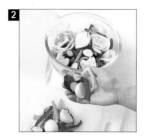

1 Place all of the vegetables in a large bowl and mix well.

2 Cut 4 large squares of baking parchment and place a quarter of the vegetables in the center of each. Bring the sides of the paper up and pinch together to make an open parcel.

3 Mix together the vermouth, lime juice, lime zest, and paprika and pour a quarter of the mixture into each parcel. Season with salt and pepper and add a tarragon sprig to each. Pinch the tops of the parcels together to seal.

4 Place the parcels in a steamer, cover, and cook for 15–20 minutes or until the vegetables are tender. Garnish with tarragon sprigs and serve.

COOK'S TIP
Vermouth is a fortified white wine flavored with various herbs and spices. It is available in both sweet and dry forms.

Thai Fragrant Coconut Rice

Basmati rice is cooked with creamed coconut, lemon grass, fresh ginger, and spices to make a wonderfully aromatic, fluffy rice.

NUTRITIONAL INFORMATION

Calories	258	Sugars	.......0.4g
Protein	.........5g	Fat	...........6g
Carbohydrate	...51g	Saturates	......4g

 5 MINS   20 MINS

SERVES 4–6

INGREDIENTS

1 inch piece fresh ginger, peeled and sliced

2 cloves

1 piece lemon grass, bruised and halved

2 tsp ground nutmeg

1 cinnamon stick

1 bay leaf

2 small thin strips lime zest

1 tsp salt

1 oz creamed coconut, chopped

2½ cups water

1¾ cups Basmati rice

ground pepper

1 Place the ginger, cloves, lemon grass, nutmeg, cinnamon stick, bay leaf, lime zest, salt, creamed coconut, and water in a large, heavy-based pan and bring slowly to a boil.

2 Add the rice, stir well, then cover, and simmer, over a very gentle heat, for about 15 minutes or until all the liquid has been absorbed and the rice is tender but still has a bite to it.

3 Alternatively, bring the rice to a boil, then cover tightly, and turn off the heat. Leave for 20–25 minutes before removing the lid—the rice will be perfectly cooked.

4 Remove from the heat, add pepper to taste, then fluff up the rice with a fork.

5 Remove the large pieces of spices before serving.

COOK'S TIP

When using a whole stem of lemon grass (rather than chopped lemon grass), beat it well to bruise it so that the flavor is fully released. Lemon zest or a pared piece of lemon peel can be used instead.

Lemony & Herby Potatoes

Choose from these two divine recipes for new potatoes. To check if new potatoes are fresh, rub the skin—the skin will come off easily if fresh.

NUTRITIONAL INFORMATION

Calories	226	Sugars	.........2g
Protein	.........5g	Fat	...........5g
Carbohydrate	...42g	Saturates	......3g

20 MINS   35 MINS

SERVES 4

I N G R E D I E N T S

L E M O N Y   N E W   P O T A T O E S

2 lb 4 oz new potatoes

2 tbsp butter

1 tbsp finely grated lemon rind

2 tbsp lemon juice

1 tbsp chopped fresh dill or chives

salt and pepper

extra chopped fresh dill or chives, to garnish

H E R B Y   N E W   P O T A T O E S

2 lb 4 oz new potatoes

3 tbsp light olive oil

1h tbsp white wine vinegar

pinch of dry mustard

pinch of sugar

salt and pepper

2 tbsp chopped mixed fresh herbs, such as parsley, chives, marjoram, basil and rosemary

extra chopped fresh mixed herbs, to garnish

1 For the lemony potatoes, either scrub the potatoes well or remove the skins by scraping off with a sharp knife. Cook the potatoes in plenty of lightly salted boiling water for about 15 minutes until just tender.

2 While the potatoes are cooking, melt the butter over a low heat. Add the lemon rind, juice, and herbs. Season with salt and pepper.

3 Drain the cooked potatoes and transfer to a serving bowl.

4 Pour over the lemony butter mixture and stir gently to mix. Garnish with extra herbs and serve hot or warm.

5 For the herby potatoes, prepare and cook the potatoes as described in step 1. Whisk the oil, vinegar, mustard, sugar, and seasoning together in a small bowl. Add the chopped herbs and mix well.

6 Drain the potatoes and pour over the oil and vinegar mixture, stirring to coat evenly. Garnish with extra fresh herbs and serve warm or cold.

Greek Green Beans

This dish contains many Greek flavors, such as lemon, garlic, oregano, and olives, for a really flavorful recipe.

NUTRITIONAL INFORMATION

Calories	115	Sugars	. . . . .4g
Protein	. . . . .6g	Fat	. . . . .4g
Carbohydrate	. . .15g	Saturates	. . . . .0.6g

 5 MINS   1 HOUR

SERVES 4

I N G R E D I E N T S

14 oz can navy beans, drained

1 tbsp olive oil

3 garlic cloves, crushed

2 cups vegetable stock

1 bay leaf

2 sprigs oregano

1 tbsp tomato paste

juice of 1 lemon

1 small red onion, chopped

1 oz pitted black olives, halved

salt and pepper

1 Put the navy beans in a flameproof casserole dish.

2 Add the olive oil and crushed garlic and cook over a gentle heat, stirring occasionally, for 4–5 minutes.

3 Add the stock, bay leaf, oregano, tomato paste, lemon juice, and red onion, cover, and simmer for about 1 hour or until the sauce has thickened.

4 Stir in the olives, season with salt and pepper to taste, and serve warm or cold.

VARIATION

You can substitute other canned beans for the navy beans—try cannellini or black-eyed peas, or garbanzo beans instead. Drain and rinse them before use as canned beans often have sugar or salt added.

Yellow Split Pea Casserole

If ever there was a winter warmer, this is it—an intensely satisfying dish, ideal for serving with rice or fresh naan bread.

NUTRITIONAL INFORMATION

Calories 358	Sugars 10g
Protein 19g	Fat 12g
Carbohydrate ...45g	Saturates 1g

2¼ HOURS   1½ HOURS

SERVES 4

I N G R E D I E N T S

2 tbsp ghee or vegetable oil

1 tsp black mustard seeds

1 onion, chopped finely

2 garlic cloves, crushed

1 carrot, grated

1 inch piece fresh ginger, grated

1 green chili, deseeded and chopped finely

1 tbsp tomato paste

1 cup yellow split peas, soaked in water for 2 hours

14 oz can chopped tomatoes

2 cups vegetable stock

1½ cups pumpkin, cubed

8 oz cauliflower, cut into florets

2 tbsp oil

1 large eggplant, cubed

1 tbsp chopped fresh cilantro

1 tsp garam masala

salt and pepper

1 Melt the ghee over a medium heat in a large pan. Add the mustard seeds, and when they start to splutter, add the onion, garlic, carrot, and ginger.

2 Cook until soft, about 5 minutes. Add the green chili and stir in the tomato paste. Stir in the split peas.

3 Add the tomatoes and stock and bring to a boil. Season well.

4 Simmer for 40 minutes, stirring occasionally. Add the pumpkin cubes and cauliflower florets and simmer for a further 30 minutes, covered, until the split peas are soft.

5 Meanwhile, heat the oil in a frying pan over a high heat. Add the eggplant and stir until sealed on all sides; remove and drain on paper towels.

6 Stir the eggplant into the split pea mixture with the cilantro and garam masala. Check for seasoning.

7 Transfer to a serving dish and serve immediately.

Colcannon

This is an old Irish recipe, usually served with a piece of bacon, but it is equally delicious with chicken or fish.

NUTRITIONAL INFORMATION

Calories 102	Sugars 4g
Protein 4g	Fat 4g
Carbohydrate . . .14g	Saturates 2g

  5 MINS 35 MINS

SERVES 4

INGREDIENTS

8 oz green cabbage, shredded

⅓ cup skim milk

8 oz russet or Idaho potatoes, diced

1 large leek, chopped

pinch of grated nutmeg

1 tbsp butter, melted

salt and pepper

1 Bring a large saucepan of salted water to a boil, add the shredded cabbage, and cook for 7-10 minutes. Drain thoroughly and set aside.

2 Meanwhile, in a separate saucepan, bring the milk to a boil, and add the potatoes and leek. Reduce the heat and simmer for 15-20 minutes or until they are cooked through.

3 Stir in the grated nutmeg and mash the potatoes and leeks together.

4 Add the drained cabbage to the potatoes and mix well.

5 Spoon the potato and cabbage mixture into a serving dish, making a

hollow in the center with the back of a spoon.

6 Pour the melted butter into the hollow and serve the colcannon immediately.

COOK'S TIP

There are many different varieties of cabbage which produce hearts at varying times of year, so you can be sure of being able to make this delicious cabbage dish all year round.

Potatoes en Papillotes

New potatoes are perfect for this recipe. The potatoes and vegetables are wrapped in waxed paper, sealed, and steamed in the oven.

NUTRITIONAL INFORMATION

Calories ....85 Sugars 4g
Protein ....2g Fat 0.5g
Carbohydrate ...15g Saturates 0.1g

 10 MINS   35 MINS

SERVES 4

I N G R E D I E N T S

16 small new potatoes

1 carrot, cut into matchstick strips

1 fennel bulb, sliced

2¾ oz green beans

1 yellow bell pepper, cut into strips

16 tbsp dry white wine

4 rosemary sprigs

salt and pepper

rosemary sprigs, to garnish

1 Cut 4 squares of waxed paper, measuring about 10 inches in size.

2 Divide the vegetables equally between the 4 paper squares, placing them in the center.

3 Bring the edges of the paper together and scrunch them together to encase the vegetables, leaving the top open.

4 Place the parcels in a shallow roasting pan and spoon 4 tablespoons of white wine into each parcel. Add a rosemary sprig and season.

5 Fold the top of each parcel over to seal it. Cook in a preheated oven, 375°F, for 30-35 minutes or until the vegetables are tender.

6 Transfer the sealed parcels to 4 individual serving plates and garnish with rosemary sprigs.

7 Open the parcels at the table in order for the full aroma of the vegetables to be appreciated.

COOK'S TIP

If small new potatoes are unavailable, use larger potatoes which have been halved or quartered to ensure that they cook through in the specified cooking time.

Carrot & Poppy Seed Bake

The poppy seeds add texture and flavor to this recipe and counteract the slightly sweet flavor of the carrots.

NUTRITIONAL INFORMATION

Calories	138	Sugars	........31g
Protein	.........2g	Fat	...........1g
Carbohydrate	...32g	Saturates	.....0.2g

10 MINS   40 MINS

SERVES 4

I N G R E D I E N T S

1½ lb carrots, cut into thin strips

1 leek, sliced

1¼ cups fresh orange juice

2 tbsp clear honey

1 garlic clove, crushed

1 tsp mixed spice

2 tsp chopped thyme

1 tbsp poppy seeds

salt and pepper

fresh thyme sprigs and orange rind, to
    garnish

1 Cook the carrots and leek in a saucepan of boiling salted water for 5–6 minutes. Drain well and transfer to a shallow baking dish until required.

2 Mix together the orange juice, honey, garlic, mixed spice, and thyme and pour the mixture over the vegetables. Add salt and pepper to taste.

3 Cover the baking dish and cook in a preheated oven, 350°F, for 30 minutes or until the vegetables are tender.

4 Remove the lid and sprinkle with poppy seeds. Garnish with fresh thyme sprigs and orange rind and serve immediately.

VARIATION

If you prefer, use 2 tsp cumin instead of the mixed spice and omit the thyme, as cumin works particularly well with carrots.

Kachumbers

Kachumbers can be made with fruit as well as vegetables. They are served at Indian tables as an appetizer or a garnish for the main meal.

NUTRITIONAL INFORMATION

Calories	55	Sugars	.........4g
Protein	.........1g	Fat	..........4g
Carbohydrate	....4g	Saturates	.....0.5g

 15 MINS   0 MINS

EACH SERVES 6

INGREDIENTS

TOMATO, ONION, & CUCUMBER KACHUMBER

3 ripe tomatoes, peeled

¼ cucumber, peeled

1 small onion, quartered

1 tsp lime juice

2 green chilies, deseeded and chopped (optional)

MANGO KACHUMBER

½ mango, peeled and chopped

1 small onion, chopped

1 tbsp chopped fresh cilantro

2 tomatoes, chopped

RADISH KACHUMBER

8 large radishes, sliced

½ cucumber, peeled and chopped

1 small onion, chopped

1 tbsp chopped fresh cilantro

1 tbsp oil

1 tbsp vinegar

1 To make the tomato, onion, and cucumber kachumber, cut the tomatoes into quarters and cut each quarter in half. The seeds can be removed at this stage, if you prefer. Cut the cucumber lengthways into quarters. Remove the seeds and cut into cubes. Cut each onion quarter into slices. Combine all the ingredients in a bowl and sprinkle with the lime juice. Add the chilies, if using, and serve.

2 To make the mango kachumber, mix all the ingredients together and serve.

3 To make the radish kachumber, combine all the ingredients in a bowl and serve.

COOK'S TIP

To peel tomatoes, make a little cross in the bottom of each one with a pointed knife, place in a bowl, and cover with boiling water. Leave for 1 minute before draining. The skins will slip off easily.

Tomato Salsa

This salad is used extensively in Mexican cooking and served as a dip or a relish, and is eaten as an accompaniment to almost any dish.

NUTRITIONAL INFORMATION

Calories	10	Sugars	. . . . .2g
Protein	. . . . .0.4g	Fat	. . . . .0.1g
Carbohydrate	. . . .2g	Saturates	. . . . . .0g

10 MINS   0 MINS

SERVES 4

INGREDIENTS

4 ripe red tomatoes

1 medium red onion or
   6 green onions

1–2 garlic cloves, crushed (optional)

2 tbsp chopped fresh cilantro

½ red or green chili (optional)

finely grated rind of ½–1 lemon
   or lime

1–2 tbsp lemon or lime juice

pepper

preferred, they may be peeled by placing them in boiling water for about 20 seconds and then plunging into cold water. The skins should then slip off easily when they are nicked with a knife.

2 Peel and slice the red onion thinly, or trim the green onions and cut into thin slanting slices; then add to the tomatoes with the garlic and cilantro and mix lightly.

3 Remove the seeds from the red or green chili (if using), chop the flesh very finely, and add to the salad. Treat the chilies with care; do not touch your eyes or face after handling them until you have washed your hands thoroughly. Chili juices can burn.

4 Add the lemon or lime rind and juice to the salsa and mix well. Transfer to a serving bowl and sprinkle with pepper.

1 Chop the tomatoes fairly finely and evenly and put into a bowl. They must be firm and a good strong red color for the best results, but if

COOK'S TIP

If you don't like the distinctive flavor of fresh cilantro, you can replace it with flat-leaf parsley instead.

Raitas

Raitas are very easy to prepare, very versatile, and have a cooling effect which will be appreciated if you are serving hot, spicy dishes.

NUTRITIONAL INFORMATION

Calories 33	Sugars 5g	
Protein 3g	Fat 0.4g	
Carbohydrate 5g	Saturates 0.3g	

 10 MINS   5 MINS

SERVES 4

I N G R E D I E N T S

MINT RAITA

¾ cup low-fat plain yogurt

4 tbsp water

1 small onion, finely chopped

½ tsp mint sauce

½ tsp salt

3 fresh mint leaves, to garnish

CUCUMBER RAITA

8 oz cucumber

1 medium onion

½ tsp salt

½ tsp mint sauce

1¼ cups low-fat plain yogurt

⅔ cup water

fresh mint leaves, to garnish

EGGPLANT RAITA

1 medium eggplant

1 tsp salt

1 small onion, finely chopped

2 green chilies, finely chopped

¾ cup low-fat plain yogurt

3 tbsp water

1 To make the mint raita, place the yogurt in a bowl and whisk with a fork. Gradually whisk in the water. Add the onion, mint sauce, and salt and blend together. Garnish with mint leaves.

2 To make the cucumber raita, peel and slice the cucumber. Chop the onion finely. Place the cucumber and onion in a large bowl, then add the salt and the mint sauce. Add the yogurt and the water, place the mixture in a liquidizer, and blend well. Serve garnished with mint leaves.

3 To make the eggplant raita, remove the top end of the eggplant and chop the rest into small pieces. Boil in a pan of water until soft, then drain, and mash. Add the salt, onion, and green chilies, mixing well. Whip the yogurt with the water and add to the mixture and mix thoroughly.

Saffron Rice

This is the classic way to serve rice, paired with saffron, so that each brings out the best in the other.

NUTRITIONAL INFORMATION

Calories 63	Sugars 0.1g
Protein 1.4g	Fat 2g
Carbohydrate 11g	Saturates 0.2g

 15 MINS    25 MINS

SERVES 8

I N G R E D I E N T S

12 saffron threads, crushed lightly

2 tbsp warm water

1¾ cups water

8 oz Basmati rice

1 tbsp toasted, slivered almonds

1 Put the saffron threads into a bowl with the warm water and leave for 10 minutes. They need to be crushed before soaking to ensure that the maximum flavor and color is extracted at this stage.

2 Put the water and rice into a medium saucepan and set it over the heat to boil. Add the saffron and saffron water and stir.

3 Bring back to a gentle boil, stir again, and let the rice simmer, uncovered, for about 10 minutes, until all the water has been absorbed.

4 Cover tightly, reduce the heat as much as possible, and leave for 10 minutes. Do not remove the lid. This ensures that the grains separate and that the rice is not soggy.

5 Alternatively, you can soak the rice overnight and drain before cooking. Cook as before but reduce the cooking time by 3–4 minutes to compensate for the presoaking.

6 Remove the rice from the heat and transfer to a serving dish. Fork through the rice gently and sprinkle on the toasted almonds before serving.

COOK'S TIP

Saffron, grown in Europe and the Middle East, is the most ancient of spices and continues to be the most expensive—literally worth its weight in gold. It is still harvested and sorted by hand and is a treasured commodity.

Sesame Seed Chutney

This chutney is delicious served with spiced rice dishes, and also makes an unusual filling to spread in sandwiches.

NUTRITIONAL INFORMATION

Calories 120	Sugars 0g	
Protein 4g	Fat 12g	
Carbohydrate ...0.2g	Saturates 2g	

 10 MINS   5 MINS

SERVES 4

I N G R E D I E N T S

8 tbsp sesame seeds

2 tbsp water

½ bunch fresh cilantro

3 fresh green chilies, chopped

1 tsp salt

2 tsp lemon juice

chopped red chili, to garnish

1 Place the sesame seeds in a large, heavy-based saucepan and dry roast them. Set the sesame seeds aside to cool.

3 Once cooled, place the sesame seeds in a food processor or pestle and mortar and grind well to form a fine powder.

4 Add the water to the sesame seeds and mix thoroughly to form a smooth paste.

5 Using a sharp knife, finely chop the cilantro.

6 Add the chilies and cilantro to the sesame seed paste and grind once again.

7 Add the salt and lemon juice to the mixture and grind once again.

8 Remove the mixture from the food processor or pestle and mortar and transfer to a serving dish. Garnish with red chili and serve.

COOK'S TIP

Dry roasting brings out the flavor of dried spices and takes just a few minutes. You will be able to tell when the spices are ready because of the wonderful fragrance that develops. Stir the spices constantly to ensure that they do not burn.

Gram Flour Bread

This filling bread goes well with any vegetarian curry and lime pickle. Store the gram flour in a cool, dark place in an air-tight container.

NUTRITIONAL INFORMATION

Calories 112	Sugars 1g
Protein 3g	Fat 2g
Carbohydrate . . .21g	Saturates 0g

30 MINS   15 MINS

SERVES 4–6

I N G R E D I E N T S

¾ cup whole wheat flour (ata or chapati flour)

½ cup gram flour

½ tsp salt

1 small onion

fresh cilantro leaves, chopped very finely

2 fresh green chilies, chopped very finely

⅔ cup water

2 tsp ghee or vegetable oil

1 Sift the whole wheat and gram flours together in a large mixing bowl. Add the salt to the flour and mix to combine.

2 Using a sharp knife, chop the onion very finely.

3 Blend the onion, cilantro, and chilies into the flour mixture.

4 Add the water and mix to form a soft dough. Cover the dough and set aside for about 15 minutes.

5 Knead the dough for 5-7 minutes. Divide the dough into 8 equal portions.

6 Roll out the dough portions to about 7 inches on a lightly floured surface.

7 Place the dough portions individually in a frying-pan and cook over a medium heat, turning three times and lightly greasing each side with the ghee each time. Transfer the gram flour bread to serving plates and serve hot.

COOK'S TIP

In Indian kitchens, gram flour is used to make breads, bhajis, and batters, and to thicken sauces and stabilize yogurt when it is added to hot dishes.

Chapati

This Indian bread contains no fat, but some people like to brush them with a little melted butter before serving.

NUTRITIONAL INFORMATION

Calories . . . . .61 Sugars 0.5g
Protein . . . . .2g Fat 0.3g
Carbohydrate . . .13g Saturates 0g

 40 MINS 25 MINS

MAKES 10–12

INGREDIENTS

1½ cups whole wheat flour (ata or chapati flour)

½ tsp salt

¾ cup water

1 Place the flour in a large mixing bowl. Add the salt and mix to combine.

2 Make a well in the middle of the flour and gradually pour in the water, mixing well with your fingers to form a supple dough.

3 Knead the dough for about 7-10 minutes. Ideally, set the dough aside and leave to rise for about 15-20 minutes, but if time is short roll out the dough immediately. Divide the dough into 10-12 equal portions. Roll out each piece to form a round on a well-floured surface.

4 Place a heavy-based frying-pan on a high heat. When steam starts to rise from the frying pan, lower the heat to medium.

5 Place a chapati in the frying pan and when the chapati starts to bubble turn it over. Carefully press down on the chapati with a clean dish cloth or a flat spoon and turn the chapati over once

again. Remove the chapati from the pan, set aside, and keep warm while you make the others.

6 Repeat the process until all of the chapatis are cooked.

COOK'S TIP

Ideally, chapatis should be eaten as they come out of the frying pan, but if that is not practical keep them warm after cooking by wrapping them up in foil. In India, chapatis are sometimes cooked on a naked flame, which makes them puff up.

Spicy Cauliflower

This is a perfectly delicious way to serve cauliflower. It can be enjoyed as a salad or at a picnic, or as a side dish to a main meal.

NUTRITIONAL INFORMATION

Calories	68	Sugars	.........3g
Protein	.........5g	Fat	..........4g
Carbohydrate	....4g	Saturates	......1g

 5 MINS   15 MINS

SERVES 4

I N G R E D I E N T S

1 lb 2 oz cauliflower, cut into florets

1 tbsp sunflower oil

1 garlic clove

½ tsp turmeric

1 tsp cumin seeds, ground

1 tsp coriander seeds, ground

1 tsp yellow mustard seeds

12 green onions, sliced finely

salt and pepper

1 Blanch the cauliflower in boiling water, drain, and set aside. Cauliflower holds a lot of water, which tends to make it over-soft, so turn the florets upside-down at this stage and you will end up with a crisper result.

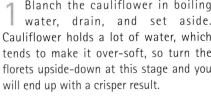

COOK'S TIP

For a special occasion this dish looks great made with baby cauliflowers instead of florets. Peel off most of the outer leaves, leaving a few for decoration, and blanch the baby cauliflowers whole for 4 minutes, then drain. Continue from step 2.

2 Heat the oil gently in a large, heavy frying pan or wok. Add the garlic clove, turmeric, ground cumin, ground coriander, and mustard seeds. Stir well and cover the pan.

3 When you hear the mustard seeds popping, add the green onions and stir. Cook for 2 minutes, stirring

constantly, to soften them a little. Season with salt and pepper to taste.

4 Add the cauliflower and stir for 3–4 minutes until coated completely with the spices and thoroughly heated.

5 Remove the garlic clove and serve immediately.

 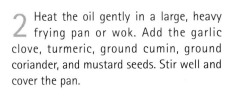 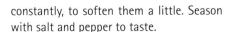

Trio of Potato Purées

These small molds filled with layers of flavored potato look very impressive. They are ideal with fish or roast meats.

NUTRITIONAL INFORMATION

Calories	170	Sugars	.........5g
Protein	.........7g	Fat	...........6g
Carbohydrate	...24g	Saturates	......3g

15 MINS   1¼ HOURS

SERVES 4

I N G R E D I E N T S

10½ oz russet or Idaho potatoes, chopped

4½ oz rutabaga, chopped

1 carrot, chopped

1 lb spinach

1 tbsp skim milk

1 tbsp butter

¼ cup all-purpose flour

1 egg

½ tsp ground cinnamon

1 tbsp orange juice

¼ tsp grated nutmeg

salt and pepper

carrot matchsticks, to garnish

1 Lightly grease four ⅔ cup ramekins.

2 Cook the potatoes in a saucepan of boiling water for 10 minutes. In separate pans, cook the rutabaga and carrot in boiling water for 10 minutes. Blanch the spinach in boiling water for 5 minutes. Drain the vegetables. Add the milk and butter to the potatoes and mash until smooth. Stir in the flour and egg.

3 Divide the potato mixture into 3 bowls. Spoon the rutabaga into one bowl and mix well. Spoon the carrot into the second bowl and mix well. Spoon the spinach into the third bowl and mix well.

4 Add the cinnamon to the rutabaga and potato mixture and season to taste. Stir the orange juice into the carrot and potato mixture. Stir the nutmeg into the spinach and potato mixture.

5 Spoon a layer of the rutabaga and potato mixture into each of the ramekins and smooth over the top. Cover each with a layer of spinach and potato mixture, then top with the carrot and potato mixture. Cover the ramekins with foil and place in a roasting pan. Half fill the pan with boiling water and cook in a preheated oven, 350°F, for 40 minutes or until set.

6 Turn out onto serving plates, garnish with the carrot matchsticks, and serve immediately.

Desserts

The healthiest ending to a meal would be fresh fruit topped with low fat yogurt. Fruit contains no fat and is naturally rich in vitamins and fiber—perfect for the low fat diet. However, there are many other ways to use fruit as the basis for a range of delicious desserts. Experiment with the unusual and exotic fruits that are increasingly

available in our supermarkets. In this chapter there is a mouthwatering range of hot and cold fruit desserts, sophisticated mousses and fools, and satisfying cakes, as well as variations on

the traditional fruit salad. There are also a number of non-fruit based desserts, such as New Age Spotted Dick and Brown Bread Ice Cream, and even some low fat treats for chocoholics such as the super-light Chocolate Cheese Pots and Chocolate & Pineapple Cake.

Strawberry Roulade

Serve this moist, light sponge rolled up with an almond and strawberry yogurt filling for a delicious tea-time treat.

NUTRITIONAL INFORMATION

Calories 166   Sugars 19g
Protein . . . . .6g   Fat 3g
Carbohydrate . . .30g   Saturates 1g

30 MINS   10 MINS

SERVES 8

I N G R E D I E N T S

3 large eggs

4½ oz sugar

4½ oz all-purpose flour

1 tbsp hot water

F I L L I N G

¾ cup low-fat plain yogurt

1 tsp almond extract

8 oz small strawberries

½ oz toasted almonds, slivered

1 tsp icing sugar

1 Preheat the oven to 425°F. Line a 14 x 10 inch Swiss roll pan with baking parchment. Place the eggs in a mixing bowl with the sugar. Place the bowl over a pan of hot water and whisk until pale and thick.

2 Remove the bowl from the pan. Sift in the flour and fold into the eggs with the hot water. Pour the mixture into the pan and bake for 8–10 minutes, until golden and set.

3 Transfer the mixture to a sheet of baking parchment. Peel off the lining

paper and roll up the sponge tightly along with the baking parchment. Wrap in a dish cloth and let cool.

4 Mix together the yogurt and the almond extract. Reserving a few strawberries for decoration, wash, hull, and slice the rest. Leave the mixture to chill in the refrigerator until required.

5 Unroll the sponge, spread the yogurt mixture over the sponge, and sprinkle with strawberries. Roll the sponge up again and transfer to a serving plate. Sprinkle with almonds and lightly dust with icing sugar. Decorate with the reserved strawberries.

 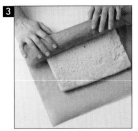 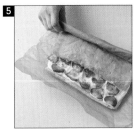

Baked Pears with Cinnamon

This simple recipe is easy to prepare and cook but is deliciously warming. For a treat, serve hot with low-fat custard.

NUTRITIONAL INFORMATION

Calories 207   Sugars 35g
Protein . . . . .3g   Fat 6g
Carbohydrate . . .37g   Saturates 2g

 10 MINS   25 MINS

SERVES 4

I N G R E D I E N T S

4 ripe pears

2 tbsp lemon juice

4 tbsp brown sugar

1 tsp ground cinnamon

2 oz low-fat spread

low-fat custard, to serve

lemon rind, finely grated, to decorate

1 Preheat the oven to 400°F. Core and peel the pears, then slice them in half lengthwise, and brush all over with the lemon juice. Place the pears, cored side down, in a small non-stick roasting pan.

2 Place the sugar, cinnamon, and low-fat spread in a small saucepan and heat gently, stirring, until the sugar has melted. Keep the heat low to stop too much water evaporating from the low-fat spread as it gets hot. Spoon the mixture over the pears.

3 Bake for 20–25 minutes or until the pears are tender and golden, occasionally spooning the sugar mixture over the fruit during the cooking time.

4 To serve, heat the custard until it is piping hot and spoon over the bases of 4 warm dessert plates. Arrange 2 pear halves on each plate.

5 Decorate with grated lemon rind and serve.

VARIATION

For alternative flavors, replace the cinnamon with ground ginger and serve the pears sprinkled with chopped stem ginger in syrup. Alternatively, use ground allspice and spoon over some warmed dark rum to serve.

Strawberry Meringues

The combination of aromatic strawberries and rose water with crisp caramelized sugar meringues makes this a truly irresistible dessert.

NUTRITIONAL INFORMATION

Calories	145	Sugars	........35g
Protein	.........3g	Fat	..........0.3g
Carbohydrate	...35g	Saturates	.....0.1g

🍯 1 HOUR   🕐 3¹/₂ HOURS

SERVES 6

I N G R E D I E N T S

3 egg whites, medium size

pinch of salt

1 cup brown sugar, crushed to be free of lumps

1½ cups strawberries, hulled

2 tsp rose water

⅔ cup low-fat plain yogurt

extra strawberries to serve (optional)

TO DECORATE

rose-scented geranium leaves

rose petals

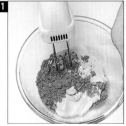  

1 In a large grease-free bowl, whisk the egg whites and salt until very stiff and dry. Gradually whisk in the sugar a spoonful at a time, until the mixture is stiff again.

2 Line a cookie sheet with baking parchment and drop 12 spoonfuls of the meringue mixture onto the sheet. Bake in a preheated oven at 250°F for 3–3¹/₂ hours, until completely dried out and crisp. Allow to cool.

3 Reserve ¹/₂ cup of the strawberries. Place the remaining strawberries in a blender or food processor and blend for a few seconds until smooth.

4 Alternatively, mash the strawberries with a fork and press through a strainer to form a purée. Stir in the rose water. Chill until required.

5 To serve, slice the reserved strawberries. Sandwich the meringues together with yogurt and sliced strawberries.

6 Spoon the strawberry rose purée onto 6 serving plates and top with a meringue.

7 Decorate with rose petals and rose-scented geranium leaves, and serve with extra strawberries (if using).

Apricot & Orange Jellies

These bright, fruity, little desserts are easy to make and taste so much better than shop-bought jellies. Serve them with low-fat ice cream.

NUTRITIONAL INFORMATION

Calories 206   Sugars 36g
Protein . . . . .8g   Fat 5g
Carbohydrate . . .36g   Saturates 3g

4¼ HOURS   25 MINS

SERVES 4

INGREDIENTS

8 oz no-need-to-soak dried apricots

1¼ cups unsweetened orange juice

2 tbsp lemon juice

2–3 tsp clear honey

1 tbsp powdered gelatine

4 tbsp boiling water

TO DECORATE

orange segments

sprigs of mint

CINNAMON "CREAM"

4½ oz medium-fat ricotta cheese

4½ oz low-fat plain yogurt

1 tsp ground cinnamon

1 tbsp clear honey

1 Place the apricots in a saucepan and pour in the orange juice. Bring to a boil, cover, and simmer for 15–20 minutes until plump and soft. Leave to cool for 10 minutes.

2 Transfer the mixture to a blender or food processor and blend until smooth. Stir in the lemon juice and add the honey. Pour the mixture into a measuring jug and make up to 2½ cups with cold water.

3 Dissolve the gelatine in the boiling water and stir into the apricot mixture.

4 Pour the mixture into 4 individual molds, each ⅔ cup, or 1 large mold, 2½ cups. Leave to chill until set.

5 Meanwhile, make the cinnamon "cream." Mix all the ingredients together and place in a small bowl. Cover the mixture and leave to chill.

6 To turn out the jellies, dip the molds in hot water for a few seconds and invert onto serving plates.

7 Decorate with the orange segments and sprigs of mint. Serve with the cinnamon "cream" dusted with extra cinnamon.

Pears with Maple Cream

These spicy cinnamon pears are accompanied by a delicious melt-in-the-mouth maple and ricotta cream—you won't believe it's low in fat!

NUTRITIONAL INFORMATION

Calories	190	Sugars	........28g
Protein	.........6g	Fat	...........7g
Carbohydrate	...28g	Saturates	......4g

 10 MINS   25 MINS

SERVES 4

INGREDIENTS

1 lemon

4 firm pears

1¼ cups hard cider or unsweetened apple juice

1 cinnamon stick, broken in half

mint leaves to decorate

MAPLE RICOTTA CREAM

½ cup low-fat ricotta cheese

½ cup low-fat plain yogurt

½ tsp ground cinnamon

½ tsp grated lemon rind

1 tbsp maple syrup

lemon rind, to decorate

1 Using a vegetable peeler, remove the rind from the lemon and place in a non-stick frying pan. Squeeze the lemon and pour into a shallow bowl.

2 Peel the pears, halve, and core them. Toss them in the lemon juice to prevent discoloration. Place in the frying pan and pour over the remaining lemon juice.

3 Add the cider or apple juice and cinnamon stick halves. Gently bring to a boil, lower the heat so the liquid simmers, and cook the pears for 10 minutes. Remove the pears using a perforated spoon; reserve the cooking juice. Put the pears in a warm heatproof serving dish, cover with foil, and put in a warming drawer or low oven to keep warm.

4 Return the pan to the heat, bring to a boil, then simmer for 8–10 minutes until reduced by half. Spoon over the pears.

5 To make the maple ricotta cream, mix together all the ingredients. Decorate the cream with lemon rind and the pears with mint leaves, and serve together.

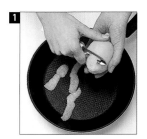

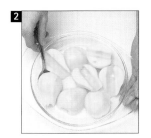

COOK'S TIP

Bartlett pears are suitable for this recipe. Pears ripen quickly and can bruise easily. It's best to buy them just before you plan to cook them.

Sticky Sesame Bananas

These tasty morsels are a real treat. Pieces of banana are dipped in caramel and then sprinkled with a few sesame seeds.

NUTRITIONAL INFORMATION

Calories	.215	Sugars	.38g
Protein	.6g	Fat	.3g
Carbohydrate	.41g	Saturates	.1g

10 MINS   20 MINS

SERVES 4

I N G R E D I E N T S

4 ripe medium bananas

3 tbsp lemon juice

4¹/₂ oz sugar

4 tbsp cold water

2 tbsp sesame seeds

²/₃ cup low-fat plain yogurt

1 tbsp icing sugar

1 tsp vanilla extract

lemon and lime rind, shredded, to decorate

1 Peel the bananas and cut into 2 inch pieces. Place the banana pieces in a bowl, spoon over the lemon juice, and stir well to coat—this will help prevent the bananas from discoloring.

2 Place the sugar and water in a small saucepan and heat gently, stirring, until the sugar dissolves. Bring to a boil and cook for 5–6 minutes until the mixture turns golden-brown.

3 Meanwhile, drain the bananas and blot with paper towels to dry. Line a cookie sheet or board with baking parchment and arrange the bananas, well spaced out, on top.

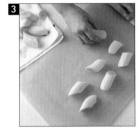

4 When the caramel is ready, drizzle it over the bananas, working quickly because the caramel sets almost instantly. Sprinkle the sesame seeds over the caramelized bananas and leave to cool for 10 minutes.

5 Mix the plain yogurt together with the icing sugar and vanilla extract.

6 Peel the bananas away from the paper and arrange on serving plates.

7 Serve the yogurt as a dip, decorated with the shredded lemon and lime rind.

Tropical Fruit Rice Mold

A rice pudding with a twist. Light flakes of rice with a tang of pineapple and lime. You can serve it with any selection of your favorite fruits.

NUTRITIONAL INFORMATION

Calories	145	Sugars	........18g
Protein	.........7g	Fat	...........1g
Carbohydrate	...30g	Saturates	.....0.3g

 4¹/₄ HOURS 25 MINS

SERVES 8

INGREDIENTS

1 cup + 2 tbsp short-grain or pudding rice, rinsed

3¾ cups skim milk

1 tbsp sugar

4 tbsp white rum with coconut or unsweetened pineapple juice

¾ cup low-fat plain yogurt

14 oz can pineapple pieces in natural juice, drained and chopped

1 tsp grated lime rind

1 tbsp lime juice

1 sachet/1 envelope powdered gelatine dissolved in 3 tbsp boiling water

lime wedges, to decorate

mixed tropical fruits, such as passion-fruit, baby pineapple, papaya, mango, or star fruit, to serve

COOK'S TIP

Try serving this dessert with a light sauce made from 1¼ cups tropical fruit or pineapple juice thickened with 2 tsp arrowroot.

1 Place the rice and milk in a saucepan. Bring to a boil, then simmer gently, uncovered, for 20 minutes until the rice is soft and the milk is absorbed.

2 Stir the mixture occasionally and keep the heat low to prevent sticking. Transfer to a mixing bowl and leave to cool.

3 Stir the sugar, white rum with coconut or pineapple juice, yogurt, pineapple pieces, lime rind, and juice into the rice. Fold into the gelatine mixture.

4 Rinse a 1¹/₂ quart non-stick ring mold or ring cake pan with water and spoon in the rice mixture. Press down well and chill for 2 hours until firm.

5 To serve, loosen the rice from the mold with a small spatula and invert onto a serving plate.

6 Decorate with lime wedges and fill the center with assorted tropical fruits.

Chocolate & Pineapple Cake

Decorated with thick yogurt and canned pineapple, this is a low-fat cake, but it is by no means lacking in flavor.

NUTRITIONAL INFORMATION

Calories	199	Sugars	........19g
Protein	.........5g	Fat	...........9g
Carbohydrate	...28g	Saturates	......3g

  10 MINS   25 MINS

SERVES 9

I N G R E D I E N T S

⅔ cup low-fat spread

4½ oz sugar

¾ cup self-raising flour, strained

3 tbsp cocoa powder, strained

1½ tsp baking powder

2 eggs

8 oz can pineapple pieces in natural juice

½ cup low-fat thick plain yogurt

about 1 tbsp icing sugar

grated chocolate, to decorate

1 Lightly grease a 8 inch square cake pan.

2 Place the low-fat spread, sugar, flour, cocoa powder, baking powder, and eggs in a large mixing bowl. Beat with a wooden spoon or electric hand whisk until smooth.

3 Pour the cake mixture into the prepared pan and level the surface. Bake in a preheated oven, 325°F, for 20–25 minutes or until springy to the touch. Leave to cool slightly in the pan before transferring to a wire rack to cool completely.

4 Drain the pineapple, chop the pineapple pieces and drain again. Reserve a little pineapple for decoration, then stir the rest into the yogurt and sweeten to taste with icing sugar.

5 Spread the pineapple and yogurt mixture over the cake and decorate with the reserved pineapple pieces. Sprinkle with the grated chocolate.

Chocolate Cheese Pots

These super-light desserts are just the thing if you have a craving for chocolate. Serve on their own or with a selection of fruits.

NUTRITIONAL INFORMATION

Calories 117	Sugars 17g
Protein 9g	Fat 1g
Carbohydrate . . .18g	Saturates 1g

 40 MINS 0 MINS

SERVES 4

INGREDIENTS

2 cups low-fat plain yogurt

1 oz icing sugar

4 tsp low-fat drinking chocolate powder

4 tsp cocoa powder

1 tsp vanilla extract

2 tbsp dark rum (optional)

2 medium egg whites

4 chocolate cake decorations

TO SERVE

pieces of kiwi fruit, orange and banana

strawberries and raspberries

COOK'S TIP

This chocolate mixture would make an excellent filling for a cheesecake. Make the base out of crushed Amaretti di Saronno biscuits and egg white, and set the filling with 2 tsp powdered gelatin dissolved in 2 tbsp boiling water.

1 Mix the yogurt in a bowl. Sift in the sugar, drinking chocolate, and cocoa powder and mix well.

2 Add the vanilla extract and rum (if using).

3 In another bowl, whisk the egg whites until stiff. Using a metal spoon, fold the egg whites into the chocolate mixture.

4 Spoon the yogurt and chocolate mixture into 4 small china dessert pots and leave to chill for about 30 minutes.

5 Decorate each chocolate cheese pot with a chocolate cake decoration and serve with an assortment of fresh fruit, such as pieces of kiwi fruit, orange, and banana, and a few whole strawberries and raspberries.

Summer Fruit Salad

A mixture of soft summer fruits in an orange-flavored syrup with a dash of port. Serve with low-fat plain yogurt.

NUTRITIONAL INFORMATION

Calories 110	Sugars 26g	
Protein 1g	Fat 0.1g	
Carbohydrate ...26g	Saturates 0g	

🍓 5 MINS   🕐 10 MINS

SERVES 6

INGREDIENTS

⅓ cup sugar

⅓ cup water

grated rind and juice of 1 small orange

2 cups red currants, stripped from their stalks

2 tsp arrowroot

2 tbsp port

1 cup blackberries

1 cup blueberries

¾ cup strawberries

1½ cups raspberries

low-fat plain yogurt, to serve

1 Put the sugar, water, and grated orange rind into a pan and heat gently, stirring until the sugar has dissolved.

2 Add the red currants and orange juice, bring to a boil, and simmer gently for 2–3 minutes.

3 Strain the fruit, reserving the syrup, and put into a bowl.

4 Blend the arrowroot with a little water. Return the syrup to the pan, add the arrowroot, and bring to a boil, stirring until thickened.

5 Add the port and mix together well. Then pour over the red currants in the bowl.

6 Add the blackberries, blueberries, strawberries, and raspberries. Mix the fruit together and leave to cool until required. Serve in individual glass dishes with low-fat yogurt.

COOK'S TIP

Although this salad is really best made with fresh fruits in season, you can achieve an acceptable result with frozen equivalents, with perhaps the exception of strawberries. You can buy frozen fruits of the forest, which would be ideal, in most supermarkets.

Fruity English Muffins

Perfect for those on a low-fat diet, these little cakes contain no butter, just a little corn oil.

NUTRITIONAL INFORMATION

Calories	162	Sugars	........11g
Protein	.........4g	Fat	..........4g
Carbohydrate	...28g	Saturates	......1g

 10 MINS   🕐 30 MINS

MAKES 10

I N G R E D I E N T S

8 oz self-raising whole wheat flour

2 tsp baking powder

1 oz brown sugar

3½ oz no-need-to-soak dried apricots, chopped finely

1 medium banana, mashed with 1 tbsp orange juice

1 tsp orange rind, grated finely

1¼ cups skim milk

1 medium egg, beaten

3 tbsp corn oil

2 tbsp oatmeal

fruit spread, honey or maple syrup, to serve

1 Preheat the oven to 400°F. Place 10 paper muffin cups in a cupcake pan. Sift the flour and baking powder into a mixing bowl, adding any husks that remain in the sieve. Stir in the sugar and chopped apricots.

2 Make a well in the center of the dry ingredients and add the banana, orange rind, milk, beaten egg, and oil. Mix together well to form a thick batter. Divide the batter evenly among the 10 paper muffin cups.

3 Sprinkle with the oatmeal and bake for 25–30 minutes until well risen and firm to the touch, or until a skewer inserted into the center comes out clean. Transfer the English muffins to a wire rack to cool slightly. Serve the English muffins warm with a little fruit spread, honey, or maple syrup.

VARIATION

If you like dried figs, they make a deliciously crunchy alternative to the apricots; they also go very well with the flavor of orange. Other no-need-to-soak dried fruits, chopped up finely, can be used as well.

Almond Trifles

Amaretti biscuits made with ground almonds have a high fat content.
Use biscuits made from apricot kernels for a lower fat content.

NUTRITIONAL INFORMATION

Calories . . . . .241 Sugars 23g
Protein . . . . .9g Fat 6g
Carbohydrate . . .35g Saturates 2g

 1¼ HOURS   0 MINS

SERVES 4

INGREDIENTS

8 Amaretti di Saronno biscuits

4 tbsp brandy or Amaretti liqueur

8 oz raspberries

1¼ cups low-fat custard

1¼ cups low-fat plain yogurt

1 tsp almond extract

½ oz slivered almonds, toasted

1 tsp cocoa powder

1 Place the biscuits in a mixing bowl and using the end of a rolling pin, carefully crush the biscuits into small pieces.

2 Divide the crushed biscuits among 4 serving glasses. Sprinkle over the brandy or liqueur and leave to stand for about 30 minutes to allow the biscuits to soften.

3 Top the layer of biscuits with a layer of raspberries, reserving a few raspberries for decoration, and spoon over enough custard to just cover.

4 Mix the yogurt with the almond extract and spoon over the custard. Leave to chill in the refrigerator for about 30 minutes.

5 Before serving, sprinkle with toasted almonds and dust with cocoa powder.

6 Decorate the trifles with the reserved raspberries and serve at once.

VARIATION

Try this trifle with assorted summer fruits. If they are a frozen mix, use them frozen and allow them to thaw so that the juices soak into the biscuit base—it will taste delicious.

Orchard Fruits Bristol

An elegant fruit salad of poached pears and apples, oranges and strawberries in a wine and caramel syrup topped with crumbled caramel.

NUTRITIONAL INFORMATION

Calories	395	Sugars	.......94g
Protein	.........3g	Fat	..........0.5g
Carbohydrate	...94g	Saturates	......0g

 30 MINS 20 MINS

SERVES 4

INGREDIENTS

4 oranges

¾ cup sugar

4 tbsp water

⅔ cup white wine

4 firm pears

4 eating apples

¾ cup strawberries

1 Pare the rind thinly from 1 orange and cut into narrow strips. Cook in the minimum of boiling water for 3–4 minutes until tender. Drain and reserve the liquid. Squeeze the juice from this and 1 other orange.

2 Lay a sheet of non-stick baking parchment on a cookie sheet or board.

COOK'S TIP

The caramel will begin to melt when added to the fruit, so do this as near to serving as possible.

3 Heat the sugar gently in a pan until it melts, then continue, without stirring, until it turns a pale golden brown. Pour half the caramel quickly on to the parchment and leave to set.

4 Add the water and squeezed orange juice immediately to the caramel left in the pan with ⅔ cup orange rind liquid. Heat until it melts, then add the wine, and remove from the heat.

5 Peel, core, and slice the pears and apples thickly (you can leave the apple skins on, if you prefer) and add to the caramel syrup. Bring gently to a boil and simmer for 3–4 minutes until just beginning to soften—they should still be firm in the center. Transfer the fruits to a bowl.

6 Cut away the peel and pith from the remaining oranges and either ease out the segments or cut into slices, discarding any seeds. Add to the other fruits. Hull the strawberries and halve, quarter, or slice thickly depending on the size and add to the other fruits.

7 Add the orange strands to the syrup and bring back to a boil for 1 minute, then pour over the fruits. Leave until cold, then break up the caramel, and sprinkle over the fruit. Cover and chill until ready to serve.

Broiled Fruit Platter

This variation of a hot fruit salad includes wedges of tropical fruits, dusted with sugar before broiling and served with a lime "butter."

NUTRITIONAL INFORMATION

Calories ....120 Sugars 20g
Protein ....1g Fat 3g
Carbohydrate ...21g Saturates 1g

40 MINS   5 MINS

SERVES 10

INGREDIENTS

1 baby pineapple

1 ripe papaya

1 ripe mango

2 kiwi fruit

4 finger bananas

4 tbsp dark rum

1 tsp ground allspice

2 tbsp lime juice

4 tbsp brown sugar

LIME "BUTTER"

2 oz low-fat spread

½ tsp finely grated lime rind

1 tbsp icing sugar

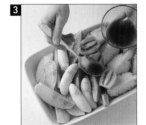

1 Using a sharp knife, quarter the pineapple, trimming away most of the leaves, and place in a shallow dish. Peel the papaya, cut it in half, and scoop out the seeds. Cut the flesh into thick wedges and place in the same dish as the pineapple.

2 Peel the mango, cut either side of the smooth, central flat pit and remove the pit. Slice the flesh into thick wedges. Peel the kiwi fruit and cut in half. Peel the bananas. Add all of these fruits to the dish.

3 Sprinkle over the rum, allspice, and lime juice, cover, and leave at room temperature for 30 minutes, turning occasionally, to allow the flavors to develop.

4 Meanwhile, make the "butter." Place the low-fat spread in a small bowl and beat in the lime rind and sugar until well mixed. Leave to chill until required.

5 Preheat the broiler to hot. Drain the fruit, reserving the juices, and arrange in the broiler pan. Sprinkle with the sugar and broil for 3–4 minutes until hot, bubbling, and just beginning to char.

6 Transfer the fruit to a serving plate and spoon over the juices. Serve with the lime "butter."

Spun Sugar Pears

Whole pears are poached in a Madeira syrup in the microwave, then served with a delicate spun sugar surround.

NUTRITIONAL INFORMATION

Calories	166	Sugars	........41g
Protein	........0.3g	Fat	...........0g
Carbohydrate	...41g	Saturates	......0g

20 MINS · 35 MINS

SERVES 4

INGREDIENTS

⅔ cup water

⅔ cup sweet Madeira wine

½ cup sugar

2 tbsp lime juice

4 ripe pears, peeled, stalks left on

sprigs of fresh mint to decorate

SPUN SUGAR

½ cup sugar

3 tbsp water

1 Mix the water, Madeira, sugar, and lime juice in a large bowl. Cover and cook on HIGH power for 3 minutes. Stir well until the sugar dissolves.

2 Peel the pears and cut a slice from the base of each one so they stand upright.

3 Add the pears to the bowl, spooning the wine syrup over them. Cover and cook on HIGH power for about 10 minutes, turning the pears over every few minutes, until they are tender. The cooking time may vary slightly depending on the ripeness of the pears. Leave to cool, covered, in the syrup.

4 Remove the cooled pears from the syrup and set aside on serving plates. Cook the syrup, uncovered, on HIGH power for about 15 minutes until reduced by half and thickened slightly. Leave to stand for 5 minutes. Spoon over the pears.

5 To make the spun sugar, mix together the sugar and water in a bowl. Cook, uncovered, on HIGH power for 1½ minutes. Stir until the sugar has dissolved completely. Continue to cook on HIGH power for about 5–6 minutes until the sugar has caramelized.

6 Wait for the caramel bubbles to subside and leave to stand for 2 minutes. Dip a teaspoon in the caramel and spin sugar around each pear in a circular motion. Serve immediately, decorated with sprigs of mint.

COOK'S TIP

Keep checking the caramel during the last few minutes of the cooking time, as it will change color quite quickly and continue to cook for several minutes after removing from the microwave oven.

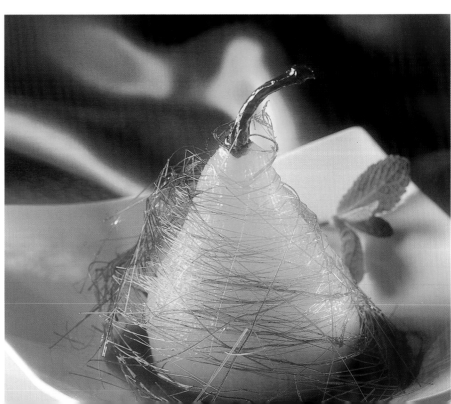

Carrot & Ginger Cake

This melt-in-the-mouth version of a favorite treat has a fraction of the fat of the traditional cake.

NUTRITIONAL INFORMATION

Calories . . . . . . .249 Sugars 28g
Protein . . . . .7g Fat 6g
Carbohydrate . . .46g Saturates 1g

 15 MINS   1¹/₄ HOURS

SERVES 10

I N G R E D I E N T S

8 oz all-purpose flour

1 tsp baking powder

1 tsp bicarbonate of soda

2 tsp ground ginger

½ tsp salt

6 oz brown sugar

8 oz carrots, grated

2 pieces stem ginger in syrup, drained and chopped

1 oz fresh ginger, grated

2 oz seedless raisins

2 medium eggs, beaten

3 tbsp corn oil

juice of 1 medium orange

F R O S T I N G

8 oz low-fat cream cheese

4 tbsp icing sugar

1 tsp vanilla extract

T O   D E C O R A T E

grated carrot

stem ginger

ground ginger

1 Preheat the oven to 350°F. Grease and line a 8 inch round cake pan with baking parchment.

2 Sift the flour, baking powder, bicarbonate of soda, ground ginger, and salt into a bowl. Stir in the sugar, carrots, stem ginger, fresh ginger, and raisins .Beat together the eggs, oil, and orange juice, then pour into the bowl. Mix the ingredients together well.

3 Spoon the mixture into the pan and bake in the oven for 1–1¹/₄ hours until firm to the touch, or until a skewer

inserted into the center of the cake comes out clean.

4 To make the frosting, place the cream cheese in a bowl and beat to soften. Sift in the icing sugar and add the vanilla extract. Mix well.

5 Remove the cake from the pan and smooth the frosting over the top. Decorate the cake and serve.

Tropical Fruit Fool

Fruit fools are always popular and this light, tangy version will be no exception. Use your favorite fruits in this recipe, if you prefer.

NUTRITIONAL INFORMATION

Calories 149   Sugars 25g
Protein ....6g   Fat 0.4g
Carbohydrate ...32g   Saturates 0.2g

35 MINS   0 MINS

SERVES 4

I N G R E D I E N T S

1 medium ripe mango

2 kiwi fruit

1 medium banana

2 tbsp lime juice

½ tsp finely grated lime rind, plus extra to decorate

2 medium egg whites

15 oz can low-fat custard

½ tsp vanilla extract

2 passion fruit

1 To peel the mango, slice either side of the smooth, flat central pit. Roughly chop the flesh and blend the fruit in a food processor or blender until smooth. Alternatively, mash with a fork.

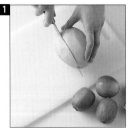  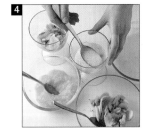

VARIATION

Other tropical fruits to try include papaya purée, with chopped pineapple, dates, or pomegranate seeds to decorate. Or make a summer fruit fool by using strawberry purée, topped with raspberries, blackberries, and cherries.

2 Peel the kiwi fruit, chop the flesh into small pieces, and place in a bowl. Peel and chop the banana and add to the bowl. Toss all of the fruit in the lime juice and rind and mix well.

3 In a grease-free bowl, whisk the egg whites until stiff and then gently fold in the custard and vanilla extract until thoroughly mixed.

4 In 4 tall glasses, alternately layer the chopped fruit, mango purée, and custard mixture, finishing with the custard on top. Leave to chill in the refrigerator for 20 minutes.

5 Halve the passion fruits, scoop out the seeds, and spoon the passion fruit over the fruit fools. Decorate each serving with the extra lime rind and serve.

Yogurt Scones

Yogurt is a suitable alternative to buttermilk, providing just the acidity needed to produce perfect scones.

NUTRITIONAL INFORMATION

Calories	109	Sugars	.........5g
Protein	.........3g	Fat	..........4g
Carbohydrate	...17g	Saturates	......2g

15 MINS   10 MINS

MAKES 16

I N G R E D I E N T S

2 cups flour, plus extra for dusting

1 tsp salt

1 tbsp baking powder

¼ cup unsalted butter, chilled, plus extra for greasing

¼ cup sugar

1 egg

6 tbsp low-fat plain yogurt

1 Sift together the flour, salt, and baking powder. Cut the butter into small pieces and rub it into the dry ingredients until the mixture resembles dry bread crumbs. Stir in the sugar.

2 Beat together the egg and yogurt and stir it quickly into the dry ingredients. Mix to form a thick dough and knead until it is smooth and free from cracks.

3 Lightly flour a pastry board or work top and rolling pin and roll out the dough to a thickness of ¾ inch.

4 Cut out rounds with a 2 inch pastry cutter, gather up the trimmings, and roll them out again. Cut out as many more rounds as possible.

5 Grease a cookie sheet lightly with butter and heat it in the oven. Transfer the dough rounds to the cookie sheet and dust lightly with flour.

6 Bake the scones in the oven for 10 minutes, or until they are well risen and golden brown. Transfer them to a wire rack to cool.

VARIATION

For spiced scones add up to 1½ teaspoons ground ginger or cinnamon to the flour.

For savory scones, omit the sugar. At the end of step 1, stir in up to ⅓ cup grated sharp Cheddar.

Aromatic Fruit Salad

The fruits in this salad are arranged attractively on serving plates with a spicy syrup spooned over.

NUTRITIONAL INFORMATION

Calories	125	Sugars	........29g
Protein	.........3g	Fat	...........1g
Carbohydrate	...29g	Saturates	.....0.2g

 25 MINS   5 MINS

SERVES 6

I N G R E D I E N T S

3 tbsp granulated sugar

⅔ cup water

1 cinnamon stick

4 cardamom pods, crushed

1 clove

juice of 1 orange

juice of 1 lime

½ honeydew melon

a good-sized wedge of watermelon

2 ripe guavas

3 ripe nectarines

18 strawberries

a little toasted, shredded coconut, for sprinkling

sprigs of mint or rose petals, to decorate

strained low-fat plain yogurt, for serving

1 First prepare the syrup. Put the sugar, water, cinnamon, cardamom pods, and cloves into a pan and bring to a boil, stirring to dissolve the sugar. Simmer for 2 minutes, then remove from heat.

2 Add the orange and lime juices to the syrup and leave to cool and infuse while preparing the fruits.

3 Peel and remove the seeds from the melons and cut the flesh into neat slices.

4 Cut the guavas in half, scoop out the seeds, then peel, and slice the flesh neatly.

5 Cut the nectarines into slices and hull and slice the strawberries.

6 Arrange the slices of fruit attractively on 6 serving plates.

7 Strain the prepared cooled syrup and spoon over the sliced fruits.

8 Sprinkle the fruit salad with a little toasted coconut. Decorate each serving with sprigs of mint or rose petals and serve with yogurt.

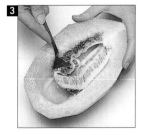

Rich Fruit Cake

Serve this moist, fruit-laden cake for a special occasion. It would also make an excellent Christmas cake.

NUTRITIONAL INFORMATION

Calories 772   Sugars 137g
Protein . . . . .14g   Fat 5g
Carbohydrate ..179g   Saturates 1g

35 MINS   1³/₄ HOURS

SERVES 4

I N G R E D I E N T S

6 oz unsweetened pitted dates

4½ oz no-need-to-soak dried prunes

¾ cup unsweetened orange juice

2 tbsp molasses

1 tsp finely grated lemon rind

1 tsp finely grated orange rind

8 oz self-raising whole wheat flour

1 tsp mixed spice

4½ oz seedless raisins

4½ oz golden sultanas

4½ oz currants

4½ oz dried cranberries

3 large eggs, separated

TO DECORATE

1 tbsp apricot jelly, softened

icing sugar, to dust

6 oz sugarpaste

strips of orange rind

strips of lemon rind

1 Preheat the oven to 325°F. Grease and line a deep 8 inch round cake pan. Chop the dates and prunes and place in a pan. Pour over the orange juice and simmer for 10 minutes. Remove the pan from the heat and beat the fruit mixture until puréed. Add the molasses and rinds. Let cool.

2 Sift the flour and spice into a bowl, adding any husks that remain in the sieve. Add the dried fruits. When the date and prune mixture is cool, whisk in the egg yolks. In a clean bowl, whisk the egg whites until stiff. Spoon the fruit mixture into the dry ingredients and mix together.

3 Gently fold in the egg whites, using a metal spoon. Transfer to the prepared pan and bake for 1¹/₂ hours. Leave to cool.

4 Remove the cake from the pan and brush the top with jelly. Dust the work counter with icing sugar and roll out the sugarpaste thinly. Lay the sugarpaste over the top of the cake and trim the edges. Decorate with orange and lemon rind.

Compôte with Honey Yogurt

Elderflower cordial is used in the syrup for this refreshing fruit compôte, giving it a delightfully summery flavor.

NUTRITIONAL INFORMATION

Calories 255	Sugars 61g
Protein 4g	Fat 1g
Carbohydrate . . .61g	Saturates 0.2g

10 MINS   15 MINS

SERVES 4

I N G R E D I E N T S

1 lemon

¼ cup sugar

4 tbsp elderflower cordial

1¼ cups water

4 eating apples

2 cups blackberries

2 fresh figs

T O P P I N G

⅔ cup thick plain yogurt

2 tbsp clear honey

1 Pare the rind from the lemon using a potato peeler. Squeeze the juice.

2 Put the lemon rind and juice into a saucepan with the sugar, elderflower cordial, and water. Heat gently and simmer, uncovered, for 10 minutes.

3 Peel, core, and slice the apples and add them to the saucepan.

4 Simmer gently for about 4–5 minutes until just tender. Leave to cool.

5 Transfer the apples and syrup to a serving bowl and add the blackberries. Slice and add the figs. Stir gently to mix. Cover and chill until ready to serve.

6 Spoon the yogurt into a small serving bowl and drizzle the honey over the top. Cover and chill before serving.

COOK'S TIP

Try to buy the apples in advance so that they can ripen at home for a day or two. Avoid apples with bruises, although the odd blemish or crack does not indicate a poor-tasting apple.

Cottage Cheese Hearts

These look very attractive when they are made in the French coeur à la crème china molds, but small ramekins could be used instead.

NUTRITIONAL INFORMATION

Calories 114   Sugars 19g
Protein . . . . .9g   Fat 1g
Carbohydrate . . .19g   Saturates 0.4g

 1¼ HOURS   0 MINS

SERVES 4

I N G R E D I E N T S

5½ oz low-fat cottage cheese

⅔ cup low-fat plain yogurt

1 medium egg white

2 tbsp sugar

1–2 tsp vanilla extract

rose-scented geranium leaves, to decorate
(optional)

S A U C E

8 oz strawberries

4 tbsp unsweetened orange juice

2–3 tsp icing sugar

1 Line 4 heart-shaped molds with clean cheesecloth. Place a strainer over a mixing bowl and using the back of a metal spoon, press through the cottage cheese. Mix in the yogurt.

2 Whisk the egg white until stiff. Fold into the cheeses, with the sugar and vanilla extract.

3 Spoon the cheese mixture into the molds and smooth over the tops. Place on a wire rack over a tray and leave to chill for 1 hour until firm and drained.

4 Meanwhile, make the sauce. Wash the strawberries under cold running water. Reserving a few strawberries for decoration, hull and chop the remainder.

5 Place the strawberries in a blender or food processor with the orange juice and process until smooth. Alternatively, push through a strainer to purée. Mix with the icing sugar to taste. Cover and leave to chill in the refrigerator until required.

6 Remove the cheese hearts from the molds and transfer to serving plates.

7 Remove the cheesecloth, decorate with strawberries and geranium leaves (if using), and serve the cheese hearts with the sauce.

Tropical Salad

Papayas are ready to eat when they yield to gentle pressure. Serve in the shells of baby pineapples for a stunning effect.

NUTRITIONAL INFORMATION

Calories 69   Sugars 13g
Protein ....1g   Fat 0.3g
Carbohydrate ...14g   Saturates 0g

10 MINS   0 MINS

SERVES 8

I N G R E D I E N T S

1 papaya

2 tbsp fresh orange juice

3 tbsp rum

2 bananas

2 guavas

1 small pineapple or 2 baby
   pineapples

2 passion-fruit

pineapple leaves to decorate

1 Cut the papaya in half and remove the seeds. Peel and slice the flesh into a bowl.

2 Pour over the orange juice together with the rum.

3 Slice the bananas, peel and slice the guavas, and add both to the bowl.

4 Cut the top and base from the pineapple, then cut off the skin.

5 Slice the pineapple flesh, discard the core, cut into pieces, and add to the bowl.

6 Halve the passion-fruit, scoop out the flesh with a teaspoon, add to the bowl, and stir well to mix.

7 Spoon the salad into glass bowls and decorate with pineapple leaves.

COOK'S TIP

Guavas have a heavenly smell when ripe—their scent will fill a whole room. They should give to gentle pressure when ripe, and their skins should be yellow. The canned varieties are very good and have a pink tinge to the flesh.

Berry Apples in Red Wine

This simple combination of apples and raspberries cooked in red wine is a colorful and tempting dessert.

NUTRITIONAL INFORMATION

Calories 221   Sugars 39g
Protein . . . . .2g   Fat 4g
Carbohydrate . . .39g   Saturates 1g

5 MINS   20 MINS

SERVES 4

INGREDIENTS

4 dessert apples

2 tbsp lemon juice

1½ oz low-fat spread

2 oz brown sugar

1 small orange

1 cinnamon stick, broken

⅔ cup red wine

8 oz raspberries, hulled and thawed if frozen

sprigs of fresh mint, to decorate

1 Peel and core the apples, then cut them into thick wedges. Place the apples in a bowl and toss in the lemon juice to prevent the fruit from discoloring.

2 In a frying pan, gently melt the low-fat spread over a low heat, add the sugar, and stir to form a paste.

3 Stir the apple wedges into the pan and cook, stirring, for 2 minutes until well coated in the sugar paste.

4 Using a vegetable peeler, pare off a few strips of orange rind. Add the orange rind to the pan along with the cinnamon pieces. Extract the juice from the orange and pour into the pan with the

red wine. Bring to a boil, then simmer for 10 minutes, stirring.

5 Add the raspberries and cook for 5 minutes until the apples are tender.

6 Discard the orange rind and cinnamon pieces. Transfer the apple and raspberry mixture to a serving plate together with the wine sauce. Decorate with a sprig of fresh mint and serve hot.

VARIATION

For other fruity combinations, cook the apples with blackberries, blackcurrants, or red currants. You may need to add more sugar if you use currants as they are not as sweet as raspberries.

Orange Syllabub

A zesty, creamy whip made from yogurt and milk with a hint of orange, served with light and luscious sweet sponge cakes.

NUTRITIONAL INFORMATION

Calories ....464 Sugars 74g
Protein ....22g Fat 5g
Carbohydrate ...89g Saturates 2g

1½ HOURS   10 MINS

SERVES 4

I N G R E D I E N T S

4 oranges

2½ cups low-fat plain yogurt

6 tbsp low-fat skimmed milk powder

4 tbsp sugar

1 tbsp grated orange rind

4 tbsp orange juice

2 egg whites

fresh orange zest to decorate

SPONGE HEARTS

2 eggs, medium size

6 tbsp sugar

6 tbsp all-purpose flour

6 tbsp whole wheat flour

1 tbsp hot water

1 tsp icing sugar

1 Slice off the tops and bottoms of the oranges and remove the skin. Cut out the segments, removing the zest and membranes between each one. Divide the orange segments between 4 dessert glasses, then chill.

2 In a mixing bowl, combine the yogurt, milk powder, sugar, orange rind, and juice. Cover and chill for 1 hour. Whisk the egg whites until stiff, then fold into the yogurt mixture. Pile onto the orange slices and chill for 1 hour. Decorate with fresh orange rind and sponge hearts.

3 To make the sponge hearts, line a 6 × 10 inch baking pan with baking parchment. Whisk the eggs and sugar until thick and pale. Sieve, then fold in the flours using a large metal spoon, adding the hot water at the same time.

4 Pour into the pan and bake in a preheated oven at 425°F for 9–10 minutes until golden and firm to the touch.

5 Turn onto a sheet of baking parchment. Using a 2 inch heart-shaped cutter, stamp out hearts. Transfer to a wire rack to cool. Lightly dust with icing sugar before serving with the syllabub.

Fruit & Fiber Layers

A good, hearty dessert, guaranteed to fill you up. Use your own favorite dried fruits in the compote.

NUTRITIONAL INFORMATION

Calories	348	Sugars	........61g
Protein	........10g	Fat	..........2g
Carbohydrate	...77g	Saturates	......1g

🍴 2 HOURS   🕐 15 MINS

SERVES 4

I N G R E D I E N T S

4½ oz no-need-to-soak dried apricots

4½ oz no-need-to-soak dried prunes

4½ oz no-need-to-soak dried peaches

2 oz dried apple

1 oz dried cherries

2 cups unsweetened apple juice

6 cardamom pods

6 cloves

1 cinnamon stick, broken

1¼ cups low-fat plain yogurt

4 oz crunchy oat cereal

apricot slices, to decorate

1 To make the fruit compote, place the dried apricots, prunes, peaches, apples, and cherries in a saucepan and pour in the apple juice.

2 Add the cardamom pods, cloves, and cinnamon stick to the pan, bring to a boil, and simmer for 10–15 minutes until the fruits are plump and tender.

3 Leave the mixture to cool completely in the pan, then transfer the mixture to a bowl, and leave to chill in the refrigerator for 1 hour. Remove and discard the spices from the fruits.

4 Spoon the compote into 4 dessert glasses, layering it alternately with yogurt and oat cereal, finishing with the oat cereal on top.

5 Decorate each dessert with slices of apricot and serve at once.

COOK'S TIP

Check the ingredients labels of dried fruit because several types have added sugar or are rolled in sugar, and this will affect the sweetness of the dish that you use them in.

Summer Fruit Clafoutis

Serve this mouth-watering French-style fruit-in-batter pudding hot or cold with low-fat plain yogurt.

NUTRITIONAL INFORMATION

Calories	228	Sugars	........26g
Protein	.........9g	Fat	...........2g
Carbohydrate	...42g	Saturates	......1g

 1¾ HOURS   50 MINS

SERVES 6

INGREDIENTS

1 lb 2 oz prepared fresh assorted soft fruits such as blackberries, raspberries, strawberries, blueberries, cherries, gooseberries, red currants, blackcurrants

4 tbsp soft fruit liqueur, such as crème de cassis, kirsch, or framboise

4 tbsp skimmed milk powder

1 cup all-purpose flour

pinch of salt

¼ cup sugar

2 eggs, medium size , beaten

1¼ cups skim milk

1 tsp vanilla extract

2 tsp sugar, to dust

TO SERVE

assorted soft fruits

low-fat plain yogurt

1 Place the assorted fruits in a mixing bowl and spoon over the fruit liqueur. Cover and chill for 1 hour for the fruit to macerate.

2 In a large bowl, mix the skimmed milk powder, flour, salt, and sugar. Make a well in the center and gradually whisk in the eggs, milk, and vanilla extract, using a balloon whisk, until smooth. Transfer to a jug and set aside for 30 minutes.

3 Line the base of a 9 inch round ovenproof baking dish with baking parchment and spoon in the fruits and juices.

4 Re-whisk the batter and pour over the fruits, stand the dish on a cookie sheet, and bake in a preheated oven at 400°F for 50 minutes until firm, risen, and golden brown.

5 Dust with sugar. Serve immediately with extra fruits and low-fat plain yogurt.

Tofu Cake

This cake has a rich creamy texture just like cheesecake, but contains no dairy produce. With crushed biscuits it is easy to make a "pastry" case.

NUTRITIONAL INFORMATION

Calories	282	Sugars	.......17g
Protein	.........9g	Fat	..........15g
Carbohydrate	...29g	Saturates	......4g

10 MINS   45 MINS

SERVES 4

INGREDIENTS

4½ oz low-fat graham crackers, crushed

10 tsp margarine, melted

1¾ oz stoned dates, chopped

4 tbsp lemon juice

rind of 1 lemon

3 tbsp water

12 oz packet firm tofu

⅔ cup apple juice

1 banana, mashed

1 tsp vanilla extract

1 mango, peeled and chopped

1 Lightly grease an 7 inch round loose-bottomed cake pan.

2 Mix together the graham cracker crumbs and melted margarine in a bowl. Press the mixture into the base of the prepared pan.

3 Put the chopped dates, lemon juice, lemon rind, and water into a saucepan and bring to a boil.

4 Simmer for 5 minutes until the dates are soft, then mash them roughly.

5 Place the mixture in a blender or food processor with the tofu, apple juice, mashed banana, and vanilla extract and process until the mixture is a thick, smooth purée.

6 Pour the tofu purée into the prepared graham cracker crumb base.

7 Bake in a preheated oven, 350°F, for 30-40 minutes until lightly golden. Leave to cool in the pan, then chill before serving.

8 Place the chopped mango in a blender and process until smooth. Serve it as a sauce with the chilled cheesecake.

New Age Spotted Dick

This is a deliciously moist low-fat pudding. The sauce is in the center of the pudding and will spill out when the pudding is cut.

NUTRITIONAL INFORMATION

Calories	529	Sugars	........41g
Protein	.........9g	Fat	..........31g
Carbohydrate	...58g	Saturates	......4g

25 MINS   1¼ HOURS

SERVES 6–8

INGREDIENTS

¾ cup raisins

generous ½ cup corn oil,
    plus a little for brushing

generous ½ cup sugar

¼ cup ground almonds

2 eggs, lightly beaten

1½ cups self-raising flour

SAUCE

½ cup walnuts, chopped

½ cup ground almonds

1¼ cups semi-skimmed milk

4 tbsp granulated sugar

1 Put the raisins in a saucepan with ½ cup water. Bring to a boil, then remove from the heat. Leave to steep for 10 minutes, then drain.

2 Whisk together the oil, sugar, and ground almonds until thick and syrupy; this will need about 8 minutes of beating (on medium speed if using an electric whisk).

3 Add the eggs, one at a time, beating well after each addition. Combine the flour and raisins. Stir into the mixture. Brush a 4 cup pudding dish with oil, or line with baking parchment.

4 Put all the sauce ingredients into a saucepan. Bring to a boil, stir, and simmer for 10 minutes.

5 Transfer the sponge mixture to the greased dish and pour on the hot sauce. Place on a cookie sheet.

6 Bake in a preheated oven at 340°F for about 1 hour. Lay a piece of baking parchment across the top if it starts to brown too fast.

7 Leave to cool for 2–3 minutes in the dish before turning out onto a serving plate.

COOK'S TIP

Always soak raisins before baking them, as they retain their moisture nicely and you taste the flavor of them instead of biting on a dried-out raisin.

Mixed Fruit Brûlées

Traditionally a rich mixture made with cream, this fruit-based version is just as tempting using plain yogurt as a topping.

NUTRITIONAL INFORMATION

Calories 165   Sugars 21g
Protein . . . . .5g   Fat 7g
Carbohydrate . . .21g   Saturates 5g

5 MINS   5 MINS

SERVES 4

I N G R E D I E N T S

1 lb prepared assorted summer
  fruits (such as strawberries, raspberries,
  blackcurrants, red currants, and
  cherries), thawed if frozen

¾ cup half-fat heavy cream alternative

¾ cup low-fat plain yogurt

1 tsp vanilla extract

4 tbsp brown sugar

1 Divide the prepared strawberries, raspberries, blackcurrants, red currants, and cherries evenly among 4 small heatproof ramekin dishes.

2 Mix together the half-fat cream alternative, yogurt, and vanilla extract until well combined.

3 Generously spoon the mixture over the fruit in the ramekin dishes, to cover the fruit completely.

4 Preheat the broiler to hot.

5 Top each serving with 1 tbsp brown sugar and broil the desserts for 2–3 minutes, until the sugar melts and begins to caramelize. Leave to stand for a couple of minutes before serving.

COOK'S TIP

Look out for half-fat creams, in light and heavy varieties. They are good substitutes for occasional use. Alternatively, in this recipe, omit the cream and double the quantity of yogurt for a lower fat version.

Eggless Sponge

This is a healthy variation of the classic Victoria sponge layer cake and is suitable for vegans.

NUTRITIONAL INFORMATION

Calories . . . . . . .273 Sugars 27g
Protein . . . . .3g Fat 9g
Carbohydrate . . .49g Saturates 1g

 1¼ HOURS 30 MINS

1 x 8" CAKE

I N G R E D I E N T S

1¾ cups self-raising whole wheat flour

2 tsp baking powder

¾ cup sugar

6 tbsp sunflower oil

1 cup water

1 tsp vanilla extract

4 tbsp strawberry or raspberry reduced-
sugar spread

sugar, for dusting

1 Grease two 8 inch sandwich cake layer pans and line them with baking parchment.

2 Strain the self-raising flour and baking powder into a large mixing bowl, stirring in any bran remaining in the sieve. Stir in the sugar.

3 Pour in the sunflower oil, water, and vanilla extract. Mix well with a wooden spoon for about 1 minute until the mixture is smooth, then divide between the prepared pans.

4 Bake in a preheated oven, 350°F, for about 25-30 minutes until the center springs back when lightly touched.

5 Leave the sponges to cool in the pans before turning out and transferring to a wire rack.

6 To serve, remove the baking parchment and place one of the sponges on to a serving plate. Spread with the jam and place the other sponge on top.

7 Dust the eggless sponge cake with a little sugar before serving.

Baked Apples with Berries

This winter dessert is a classic dish. Large, fluffy apples are hollowed out and filled with spices, almonds, and blackberries.

NUTRITIONAL INFORMATION

Calories 228	Sugars 31g
Protein 1g	Fat 2g
Carbohydrate ...31g	Saturates 0.2g

  10 MINS   45 MINS

SERVES 4

I N G R E D I E N T S

4 medium-sized cooking apples

1 tbsp lemon juice

3½ oz prepared blackberries, thawed if frozen

½ oz slivered almonds

½ tsp ground allspice

½ tsp finely grated lemon rind

2 tbsp brown sugar

1¼ cups port

1 cinnamon stick, broken

2 tsp cornstarch, blended with 2 tbsp cold water

low-fat custard, to serve

1 Preheat the oven to 400°F. Wash and dry the apples. Using a small sharp knife, make a shallow cut through the skin around the middle of each apple—this will help the apples to cook through.

2 Core the apples, brush the centers with the lemon juice to prevent browning, and stand in an ovenproof dish.

3 In a bowl, mix together the blackberries, almonds, allspice, lemon rind, and sugar. Using a teaspoon, spoon the mixture into the center of each apple.

4 Pour the port into the dish, add the cinnamon stick, and bake the apples in the oven for 35–40 minutes or until tender and soft. Drain the cooking juices into a pan and keep the apples warm.

5 Add the cornstarch mixture to the cooking juices. Heat, stirring, until thickened.

6 Heat the custard until piping hot. Pour the sauce over the apples and serve with the custard.

Pavlova

This fruit meringue dish was created for Anna Pavlova, and it looks very impressive. Use fruits of your choice to make a colorful display.

NUTRITIONAL INFORMATION

Calories 321   Sugars 37g
Protein . . . . .3g   Fat 18g
Carbohydrate . . .37g   Saturates 11g

 1¹/₂ HOURS   1¹/₂ HOURS

SERVES 8

INGREDIENTS

6 egg whites

½ tsp cream of tartar

1 cup superfine sugar

1 tsp vanilla extract

1¼ cups whipping cream

2½ cups strawberries, hulled and halved

3 tbsp orange-flavored liqueur

fruit of your choice, to decorate

1 Line a cookie sheet with baking parchment and mark out a circle to fit your serving plate. The recipe makes enough meringue for a 12 inch circle.

2 Whisk the egg whites and cream of tartar together until stiff. Gradually beat in the superfine sugar and vanilla extract. Whisk well until glossy and stiff.

3 Either spoon or pipe the meringue mixture into the marked circle, in an even layer, slightly raised at the edges, to form a dip in the center.

4 Baking the meringue depends on your preference. If you like a soft chewy meringue, bake at 275°F for about 1¹/₂ hours until dry but slightly soft in the center. If you prefer a drier meringue, bake in the oven at 225°F for 3 hours until dry.

5 Before serving, whip the cream to a piping consistency, and either spoon or pipe on to the meringue base, leaving a border of meringue all around the edge.

6 Stir the strawberries and liqueur together and spoon onto the cream. Decorate with fruit of your choice.

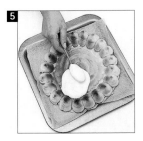

COOK'S TIP

If you like a dry meringue, you can leave it in the oven on the lowest setting overnight. However, do not use this technique with a gas oven—but in an electric oven or solid fuel cooker it would be fine.

Fruit Loaf with Apple Spread

This sweet, fruity loaf is ideal served for tea or as a healthy snack. The fruit spread can be made quickly while the cake is in the oven.

NUTRITIONAL INFORMATION

Calories	733	Sugars	.......110g
Protein	........12g	Fat	...........5g
Carbohydrate	...171g	Saturates	......1g

  1¼ HOURS   2 HOURS

SERVES 4

INGREDIENTS

6 oz oatmeal

3½ oz brown sugar

1 tsp ground cinnamon

4½ oz golden raisins

6 oz seedless raisins

2 tbsp malt extract

1¼ cups unsweetened apple juice

6 oz self-raising whole wheat flour

1½ tsp baking powder

strawberries and apple wedges, to serve

FRUIT SPREAD

8 oz strawberries, washed and hulled

2 dessert apples, cored, chopped, and mixed with 1 tbsp lemon juice to prevent browning

1¼ cups unsweetened apple juice

1 Preheat the oven to 350°F. Grease and line a 2 lb loaf pan.

2 Place the oatmeal, sugar, cinnamon, golden raisins, raisins, and malt extract in a mixing bowl. Pour in the apple juice, stir well, and leave to soak for 30 minutes.

3 Sift in the flour and baking powder, adding any husks that remain in the sieve, and fold in using a metal spoon.

4 Spoon the mixture into the prepared pan and bake for 1½ hours until firm or until a skewer inserted into the center comes out clean.

5 Leave to cool for 10 minutes, then turn onto a rack, and leave to cool.

6 Meanwhile, make the fruit spread. Place the strawberries and apples in a saucepan and pour in the apple juice. Bring to a boil, cover, and simmer for 30 minutes. Beat the sauce well and spoon into a clean, warmed jar. Leave to cool, then seal, and label.

7 Serve the loaf with 1–2 tablespoons of the fruit spread and an assortment of strawberries and apple wedges.

Almond Cheesecakes

These creamy cheese desserts are so delicious that it's hard to believe that they are low in fat.

NUTRITIONAL INFORMATION

Calories 361   Sugars 29g
Protein . . . . .16g   Fat 15g
Carbohydrate . . .43g   Saturates 4g

1¼ HOURS   10 MINS

SERVES 4

I N G R E D I E N T S

12 Amaretti di Saronno cookies

1 medium egg white, lightly beaten

8 oz skim cream cheese

½ tsp almond extract

½ tsp finely grated lime rind

1 oz ground almonds

1 oz sugar

2 oz golden raisins

2 tsp powdered gelatin

2 tbsp boiling water

2 tbsp lime juice

TO DECORATE

1 oz slivered almonds, toasted

strips of lime rind

1 Preheat the oven to 350°F. Place the cookies in a clean plastic bag, seal the bag, and using a rolling pin, crush them into small pieces.

2 Place the crumbs in a bowl and bind together with the egg white.

3 Arrange 4 non-stick pastry rings or poached egg rings, 3½ inches across, on a cookie sheet lined with baking parchment. Divide the cookie mixture into 4 equal portions and spoon it into the rings, pressing down well. Bake for 10 minutes until crisp and leave to cool in the rings.

4 Beat together the cream cheese, almond extract, lime rind, ground almonds, sugar, and sultanas until well mixed.

5 Dissolve the gelatin in the boiling water and stir in the lime juice. Fold into the cheese mixture and spoon over the cookie bases. Smooth over the tops and chill for 1 hour or until set.

6 Loosen the cheesecakes from the pans using a spatula and transfer to serving plates. Decorate with slivered toasted almonds and strips of lime rind, and serve.

Warm Currants in Cassis

Crème de cassis is a blackcurrant-based liqueur which comes from France and is an excellent flavoring for fruit dishes.

NUTRITIONAL INFORMATION

Calories 202	Sugars 35g
Protein 2g	Fat 6g
Carbohydrate ...35g	Saturates 4g

 10 MINS 10 MINS

SERVES 4

INGREDIENTS

12 oz blackcurrants

8 oz red currants

4 tbsp sugar

grated rind and juice of 1 orange

2 tsp arrowroot

2 tbsp crème de cassis

whipped cream or low-fat plain yogurt, to serve

1 Using a fork, strip the blackcurrants and red currants from their stalks and put in a saucepan.

2 Add the sugar and orange rind and juice, and heat gently, stirring, until the sugar has dissolved. Bring to a boil and simmer gently for 5 minutes.

3 Strain the currants and place in a bowl. Then return the juice to the pan.

4 Blend the arrowroot with a little water and mix into the juice in the pan. Boil the mixture until thickened.

5 Leave to cool slightly, then stir in the cassis.

6 Serve in individual dishes with whipped cream or yogurt.

Chocolate Brownies

You really can have a low-fat chocolate treat. These moist bars contain a dried fruit purée, which enables you to bake without adding any fat.

NUTRITIONAL INFORMATION

Calories 271	Sugars 45g	
Protein 5g	Fat 4g	
Carbohydrate . . .57g	Saturates 2g	

  30 MINS   40 MINS

MAKES 12

I N G R E D I E N T S

2 oz unsweetened pitted dates, chopped

2 oz no-need-to-soak dried prunes, chopped

6 tbsp unsweetened apple juice

4 medium eggs, beaten

10½ oz brown sugar

1 tsp vanilla extract

4 tbsp low-fat drinking chocolate powder, plus extra for dusting

2 tbsp cocoa powder

6 oz all-purpose flour

2 oz dark chocolate chips

I C I N G

4½ oz icing sugar

1–2 tsp water

1 tsp vanilla extract

1 Preheat the oven to 350°F. Grease and line a 7 x 11 inch cake pan with baking parchment. Place the dates and prunes in a small saucepan and add the apple juice. Bring to a boil, cover, and simmer for 10 minutes until soft. Beat to form a smooth paste, then set aside to cool.

2 Place the cooled fruit in a mixing bowl and stir in the eggs, sugar, and vanilla extract. Sift in 4 tbsp drinking chocolate, the cocoa, and the flour, and fold in along with the chocolate chips until well incorporated.

3 Spoon the mixture into the prepared pan and smooth over the top. Bake for 25–30 minutes until firm to the touch or until a skewer inserted into the center comes out clean. Cut into 12 bars and leave to cool in the pan for 10 minutes. Transfer to a wire rack to cool completely.

4 To make the frosting, sift the sugar into a bowl and mix with sufficient water and the vanilla extract to form a soft, but not too runny frosting.

5 Drizzle the frosting over the chocolate brownies and allow to set. Dust with the extra chocolate powder before serving.

COOK'S TIP

To make double the amount, cut one of the cakes into bars and open freeze, then store in plastic bags. Take out pieces of cake as and when you need them—they'll take no time at all to defrost.

Winter Puddings

An interesting alternative to the familiar Summer Pudding that uses dried fruits and a tasty malt loaf.

12 HOURS   15 MINS

SERVES 4

INGREDIENTS

11½ oz fruit malt loaf

1 cup no-need-to-soak dried apricots, chopped coarsely

½ cup dried apple, chopped coarsely

2 cups orange juice

1 tsp grated orange rind

2 tbsp orange liqueur

grated orange rind, to decorate

low-fat crème fraîche or low-fat plain yogurt, to serve

1 Cut the malt loaf into ½ inch slices.

2 Place the apricots, apple, and orange juice in a saucepan. Bring to a boil, then simmer for 10 minutes. Remove the fruit using a perforated spoon and reserve the liquid. Place the fruit in a dish and leave to cool. Stir in the orange rind and liqueur.

3 Line 4 × ¾ cup pudding dishes or ramekin dishes with baking parchment.

4 Cut 4 circles from the malt loaf slices to fit the tops of the molds and cut the remaining slices to line them.

5 Soak the malt loaf slices in the reserved fruit syrup, then arrange around the base and sides of the molds. Trim away any crusts which overhang the edges. Fill the centers with the chopped fruit, pressing down well, and place the malt loaf circles on top.

6 Cover with baking parchment and weigh each dish down with a 8 oz weight or a food can. Chill in the refrigerator overnight.

7 Remove the weight and baking parchment. Carefully turn the puddings out onto 4 serving plates. Remove the lining paper.

8 Decorate with orange rind and serve with crème fraîche or yogurt.

Red Fruits with Frothy Sauce

A colorful combination of soft fruits, served with a marshmallow sauce, is an ideal dessert when summer fruits are in season.

NUTRITIONAL INFORMATION

Calories 219	Sugars 55g
Protein 2g	Fat 0.3g
Carbohydrate . . .55g	Saturates 0g

1¼ HOURS   20 MINS

SERVES 4

I N G R E D I E N T S

8 oz red currants, washed and trimmed, thawed if frozen

8 oz cranberries

2¾ oz brown sugar

¾ cup unsweetened apple juice

1 cinnamon stick, broken

10½ oz small strawberries, washed, hulled, and halved

S A U C E

8 oz raspberries, thawed if frozen

2 tbsp fruit cordial

3½ oz marshmallows

1 Place the red currants, cranberries, and sugar in a saucepan. Pour in the apple juice and add the cinnamon stick. Bring the mixture to a boil and simmer gently for 10 minutes until the fruit is soft.

COOK'S TIP

This sauce is delicious poured over low-fat ice cream. For an extra-colorful sauce, replace the raspberries with an assortment of summer berries.

2 Stir the strawberries into the fruit mixture and mix well. Transfer the mixture to a bowl, cover, and leave to chill in the refrigerator for about 1 hour. Remove and discard the cinnamon stick.

3 Just before serving, make the sauce. Place the raspberries and fruit cordial in a small saucepan, bring to a boil, and

simmer for 2–3 minutes until the fruit is just beginning to soften. Stir the marshmallows into the raspberry mixture and heat through, stirring, until the marshmallows begin to melt.

4 Transfer the fruit salad to serving bowls. Spoon over the raspberry and marshmallow sauce and serve.

Fruity Potato Cake

Sweet potatoes mix beautifully with fruit and brown sugar in this unusual cake. Add a few drops of rum or brandy to the recipe if you like.

NUTRITIONAL INFORMATION

Calories	275	Sugars	.......44g
Protein	.........6g	Fat	..........5g
Carbohydrate	...55g	Saturates	......2g

15 MINS   1½ HOURS

SERVES 6

INGREDIENTS

1½ lb sweet potatoes, diced

1 tbsp butter, melted

4½ oz brown sugar

3 eggs

3 tbsp skim milk

1 tbsp lemon juice

grated rind of 1 lemon

1 tsp caraway seeds

4½ oz dried fruits, such as apple,
    pear, or mango, chopped

2 tsp baking powder

1 Lightly grease a 7 inch square cake pan.

2 Cook the sweet potatoes in boiling water for 10 minutes or until soft. Drain and mash until smooth.

3 Transfer the mashed sweet potatoes to a mixing bowl whilst still hot and add the butter and sugar, mixing to dissolve.

4 Beat in the eggs, lemon juice and rind, caraway seeds, and chopped dried fruit. Add the baking powder and mix well.

5 Pour the mixture into the prepared cake pan.

6 Cook in a preheated oven, 325°F, for 1-1¼ hours or until cooked through.

7 Remove the cake from the pan and transfer to a wire rack to cool. Cut into thick slices to serve.

COOK'S TIP

This cake is ideal as a special occasion dessert. It can be made in advance and frozen until required. Wrap the cake in plastic wrap and freeze. Thaw at room temperature for 24 hours and warm through in a moderate oven before serving.

Banana & Lime Cake

A substantial cake that is ideal served for tea. The mashed bananas help to keep the cake moist, and the lime icing gives it extra zing and zest.

NUTRITIONAL INFORMATION

Calories	235	Sugars	.......31g
Protein	.........5g	Fat	...........1g
Carbohydrate	...55g	Saturates	.....0.3g

 35 MINS 45 MINS

SERVES 10

INGREDIENTS

10½ oz all-purpose flour

1 tsp salt

1½ tsp baking powder

6 oz brown sugar

1 tsp lime rind, grated

1 medium egg, beaten

1 medium banana, mashed with 1 tbsp lime juice

⅔ cup low-fat plain yogurt

4 oz sultanas

banana chips, to decorate

lime rind, finely grated, to decorate

TOPPING

4 oz icing sugar

1–2 tsp lime juice

½ tsp lime rind, finely grated

VARIATION

For a delicious alternative, replace the lime rind and juice with orange and the sultanas with chopped apricots.

1 Preheat the oven to 350°F. Grease and line a deep 7 inch round cake pan with baking parchment.

2 Sift the flour, salt, and baking powder into a mixing bowl and stir in the sugar and lime rind.

3 Make a well in the center of the dry ingredients and add the egg, banana, yogurt, and sultanas. Mix well until thoroughly incorporated.

4 Spoon the mixture into the pan and smooth the surface. Bake for 40–45 minutes until firm to the touch or until a skewer inserted in the center comes out clean. Leave to cool for 10 minutes, then turn out onto a wire rack.

5 To make the topping, sift the icing sugar into a small bowl and mix with the lime juice to form a soft, but not too runny frosting. Stir in the grated lime rind. Drizzle the frosting over the cake, letting it run down the sides.

6 Decorate the cake with banana chips and lime rind. Let the cake stand for 15 minutes so that the frosting sets.

Exotic Fruit Parcels

Delicious pieces of exotic fruit are warmed through in a deliciously scented sauce to make a fabulous barbecue dessert.

NUTRITIONAL INFORMATION

Calories 43	Sugars 9g
Protein 2g	Fat 0.3g
Carbohydrate 9g	Saturates 0.1g

40 MINS   20 MINS

SERVES 4

INGREDIENTS

1 papaya

1 mango

1 star fruit

1 tbsp grenadine

3 tbsp orange juice

light cream or low-fat plain yogurt,
    to serve

1 Cut the papaya in half, scoop out the seeds, and discard them. Peel the papaya and cut the flesh into thick slices.

2 Prepare the mango by cutting it lengthways in half either side of the central pit.

3 Score each mango half in a criss-cross pattern. Push each mango half inside out to separate the cubes and cut them away from the peel.

4 Using a sharp knife, thickly slice the star fruit.

5 Place all of the fruit in a bowl and mix them together.

6 Mix the grenadine and orange juice together and pour over the fruit. Leave to marinate for at least 30 minutes.

7 Divide the fruit among 4 double thickness squares of kitchen foil and gather up the edges to form a parcel that encloses the fruit.

8 Place the foil parcel on a rack set over warm coals and barbecue the fruit for 15–20 minutes.

9 Serve the fruit in the parcel, with the low-fat plain yogurt.

COOK'S TIP

Grenadine is a sweet syrup made from pomegranates. If you prefer you could use pomegranate juice instead. To extract the juice, cut the pomegranate in half and squeeze gently with a lemon squeezer—do not press too hard or the juice may become bitter.

Brown Bread Ice Cream

Although it sounds unusual, this yogurt-based recipe is delicious. It contains no cream and is ideal for a low-fat diet.

NUTRITIONAL INFORMATION

Calories 264   Sugars 25g
Protein . . . . .12g   Fat 6g
Carbohydrate . . .43g   Saturates 1g

2¹/₄ HOURS   5 MINS

SERVES 4

I N G R E D I E N T S

6 oz fresh whole wheat bread crumbs

1 oz finely chopped walnuts

2 oz sugar

½ tsp ground nutmeg

1 tsp finely grated orange rind

2 cups low-fat plain yogurt

2 large egg whites

TO DECORATE

walnut halves

orange slices

fresh mint

1 Preheat the broiler to medium. Mix the bread crumbs, walnuts, and sugar and spread over a sheet of foil in the broiler pan.

2 Broil, stirring frequently, for 5 minutes until crisp and evenly browned. (Take care that the sugar does not burn.) Remove from the heat and leave to cool.

3 When cool, transfer to a mixing bowl and mix in the nutmeg, orange rind, and yogurt. In another bowl, whisk the egg whites until stiff. Gently fold into the bread crumb mixture, using a metal spoon.

4 Spoon the mixture into 4 mini-dishes, smooth over the tops, and freeze for 1½–2 hours until firm.

5 To serve, hold the bases of the molds in hot water for a few seconds, then turn onto serving plates.

6 Serve immediately, decorated with the walnuts, oranges, and fresh mint.

COOK'S TIP

If you don't have mini-dishes, use ramekins or teacups or, if you prefer, use one large bowl. Alternatively, spoon the mixture into a large, freezing container to freeze and serve the ice cream in scoops.

Citrus Meringue Crush

This is an excellent way to use up left-over meringue shells and is very simple to prepare. Serve with a spoonful of tangy fruit sauce.

NUTRITIONAL INFORMATION

Calories ....165 Sugars 32g
Protein ....5g Fat 1g
Carbohydrate ...37g Saturates 0.4g

  2 HOURS   10 MINS

SERVES 4

INGREDIENTS

8 ready-made meringue nests

1¼ cups low-fat plain yogurt

½ tsp finely grated orange rind

½ tsp finely grated lemon rind

½ tsp finely grated lime rind

2 tbsp orange liqueur or unsweetened orange juice

TO DECORATE

sliced kumquat

lime rind, grated

SAUCE

2 oz kumquats

8 tbsp unsweetened orange juice

2 tbsp lemon juice

2 tbsp lime juice

2 tbsp water

2–3 tsp sugar

1 tsp cornstarch mixed with 1 tbsp water

1 Place the meringues in a plastic bag and using a rolling pin, crush into small pieces. Place in a mixing bowl. Stir in the yogurt, grated citrus rinds, and the liqueur or juice. Spoon the mixture into 4 mini-dishes and freeze for 1½–2 hours until firm.

2 Thinly slice the kumquats and place them in a small saucepan with the fruit juices and water. Bring gently to a boil and then simmer over a low heat for 3–4 minutes until the kumquats soften.

3 Sweeten with sugar to taste, stir in the cornstarch mixture, and cook, stirring, until thickened. Pour into a small bowl, cover the surface with plastic wrap, and leave to cool—the film will help prevent a skin forming. Leave to chill until required.

4 To serve, dip the meringue dishes in hot water for 5 seconds or until they loosen, and turn onto serving plates. Spoon over a little sauce, decorate with slices of kumquat and lime rind, and serve immediately.

Paper-Thin Fruit Pies

These extra-crisp pastry cases, filled with slices of fruit and glazed with apricot jelly, are best served hot with low-fat custard.

NUTRITIONAL INFORMATION

Calories 158	Sugars 12g
Protein 2g	Fat 10g
Carbohydrate ...14g	Saturates 2g

  20 MINS 15 MINS

SERVES 4

INGREDIENTS

1 medium dessert apple

1 medium ripe pear

2 tbsp lemon juice

2 oz low-fat spread

4 rectangular sheets of filo pastry, thawed if frozen

2 tbsp low-sugar apricot jelly

1 tbsp unsweetened orange juice

1 tbsp finely chopped natural pistachio nuts, shelled

2 tsp icing sugar, for dusting

low-fat custard, to serve

1 Preheat the oven to 400°F. Core and thinly slice the apple and pear and toss them in the lemon juice.

2 Over a low heat, gently melt the low-fat spread.

3 Cut the sheets of pastry into 4 and cover with a clean, damp dish cloth. Brush 4 non-stick large muffin pans, measuring 4 inch across, with a little of the low-fat spread.

4 Working on each pie separately, brush 4 sheets of pastry with low-fat spread. Press a small sheet of pastry into the base of one pan. Arrange the other sheets of pastry on top at slightly different angles. Repeat with the other sheets of pastry to make another 3 pies.

5 Arrange the apple and pear slices alternately in the center of each pastry case and lightly crimp the edges of the pastry of each pie.

6 Mix the jelly and orange juice together until smooth and brush over the fruit. Bake for 12–15 minutes. Sprinkle with the pistachio nuts, dust lightly with confectioners' sugar, and serve hot with low-fat custard.

VARIATION

Other combinations of fruit are equally delicious. Try peach and apricot, raspberry and apple, or pineapple and mango.

Lace Crêpes with Fruit

These super-light crêpes melt in the mouth. They are filled with a gingered fruit salad of melon, grapes, and lychees.

NUTRITIONAL INFORMATION

Calories ....176 Sugars 22g
Protein ....3g Fat 2g
Carbohydrate ...36g Saturates 0.2g

10 MINS   5 MINS

SERVES 4

I N G R E D I E N T S

3 medium egg whites

4 tbsp cornstarch

3 tbsp cold water

1 tsp vegetable oil

F R U I T   F I L L I N G

12 oz fresh lychees

¼ Galia melon

6 oz seedless green grapes

½ inch piece fresh ginger

2 pieces stem ginger in syrup

2 tbsp ginger wine or dry sherry

1 To make the fruit filling, peel the lychees and remove the pits. Place the lychees in a bowl. Scoop out the seeds from the melon and remove the skin. Cut the melon flesh into small pieces and place in the bowl.

2 Wash and dry the grapes, remove the stalks, and add to the bowl. Peel the ginger and cut into thin shreds or grate finely. Drain the stem ginger pieces, reserving the syrup, and chop the ginger pieces finely.

3 Mix the gingers into the bowl along with the ginger wine or sherry and the stem ginger syrup. Cover and set aside.

4 Meanwhile, prepare the crêpes. In a small jug, mix together the egg whites, cornstarch, and cold water until very smooth.

5 Brush a small non-stick crêpe pan with oil and heat until hot. Drizzle the surface of the pan with a quarter of the cornstarch mixture to give a lacy effect. Cook for a few seconds until set, then carefully lift out and transfer to absorbent paper towels to drain. Set aside and keep warm. Repeat with the remaining mixture to make 4 crêpes in total.

6 To serve, place a crêpe on each serving plate and top with the fruit filling. Fold over the pancake and serve hot.

Fruit & Nut Loaf

This loaf is like a fruit bread which may be served warm or cold, perhaps spread with a little margarine or butter, or topped with jam.

NUTRITIONAL INFORMATION

Calories	.531	Sugars	.53g
Protein	.12g	Fat	.14g
Carbohydrate	.96g	Saturates	.2g

1 HOUR • 40 MINS

SERVES 4

INGREDIENTS

1¾ cups white bread flour, plus extra for dusting

½ tsp salt

1 tbsp margarine, plus extra for greasing

2 tbsp soft light brown sugar

⅔ cup golden raisins

½ cup no-need to soak dried apricots, chopped

½ cup chopped hazelnuts

2 tsp easy-blend dried yeast

6 tbsp orange juice

6 tbsp low-fat plain yogurt

2 tbsp sieved apricot jelly

1 Sieve the flour and salt into a mixing bowl. Rub in the margarine and stir in the sugar, golden raisins, apricots, nuts, and yeast.

2 Warm the orange juice in a saucepan but do not allow to boil.

3 Stir the warm orange juice into the flour mixture with the yogurt and bring the mixture together to form a dough.

4 Knead the dough on a lightly floured surface for 5 minutes until smooth and elastic. Shape into a round and place on a lightly greased cookie sheet. Cover with a clean dish cloth and leave to rise in a warm place until doubled in size.

5 Cook in a preheated oven, 425°F, for 35–40 minutes until cooked through. Transfer to a cooling rack and brush the cake with the apricot jelly. Leave the cake to cool before serving.

COOK'S TIP

To test whether the cake is done, tap the pan from underneath. If it sounds hollow, the cake is ready. This method applies to yeasted bread, too.

Brown Sugar Pavlovas

This simple combination of fudgey meringue topped with yogurt and raspberries is the perfect finale to any meal.

NUTRITIONAL INFORMATION

Calories 155	Sugars 34g
Protein 5g	Fat 0.2g
Carbohydrate . . .35g	Saturates 0g

   1 HOUR   1 HOUR

SERVES 4

I N G R E D I E N T S

2 large egg whites

1 tsp cornstarch

1 tsp raspberry vinegar

3½ oz brown sugar, crushed free of lumps

2 tbsp red currant jelly

2 tbsp unsweetened orange juice

¾ cup low-fat plain yogurt

6 oz raspberries, thawed if frozen

rose-scented geranium leaves, to decorate (optional)

1 Preheat the oven to 300°F. Line a large cookie sheet with baking parchment. Whisk the egg whites until very stiff and dry. Fold in the cornstarch and vinegar.

2 Gradually whisk in the sugar, a spoonful at a time, until the mixture is thick and glossy.

3 Divide the mixture into 4 and spoon onto the cookie sheet, spaced well apart. Smooth each into a round, about 4 inches across, and bake in the oven for 40–45 minutes until lightly browned and crisp. Leave to cool on the cookie sheet.

4 Place the red currant jelly and orange juice in a small pan and heat, stirring, until melted. Leave to cool for 10 minutes.

5 Using a spatula, carefully remove each pavlova from the baking parchment and transfer to a serving plate. Top with the yogurt and the raspberries. Glaze the fruit with the red currant jelly, and decorate with the geranium leaves (if using).

COOK'S TIP

Make a large pavlova by forming the meringue into a round, measuring 7 inches across, on a lined cookie sheet and bake for 1 hour.

Crispy-Topped Fruit Bake

The sugar cubes give a lovely crunchy tasted to this easy-to-make pudding.

NUTRITIONAL INFORMATION

Calories	227	Sugars	........30g
Protein	.........5g	Fat	...........1g
Carbohydrate	...53g	Saturates	.....0.2g

15 MINS   1 HOUR

SERVES 10

INGREDIENTS

12 oz cooking apples

3 tbsp lemon juice

10½ oz self-raising whole wheat flour

½ tsp baking powder

1 tsp ground cinnamon, plus extra for dusting

6 oz prepared blackberries, thawed if frozen, plus extra to decorate

6 oz brown sugar

1 medium egg, beaten

¾ cup low-fat plain yogurt

2 oz white or brown sugar cubes, lightly crushed

sliced dessert apple, to decorate

1 Preheat the oven to 375°F. Grease and line a 2 lb loaf pan. Core, peel, and finely dice the apples. Place them in a saucepan with the lemon juice, bring to a boil, cover, and simmer for 10 minutes until soft and pulpy. Beat well and set aside to cool.

2 Sift the flour, baking powder, and 1 tsp cinnamon into a bowl, adding any husks that remain in the sieve. Stir in 4 oz blackberries and the sugar.

3 Make a well in the center of the ingredients and add the egg, yogurt, and cooled apple purée. Mix well to incorporate thoroughly. Spoon the mixture into the prepared loaf pan and smooth over the top.

4 Sprinkle with the remaining blackberries, pressing them down into the cake mixture, and top with the crushed sugar lumps. Bake for 40–45 minutes. Leave to cool in the pan.

5 Remove the cake from the pan and peel away the lining paper. Serve dusted with cinnamon and decorated with extra blackberries and apple slices.

1

2

4

VARIATION

Try replacing the blackberries with blueberries. Use the canned or frozen variety if fresh blueberries are unavailable.

Fall Fruit Bread Pudding

This is like a summer pudding, but it uses fruits which appear later in the year, such as apples, pears, and blackberries, as a succulent filling.

NUTRITIONAL INFORMATION

Calories	178	Sugars	........31g
Protein	.........3g	Fat	...........1g
Carbohydrate	...42g	Saturates	.....0.1g

 12 HOURS   10 MINS

SERVES 8

I N G R E D I E N T S

4 cups mixed blackberries, chopped apples, chopped pears

¾ cup soft light brown sugar

1 tsp cinnamon

8 oz white bread, thinly sliced, crusts removed

1 Place the prepared fruit in a large saucepan with the soft light brown sugar, cinnamon, and 3½ fl oz of water, stir, and bring to a boil.

2 Reduce the heat and simmer for 5–10 minutes so that the fruits soften but still hold their shape.

3 Meanwhile, line the base and sides of a 1½ pint pudding dish with the bread slices, ensuring that there are no gaps between the pieces of bread.

4 Spoon the fruit into the center of the bread-lined bowl and cover the fruit with the remaining bread.

5 Place a saucer on top of the bread and weight it down. Leave the pudding to chill in the refrigerator overnight.

6 Turn the fall fruit bread pudding out onto a serving plate and serve immediately.

VARIATION

You can use thin slices of plain sponge cake instead of sliced bread. The sponge will t color from the fruit brown edges of the c attractive pat

Mocha Swirl Mousse

A combination of feather-light yet rich chocolate and coffee mousses, whipped and attractively served in serving glasses.

NUTRITIONAL INFORMATION

Calories 130   Sugars 10g
Protein ....5g   Fat 8g
Carbohydrate ....11g   Saturates 5g

1¼ HOURS   0 MINS

SERVES 4

INGREDIENTS

1 tbsp coffee and chicory extract

2 tsp cocoa powder, plus extra for dusting

1 tsp low-fat drinking chocolate powder

⅔ cup low-fat crème fraîche, plus 4 tsp to serve

2 tsp powdered gelatin

2 tbsp boiling water

2 large egg whites

2 tbsp sugar

4 chocolate coffee beans, to serve

1 Place the coffee and chicory extract in one bowl, and 2 tsp cocoa powder and the drinking chocolate in another bowl. Divide the crème fraîche between the 2 bowls and mix both well.

2 Dissolve the gelatin in the boiling water and set aside. In a grease-free bowl, whisk the egg whites and sugar until stiff and divide this evenly between the two mixtures.

3 Divide the dissolved gelatin between the 2 mixtures and, using a large metal spoon, gently fold until well mixed.

4 Spoon small amounts of the 2 mousses alternately into 4 serving glasses and swirl together gently. Chill for 1 hour or until set.

5 To serve, top each mousse with a teaspoonful of crème fraîche, a chocolate coffee bean, and a light dusting of cocoa powder. Serve immediately.

COOK'S TIP

Vegetarians should not be denied this delicious chocolate dessert. Instead of gelatin use the vegetarian equivalent, gelozone, available from health-food shops. However, be sure to read the structions on the packet first as it ared differently from gelatin.

Summer Pudding

Use whatever summer fruit you have available. Avoid strawberries as they do not give a good result, but cherries are delicious.

NUTRITIONAL INFORMATION

Calories 174   Sugars 42g
Protein . . . . .2g   Fat 0.4g
Carbohydrate . . .43g   Saturates 0g

 12 HOURS   0 MINS

SERVES 4–6

INGREDIENTS

2 lb 4 oz mixed summer fruit,
   such as blackberries, red currants,
   blackcurrants, raspberries,
   loganberries, and cherries

¾ cup sugar

8 small slices white bread

low-fat plain yogurt, to serve

1 Stir the fruit and sugar together in a large saucepan, cover, and bring to a boil. Simmer for 10 minutes, stirring once.

2 Cut the crusts off the bread slices.

3 Line a 4½ cup pudding dish with the bread, ensuring there are no gaps between the bread slices.

4 Add the fruit and as much of the cooking juices as will fit into the bread-lined bowl.

5 Cover the fruit with the remaining bread slices.

6 Put the pudding dish onto a large plate or a shallow cookie sheet. Place a plate on top and weigh it down with cans. Leave to chill overnight in the refrigerator.

7 When ready to serve, turn the summer pudding out onto a serving plate or shallow bowl, cut into slices, and serve cold with low-fat yogurt.

COOK'S TIP

To make the pudding set for longer, dissolve 2 envelopes or 2 tablespoons of powdered gelatin in water and stir into the fruit mixture. This enables you to turn it out onto the serving plate a couple of hours before serving.

Index

Index compiled by Sandra Shotter.